The Wrong House:
The Architecture of Alfred Hitchcock

Steven Jacobs

010 Publishers, Rotterdam, 2007

for Hilde

"Settings, of course, come into the preliminary plan, and
usually I have fairly clear ideas about them; I was an art
student before I took up with films. Sometimes I even
think of backgrounds first."
Alfred Hitchcock, *Direction* (1937)

"*Rope* contributed in no small way to freeing the film-
maker from his obsession with painting and making of
him what he had been in the time of Griffith and the
pioneers – an *architect*."
Eric Rohmer & Claude Chabrol, *Hitchcock* (1957)

"I do not follow the geography of a set, I follow the
geography of the screen."
Alfred Hitchcock, in Peter Bogdanovich, *Who the Devil
Made It* (1997)

"There is violence that all individuals inflict on spaces by
their very presence, by their intrusion into the controlled
order of architecture. Entering a building may be a delicate
act, but it violates the balance of a precisely ordered geom-
etry (do architectural photographs ever include runners,
fighters, lovers?)."
Bernard Tschumi, *Violence of Architecture* (1981)

"If one would ask us what is the most precious benefaction
of the house, we would say: the house accommodates
dreaming, the house protects the dreamer, the house allows
us to dream in peace."
Gaston Bachelard, *La poétique de l'espace* (1957)

"The uncanny might be characterized as the quintessential
bourgeois kind of fear: one carefully bounded by the limits
of real material security and the pleasure principle afforded
by a terror that was, artistically at least, kept well under
control. The uncanny was, in this first incarnation, a sensa-
tion best experienced in the privacy of the interior."
Anthony Vidler, *The Architectural Uncanny* (1992)

"If you rip the fronts off houses, you'd find swine."
Uncle Charlie in *Shadow of a Doubt* (1943)

"One of television's greatest contributions is that it
brought murder back into the home where it belongs."
Alfred Hitchcock, *After-Dinner Speech at the Screen
Producers Guild Dinner* (1965)

Contents

Country Houses and Mansions

Modern Hide-Outs and Look-Outs

Appendix: Hitchcock's Art Directors

Filmography

Bibliography

Index

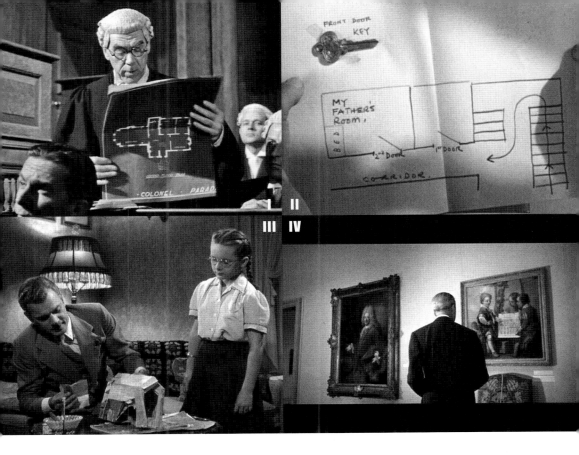

Acknowledgments

First of all, I would like to thank 010 Publishers for believing in this project, which was realized thanks to some financial support provided by Sint Lukas College of Art Brussels and the Ghent Urban Studies Team (GUST) at the University of Ghent.

Large parts of my research were carried out in the Hitchcock Archive at the Margaret Herrick Library of the Academy of Motion Picture Arts and Sciences, Los Angeles. Members of the staff were of valuable assistance. In particular, I would like to express my deepest gratitude to Barbara Hall and Faye Thompson. In addition, I would like to thank Ned Comstock and Noelle Carter at the Warner Brothers Archives at the University of Southern California, Los Angeles; Stefan Franck and Tim Van Der Poel of the Vlaamse Dienst voor Filmcultuur in the Royal Film Archive Brussels; and Nina Harding at the British Film Institute in London.

Many other people have been helpful. Eline Dehullu, Hilde D'haeyere, Bart Eeckhout, and Annelies Staessen were of valuable assistance in the logistical process. Rob King, Zoe Strother, Jonathan Reynolds, Anita Witek, and Gregor Neuerer offered me hospitality in Los Angeles and London and questioned me critically about my plans to make a book on the architecture of a non-existing architect.

No less deserving of my gratitude are David Claus and Linde Vertriest. A few years ago, I enjoyed supervising their master dissertation on Hitchcock at the Department of Architecture and Urban Planning at the University of Ghent. Our exchange of ideas, no doubt, resonate in this volume. In addition, discussions and/or correspondences with Nandor Bokor, Edwin Carels, Dirk De Meyer, Hilde D'haeyere, Fredie Floré, Stefan Franck, Tina Gillen, Johan Lagae, Alan Marcus, Amy Murphy, Marie-Leen Ryckaert, Will Straw, Frank van der Kinderen, Yves Schoonjans, and Merrill Schleier allowed me to sharpen my ideas. Some of them proved critical readers of some parts of the rough copy.

Furthermore, some fragments of the text can be considered as (generally radical) revisions of earlier published material: essays on Hitchcock's monuments, the architecture in the Gothic Romance film, and set design in *The Birds* were published in Dutch in *De Witte Raaf*; an article on Hitchcock's museum scenes was published in a 2006 issue of *The Journal of Architecture*. Comments of the editors of these publications and, in some cases, readers as well, have been very useful. This also applies to organizers of lecture series, panel members, and chairs of conferences and workshops, at which I presented papers on Hitchcock's architecture: on set design in *Rear Window* and *The*

Birds (Royal Film Museum, Brussels), and on Hitchcock's preference for tourist sites (successively at the 2005 *Visualizing the City* conference at the University of Manchester, the Institute of Media and Representation at the University of Utrecht, and at the *Tourist Traps* symposium organized by GUST in Ghent).

In addition, I would like to thank Moritz Küng, curator at deSingel International Arts Centre Antwerp, who stimulated me to finalize this book and turn it into an exhibition made in collaboration with Michael Hofstätter & Wolfgang Pauzenberger of PauHof Architects Vienna. The opening of this Antwerp exhibition (Fall 2007) coincides with the publication of this volume.

Last but not least, I would like to thank Petra Van der Jeught, who provided indispensable linguistic and editorial assistance, and Wesley Aelbrecht, Anna Barborini, Bartel Bruneel, David Claus, Thomas De Keyser, Bruno Poelaert, Annelies Staessen, and Linde Vertriest, who drew the fascinating floor plan reconstructions included in this volume.

Introduction

The history of architecture not only comprises the history of built constructions and unrealized projects designed by prominent architects but also the representations and evocations of architecture in the arts and popular culture. This is why the architectural historian should address the imaginary architecture of cinema. On the one hand, the medium of film has offered designers possibilities to create visionary buildings and utopian cities that could not be built in reality. On the other hand, all kinds of vernacular architecture represented on the screen express opinions and feelings that people nourished about small, big, beautiful, and ugly buildings. Screen architecture demonstrates the ways people have put meaning on the notions of the home, domestic culture, public spaces, landscapes, monuments, the difference between inside and outside, and so forth. Apart from a specialized group of high-style movies, in film architecture, use and meaning rather than form are given priority.[1] Creating a narrative space in the first place, cinema shows an architecture in use and, to a certain extent, an environment that answers to such notions as *lived space* (Henri Lefebvre) or *everyday space* (Mary McLeod), which have become important in recent architectural and urban debates.[2] The physical realm and abstract notions of space cannot be disconnected from our memories, dreams, fears, desires, and our everyday existence. In collaboration with directors and cinematographers, production designers and set decorators have created spaces that inspire the viewers to daydream in the way Gaston Bachelard wrote about places and spaces in his seminal *Poétique de l'espace* (1957). Cinematic spaces unmistakably play on the ways in which, for instance, attics, basements, and bedrooms hold different roles in our daily and imaginary lives. In relation to the film's plot and characters, cinematic spaces evoke the places where we all have lived, grown up, felt comfortable or alienated, and had a feeling of wonder or fear.

Alfred Hitchcock (1899-1980) was certainly aware of that. Space, in Hitchcock, is far from neutral and architecture plays an important role in his films. According to Camille Paglia, Hitchcock even expresses his partiality for architecture in his own peculiar world view and portrayal of mankind. As Paglia noted, "Hitchcock's vision of architecture as the grand but eternally provisional frame of human meaning is evident everywhere in his major films, from the glass-skinned towers of *North by Northwest* and the arched suspension bridge of *Vertigo* to the cantilevered brassieres designed by Barbara Bel Geddes in the same film."[3]

10

1 Wollen, "Architecture and Film," 211.
2 Lefebvre, *The Production of Space*, 39-42; McLeod, "Everyday and 'Other' Spaces." See also Harris & Berke, *Architecture of the Everyday*.
3 Paglia, *The Birds*, 66.
4 Bonitzer, "Notorious," 152.
5 Alfred Hitchcock, quoted in Lightman, "Hitchcock Talks About Lights, Camera, Action," 351.
6 Mallet-Stevens, "Le décor."

First and foremost, Hitchcock's architecture, of course, is an achievement of art direction or production design. Consequently, several famous Hitchcock sets, their construction, and their designers and decorators will be discussed in the following pages. According to Pascal Bonitzer, "the set in Hitchcock is more than just a mere set; rather, it is a labyrinth in which everyone – characters, director and audience – loses and finds themselves, in the intensity of their emotions."[4] Hitchcock himself stated that "a rule I've always followed is: Never use a setting simply as a background. Use it one hundred percent. (…) You've got to make the setting work dramatically. You can't use it just as a background. In other words, the locale must be functional."[5] Hitchcock's sets can be considered perfect examples of the way Robert Mallet-Stevens, the famous French architect who worked for the cinema, spoke of them in a seminal text on screen design: they tell you about the characters who inhabit them before they appear on screen.[6] However, screen buildings are not only constructed by the architectural practices of production design. The art of framing characters within diegetic architecture, cinema also creates architecture through the camera. In the process of creating cinematic space, phenomena such as lighting, sound, editing, camera positions, and camera movements can and should be interpreted as *architectonic* practices. As a result, this book not only deals with production design but also with the way Hitchcock creates cinematic space by means of cinematic devices.

Nonetheless, this book takes Hitchcock as an architect. It starts from the absurd premise that all the important buildings in his films are designed by one and the same architect whose *œuvre* includes a modernist villa in South Dakota, a Manhattan penthouse, a London apartment, a suburban house in a Californian small-town, numerous

11

I Golden Gate Bridge, San Francisco (Joseph Strauss, 1937)
Vertigo (1958) (Digital Frame)
II "A brassiere… It works on the principle of the cantilever bridge."
Vertigo (1958) (Digital Frame)

Victorian mansions, and a colorful collection of other buildings. The resulting image would be that of a timeless, architectural chameleon who excelled in a wide variety of architectural styles. More than a study of the set design in Hitchcock's works, this book deals with the architectural imagery in his films. Apart from discussing the achievements of art directors, production designers, and set decorators, this book links these imaginary buildings to the history and theory of architecture.

There are many reasons why it is interesting to study Hitchcock's architecture – this book addresses five of them in particular.

First, having worked as a set designer in the early 1920s, Hitchcock remained intensely concerned with the art direction of the fifty odd films he directed between 1926 and 1976. In close collaboration with production designers, many of them prominent ones, Hitchcock created a series of memorable cinematic buildings that often play an important part in the narrative.

Second, Hitchcock has been regarded repeatedly as a director who privileged visual presence over narration. Architecture and set design contribute largely to this predominance of the visual and to the development of Hitchcock's idea of 'pure cinema.' Specific architectural motifs such as stairs and windows are closely connected to Hitchcockian narrative structures, such as suspense, or typical Hitchcock themes, such as voyeurism.

Third, throughout his career, Hitchcock made four remarkable single-set films. Three of them, *Rope*, *Dial M for Murder*, and *Rear Window* explicitly deal with the way the confines of the set relate to those of the architecture on screen.

Fourth, spaces of confinement also turn up in the 'Gothic plot' of a series of motion pictures Hitchcock made during the 1940s, such as *Rebecca*, *Suspicion*, *Shadow of a Doubt*, *The Paradine Case*, *Notorious*, and *Under Capricorn*, but also in later masterpieces such as *The Birds*. In these films, the house is presented as an uncanny labyrinth and a trap.

Fifth, it became a Hitchcock hallmark to use famous buildings or monuments, such as the National Gallery, the Statue of Liberty, or the Golden Gate Bridge, as the location for a climactic scene.

These topics are discussed in the following pages. The first chapter deals with Hitchcock's involvement in production design and it contains some general, introductory remarks on his visualizations of specific architectural forms, his experiments with single sets, and his preference for uncanny interiors and the 'Gothic' plot. The second chapter focuses on Hitchcock's use of public spaces such as cities, monuments, and museums.

7 Alfred Hitchcock, quoted in a *Strangers on a Train* press release, Warner Brothers Archives.
8 Kraft & Leventhal, *Footsteps in the Fog*, 262-69.
9 Henry-Russell Hitchcock, *Architecture: Nineteenth and Twentieth Centuries*, 294 and 360.
10 Horton, *Henry Bumstead and the World of*

Hollywood Art Direction, 59.

The third chapter, finally, comprises detailed reviews of a series of specific buildings. Discussing several bourgeois houses, grand mansions and country houses, and some modern dwellings, this chapter clarifies Hitchcock's peculiar visualization of domestic buildings.

The house and the home, after all, developed into major themes of the director who replied without hesitation "domestic tranquility at its most blissful" when asked to describe his own story. "My house hasn't a shadow in it," he declared.[7] Living in a house at Belagio Road in Bel-Air, "a fashionable residential section of Los Angeles given over to large homes and gardens," Hitchcock presented himself as a family man surrounded by his wife, daughter, pets, and pieces of modern art – photographs of his house became part of his public persona and were published in life-style magazines, such as in an August 1942 issue of *House and Garden*. In addition, in September 1940, Alfred and Alma Hitchcock purchased a Scotts Valley estate, near Santa Cruz in Northern California.[8] The floor plan of the building in the Monterey Spanish style shows an asymmetrical combination of volumes that constitute what Hitchcock – not Alfred, the filmmaker, but Henry-Russell, the prominent architectural historian – has called the "agglutinative plan,"[9] which is typical of the Victorian mansions that pervade in Alfred's œuvre. Irregular rooms, rounded corners, inner courtyards, and staircases turn the house into one of the domestic labyrinths he loved to explore in his pictures. The interventions by Henry Bumstead, the art director of *The Man Who Knew Too Much*, *Vertigo*, *Topaz*, and *Family Plot*, confirmed the mansion's cinematic connotations. Bumstead also worked on one of the rooms in Hitchcock's Bel-Air house, which had also been redesigned by Emile Kuri, the set decorator of *Spellbound*, *The Paradine Case*, *Rope*, and *The Trouble with Harry*. For Hitchcock's Santa Cruz mountain residence, Bumstead designed some outdoor furniture and some iron gates and grilles.[10]

Since this book takes Hitchcock as an architect, it presents itself as an architectural monograph focusing on individual buildings. In order to do so, it uses conventional illustrations such as photographs and floor plans. However, the floor plans included in this book are not based on original plans of the sets found in archives. In only a few occasions was I able to localize and consult original drawings or blueprints. The Warner Brothers Archives contain fascinatingly detailed materials of Anthony House (*Strangers on a Train*) and Balestrero House (*The Wrong Man*). The Hitchcock Archive in the Margaret Herrick Library includes drawings of the Vandamm House (*North by Northwest*) and rough sketches of Manderley (*Rebecca*). Plans of the Bates House (*Psycho*) can be found on the Internet. However, complete plans of the domestic buildings discussed in this

book usually did not exist simply because these fictitious buildings were never built. Only parts of them were constructed in the studio. Studio shots of these partial buildings were carefully combined with location shots, shots of scale models, and matte shots. Consequently, the plans included in this book were made exclusively on the basis of repeated careful viewing sessions of the films. They are first and foremost *interpretations* of Hitchcock buildings. By taking into account perspectival distortions and by 'simple' (but complicated and labor-intensive) tricks such as counting footsteps or paving tiles, Hitchcock's inherently fragmented cinematic spaces were translated – if possible – into spatially coherent architectural drawings.

In some cases, drawings exposed architectural inconsistencies: in *The Lodger*, for instance, the two rooms separated by a glass ceiling are not situated above one another at all and the protagonist's room is situated on the second floor in one scene and on the third in another. A wall in Manderley's library has a window in one scene and no window in another. At a certain moment, Manderley's dining room seems to have turned 180 degrees. Often, rooms rendered in detail could not be matched with the rest of the floor plan, or only with great difficulty. Hence the oblique position of the study in

14

11 Tschumi, *Architecture in/ of Motion*, 21.

I Hitchcock Residence, Santa Cruz County, California First Floor Plan Bowman & Williams (1960) (Academy of Motion Picture Arts and Sciences)
II Hitchcock with a scale model of the set of *Rope* (1948) (Warner Brothers Release Leaflet)

the Aysgarth House, which is highly implausible in a Georgian mansion. Norman Bates' room, isolated by a small flight of stairs, can be situated on the same floor as his mother's (this would imply that the mansion's roof would be asymmetrical) or on a higher floor. Some floor plans lack rooms that should be there: there are no whereabouts of Maxim De Winter's rooms in Manderley, Roger's bedroom in the Newton House, or Mitch' room in the Brenner House. Conversely, some plans contain large spaces that have no specific function other than shaping the mass of a building.

Some interpretations resulted in fairly complete drawings that resemble 'real' floor plans of 'real' buildings. Other drawings, however, contain rooms or outside spaces which could be indicated only partially. Such drawings articulate the 'negative,' 'absent,' or invisible spaces in the plan – a feature that is also important in the Hitchcock narrative. Not coincidentally, particularly in films characterized by extensive point-of-view cutting, the drawings show fragmented constructions highly determined by lines of sight. These drawings evoke the deconstructivist designs of Bernard Tschumi, who, in his *Screenplay Series* (1978-82), took a crossfade of *Psycho* as a point of departure to explore the relation between architectural space and its activation by the motions of bodies. Tschumi further stated that "architecture is about designing conditions, rather than conditioning designs" and that it is "about identifying, and ultimately, releasing potentialities hidden in a site."[11] Designing architecture is a Hitchcockian activity.

1 Space Fright

The Art Director Vanishes: Hitchcock and Production Design Although the architecture in Hitchcock's films was created by the combined forces of cinematographers, editors, art directors, production designers, interior designers, and set decorators, Hitchcock was renowned for the meticulous supervision he exercised over his sets. In light of this, one should acknowledge that Hitchcock was an art director in his own right. Before he started directing films in 1925, Hitchcock served as a graphic designer of intertitles, assistant director, co-screenwriter, and eventually art director. "As a young man and as an art director, I was quite dogmatic," Hitchcock stated. "I mean, I would build a set and say to the director, 'Here's where it's shot from.'"[1] In particular, Hitchcock designed sets for some films directed by Graham Cutts and produced by Michael Balcon. For Cutts' *The Blackguard* (1925), Hitchcock created the sets on the stages of the vast Neubabelsberg studio of UFA in Berlin. In addition, his first two credits as director, *The Pleasure Garden* (1925) and *The Mountain Eagle* (1926), were largely shot in the Emelka studio near Munich. Numerous commentators have traced back Hitchcock's lifelong interest in production design to his personal experiences in the sophisticated German studios during the 1920s. Undoubtedly, Weimar cinema left its mark on Hitchcock because of its 'architectural' qualities. Hitchcock biographer Patrick McGilligan noted that "German cinema was more architectural, more painstakingly designed, more concerned with atmosphere. The Germans shot the set, not the stars, and when they shot the stars they anatomized them into eyes and mouths and hands. The Germans loved shadows and glare, bizarre camera angles, extreme close-ups, and mobile camera work; the 'floating camera' that became a Hitchcock trademark was first Murnau's."[2] Apart from the importance of the image of the double and a fascination for terrors, Hitchcock particularly borrowed spatial and architectural characteristics from German cinema such as shadows, stairs, mirrors, and dark foreboding landscapes.[3] As in the works by German expressionism, Hitchcock presented the physical world as a dark, frightening, violent, and unstable place, which is often a projection of a disturbed person shown through striking set designs and lighting effects as well as subjective camera shots. However, in contrast with some trendsetting examples of expressionist cinema, Hitchcock seldom favored highly artificial environments or stylized sets but immersed his stories in the everyday. Apart from his scenes situated in the environs of famous monuments, he seldom preferred big architecture that dwarfs the characters. Rather than expressionism, the *Kammerspielfilm*, which also developed in German film culture of

[1] Bogdanovich, *Who the Devil Made It*, 487.
[2] McGilligan, *Alfred Hitchcock*, 63.
[3] Gottlieb, "Early Hitchcock," 103-106. See also Garncarz, "German Hitchcock," 73-99.

the 1920s, proved influential for Hitchcock's entire career. These filmed chamber plays focused, with a meticulous attention to details, on the life of individuals in everyday claustrophobic environments. The combination of intimacy, careful exploration of domestic interiors, use of highly charged objects, and mobile camera work, which are typical of the *Kammerspielfilm*, also characterize several of Hitchcock films such as *The Lodger*, *Notorious*, *Rope*, *Under Capricorn*, or *Dial M for Murder*.

However, the careful attention to an everyday environment that characterized the *Kammerspielfilm*, was dependent on a sophisticated studio recreation of mundane settings. Consequently, Hitchcock's 'German' background determined his reliance on the studio throughout his British and American careers. Collaborating with German art directors such as Alfred Junge and Oscar Werndorff, Hitchcock relied on studio shooting and special effect departments in his 1930s Gaumont British thrillers, which are nonetheless characterized by rapid successions of often exotic locations. Bits and pieces of precisely stipulated second-unit footage were skillfully combined with painted backdrops. The Schüfftan process, first used by Fritz Lang in *Metropolis* and used by Hitchcock in *The Ring* and *Blackmail*, was also applied in the famous Albert Hall sequence of the 1934 version of *The Man Who Knew Too Much*. Hitchcock's penultimate British film, *The Lady Vanishes*, combines back projection, trick-shots, and miniatures to maintain the illusion of a real train in constant motion.

In his American period as well, Hitchcock favored the studio although he drew a lot of attention with extensive location shooting in films such as *Shadow of a Doubt*, *I Confess*, and *The Wrong Man* before that became common practice in the 1960s. Hitchcock arrived in Hollywood in 1939, when the classical studio system reached its technical and

I *Woman to Woman* (Graham Cutts, 1923)
Art Direction by Alfred Hitchcock (Still, Royal Film Archive, Brussels)
II *Foreign Correspondent* (1940)
Art Direction by Alexander Golitzen (Still, Royal Film Archive, Brussels)

artistic zenith. In the 1960s a predilection for location shooting came about; prior to that time, the classical mode of production was heavily based on filming on the sound stage. Within this mode of production, art departments fulfilled very specific tasks. Although it is difficult to draw sharp demarcations and give strict definitions, each studio had its house style shaped by its art directors and set decorators. To a large extent, the look of a film actually was set by the art department. Even the visual styles of highly individualistic directors like Alfred Hitchcock varied noticeably as they moved from studio to studio. The look of a Universal Hitchcock film, such as *Shadow of a Doubt*, differs considerably from a RKO Hitchcock film, such as *Suspicion*, made two years earlier. Unmistakably, this difference is due to the influence of the unit art directors who worked on each film, and above them, each studio's supervising art director.[4] According to Mary Corliss and Carlos Clarens, "even Hitchcock is amenable to changing his style; he is not immune to the influence of a house style or an individual designer, like Lubitsch and other major directors. For the alert viewer, a new system of correspondences begins to appear among the films of one designer. Hitchcock's *Rebecca* (1940) seems closer to Otto Preminger's *Laura* (1944) than to other Hitchcock films, for instance. Made at different studios four years apart, both derive from novels written by women and both feature the actress Judith Anderson. Could that be the reason? Or could it be that the other signature common to both is that of Lyle Wheeler, the art director?"[5]

According to Robert Boyle, who designed sets for five Hitchcock pictures (*Saboteur, Shadow of a Doubt, North by Northwest, The Birds,* and *Marnie*), it was "very easy to work in the studio in those days, because each studio had a complete complex of arts and crafts and a lot of equipment. Each studio had a staff shop with sculptors, and all the plaster work was done there. Each studio had a paint department and a construction department. They had property departments that were like museums. Each studio went to Europe every year and bought millions of dollars worth of antiques and props that were just there for you to check out. Each studio had a matte department that took care of matte paintings. All of this was within three hundred yards of your office, so you had no problem."[6] "There was also location work," Boyle nuances. "You'd make your long shot on location, but you didn't have a whole company standing around on a street waiting for you to move the cameras in for the close shot as somebody knocks on the door. In those days if we were shooting in New York on a street, we would shoot somebody driving up to a building in a cab and the next shot you're in the studio. The front door was built to match the location and be a part of the studio-built interior. What you saw out the windows of the interior were painted or photographic backings."[7] The long

4 Stephens, *Art Directors in Cinema*, 1.
5 Corliss & Clarens, "Designed for Film," 31.
6 Robert Boyle, in LoBrutto, *By Design*, 4.
7 Ibid.

shots made on location were often based on still photographs made by location scouts, who often were instructed by the producer, the art department, or, in some cases, the director. Production files of several films demonstrate that Hitchcock himself, who produced his own films from the late 1940s onwards, often elaborately primed the studio's location scouts.

Boyle enjoyed working for Hitchcock in particular because of the latter's preference for shooting in the studio over location – something which the director himself expressed on several occasions. Disliking the location chaos, Hitchcock preferred the control that was possible in the studio situation. Hitchcock's control of the set's details has become legendary. Many statements in interviews as well as production files confirm his almost maniacal interest in every prop and his concern about the authenticity of settings and furnishings. This authenticity was crucial to Hitchcock because he often situated his story in everyday environments. Instead of in haunted castles, gruesome events take place in a suburban house, a sanitary motel bathroom, or a farm kitchen.

Location photograph of a suburban house for *Saboteur* (1942)
(Academy of Motion Picture Arts and Sciences)

I A London street set with scenic backing
Sabotage (1936) (Set Photograph, British Film Institute)
II Shooting on location in Manhattan
North by Northwest (1959) (Set Photograph, Royal Film
Archive, Brussels)
III Copacabana rear projection
Notorious (1946) (Digital Frame)

With its preference for shooting on the sound stage, the studio system made the work of art directors possible – according to Boyle, this work entailed the interpretation of the script through decor.[8] In an entry on film production written for the *Encyclopaedia Britannica*, Hitchcock stated that "an art director must have a wide knowledge and understanding of architecture. On the other hand, he must be able to distinguish between what characterizes a type of dwelling and what individuates the inhabitant of that dwelling. The profession of a man may be characterized by what is on his walls. His untidiness, however, will be personal to him. Indeed, it is only the more imaginative aspects of art direction that require the art director to depart from the letter of his research. His basic information is not the answer to the actual requirements of a character or a scene."[9] In short, a director such as Hitchcock not only preferred studio shooting to locations because of all kinds of practical reasons such as control of lighting, color, sound, etcetera. Known for his use of meaningful and symbolically charged objects, Hitchcock also favored designed sets because they interpret and punctuate the narrative. "I learned a lot from Hitch," said art director Henry Bumstead, who worked on the American version of *The Man Who Knew Too Much*, *Vertigo*, *Topaz*, and *Family Plot*. "He knew how to make sets look like the characters he was filming."[10] Whereas Hitchcock, as the following paragraphs will show, often used narratives with characters that are determined, frightened, or suppressed by their architectural environments, he definitely also shaped his sets in relation to his characters. Showing preference for 'expressive décor,' Hitchcock certainly was not keen on locations since they, as C.S. Tashiro puts it, "might submit the script to the tyranny of circumstance."[11] Edward Haworth, art director of *Strangers on a Train* and *I Confess*, noted about shooting on location that "what you see in real life starts to tell a story better than the script you are shooting."[12]

Hitchcock's reluctance toward location shooting also resulted in his long-standing interest in rear projection. Although this procedure became common practice in Hollywood cinema, it also became a hallmark of the Hitchcock style. The projection of a film onto the rear of a translucent screen in front of which live action is being filmed made it very easy to merge actors and remote natural or urban settings, such as Copacabana beach (*Notorious*) or Washington, DC (*Topaz*). However, many critics gave emphatically aesthetic reasons to explain Hitchcock's being so attached to this illusory device, which he continued using also later in his career, when it was already considered an outdated special effect.[13] In some of Hitchcock's and other directors' films, the rear projection is scarcely visible. Sometimes, however, Hitchcock and his technicians took little efforts to conceal it. According to some commentators, this shameless artificiality is even the essence of Hitchcock's modernism.[14] Especially in the 1940s, Hitchcock used it in a

8 Robert Boyle, quoted in Affron & Affron, *Sets in Motion*, 15.
9 Alfred Hitchcock, "On Film Production," 219-220.
10 Horton, *Henry Bumstead and the World of Hollywood Art Direction*, 52.
11 Tashiro, *Pretty Pictures*, 33.
12 Edward Haworth, in LoBrutto, *By Design*, 32.

13 Païni, "The Wandering Gaze," 51-78.
14 See Carcassonne, "L'ordre et l'insécurité du monde," 13-16; Yacowar, "Hitchcock's Imagery and Art," 22-23; and McElhaney, "Touching the Surface," 87.

self-consciously dramatic, at times even excessive or voyeuristic way. Rather than blending actors and spatial context, the rear-projection technique outlines them and sets them apart. The space behind the characters dissolves in a maelstrom. The landscape is presented as a distant unreachable realm. When used to maximum poetic effect, rear projections mimic the effect of a (day)dream.

This also applies to Hitchcock's use of matte shots that combine images of separate shots or live action with painted backgrounds. "The beauty of matte is that you can become God. From an art-direction point of view, you can do whatever you like," Hitchcock stated.[15] The matte technique was often used to create architectural surroundings such as the ceilings of Manderley, the castle in *Rebecca*, or the bird's-eye view of the town of Bodega Bay in *The Birds*, which combined a matte painting with a fire filmed on a parking lot at Universal. Matte shots were also used in *Marnie*, a film that has been criticized for its artificiality and Hitchcock's blatant disregard of realism. The matte shots in *The Birds* and *Marnie* were made by Albert Whitlock, who can be considered the dean of this technique. Already at the time of Hitchcock's British period, Whitlock began a long association with the director, doing all the signs for *The 39 Steps* and assisting in the miniature effects for *The Man Who Knew Too Much*. Apart from *The Birds* and *Marnie*, Whitlock created matte shots and all kinds of visual effects for *Torn Curtain*, *Topaz*, *Frenzy*, and *Family Plot*. According to Robert Boyle, "it starts with the production designer's concept, and then you get somebody who's such a wonderful painter as Whitlock, and he takes it a step further and makes it better. Suppose it's a big building, a house, or a mansion that you can't afford to build. You're going to build the door of the mansion, and everything else is painted. You make a sketch of the whole composition and you give it to Albert, who adds his own special flavor to it, and it invariably becomes better."[16]

Since Hitchcock insisted on controlling all visual details, he also objected to the usual division of labor that attributed specific and even separate tasks to art director and set dresser. Consequently, Hitchcock had more faith in the role of a production designer – a screen credit that had been established in 1939, the very year he came to Hollywood. As Leo Kuter wrote in a 1951 article, the production designer was not only concerned with "the setting, the then normal field of endeavor, but also the design of much that goes within it. Indeed, in many cases, it has since become the responsibility of the art director to design the entire format and procedure of the film and, by means of illustration, to establish the preliminary concept of dramatic action, mood and pictorial content – long before actual production is set in motion."[17] The first art director getting

15 Bogdanovich, *Who the Devil Made It*, 488.
16 Robert Boyle, in LoBrutto, *By Design*, 13.
17 Kuter, "Production Designer."
18 "Hitchcock on Style," 4.
19 Lightman, "Hitchcock Talks About Lights, Camera, Action," 334.
20 Horton, *Henry Bumstead and the World of*

Hollywood Art Direction, 51.

screen credit as production designer was William Cameron Menzies for *Gone With the Wind*. Menzies also collaborated on Hitchcock's *Foreign Correspondent* and *Spellbound*. According to Hitchcock, Menzies "would take a sequence (...) and by a series of sketches indicate camera set-ups. Now this has, in a way, nothing to do with art direction. The art direction is set designing. Production design is definitely taking a sequence and laying it out in sketches."[18] Hitchcock also stated that he himself was involved in the production design of his films and that a production designer should already be present at the first versions of the screenplay. "When I'm writing a script, I bring in the production designer very early on," Hitchcock told. "When I'm sitting there with a writer and we're designing a scene, I'll say, 'I wonder whether we can do that. What sort of setting should we write this for?' We bring in the production designer while the script is being written. We have another strange anomaly in our business: the art director leaves the set the moment it's painted. Then the set dresser comes on. And yet the art director plays no part in the set dressing. That's standard practice. That's why, on *Torn Curtain*, I brought Hein Heckroth as an over-all coordinator of production design."[19] Henry Bumstead admitted that he designed not only for but also with Hitchcock and, as a result, was able to intuit the moods and emotional states that the master of suspense was after.[20]

Production designers could depart from the legendary sketches or storyboards made roughly by Hitchcock himself or by a sketch artist under the director's supervision. Referring to his work on *Strangers on a Train*, Edward Haworth told that Hitchcock "had a great sense of line – that was his language. (...) I would make sketches, and

23

Matte shot of Bodega Bay
The Birds (1963) (Digital Frame)

Hitch would approve or not approve them. Hitch was one of the few directors who knew *exactly* what it was going to be by the time he went on the set. He would say, 'I need space here because when two people are angry, they almost always distance themselves from each other and start yelling.' You knew he wanted to have a staircase connected to the staircase upstairs, the scale of the staircase, the look of it. You knew at what point on the staircase Hitch was going to stop the actor to look back at the dog, at what point you wanted the actor to get up to the door of the bedroom he is going to start to open, and at what point you cut to a set that is down on the stage floor and how you match the two together. Hitch kept it alive in your mind. (…) He would sit down and think about what he wanted to do with the set in detail. He would say, 'Everybody get lost for a few minutes,' and chase everybody out of the room but never the art director."[21]

Nonetheless, several art directors who worked for Hitchcock also emphasized their personal freedom in shaping a character through set design. Henry Bumstead, for instance, contributed to the creation of James Stewart's character in *Vertigo*: "An ex-cop, probably not a great reader. I made him a philatelist, and dressed a corner of his living rooms with stamp magazines, magnifying glass and all the equipment a stamp collector has. That's the kind of detail Hitchcock loved to see," Bumstead told.[22]

Pure Doorknob Cinema: Doors, Windows, and Stairs   Although working within the standards of classical Hollywood cinema, Hitchcock has often been considered a direc-

21 Edward Haworth, quoted in LoBrutto, *By Design*, 22.
22 Ettedgui, *Production Design and Art Direction*, 20.
23 Jack Cardiff, quoted in Auiler, *Hitchcock's Notebooks*, 465.
24 Wood, *Hitchcock's Films Revisited*, 213.
25 Truffaut, *Hitchcock*, 218.

Sketch for Scottie's apartment
Vertigo (1958)
Production design by Henry Bumstead

tor who privileged visual presence over narration. Jack Cardiff, the famous cinematographer who collaborated with Hitchcock on *Under Capricorn*, said that "practically all of Hitchcock's dramatic ideas were visual. If a cameraman is supposed to 'paint with light,' Hitchcock painted with a moving camera."[23] This notion of the predominance of the visual answers perfectly to the concept of 'pure cinema,' which Hitchcock advocated in a series of influential interviews in the early 1960s, and to the opinion that his seminal films are self-referential or self-reflexive meditations on the nature of the medium of cinema itself – an idea fostered by critics such as Jean Douchet, Robert Stam, Stefan Sharff, and William Rothman, among many others. Robin Wood presented Hitchcock as a director who favored an image-centered cinema instead of an actor-centered style of filmmaking. Whereas the latter, as typified by the films of Jean Renoir, Howard Hawks or Leo McCarey, implies a 'humanist' philosophy and a certain form of 'realism,' directors such as Hitchcock, Josef von Sternberg, or Michelangelo Antonioni create films in which the characters are, in Wood's words, "trapped, isolated, and unable to communicate."[24] In Hitchcock films, the characters become one of the many precisely calculated details in the décor. Given this perspective, Hitchcock paid a lot of attention to the placement of his characters in the frame and, consequently, to the visual, compositional but also psychological and social relation between the characters and their surroundings. Hitchcock intensifies this relation by his characteristic point-of-view shots, elaborate camera movements, or impressive editing techniques. Whereas the long takes in *Young and Innocent, The Paradine Case, Rope,* or *Under Capricorn* make the space palpable to the viewer, his point-of-view shots in *Rear Window* or *Vertigo* freeze the characters into *tableaux* that turn the actors into 'architectural' components. His sophisticated editing, moreover, fragments and manipulates cinematic space. Robin Wood has noted that spatial deception through editing is common practice in Hitchcock. Tellingly, he doesn't refer to one of Hitchcock's impressive sets but to a seemingly simple scene in *Notorious*, in which Ingrid Bergman hides and drops the key while she is kissed by Claude Rains. Filmed by, say, Preminger, as a single-take long shot from across the room, this simple action would be implausible. Often, Hitchcock breaks down both the action and the space into a characteristically detailed and fragmented montage that culminates in a series of close-ups. Moreover, Hitchcock often does not give an over-all view of the setting until a scene reaches its dramatic peak. The court-room scene in *The Paradine Case* and the scene with the death of the dog in *Rear Window* are examples of this. "The size of the image is used for dramatic purposes," Hitchcock said, "and not merely to establish the background."[25] Nevertheless, Hitchcock often makes a special effort to give the audience the geography of the room, to

25

orient them. "Otherwise, they get confused. And you can't do it in a long shot. The eye can't absorb it," Hitchcock noted. "In the theatre the audience can look at a set for thirty-nine minutes and orient themselves. But in a film, if you use a long shot – which I don't – it's on the screen for ten feet: seven and a half seconds. You can't possibly absorb it, so you orient the audience in the course of playing the scene."[26]

Hitchcock's visual way of thinking has also been noted by Jean-Luc Godard, who stated that Hitchcock "proves that the cinema today is better fitted than either philosophy or the novel to convey the basic data of consciousness."[27] According to Godard, with Hitchcock one remembers shots rather than scenes.[28] In the episode dedicated to Hitchcock in his *Histoire(s) du cinéma* (1998), Godard remarks that we never remember plots of Hitchcock's films, for example, the reason why Joan Fontaine leans from a cliff in *Suspicion*, why Joel McCrea goes to Holland in *Foreign Correspondent*, or why Janet Leigh stops at Bates Motel in *Psycho*. What we remember are merely images. More precisely, we remember shots focusing on some key objects: a handbag, a glass of milk, wings of a mill, a curl of hair, a row of bottles, a pair of glasses, a score of music, a cigarette lighter, and so forth.[29] Moreover, Hitchcock's objects are never mere props. According to Andrew Sarris, they are the very substance of his cinema. "These objects embody the feelings and fears of characters as object and character interact with each other in dramas within dramas."[30] Through their emphasis, objects but also spaces seem to come alive.

Hitchcock's cinema is permeated by fetish objects, many of which have highly architectural or domestic connotations such as a bunch of keys, a doorknob, a closed door, a darkened window, or the top of a staircase. In a way, these doors, windows, and stairs can be interpreted as instances of the hypersignification typical of a number of films of the 1940s.[31] Turned into focal points, architectural details are part of the kind of "doorknob cinema" that André Bazin deplored because it presents every detail as a sign rather than a fact.[32] In Hitchcock, several of these architectural motifs are intrinsically connected to typically Hitchcockian themes or narrative structures. The motif of the closed door – accompanied by that of the key – relates to the theme of a secret hidden within the house or the family, for instance. Activating a dialectic of concealing and revealing, famous instances of this motif can be found in *Rebecca*, *Spellbound*, *Notorious*, *Strangers on a Train*, *Dial M for Murder*, *Psycho*, and *The Birds*. Hitchcock makes the viewer focus on another articulation of the border between interior and exterior: the window. Apart from being convenient mediators between light and shadow and conventional tokens of meditation, windows are closely linked to Hitchcock's favorite theme of voyeurism. *The Lady Vanishes*, *Foreign Correspondent*, *Shadow of a Doubt*, *Rope*, *I Confess*, *Rear Window*,

26 Bogdanovich, *Who the Devil Made It*, 517.
27 Godard, "The Wrong Man," 50.
28 Godard, "Georges Franju," 101.
29 See Volume 4A, entitled "Le contrôle de l'univers," of the book version of Jean-Luc Godard's *Histoire(s) du cinéma*, 76-93.
30 Sarris, *The American Cinema*, 59.
31 Doane, *The Desire to Desire*, 137.
32 Bazin, *What Is Cinema?*, II, 37.
33 Mulvey, "Visual Pleasures and Narrative Cinema," 23.

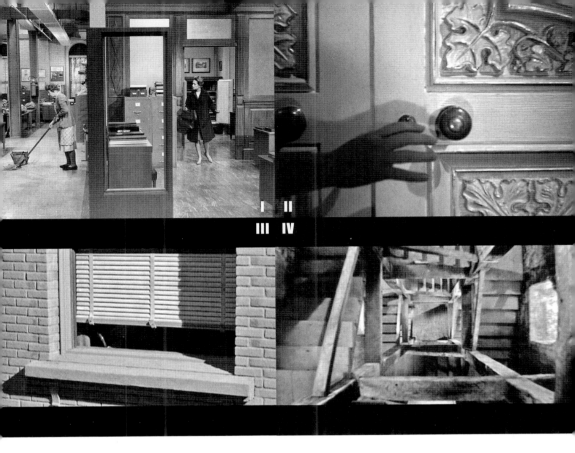

and *Psycho* even open with the image of a window that marks the transition from an urban exterior to the seclusion and mysteries of an interior. Carrying the word in its title, *Rear Window* is the preeminent example of the Hitchcock formula in which, according to Laura Mulvey, "the spectator is absorbed into a voyeuristic situation within the screen scene and diegesis, which parodies his own in the cinema."[33]

Another favorite Hitchcock architectural motif is the staircase, which even developed into a quintessential Hitchcock image – noted by commentators Lesley Brill, Jean Funck, Michael Walker, Maurice Yacowar, and Dennis Zirnite, among many others. Already in 1929, after the release of *Blackmail*, the London correspondent for *Variety* noted the director's "staircase complex." Dynamic and spatially fragmented structures, staircases are often places of crisis and their perspectival effects seem to isolate and

I Framing Marnie in the Ruttland office
Marnie (1964) (Still, Royal Film Archive, Brussels)
II Doorknob cinema
Rebecca (1940) (Digital Frame)
III Phoenix hotel room window
Psycho (1960) (Digital Frame)
IV Staircase of mission bell tower
Vertigo (1958) (Digital Frame)

confine characters. A central spine of domestic space, the staircase presents itself as an arena for psychological tensions. Furthermore, in Hitchcock's films, staircases lead to trouble since they accompany the cognitive hubris of the characters. Inquisitiveness drives characters upstairs or downstairs. In addition, Hitchcock integrates his staircases perfectly into his technique of suspense: each step advances but also delays the dénouement.

Last but not least, the activity of climbing or descending staircases is also often connected to another recurrent Hitchcock motif: that of the hanging figure, which elicits anxiety from moviegoers and rouses *suspense* – a word derived from the Latin *pendere*, meaning 'to cause to hang.'[34] Being the art that, according to Schopenhauer, makes visible the relation between support and weight, architecture simultaneously defies and obeys gravity. In films such as *Murder, Number 17, Foreign Correspondent, Saboteur, Rear Window, Vertigo*, and *North by Northwest*, characters climb buildings. Endangering their bodies, architecture is presented as something vertiginous – something that Hitchcock perfectly visualized in the famous *Vertigo* tower scene by means of a combination of a zoom in and a track back resulting in a dizzying effect that relies on the strong architectural spatial cues of the staircase seen from the vantage point of the character.

Family Plots on Single Sets: Cinematic Confinement   Another instance of Hitchcock's outspoken interest in architecture are his remarkable single-set films that explicitly explore the confines of cinematic space: *Lifeboat, Rope, Dial M for Murder*, and *Rear Window*. Apart from that, one should note that in many other Hitchcock films, large parts of the story take place within the confines of one or two buildings: this is the case in *The Lodger, Easy Virtue, Juno and the Paycock, The Skin Game, Number 17, Jamaica Inn, Rebecca, Suspicion, Shadow of a Doubt, Notorious, Under Capricorn*, and *Psycho*. Strikingly, in these pictures, space is gradually constructed through the mise-en-scène but eventually acquires an autonomous quality: although architecture is created through cinematic processes, everything suggests that it exists independent of the camera. Since he relied upon point-of-view cutting to an almost unique degree, Hitchcock creates cinematic space by having the characters discover the space and taking up their point of view. Hence the importance of a character's first arrival in a building in films such as *The Lodger, Number Seventeen, Jamaica Inn, Rebecca, Notorious, Under Capricorn, Psycho*, or *The Birds*. Such a gradual exploration of space and the suggestion of architecture's autonomy independent of the camera acquire new dimensions, of course, when the entire film is situated in a single spot. As such, Hitchcock encompasses a total world as complete as human perception will permit. His shot of the interior of the jail cell in *Frenzy*, that

28

34 Morris, *The Hanging Figure*, 53.
35 Sharff, *Hitchcock's High Vernacular*, 241. See also Chabrol, "Variations sur le huis clos," 30-34.
36 Bogdanovich, *Who the Devil Made It*, 511.
37 Affron & Affron, *Sets in Motion*, 39.
38 Wollen, "Architecture and Film," 214.

shows all four walls in a most stylized way, is a perfect instance of this. This scene also illustrates perfectly how Hitchcock is highly aware of the so-called 'fourth wall,' which is never conspicuous in his films. According to Stefan Sharff, Hitchcock's 'fourth wall' is rarely concerned with information or exposition, since his reverse shots are usually closer and contain little background and, consequently, little information.[35] Yet, they carry an emotional and cinesthetic impact since they unveil, sometimes in a somewhat delayed way, the confines of the space – an effect that is particularly striking in the single-set films.

The first of Hitchcock's single-set films is *Lifeboat*, the story of which is entirely situated in the lifeboat of a ship torpedoed by a German submarine. The uncanny situation of a *huis clos* on the infinite surface of the ocean was skillfully created in the studio. Whereas *Lifeboat* is, in Hitchcock's own words, "a film without scenery,"[36] *Rope, Dial M for Murder*, and *Rear Window* foreground their architectural contexts. Reducing their field of reading to a single locale, these films challenge the moviegoer's fundamental expectation that, through editing, the spectator will be transported from place to place, and, consequently, from set to set.[37] Instead of merely advancing or punctuating the narrative, the single set becomes one with it. Peter Wollen noted that such single-set films as *Rear Window, Rope, Le jour se lève* (Marcel Carné, 1939), *Die bitteren Tränen der Petra von Kant* (Rainer Werner Fassbinder, 1972), or *Wavelength* (Michael Snow, 1967) are the films most fascinating in their use of space. "In these films," Wollen writes, "we become gradually familiar with a place, building up our own set of memories, associations and expectations, creating our own symbolizations, our own mental maps."[38] In such films, sets transcend their usual function and become inseparable from the narra-

Lifeboat (1944) (Digital Frame)

tive. What happens cannot be disconnected from where it happens. Action and place, narrative and set, are completely of a piece. Consequently, with their deliberate visual restriction, the narrative of Hitchcock's single-set films depends greatly on the tension between inside and outside space. This coincides with the motif of intrusion, which is important in *Rope*, *Dial M for Murder*, and *Rear Window* but it also recurs in many of his other films. The spaces may or may not be factual (a room literally exists for the characters; a frame does not), but ultimately they are psychological; the interior space represents subjective perception, which is often threatened by reality from outside.[39] Furthermore, the single-set films not only hypostatize the difference between inside and outside but also that between onscreen and offscreen space. In single set films, the off-screen acquires highly specific meanings both in the diegetic (the space of the film) and extradiegetic sense (the space of the shooting of the film). In both cases, the offscreen is emphasized as an absence: an absent space summoned up by the looks of the characters on the one hand, or by the spectator's gaze via the look of the camera on the other. In single-set films, both kinds of absent space interfere with each other constantly. Hitchcock often created anguish and suspense by prolonging such an absence – a tactic frequently used in horror films, where the offscreen can hide nameless terrors.[40]

Interestingly, in his single-set films, Hitchcock in each case combined the single set with striking experiments in cinematic style and technique. In *Rope*, he explored the single set by means of a (supposedly) single take. In *Dial M for Murder*, he used the short-lived 3-D process to create dramatic effects in a furnished interior. In *Rear Window*, he shifted to the widescreen VistaVision format and its demand for space-filling detail, which enabled him to work with a more lavish kind of art direction. Each time, the restrictions of the single set prompted Hitchcock to sculpt cinematic space in innovating ways. In *Rope*, the camera moves through the rooms of the protagonists' apartment, its frame constantly shifting. In *Dial M for Murder*, the layout of the apartment is clarified by means of striking high angle shots. In *Rear Window*, Hitchcock explores the courtyard and its adjacent apartments by combining fluent crane shots with point-of-view editing. In these films, Hitchcock had to construct an integrated space. According to Claude Chabrol and Eric Rohmer, "*Rope* contributed in no small way to freeing the film-maker from his obsession with painting and making of him what he had been in the time of Griffith and the pioneers – an architect."[41]

39 Weis, *The Silent Scream*, 125-35.
40 Vernet, "Espace (Structuration de l')," 86-95.
41 Chabrol & Rohmer, *Hitchcock*, 96-97.

I *Rope* (1948) (Set Photograph, Royal Film Archive, Brussels)
II *Rear Window* (1954) (Set Photograph, Royal Film Archive, Brussels)

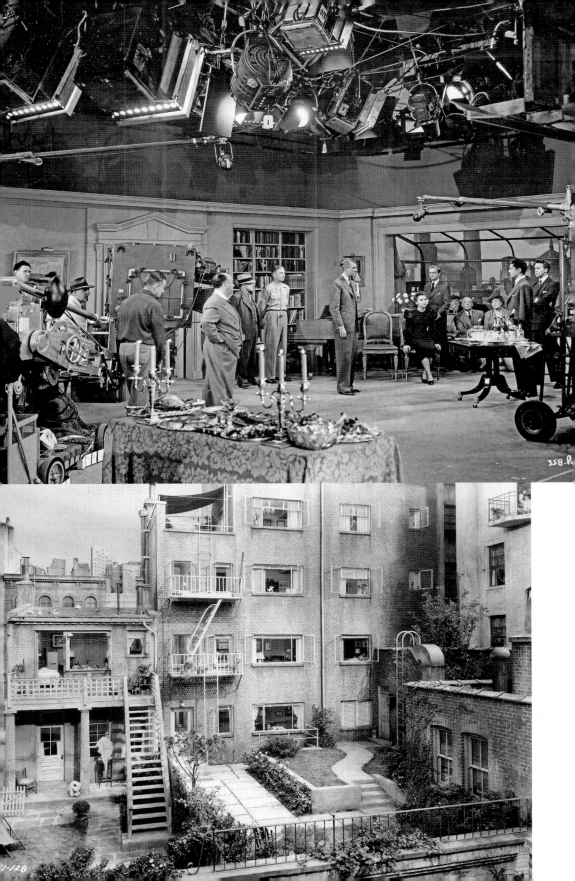

358-R

1-128

Torn Curtains in Rear Windows: Uncanny Homes and Gothic Plots

Hitchcock did not only explore the confines of cinematic space by single sets. Spaces of confinement pervade in his entire œuvre. "Hitchcock's architectural symbolism is evident as early as *Murder*, which ends with a magnificent shot of a stony prison façade," Camille Paglia writes. "As a British Romantic, he inherited from William Blake and Charles Dickens that understanding of prison spaces traced by so many ill-informed persons to Michel Foucault."[42] However, in Hitchcock, not the literal prison but rather the house and the home are presented as eminent places of confinement. In a way, many Hitchcock films are stories about a house or about the juxtaposition between two houses: *The Lodger*, *Easy Virtue*, *The Skin Game*, *Number 17*, *Jamaica Inn*, *Rebecca*, *Suspicion*, *Shadow of a Doubt*, *Notorious*, *The Paradine Case*, *Rope*, *Under Capricorn*, *Dial M for Murder*, *Rear Window*, *Psycho*, and *The Birds* are films, the plot and characters of which can be considered MacGuffins for the houses themselves. In addition, as Thomas Leitch has noted earlier, virtually all of Hitchcock's films deal with the idea of the home.[43] In most of his British pictures, the home is a stable resting place for the characters. However, already in several early films, such as *The Lodger*, *Downhill*, *Easy Virtue*, *The Manxman*, *A Farmer's Wife*, *Rich and Strange*, or *The Skin Game*, tensions within the family undermine the idea of the home as a realm of stability, security, and family relationships. In Hitchcock, as Tom Cohen wrote, "the family is always involved in a family plot."[44] This dialectic of hominess and homelessness also characterizes the Gaumont-British thrillers of the 1930s with their adventurous protagonists separated from their homes and looking for shelter and refuge. The theme of the home as a site of disturbance is elaborated and

42 Paglia, *The Birds*, 98.

43 Leitch, *Find the Director and Other Hitchcock Games*, 108-129.

44 Cohen, *Hitchcock's Cryptonymies*, I, 147.

45 See Michie, "Unveiling Maternal Desires," 29-54.

46 Cohen, *Alfred Hitchcock: The Legacy of Victorianism*.

47 Ruskin, *Sesame and Lilies*, 145-46.

48 See Albrecht, *Designing Dreams*, 104; and Mandel-baum & Myers, *Forties Screen Style*.

49 Edwards, "Brand-Name Literature," 32-58.

50 Mandelbaum & Myers, *Forties Screen Style*, 12.

Murder (1930) (Still, Royal Film Archive, Brussels)

even foregrounded in his American films.[45] In films such as *Rebecca, Suspicion, Shadow of a Doubt, The Paradine Case, Rope, Under Capricorn, Strangers on a Train, Dial M for Murder, The Wrong Man, Psycho,* and *The Birds*, domestic values are undermined and the theme of the home is used to link motifs of instability, alienation, fear, claustrophobia, and the loss of identity. Similarly, *Mr. and Mrs. Smith*, Hitchcock's atypical 1941 domestic comedy, can be considered a comedy of homelessness.

Presenting the house and the home as sites of anxiety and disturbance, Hitchcock has been situated in the tradition of the Victorian novel, which cultivated the dramatic potential of the domestic sphere.[46] After all, popular culture in the 1940s saw the Victorian home no longer exclusively the way John Ruskin described it as "the place of Peace; the shelter not only from all injury, but from all terror, doubt, and division" and a "sacred place, a vestal temple, a temple of the hearth watched over by Household Gods."[47] On the contrary, with its exaltation of the concealed, Victorian domesticity was also associated with the bourgeois hypocrisy, bigotry and cruelty that pervade Samuel Butler's autobiographical novel *The Way of All Flesh* (1880).

Victorian houses and interiors are omnipresent in Hitchcock's œuvre: *Easy Virtue, The Skin Game, The 39 Steps, Jamaica Inn, Rebecca, Suspicion, Saboteur, Notorious, The Paradine Case, Under Capricorn, Strangers on a Train, Vertigo,* and *Psycho* contain important scenes situated in impressive Victorian mansions. Hitchcock's preference for Victorian interiors reached its peak in the 1940s, when modernism and art deco had made room for a renewed interest in traditional styles. In the late 1930s and 1940s, Hollywood set design was dominated by several variants of so-called *High Pastiche*: Early American, Tropical, Surrealist, Contemporary, and diverse forms of Period Revivalism such as Neo-Baroque.[48] The share of sets in Victorian style is striking and this Victorian renaissance was not restricted to the realm of cinema but had a strong impact on life style in general. The merchandising campaign of *Rebecca*, for instance, included the launch of an expensive furniture line.[49] A taste for Victorian furniture, however, did not imply a turn to Victorian morals. A 1937 article in *Harper's Bazaar* states that "the modern young woman has not turned herself into a Victorian. She has decided to become more feminine, and being bold adventurous and having filled her flat with glass and steel furniture, she realizes that it will make an excellent setting for the Victorian decorative objects which she was taught in her childhood to despise."[50] Fashion magazines, home decorating manuals, and advertisings of the 1930s reflected the drastic changes that the home had undergone since the Victorian era. Whereas the bourgeois home of 1850 tended to serve as a showplace of male class and occupational status, the late nineteenth-century and early twentieth-century interior emerged as a separate sphere of feminine aesthetic self-expression and identity formation.[51]

Undoubtedly, this Victorian revival in films dealing with the home was also stimulated by the identity crisis of contemporary dwelling itself. Popular culture often associated the idea of the house with Victorian interiors whereas architectural modernism, with its celebration of transparency, bare white walls, geometrical simplicity, and the open spaces of the *plan libre*, came to be seen as antagonistic *vis-à-vis* domesticity as such. According to architectural historians such as Francesco Dal Co and Massimo Cacciari, the many experiments with domestic building types of the late nineteenth and early twentieth centuries illustrate that the house was in a state of crisis. This identity crisis was based on the paradox of the bourgeois interior and its cult of the domestic: it developed along with the modern metropolis, but lost its validity precisely because of the processes of industrialization and urbanization.[52] Leading modern architects were convinced that the old antagonisms between exterior and interior, and private and public, could no longer be repaired but, at the most, only ritualized. The Victorian revival of the late 1930s and early 1940s clearly expresses this nostalgia for domestic safety.

Fascinated by the house as a place of secrets and concealment, Hitchcock preferred Victorian houses because of their closed and stuffed interiors. Moat House (*Easy Virtue*), Manderley (*Rebecca*), Aysgarth House (*Suspicion*), Sutton House (*Saboteur*), Sebastian House (*Notorious*), Hindley Hall (*The Paradine Case*), and Minyago Yugilla (*Under Capricorn*) are products of a bourgeois culture characterized, as Peter Gay explains in *The Bourgeois Experience*, by an incredible "lust to conceal" and to retreat into the sanctity of the family.[53] In addition, these houses are crammed spaces by all means. Their owners and inhabitants are fanatic collectors of all kinds of domestic objects. From time immemorial the house has been presented as an expression of the personality of the inhabitant. According to Mario Praz, this is the house in its deepest essence: "a projection of the ego. And furnishing is nothing but an indifferent form of ego-worship."[54] Next to an articulated system of comfort, the Victorian house is an expression and expansion of self-consciousness. The inhabitant, after all, creates a private world in which the ego wants to see its reflection daily. Referring to fictitious dwellers as Walter Pater's Carl of Rosenmold and Joris Karl Huysmans' des Esseintes, Praz states that "hypersensitive nerves and love of furniture are indeed connected phenomena."[55] In films such as *Easy Virtue*, *Jamaica Inn*, *Rebecca*, *Suspicion*, *Notorious*, and *The Paradine Case* too, one is confronted with a parade of psychopathological characters packing their interiors with furniture, decorations and art objects. This, of course, fits perfectly

51 Tiersten, "The Chic Interior and the Feminine Modern," 18.
52 See Reed, *Not at Home*; Dal Co, *Figures of Architecture and Thought*, 13.
53 Gay, *The Education of the Senses: The Bourgeois Experience*.
54 Praz, *An Illustrated History of Interior Decoration*, 17.

55 Ibid., 27.
56 Walker, *Art and Artists on Screen*; Waldman, "The Childish, the Insane, and the Ugly," 52–65.
57 Benjamin, "Das Passagen-Werk: Paris, die Hauptstadt des XIX. Jahrhunderts," in *Gesammelte Schriften*, V, 1, 53.

into the Hollywood world-view which usually associates sophisticated art lovers and art collectors with decadent and criminal qualities.[56] In addition, the abundance of domestic objects illustrates the wealth and power of the inhabitants. These crammed interiors, moreover, have to make clear that the characters are stuck in their past and are haunted by demons of past times.

Such an accumulation of furniture, artworks and knick-knacks is, as the eclectic contamination of classical, Gothic and exotic forms, a typical product of nineteenth-century bourgeois culture, which considered the rigorous division between private and public domain of paramount importance. In his influential analysis of the bourgeois interior, Walter Benjamin states that "the interior is the refuge of art. The true inhabitant of the interior is the collector. He undertook the heavy task to worship things. By owning them, he assumes the Sisyphus-task of scraping off the commodity value of things."[57] Both collecting and eclecticism, or the ability to absorb and recontextualize elements of the past, signified individual sensibility and, at the same time, of bourgeois modernity.

Hitchcock's (neo-)Victorian houses illustrate Benjamin's interpretation of the bourgeois interior perfectly. All objects seem to have put aside their commodity and use value. As fetishes, they seem to put a spell on the characters. In addition, Benjamin states that the interior is both the universe and the container of a private person. "Dwelling," Benjamin writes, "means to leave traces behind. These are stressed by the interior. Dust covers, upholsters, cases, *étuis*, all in which the traces of everyday objects are imprinted, are invented in abundance. The traces of the inhabitants are imprinted in the interior too." Not coincidentally, Benjamin notes, the detective story, in which traces are

Entering the Victorian mansion in *Rebecca* (1940) (Still, Royal Film Archive, Brussels)

searched for continuously, developed within that very culture. Benjamin calls Poe, who not only wrote mysterious crime stories but also was the author of the essay *Philosophy of the Furniture*, "the first physiognomist of the interior."

Benjamin also hinted at the double connotation of the idea of dwelling. On the one hand it implies an age-old, presumably timeless element that answers to the image of staying in the mother's womb. According to Benjamin, this archetype does not consist of a sojourn in a house (*Haus*) but in casings (*Gehäuse*) that carry the imprints of their inhabitants. On the other hand, dwelling in its more extreme capacity, responds to the specific lifestyle of nineteenth century bourgeois culture, which was swept away in the twentieth century with its predilection for transparency and open air.[58] Finally, Benjamin notes, in a world in which everything is draped and covered, superficial appearances reign and, eventually, the inhabitant seems to submit himself to the interior. Things seem to take possession of the house. The interior, Benjamin concludes, appears to be determined by customs which are rather beneficial to the interior itself than to the inhabitants.[59]

In this perspective as well, Hitchcock's Victorian houses meet Benjamin's interpretation of the bourgeois interior. They appear to be bottomless reservoirs of traces. To the (mostly) female protagonist and the viewer alike, the house is presented as a network of signs. In addition, Hitchcock's houses seem to absorb their women residents. On the one hand, this tallies with modern bourgeois domestic culture. Decorating handbooks and magazine columns emphasized the need for aesthetic harmony and unity between the woman and her home to such an extent that the *body* of the bourgeois housewife became an integral part of the interior. As a result, the objects in a woman's home played a synecdochal rather than a symbolic role in relation to her identity; a room decorated by the bourgeois housewife was ultimately not so much her creation as an extension of her very being.[60] On the other hand, Hitchcock's heroines are never fully absorbed by the interior because they end up in homes decorated by others: the first Mrs. De Winter in *Rebecca*, the interior designer Mr. Bailey acting according to guidelines by Johnny Aysgarth in *Suspicion*, Mrs. Sebastian in *Notorious*, and Milly in *Under Capricorn*. As a result, every part of the interior is laden with symbolical meanings and every domestic object appears to be haunted by mysterious and sometimes fatal powers. In contrast with the castles and ruins of horror films, fear is interiorized. Haunting ghosts or bloodsucking monsters are exchanged for paranoia, traumas or neurotic and psychotic experiences, which destabilize the spatial coordinates of the house.[61] Instead of an organic unity, the architecture becomes a discontinuous montage of known and unknown, visible and invisible spaces. The architecture becomes a mental construction, perfectly suited for

58 Benjamin, "Das Passagen-Werk: Aufzeichnungen und Materialien," in *Gesammelte Schriften*, v, 1, 291-292.
59 Benjamin, "Erfahrung und Armut," in *Gesammelte Schriften*, 11, 1, 217.
60 Tiersten, "The Chic Interior and the Feminine Modern," 30-32.
61 See Mulvey, "Pandora:

Topographies of the Mask and Curiosity," 57.
62 Goliot, "Introduction à une narratologie de l'espace," 71-83.
63 Doane, *The Desire to Desire*, 123-54; Waldman, "Architectural Metaphor in the Gothic Romance Film," 55-70. See also Gallefant, "Black Satin," 84-103; Modleski, *The*

Women Who Knew Too Much, 43-71; and Jacobs, "Interieur en introspectie," 15-17.

cinematic evocations. One can apply Anne Goliot's remark regarding the house in George Cukor's *Gaslight* (1944) to many of Hitchcock's architectural constructions: "The space is part of the story and seems to move with it. The space is not a static frame but takes on a dynamic function. It is not a stabile place but must be considered in terms of action, perception, trajectory, movement, change, instability. (…) The film does not show us the built house but a house constructing itself."[62]

Such haunted interiors are part of the 'Gothic plot' that marks several of Hitchcock's films. In so doing, Hitchcock contributed significantly to a cycle of Hollywood pictures of the 1940s, which critics such as Mary Ann Doane and Diane Waldman have called *paranoid woman's films* and *Gothic romance films* respectively.[63] Both authors present *Rebecca* as the starting point of this genre. *Suspicion*, *Notorious* and *Under Capricorn* can certainly be considered variations on the Gothic theme, which is characterized by a plot in which a young, female protagonist feels attracted to a mysterious man. They get married and after the honeymoon, the woman finds herself in the ancestral home of her husband. Here, the heroine gets involved in a series of bizarre and astonishing events in which the husband increasingly frightens her. Eventually, the suspicion arises that the mysterious and tormented husband wants to kill his young bride. In their psychoana-lytical or gender based perspectives, Doane en Waldman have already demonstrated convincingly the importance of a domestic environment and architectural elements such as walls, stairs, doors, and windows in these films.

As suggested by the term, such films can be considered as descendants of the Gothic novel, a literary genre that developed, almost simultaneously with the Gothic revival in architecture, in the second half of the eighteenth century. Indeed, the stories of the first Gothic novels were situated amongst ruins or in medieval castles, which were associated with the exploration of the spiritual. Stemming from an age permeated with religion, Gothic buildings, with their high walls, moats, grotesque sculptures, pinnacles, towers, spiral staircases, ramps, battlements, dark dungeons, secret passageways, subterranean vaults, and concealed rooms, became the perfect metaphor for the hidden, irrational and inscrutable aspects of the soul. However, quite early on, medieval castles and abbeys were exchanged for the domesticity and coziness of the bourgeois dwelling. This reflects, of course, the social evolution from an aristocratic to a bourgeois society. This is also the case in Hitchcock's architectural variations on the Gothic theme. The demonic houses in *Jamaica Inn* and *Under Capricorn* are determined by the conventions of the historical costume drama. *Rebecca* is situated in a grand Victorian country house that evokes the spirit of an old castle and its opening sequence shows a ruin in moonlight. However, the

plots of *Suspicion*, *Shadow of a Doubt*, *Spellbound*, *Notorious*, and *The Paradine Case* are 'plain-clothes Gothic' and their houses and interior decorations breathe a more modern and bourgeois atmosphere.

Many 1940s Gothic romance films contain the so-called Bluebeard motif: a certain part of the house is taboo or even literally forbidden to be used and closed off: the attic in Cukor's *Gaslight*, the seventh basement room in Fritz Lang's *Secret Beyond the Door*, the artist's studio in Peter Godfrey's *The Two Mrs. Carrolls*, the tower chambers in Robert Stevenson's *Jane Eyre* and Joseph L. Mankiewicz' *Dragonwyck*, and so forth. This intrusion in the mysterious or forbidden room also characterizes several seminal Hitchcock films: the first Mrs. De Winter's bedroom in *Rebecca*, the wine cellar in *Notorious*, the bedroom and the valet's room in Hindley Hall in *The Paradine Case*, father's bedroom in *Strangers on a Train*, the McKintrick Hotel room in *Vertigo*, mother's bedroom in *Psycho*, or the attic room in *The Birds*. Hence the importance of keys in Hitchcock's films. Already in some of the British films the locking and unlocking of doors is given dramatic focus, through close-ups, for instance, but in some of his American films, such as *Notorious*, *Under Capricorn*, *Strangers on a Train*, and *Dial M for Murder*, they become an elaborated motif.

    In *Rebecca*, as in other films of the 1940s cycle, what is hidden behind the closed doors of these forbidden rooms seems always to contain an explanation for the strange behavior of the owner of the house. The plot structure is even constructed as a gradual revelation of the content of the forbidden room, both to the protagonist and the viewer. Referring to a kind of textbook version of psychoanalytical therapy, which Hollywood

38

64 Waldman, "Architectural Metaphor in the Gothic Romance Film," 63-64.
65 Wigley, "Untitled: The Housing of Gender," 347.
66 Girouard, *Life in the English Country House*, 298; Girouard, *The Victorian Country House*, 34-38.
67 Freud, "The Uncanny."

68 Vidler, *The Architectural Uncanny.*

I *Gaslight* (George Cukor, 1944) (Digital Frame)
II *Secret Beyond the Door* (Fritz Lang, 1948) (Digital Frame)

helped to popularize in the 1940s, several Gothic romance films can be considered examples of the so-called *cathartic method film*, of which Hitchcock's *Spellbound* is undoubtedly the most famous one.[64] In this category, characters relive a repressed traumatic experience blocked from memory. In Gothic romance films, the forbidden room is a metaphor for the repressed experience. The heroine attempts to disclose and visualize the secrets and mysteries, just like the psychoanalyst opens up the mysterious depths of the soul. Opening the forbidden room is, of course, especially in the films with the Bluebeard motif, the cathartic moment in the story. Hitchcock played on the power of the metaphor of opening doors in the famous point-of-view shot, in which Joan Fontaine's hand reaches for the door handle that gives access to Rebecca's bedroom, and in the equally famous staggering kissing scene in *Spellbound*, in which a series of doors open one behind the other. Because this film deals with psychoanalysis explicitly, this motif, undoubtedly, acts as a metaphoric representation of the opening and closing of the mind.

This spatiality of secrets joins the gender-based division of the house, in which, according to Mark Wigley, "the first truly private space was the man's study, a small locked room off his bedroom which no one else enters, an intellectual space beyond sexuality."[65] The motifs of doors that are locked and rooms that are forbidden to women protagonists present the house as a space that is controlled, guarded, and surveyed. The difference between the public and masculine space of the city and the private, feminine space of the house is repeated and reinforced by a form of segregation in the house itself. Even in the feminine domestic realm, women cannot enter some parts. Victorian mansions and country houses, such as Manderley in *Rebecca*, had exclusively male preserves (often with a billiard room or smoking room as nucleus), which were the natural result of the 'remember-there-are-ladies-present-sir' attitude.[66]

The house as a site of mysteries, secrets, and forbidden sections answers to the principle of what Freud has called the uncanny or unhomely (das *Unheimliche*).[67] According to Freud, feelings of anxiety and fear are often based on a confrontation with the strange, the unknown and the unfamiliar. The uncanny, however, is a form of the fearful that stems from the familiar. It is something secret or concealed that has become visible nevertheless. The *Unheimliche*, as it were, hides behind the *Heimliche*. It is something which is familiar to the soul but has become estranged as the result of a process of psychic suppression. Although the home encloses and thus gives comfort, it also encloses and hides secrets.[68] In presenting the house as the preeminent site of the 'Return of the Repressed,' Hitchcock became a master of the cinematic Uncanny. Situating his dramas in the safety of the intimate realm of the home, rather than in dungeons and medieval ruins, the threat is more intense. The bourgeois domestic interior, which was originally a refuge that offered protection from the hostility of the developing industrial metropolis, becomes, in its turn, the ultimate place of fear. His partiality for Victorian houses, however, enabled him to combine the bourgeois interior with references to the Gothic tradition. In the end, the Neogothic architectural elements that characterized Manderley, Hindley Hall, or the Bates House, would disappear completely. In 1955, when he made his first television shows, Hitchcock stated that he would bring "murder back into the American home where it had always belonged."[69] In *Psycho*, danger and perversion lurk both in a Victorian house and a modern motel. In *Rope*, *Rear Window*, *North by Northwest*, and *The Birds*, the logics of the uncanny operate in the generic apartments and houses of modern architecture. However, although unmistakably situated in a modern world in which domesticity has disintegrated, Hitchcock's houses answer to an almost sacred, quasi religious idea of the home celebrated in both Heidegger's and Bachelard's writings.

69 Naremore, "Hitchcock and Humor," 31. See also Hitchcock, "After-Dinner Speech at the Screen Producers Guild Dinner," 58.

City Symphonies and Cameos in the Crowd: The Suspense of Urban Modernity

Although he stated on many occasions that he preferred working in the studio, Hitchcock has always had an interest in location shooting from the beginning of his career. In addition, an idea about a particular topography or a juxtaposition of specific sites often preceded the story of his films. Instead of plot or characters, Hitchcock rather based his screenplays on objects and places.[1] From the very outset, "the contrast between the snowy Alps and the congested streets of London" was a visual concept that triggered off the production of the first version of *The Man Who Knew Too Much*.[2] *Foreign Correspondent* started with the famous sequence of windmills with wings turning against the wind and the image of a rainy square full of umbrellas. The idea of a chase on top of Mount Rushmore existed before there was the plot of *North by Northwest*.[3] The primacy of locations also determined Hitchcock's plans of the mid 1960s to make a film entitled *Frenzy* (not to be confused with the 1972 film with the same title) that entirely should take place in New York. In order to polish the screenplay, Hitchcock approached playwright Herb Gardner. When Gardner saw the storyboards, he was surprised to see a character successively being choked, pushed off the Verrazano-Narrows Bridge, and, two frames later, sitting at an outdoor café on Fifth Avenue. "How do we get from the guy being pushed off the Verrazano-Narrows Bridge to the same guy at a Fifth Avenue cafe?" Gardner asked.

"The crew goes there," said Hitchcock without cracking a smile.

"Wait a minute. How do we get the audience there, is what I mean."

"Mr. Gardner," said Hitchcock, "The audience will go wherever I take them and they'll be very glad to be there, I assure you."[4]

Many Hitchcock films contain a carefully constructed certain urban *couleur locale*. The producers of *Sabotage* praised the film because it would "feature more of the real London than any film yet made."[5] This attention to London street life harks back to the very start of Hitchcock's film career. "I have a penchant for including scenes of London in my films and in the old silent days we made endless excursions into the capital, shooting where and when we liked," Hitchcock wrote in a 1937 *New York Times* article.[6] Such an endless excursion was reflected in *Blackmail*. Images shot by a second unit headed by the director himself were used in the impressive opening sequence, which shows a police car driving through the streets of the metropolis.[7] *Downhill* even contains a sequence

1 Leff, *Hitchcock and Selznick*, 127.

2 Truffaut, *Hitchcock*, 90; see also Hitchcock, "Direction," 255.

3 Leff, "Hitchcock at Metro," 51.

4 McGilligan, *Alfred Hitchcock*, 686.

5 Krohn, *Hitchcock at Work*, 24.

6 Hitchcock, "Search for the Sun," 251.

7 Barr, *English Hitchcock*, 83. See also Ryall, *Blackmail*.

reminiscent of the so-called city symphonies made by avant-garde filmmakers in the 1920s and early 1930s. Completely being prey of poverty and despair, the delirious protagonist returns to his parental home, wandering through the London streets filled with traffic and anonymous pedestrians. As in the famous examples of the genre – *Berlin: Symphonie einer Großstadt* (Walther Ruttmann, 1927) or *The Man with the Movie Camera* (Dziga Vertov, 1929) – the hectic rhythm and bustle of the metropolis are evoked by means of fast editing, superpositions, double exposures, unusual viewpoints, and dizzying camera movements. Hitchcock himself, moreover, flirted with the idea to make an experimental "film symphony" entitled *London* or *Life of a City* in collaboration with Walter Mycroft: "The story of a big city from dawn to the following dawn. I wanted to do it in terms of what lies behind the face of a city – what makes it thick – in other words, backstage of a

42

8 McGilligan, *Alfred Hitchcock*, 102. See also Bogdanovich, *Who the Devil Made It*, 494.

9 Alfred Hitchcock in an interview with the *New York Herald Tribune* (22 April 1945), quoted in McGilligan, *Alfred Hitchcock*, 382-83. See also Hunter, *Me and Hitch*, 89.

10 See Frisby, *Simmel and*

Since, 103.

I Dissolve from the Alps to London
The Man Who Knew Too Much (1934) (Digital Frame)
II Hectic London street life
Downhill (1927) (Digital Frame)
III The urban crowd
Foreign Correspondent (1940) (Digital Frame)
IV The anonymous pedestrian
The Birds (1963) (Digital Frame)

city."[8] Years later, Hitchcock spoke of a similar project on New York to a *New York Herald Tribune* reporter: New York is "too big, too hard to get it with the camera. It would be wonderful to do a story entirely about New York in color. What I mean is not the New York as it exists to the tourist or the casual observer, but inside New York, a behind-the-scenes, backstage New York, something that would show the inner life of the city, like the things that go on in the kitchens of big hotels." "I would begin the story at four o'clock in the morning and end it at two the following morning," Hitchcock continued. "I'd like to open with a scene in the Bowery showing a bum drowsing in a saloon, a fly walking on his nose: starting with the lowest form of life in the metropolis. And I'd end up, ironically of course, with the highest form of life, a scene the following morning in a swank nightclub, with well-dressed drunks slouching over their tables and passing out. I don't know what the story would be in between. That's the problem."[9]

In contrast with the city symphonies by Ruttmann or Vertov, Hitchcock did not see his unrealized London project as a "mechanical film" but as a work that would offer a heaping slice of humanity and in which "everything would have to be used dramatically." In *Downhill* as well, the whole repertory of experimental techniques are humanized, as it were, and integrated into a 'classic' framework: all avant-garde extravaganzas are justified by the narrative since we see the city through the eyes of a delirious character. Nonetheless, similar to the paintings and films of the 1920s avant-garde, the city is represented as a fragmented accumulation of sensory impressions and as a space filled and determined by the bustling density of crowds.

Furthermore, urban crowds are a recurrent motif in climactic Hitchcock scenes. Every Hitchcock fan remembers the images of a lynching mob in *The Lodger*, the fighting crowds in *Juno and the Paycock*, the bystanders on the pavement in *Sabotage*, the music hall audience in *The 39 Steps*, the umbrellas in *Foreign Correspondent*, the factory workers in *Saboteur*, the army of clerks and secretaries in the opening sequence of *North by Northwest*, the theater audience in *Torn Curtain*, and so forth. The concept of a man being more isolated in the middle of a crowd than in a deserted spot recurs in many of Hitchcock's films. The hero is often trapped in a movie house, in a music hall, at a political rally, at an auction sale, in a ballroom, or at a fund-raising event. In addition, it is striking that the crowds and spaces of urban modernity provide in most cases the context for Hitchcock's infamous cameo appearances. Hitchcock himself pops up in his films as an anonymous stranger – a character that, according to the urban sociologist Georg Simmel, precisely typifies life in the public spaces of the modern metropolis.[10] In contrast with the village of the small town, it is on the sidewalks and in the subways of the metropolis

43

that we are constantly confronted with unknown and anonymous faces. Sometimes, the director hides himself in the crowd, such as in *The Lodger*, *Under Capricorn*, *Frenzy*, or the American version of *The Man Who Knew Too Much*. In *Rear Window*, he shows up in the room of one of the neighbors. For *Rope*, Hitchcock flirted with the idea to merge literally into the abundance of signs in the urban landscape: his trademark silhouette would be noticeable as a blinking neon light from the window of the penthouse in which the entire film takes place. Eventually, he abandoned the plan and he appears as an anonymous pedestrian walking in the streets of the city – something that is also the case in *Murder*, *The 39 Steps*, *Young and Innocent*, *Rebecca*, *Foreign Correspondent*, *Mr. and Mrs. Smith*, *Suspicion*, *Saboteur*, *Stage Fright*, *I Confess*, *Vertigo*, *Psycho*, and *The Birds*. In other films, he appears in the public and heterogeneous spaces of corridors (*Marnie*), lobbies (*Torn Curtain*), and elevators (*Spellbound*) of hotels – a locale that, according to Siegfried Kracauer, epitomized the conditions of modern urban life in their anonymity and fragmentation.[11] From the mid 1930s, Hitchcock, who enjoyed the luxury of exclusive hotels, toyed for decades with the idea to shoot a film in a hotel that is an urban microcosm in itself.[12]

In addition, many of Hitchcock's sneaky appearances are closely connected to motorized traffic, another preeminent icon of urban modernity. Hitchcock is a passenger of the subway (*The Lodger*) or finds himself in train stations (*The Lady Vanishes*) or airports (*Topaz*). He regularly travels by train (*Shadow of a Doubt*, *The Paradine Case*, *Strangers on a Train*) or bus (*To Cath a Thief*, *North by Northwest*). This predilection for motorized traffic also resulted in a series of memorable car scenes – a motif perfectly tailored to the characteristics of Hitchcock's style: a sophisticated editing technique, fluid camera

44

11 Kracauer, "The Hotel Lobby."

12 See McGilligan, *Alfred Hitchcock*, 660-62; and Gottlieb, "Unknown Hitchcock," 100-101.

13 See Jacobs, "From Flaneur to Chauffeur," 213-28.

14 Silver, "Fragments of the Mirror," 117.

movements, the excessive but always well-considered use of point-of-view shots, and the predilection for rear-projections. In addition, Hitchcock perfectly geared the perception of a shifting landscape through the windshield to the cinematic experience itself. Consequently, as in the works of modernist auteurs such as Rossellini, Antonioni, or Godard, in Hitchcock's films, the motif of the car drive became a perfect instrument of cinematic self-reflection.[13] This is clearly the case in what Alain Silver called "the landmarking effect" of the prolonged car drives through San Francisco in *Vertigo*.[14] As a flaneur, Scottie (James Stewart), wanders through San Francisco, which is presented as a dead city in the spell of the past. Reminiscent of the city imagery of symbolist novels such as Georges Rodenbach's famous *Bruges-la-morte* (1892), which has been mentioned as a source of inspiration of *Vertigo*'s source novel *D'entre les morts* by Pierre Boileau and Thomas Narcejac, the city is transformed into a symbolic landscape. This landscape – "ignore geography; consider length only regardless of turns," Hitchcock wrote to editor George Tomasini – is explored by the car, which is presented as a tool of the gaze and a device of sightseeing.

Montage of Tourist Attractions: Hitchcock's Creative Geography   This "landmarking effect" and this form of sightseeing brings us to another striking urban icon playing an important part in Hitchcock films: the tourist site. The British Museum, the Royal Albert Hall, the Statue of Liberty, the Jefferson Memorial, the Golden Gate Bridge, the United Nations Headquarters, and Mount Rushmore are eternally connected to films such as *Blackmail*, *The Man Who Knew Too Much*, *Saboteur*, *Strangers on a Train*,

45

i Hotel cameo
Marnie (1964) (Digital Frame)
ii Traffic cameo
North by Northwest (1959) (Digital Frame)
iii Car driving as a cinematic experience
Vertigo (1958) (Digital Frame)

Vertigo, and *North by Northwest* respectively. Writing the screenplay of *Strangers on a Train*, Raymond Chandler complained: "Every time you get set, he jabs you off balance by wanting to do a love scene on top of the Jefferson Memorial or something like that."[15]

This interest in monuments tallies with his predilection for exotic locations such as Lake Como (*The Pleasure Garden*), the isle of Man (*The Manxman*), Vienna (*Waltzes from Vienna*), Switzerland (*Secret Agent* and the British version of *The Man Who Knew Too Much*), the Scottish highlands (*The 39 Steps*), Holland (*Foreign Correspondent*), Quebec (*I Confess*), the French Riviera (*To Catch a Thief*), Morocco (the American version of *The Man Who Knew Too Much*) or Copenhagen (*Topaz*). Exotic locations emphasize the adventurous character of these films. Unmistakably, they situate Hitchcock's films in the tradition of the adventure story, which is characterized by a series of changing locations to which the hero has to adapt himself. Hitchcock, however, often selects monuments as locations – in other words, places that are already part of a tourist ritual. Although he wanted to evoke the backside of a city in his unrealized films on London and New York, Hitchcock's urban imagery is closely connected to tourist attractions. Undoubtedly, famous buildings and places even acquired more tourist attention because of their prominent role in Hitchcock's films. Hitchcock, consequently, both tailed and stimulated tourism. "In the town of Bodega (65mi N of San Francisco), you will find the building (17110 Bodega Lane) that served as the schoolhouse in Alfred Hitchcock's film *The Birds* (1963). Originally the Potter School (1873), the Italianate structure has been converted into a bed-and-breakfast inn," the Michelin travel guide of California states. Also the gravestone of the fictitious character of Carlotta Valdez (*Vertigo*) at the Mission Dolores cemetery in San Francisco turned into an important tourist attraction. Meanwhile, the stone was removed because it was not 'authentic' enough to reside in the hallowed grounds of the Mission cemetery.[16]

In order to evoke a specific topographical context, Hitchcock often integrated monuments in conventional techniques such as establishing shots, montage-sequences, or rear projections, which Hollywood cinema put at a director's disposal. At first sight, Hitchcock seems to operate as an orthodox filmmaker respecting the rules of classical cinema. Nonetheless, in Hitchcock, these technical and stylistic conventions go hand in hand with a specific logic and a peculiar sensibility.

In line with classical cinema conventions, Hitchcock often included tourist attractions in his establishing shots as a kind of visual synecdoche. Famous buildings and sites identify not only themselves but also act as convenient shorthand for the entire cities that encompass them. Some aerial and panoramic views in *Notorious*, which were shot

15 McGilligan, *Alfred Hitchcock*, 444.
16 Kraft & Leventhal, *Footsteps in the Fog*, 101.
17 Monaco, *How to Read a Film*, 323.
18 Eisenstein, "The Montage of Film Attractions."
19 Urry, *The Tourist Gaze*, 138-40.

by a second unit, for instance, make us clear that the story is situated in Rio de Janeiro although the film was entirely made in the Hollywood studio. Answering perfectly to the continuity laws of classical cinema, Hitchcock made full use of what Kuleshov had called "creative geography" – the composite of shots made at varying times and places making a unified piece of film narrative.[17] Opening shots or entire opening credit sequences in particular establish a topographical context for the narrative. The opening credits showing images of Park Avenue in *Mr. and Mrs. Smith* make clear that the story is set in New York City. In addition, the opening shots of *Sabotage*, *Stage Fright*, and *Frenzy* immediately situate the story in London. Such views – in *Frenzy*, they even include the city arms – have an unmistakably postcard quality. The role of famous monuments, such as the Houses of Parliament, Trafalgar Square, and Piccadilly Circus (*Sabotage*), St Paul's Cathedral (*Stage Fright*) or the Tower Bridge (*Frenzy*), is clearly to construct a topographical context. Paradoxically, the famous panning shot that does *not* show a tourist attraction proves this. In the opening shot of *Psycho*, the place of action is also indicated by means of a text: a typical example of the postwar urban condition, the generic city of Phoenix, after all, lacks the world-famous monuments bringing the viewer immediately to the right place.

Another conventional technique to situate a story geographically is the so-called 'montage sequence,' which shows a series of short shots in a brief time span. Some stereotypical examples of montage sequences, moreover, are associated with the realm of traveling and tourism, such as the superposition of hotel stickers on a traveling case (as in *Suspicion*). In *Rich and Strange*, an expository title card that reads "To get to the Folies Bergere, you have to cross Paris" is followed by a swiftly edited montage of sights of monuments, hectic street life, and vibrant nightlife, intercut with fast motion reaction shots of both protagonists. As a kind of incorporation of Soviet montage techniques within the classical Hollywood style, this Paris montage sequence shows striking resemblances with the aesthetics of the avant-garde city symphony. The city is not only presented as a series of tourist 'attractions' but also as a space that lends itself to a representation by means of an Eisensteinian 'montage of attractions' – a kind of calculated assemblage of powerful shock moments and surprise effects, which is rather based on psychological stimulation than on narrative logic.[18]

The urban imagery produced by the establishing shots and montage sequences of classical cinema shows a striking resemblance with what John Urry has called the "tourist gaze" – a kind of look that transforms the city into a series of static postcards.[19] Tourism has been connected with industrial image production from the very first. A search for the photogenic, tourism turned travel into an accumulation of pictures. Supported by photography and film or video equipment, traveling is transformed into a movement from one sight to another. In addition, the tourist ritual implies the sacralization of specific places – a process to which photography and cinema contribute largely. Mechanical reproductions not only elicit the tourist to see the original – a monument even becomes 'authentic' because of the production, distribution and consumptions of its copies. In a brilliant and ironic inversion of Walter Benjamin's thesis on mechanical reproduction, Dean MacCannell stated that the age of mechanical reproduction does not imply the final blow to the aura.[20] On the contrary, photographic reproductions themselves have become the aura of the original. The widespread pictures of the Statue of Liberty, Mount Rushmore, and Golden Gate Bridge lend luster to these monuments.

That type of tourist gaze is literally used in the typical Hollywood view on European cities, for instance. A latent urban whole is constructed through the accumulation of fragments. Warping the city's topography and presenting stereotypes of its culture and physical constitution, such films are intimately tied to the phenomenon of tourism.[21] As if in a lazy tourist's dream, routes jump-cut throughout the city, taking in all the major sites, in a visually glorious but topographically nonsensical sequence. The film becomes a kind of moving postcard collection, showing the tourist what to see and also adding the obligation of the right way to experience the landmarks by selecting viewpoints and approaches. A perfect application of what Dean MacCannel called tourism's preference for "staged authenticity," places are altered in relation to an ideal image. Hitchcock, as well, did not hesitate to "correct" one of his tourist sites, making them more "authentic." In *Vertigo*, he added a bell tower to the mission church of San Juan Bautista by means of matte shots.[22]

An ardent tourist himself, Hitchcock frequently used these picture-postcard or sightseeing clichés in static establishing shots or hectic montage-sequences. In addition, Hitchcock, as already mentioned in the previous chapter, frequently establishes a setting by means of rear projection. It should be noted that this procedure, which he continued using also later in his career when it was already considered outdated, is especially used in car and train scenes – linking it with travel, travelogues, sightseeing, and tourism.

Sightseeing Terror: Metatourism and National Monuments

The incorporation of famous monuments in establishing shots, montage sequences, and rear projections can be interpreted as an indication of Hitchcock's servile dedication to Hollywood's tourist gaze. However, in some of his most memorable scenes showing famous monuments, this tourist view is shattered. First of all, in some of his films, Hitchcock made some

48

20 MacCannel, *The Tourist*, 91-107.
21 Bass, "Insiders and Outsiders," 84-99.
22 Kraft & Leventhal, *Footsteps in the Fog*, 140.

I Establishing shot of London
Frenzy (1972) (Digital Frame)
II Establishing shot of London
Stage Fright (1949) (Digital Frame)
III Establishing shot of Phoenix
Psycho (1960) (Digital Frame)
IV Paris montage sequence
Rich and Strange (1932) (Digital Frame)
V Mission of San Juan Bautista, California
Vertigo (1958) (Digital Frame)
VI Mission of San Juan Bautista, California
(Postcard)

explicit references to the phenomenon of tourism itself. *Rich and Strange* is a film about a tourist trip; Manderley, the castle in *Rebecca*, is visited by tourists; in *Topaz*, a Russian spy hides between a group of tourists visiting a Copenhagen porcelain factory; the first shot of the British version of *The Man Who Knew Too Much* shows travel brochures for Switzerland; in *Suspicion*, a montage-sequence of hotel stickers on a suitcase tells the audience where Cary Grant and Joan Fontaine honeymooned; the opening shot of *To Catch a Thief* shows the sidewalk window of a travel bureau and actor John Williams described the environment in which the film takes place as a "travel folder heaven."[23] *North by Northwest*, finally, is characterized by an episodic succession of changing locations as if "pinned side by side in some photograph album"[24] or a tourist guidebook. In its hilarious trailer, Hitchcock presents himself as a travel agent – in the late 1950s, clearly, tourism has become a Hitchcock trademark and an aspect of his persona as is shown in a 1956 *Newsweek* article containing a world map on which some locations of his "globe-trotting movies" are marked. "The world of Alfred Hitchcock includes quite a few places that no Cook's tourist would ever wish to visit," the article tells us.[25]

The master of suspense, in short, does not only rely on the tourist gaze, he also comments on it. Some scholars claim that, in some of his films, Hitchcock even exhibits the outmost contempt for tourism – and most especially for what one might call cinema as tourism.[26] Hitchcock transcends and undermines the tourist gaze. His postcard-like views, however, were often a sham manœuvre. He made a habit of wielding postcard views in his films to lull his audiences into false security. In the end, however, in a Hitchcock movie, it's always dangerous to hang about monuments – the word 'hanging' can be used here literally. Famous buildings and sites are more than mere backdrops, they are emotionally charged with a dramatic intensity as well.

Hitchcock made the most of the emblematical power of monuments, which are symbolic by definition. Undoubtedly, he was interested in monuments because they allude to the passing of time. On the one hand, a monument, in particular an easily identifiable one, also exists before and beyond the film. As a result, it acquires a substantial reality that transcends the diegesis. On the other hand, because of the monument, the environment becomes the ground for a communication with the past – a theme perfectly elaborated in the San Francisco locations of *Vertigo*: the church and graveyard of Mission Doleres, the mission church of San Juan Bautista, the redwood forest with the age-old trees, the Victorian McKittrick hotel, the museum collection in the California Palace of the Legion of Honor, and Bernard Maybeck's neoclassical Palace of Fine Arts, which almost looks like a romantic ruin.

23 Quoted in McGilligan, *Alfred Hitchcock*, 496.
24 Jameson, "Spatial Systems in *North by Northwest*," 50.
25 "Alfred Hitchcock – Director: On TV or at the Movies, Suspense Is Golden," *Newsweek* (June 11, 1956), 105-108.
26 Modleski, *The Women Who Knew Too Much*, 104; see also Cohen, *Hitchcock's Cryptonymies*, II, 201-202.
27 Leff, "Hitchcock at Metro," 51.

Embodying collective memories and civic identities, monuments are often connected to ideological values. In particular, Hitchcock included monuments of American democracy, such as the Statue of Liberty, Mount Rushmore, and the government buildings in Washington in spy thrillers such as *Saboteur*, *North by Northwest*, and *Topaz* respectively. Initially, MGM's location manager obtained permission (later withdrawn) from the South Dakota Park authorities to film *North by Northwest*'s climax on Mount Rushmore because the monument would play a role in the elimination of the film's villains: "We sincerely believe that it will be symbolically and dramatically satisfying to the people of the United States that this great national memorial, standing there in all its granite glory, becomes the very stumbling block of those who would undermine our country. In the end, the enemies of democracy are defeated by the Shrine of Democracy itself."[27]

I Travel brochures
The Man Who Knew Too Much (1934) (Digital Frame)
II Travel bureau
To Catch a Thief (1954) (Digital Frame)
III Hitchcock as travel agent
North by Northwest trailer (1959) (Digital Frame)

North by Northwest starts with a murder in the United Nations headquarters and ends atop the megalomaniac presidential heads. Halfway the story, American intelligence agents assemble near the Capitol – in each case, monumental architecture becomes a token of terrifying power. In *Strangers on a Train*, Hitchcock and his screenwriters moved the setting of Patricia Highsmith's novel from New York City to Washington, DC. In so doing, Hitchcock, according to Robert Corber, linked the homophobic subtext of the film to national security discourses.[28] In a memorable scene of the film, the villainous character of Bruno Anthony is dwarfed by the size of the Jefferson Memorial but his black shadow on the white monument "creates a blemish on the nation."

However, rather than referring to specific patriotic or moral meanings of landmarks, Hitchcock, in the first place, exploits their dramatic potentials.[29] Monuments and famous places are turned into landscapes of terror. In *Vertigo*, all landmarks are in the grip of death. In *Blackmail*, *Foreign Correspondent*, *Saboteur*, *Vertigo*, and *North by Northwest* people fall from monuments. On more than one occasion, Hitchcock showed that, in the words of Leonard Leff, "monuments to humanity were particularly indifferent to humanity."[30]

As his theaters, concert halls, and cinemas, Hitchcock's landmarks are sites of crime and treason, and "perfect places to die."[31] By linking them to fears and phobias, Hitchcock subverts monuments. Whereas the tourist gaze selects, censors, and literally keeps the dangers of modernity outside of the image, Hitchcock presents the most familiar places and buildings as threatening sites. Hitchcock's suspense, after all, is based on a detailed rendering of a familiar environment. The more familiar, the stronger it can be disrupted and the easier it can be presented as threatening and dangerous.[32] Sites

52

28 Corber, *In the Name of National Security*, 72.
29 Midding, "Aus angemessen bequemer Distanz," 137.
30 Leff, *Hitchcock and Selznick*, 184.
31 Zupancic, "A perfect Place to Die," 73-105.
32 Bonitzer, "Hitchcockian Suspense," 23.

usually associated with amusement are used as loci for mayhem. In a Hitchcock film, danger does not lurk in dark alleys or inaccessible ruins but in the most intimate parts of the house or in precisely that part of the public realm that is known and made domestic by monuments and tourist attractions.

A visible and public place par excellence, the monument also becomes a mirror for individual fears and hidden traumas. The huge, white, marble staircase of the Jefferson Memorial in *Strangers on a Train* may express national or moral values but, in the first place, it functions as a stage for a sinister shadow haunting the protagonist. Washington's urban landscape seems to acquire the both mysterious and ominous character of the deserted and timeless streets and squares of Giorgio De Chirico. An impressive shot, seen from the moving viewpoint of the protagonist, illustrates perfectly how Hitchcock exploits such urban monuments and how he shapes a cinematic space in relation to the architecture. The sequence consists of a skillful puzzle of circular patterns: the Pantheon-based building designed by John Russell Pope, the course made by the characters walking around the building, the rounded car window through which the memorial is looked at.

The opening sequence of *I Confess*, a film shot in Quebec, does not only contain urban views to indicate a specific geographic location. From the very first shot, Hitchcock transforms the urban topography in a symbolic landscape. After a forward tracking shot – in classical Hollywood almost always a token of threat – over a river toward the skyline of a city, Hitchcock shows us a series of medium long shots of deserted and shadowy streets. These images are intercut with close shots, slightly distorted by a wide angle lens, of one way street signs. As a result, the city is presented as a claustrophobic

53

I Statue of Liberty, New York
Saboteur (1942) (Digital Frame)
II Mount Rushmore
North by Northwest (1959) (Digital Frame)
III Jefferson Memorial, Washington, DC
Strangers on a Train (1951) (Digital Frame)

and determinist labyrinth – a perfect topographical reflection of the fatalistic *noir* world view.[33] As in *Psycho*, *Rope*, or *Shadow of a Doubt*, the sequence ends with the image of an open window.

Both the scene at the Jefferson Memorial in *Strangers on a Train* and the opening sequence of *I Confess* demonstrate that, Hitchcock associates the city's monuments with threat, danger, and a feeling of oppression. The compositions of the shots often emphasize this. Alain Silver interprets the grid motif in the shot of the Forth Bridge in *The 39 Steps* and in the abstract linear patterns of the curtain wall of skyscraper in the opening credit sequence of *North by Northwest* as allusions to the traps in which the protagonists found themselves.[34] The metropolis or natural landscape, often presented as the background for a fugitive, are transformed into a prison or labyrinth.

54

33 Silver, "Fragments of the Mirror," 110-12.

34 Ibid., 112-15.

35 Pomerance, *An Eye for Hitchcock*, 26.

36 On Hitchcock as art collector, see Krohn, "Le musée secret de M. Hitchcock," and Bondil-Poupard, "Alfred Hitchcock: An Artist in Spite of Himself," 179-88.

37 Initially, Hitchcock also thought about situating one of the early key scenes of *Topaz* in the Copenhagen Glyptothek or the Rosenborg Castle (which is also a museum). Eventually, he selected the Royal Copenhagen Porcelain Manufactury as location. See folders 755 and 756 in the Alfred Hitchcock Collection,

Margaret Herrick Library, Academy of Motion Picture Arts and Sciences, Los Angeles.

I, II The streets of Quebec
I Confess (1953) (Digital Frame)
III Forth Bridge
The 39 Steps (1935) (Digital Frame)

Since monuments are connected and subjected to sightseeing, they are ultimate motifs of Hitchcockian cinema, which functions as a meditation on the gaze. Situating climactic scenes in and around monuments implies that the spectacle has its own built-in or ready-made audience. Sightseeing becomes thus a perfect motif to investigate the cinematic tension between objective and subjective viewpoints. A master of the point-of-view shot, Hitchcock realizes that monuments are not mere passively subjected to the gaze, they also organize their own perception. By privileging certain viewpoints or by starting off a cycle of production, distribution, and consumption of images, they structure our viewing habits. Hitchcock plays on this. He disorders the viewing patterns enforced by the monument. Monuments are often looked at from a 'wrong' position. The characters do not admire the monument; they find themselves in the middle or on top of it and, consequently, in the focus of the tourist gaze. In *Foreign Correspondent*, *Blackmail*, *Saboteur*, and *North by Northwest*, monuments are clambered. In the museum rooms of *Blackmail*, *Vertigo*, and *Torn Curtain*, characters become a kind of *punctum*, which draws all the attention to themselves instead of to the artworks. The familiar and meanwhile ubiquitously reproduced image of the monument is disrupted. We watch the theater, as it were, from behind the scenes. Suddenly, characters are on a place that no longer offers a view on the monument but that is looked at itself. It answers to Hitchcock's formula of putting a character or spectator in another viewing position – the hero on the monument is like the voyeur who suddenly discovers that he is being watched in his turn.[35]

The Trouble with Museums: Mausoleums of the Gaze   All these aspects have also an important part in a series of key scenes that Hitchcock, an art lover and enthusiast art collector himself, situated in museums.[36] At first sight, Hitchcock plays on the associations that museums usually evoke in Hollywood films: as other monuments, they function as a *pars pro toto* for an entire city; they are presented as a habitat for snobs or dandies; they are secret meeting places for lovers or spies; or, they are presented as dreamy realms dominated by mysterious or atavistic forces.

In four memorable museum scenes, which are scattered all over his entire *œuvre*, Hitchcock situates his characters in buildings that answer perfectly to the conventional architectural museum typology.[37] This museum type, which goes back to late eighteenth- and early nineteenth-century designs of architects such as Durand, Leo von Klenze, Karl Friedrich Schinkel, and John Soane, remained the dominant model for more than hundred fifty years. It is characterized by long rows of rooms, the presence of overhead light, and elements borrowed from classical temple architecture, such as a colonnade, a monumental staircase, and a rotunda topped by a dome.[38]

A prominent example of the first generation of museum buildings, Robert Smirke's British Museum (1823-47) in London is the location of the climactic scene in *Blackmail*. Because the museum did not allow a full cast and crew to occupy its premises, the famous backdrops were photographed first with half-our exposures and made into backlighted transparencies. The actors were integrated into the museum interior by means of the famous Schüfftan process, which Hitchcock probably learned to know in the sophisticated film studios in Germany. The film contains one of the first examples of the typical Hitchcock climax at a famous or bizarre location that is entertaining itself. The blackmailer tries to evade the police by sneaking into the museum. He ends up in the rooms with ancient Egyptian statues and the famous circular reading room of the library. One shot, in particular, appeals to the imagination: foreshadowing the surreal landscapes of the Statue of Liberty in *Saboteur* or Mount Rushmore in *North by Northwest*, a man climbs a rope next to the huge stone face of an Egyptian colossus. Also here, the scene ends with a fall from a great height – a man thrusts himself through the skylight of the museum's dome.

In the second example, *Strangers on a Train*, the sinister character of Bruno Anthony turns up from behind the columns of the interior of the National Gallery in Washington D.C. This building was designed in the 1930s by John Russell Pope and is situated roughly halfway between the Capitol and the Washington Memorial. Its architecture, which is in harmony with the nineteenth-century architectural style of the federal government buildings, is a typical product of the Washington Classical Re-revival from that era. However, it is also one of the very last orthodox applications of the classical museum typology. The scene in question, constructed by means of rear projections, takes place in the monumental rotunda of the building. A messenger of fate, Giambologna's *Mercurio* is visible above the heads of the protagonist and his girlfriend – the set decorator of Gus Van Sant's 1998 remake of *Psycho* put a replica of the statue in the room of Norman Bates' mother.

The third example is from *Vertigo*, which contains two San Francisco settings related to the arts. In the last part of the film, Scottie (James Stewart) and Judy/Madeleine (Kim Novak) walk along the Palace of Fine Arts, a grandiose rotunda and peristyle replicated from the structures designed by Bernard Maybeck to house the Impressionist art exhibits for the 1915 Panama-Pacific International Exposition. Earlier in the film, Scottie, shadowing Madeleine, finds himself in the California Palace of the Legion of Honor, a museum building opened in 1924. It is a permanent reconstruction of the French

56

38 See Searing, "The Development of a Museum Typology," and Pevsner, *A History of Building Types*, 111-138.

I, II, III British Museum, London
Blackmail (1929) (Digital Frame)
IV, V National Gallery, Washington, DC
Strangers on a Train (1951) (Digital Frame)

pavilion on the same Panama-Pacific International Exposition – in its turn a reduced replica of the Palais de la Légion d'Honneur in Paris. In this building, Madeleine visits the painting collection where she muses near the portrait of the deceased Carlotta Valdez. According to Dan Auiler, the portrait was painted especially for the film by John Ferrer, who had worked with Hitchcock on *The Trouble with Harry* and who also provided the storyboards of *Vertigo*'s dream sequence.[39]

In *Torn Curtain*, finally, Hitchcock takes us to the Alte Nationalgallerie in Berlin, built between 1866 and 1876 by Johann Heinrich Strack based on drawings by Friedrich August Stüler. Riding on an East Berlin bus, Paul Newman's character looks at a tourist brochure that contains a frontal view of the museum's neoclassical facade. The next shot shows the symmetrical building with its temple front and colonnades from the same viewpoint *in situ*. After that, Newman walks through the uncanny empty and silent rooms of the museum, the classicist architecture of which is mirrored by the sculptures of Bertel Thorvaldsen, Johann Gottfried Schadow, and Antonio Canova among others. As in *Blackmail* and *Strangers on a Train*, the confrontation between actors and the museum collection is the result of special effects. When Paul Newman is seen walking through vast galleries of artworks, only the floor is a 'real' studio floor; the galleries are paintings optically printed into the film.[40] In the case of the exterior, only the doorway and front pillars were constructed full-size. The rest was a painting. Here, the museum functions as a labyrinth in which Newman tries to get rid of his pursuer.

By selecting classical museum buildings and by emphatically depicting their obligatory architectural components, Hitchcock refers to one of the sacral origins of the museum. These museum buildings do not refer coincidentally to classical temple architecture. By means of monumental staircases, art is isolated from the everyday and turned into the object of a ritual experience. From the beginning, this museum concept was fiercely criticized by artists, architectural theorists (such as Quatremère de Quincy), and poets (Paul Valéry).[41] Museums would freeze and suffocate the artworks – "museum and mausoleum are connected by more than phonetic association," Adorno wrote in a famous paraphrase of this idea.[42]

Hitchcock rewardingly took advantage of these associations. The room, in which the fugitive ends up in *Blackmail*, is full of archaeological objects from Ancient Egypt, a culture practically completely in the sign of death, the tomb, or life in the hereafter. The British Museum also becomes literally the tomb of a character who falls off the dome. In *Strangers on a Train*, a museum is visited by a character who is not only a murderer but also morbidly proposes to swap murders. In *Vertigo*, the protagonists walk along a

39 See Auiler, *Vertigo*, 43 and 83. Paramount production files (folder 997) in the Margaret Herrick Library indicate that also other artists, such as the Italian painter Manlio Sarra, painted a version of the portrait.
40 Loring, "Filming *Torn Curtain* by Reflected Light," 680-83.
41 See Duncan, *Civilizing Rituals*, 7-20; and Newhouse, *Towards a New Museum*, 46-51.
42 Adorno, "Valéry Proust Museum," 175.

I Palace of Fine Arts, San Francisco
Vertigo (1958) (Digital Frame)
II Palace of the Legion of Honor, San Francisco
Vertigo (1958) (Digital Frame)
III, IV, V Alte Nationalgallerie, Berlin
Torn Curtain (1966) (Digital Frame)

Palace of Fine Arts, which is no more than a romantic ruin, and they also visit a museum where the portrait of a deceased woman keeps the living in her grasp. Furthermore, the entire Palace of the Legion of Honour, where the painting is situated, was conceived as a shrine for Californian soldiers who fell in the First World War. Finally, the Berlin museum of *Torn Curtain* is dominated by a solemn silence which tallies perfectly with the polished surfaces and frozen positions of the neo-classicist statues. In a long scene without dialogue, the Berlin museum is not only presented as a sinister or mysterious space but also as an environment where the senses are fine-tuned. Newman's central character regularly halts to localize the off-screen footsteps of his pursuer in the corridors and staircases of the museum. The entire sequence emphasizes that museum spaces are laboratories of sensory perception and, consequently, perfectly appropriate for cinematic self-investigation. Moreover, they are the home of a concentrated and contemplative gaze that is also fundamental for Hitchcock's cinema. Although unmistakably structured by dynamic narratives, Hitchcock's films are intensely preoccupied with the stasis of paintings and sculptures, suggestive of the death around which every Hitchcock plot inevitably turns.[43]

The *Vertigo* museum scene is a perfect illustration of Hitchcock's concept of a pure cinema highly based on point-of-view cutting. Scottie shadows Madeleine into the museum where he watches her staring at the painted portrait of Carlotta Valdez in peace and quiet. The scene, in which cinematic space is constructed by means of a subtle interaction between subjective and objective viewpoints, aptly illustrates Deleuze's statement that "Hitchcock is at the juncture of two cinemas, the classical that he perfects and the modern that he prepares."[44] The theme of the film, after all, is looking and the ways in which the gaze finds connections and constructs meanings. In the voyeurist universe of Hitchcock's modernism, it is the gaze that creates fiction. More than stimulating character identification by the spectator, the protagonist is transformed into a beholder. *Rear Window* and *Vertigo* are examples of a cinema that is about someone who looks instead of acts. Of course, there is diegetic support for the protagonist's immobility in the narrative: in both films, Stewart's characters have to watch, they simply cannot intervene in the action.

Such a static character is reminiscent of figures in the modern cinema of Roberto Rossellini, Robert Bresson, Michelangelo Antonioni, or Alain Resnais. In particular, the museum scene in *Vertigo* interestingly relates to the scene situated in the Naples archeological museum in Rossellini's *Viaggio in Italia* (1954), starring Hitchcock's fetish actress Ingrid Bergman. In both films, the theme of the erotic desire of the gaze is elab-

60

43 Peucker, *Incorporating Images*, 53.
44 Deleuze, *Cinema 1: The Movement-Image*, x. See also Ishii-Gonzalez, "Hitchcock with Deleuze," 128-45.

orated by means of the motifs of tourist attractions and the contemplation of artworks. As the masterpieces of European modernism of the 1950s and 1960s, *Vertigo* comprises many elaborate scenes without dialogue that are marked by a slow, contemplative rhythm, which matches perfectly the solemn silence and circumspectness of classical museum spaces. The museum setting in particular enables the director to investigate the theme of looking by means of emphatic close-ups of faces, highly unusual juxtapositions of action and reaction shots, and bravura camera movements tied to optical point of view.

In short, in the museum, the protagonist is reduced to a gaze. With its sacral and funerary connotations, the museum is the perfect place for the concentrated and contemplative gaze. At first sight, Hitchcock complies with the traditional Hollywood editing logic of shot/reaction shot: we see a character, then what it sees, and, finally, the character's reactions. In *Vertigo*'s museum scene, however, this convention is followed very emphatically. The camera switches from the real to the realm of representation: between the bouquet on the museum bench and the identical flower piece on the painting, between Madeleine's curl of hair and the identical one on the painted portrait. This curl is one of the many spiral motifs in *Vertigo*, in which the characters wander through a labyrinthine city and the camera moves invariably from exteriors to interiors. However, the vertiginous feeling is first and foremost the result of the confrontation and contamination of a 'real' and a 'fictitious' world. In the end, Madeleine turns out to be just as well an artificial construction as the painted portrait of Carlotta Valdez. In addition, as a modern Pygmalion, Scottie transforms Judy into a kind of Madeleine who answers to his idealized image. In the sacral space of the museum, 'real' characters are as artificial and immobile as the characters on the paintings on the wall. Next to visiting old mis-

61

I Looking at the portrait of Carlotta Valdez
Vertigo (1958) (Digital Frame)
II *Viaggio in Italia* (Roberto Rossellini, 1954) (Digital Frame)

sion churches, a graveyard, and other dreamlike settings of the city (the McKintrick Hotel, the Palace of Fine Arts, and Fort Point, directly under the Golden Bridge), the characters end up in the museum, which is "the cultural edifice in which the exchange between 'real' body and image is finalized."[45] The *Vertigo* museum scene is the ultimate example of this exchange that also occurs in other Hitchcock films. In *The Manxman*, there is the portrait of the judge that urges the liar to reveal himself. In *Rebecca*, the portrait of Lady Caroline de Winter provides the heroine a visual point of identification with the dead Rebecca. In *Suspicion*, characters talk to the portrait of General McLaidlaw. As Susan Felleman has noted, such scenes of interaction between characters and portraits literalize the effect of narrative cinema on its viewers that has been called 'suture:' "the propensity to secure the imaginary identification of the viewer with and in its narrative."[46] However, Felleman further notices that the inert portraits also disturb the smooth working of the narrative. The *Vertigo* museum scene completes this logic: Madeleine is as dead as the portrayed Carlotta Valdez.

Apart from Carlotta Valdez' portrait, other artworks in the same museum room can easily be identified, such as a *Portrait of a Gentleman* by Nicolas de Laviglière and *Flowers before a Window* (1789) by Jan-Frans van Dael, which are still part of the permanent collection of the San Francisco Palace of the Legion of Honor. However, the museum piece that compels most of Scottie's attention is a remarkable allegorical representation of architecture painted in 1753 by Charles-André Van Loo, an artist at that time praised by Caylus, Diderot, and Voltaire and whom Grimm called "the foremost painter of Europe."[47] The painting shows three children presenting to the beholder a drawing of the façade of Madame de Pompadour's *Chateau de Bellevue* at Meudon – a strikingly

62

45 Peucker, "The Cut of Representation," 150.
46 Felleman, *Art in the Cinematic Imagination*, 16-17 and 37-38.
47 See Wakefield, *French Eighteenth-Century Painting*, 101; and Levey, *Painting and Sculpture in France 1700-1789*, 174.

I Scottie looking at *Architecture* (1753) by Charles-André Van Loo
Vertigo (1958) (Digital Frame)
II Charles-André Van Loo, *Architecture* (1753)
(Palace of the Legion of Honor, San Francisco)

emblematic image in a film dealing entirely with the illusions of appearances, staged realities, and mistaken identities. Furthermore, the painting, which associates architecture with a kind of childlike innocence, seems a bit at odds in a film in which people mysteriously fall from rooftops or church towers. Hitchcock's museums and buildings do not go hand in hand with this childlike innocence.

3 Selected Works: Hitchcock's Domestic Architecture

Houses

Country Houses and Mansions

Modern Hide-Outs and Look-Outs

Under Glass Ceilings: Bunting House

13 Bessborough Gardens,
Pimlico, London, England

The Lodger: A Story of the London Fog

Black-and-white
Gainsborough Pictures
1926

ART DIRECTION:
C. Wilfrid Arnold
Bertram Evans

Drawings by Bartel Bruneel

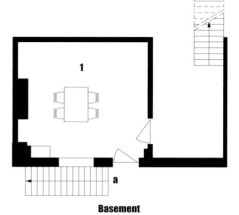

Basement

1m

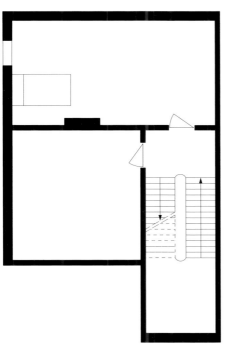
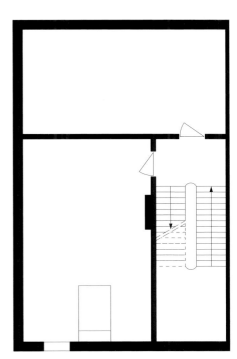

Level with Bunting Bedroom (2 versions)

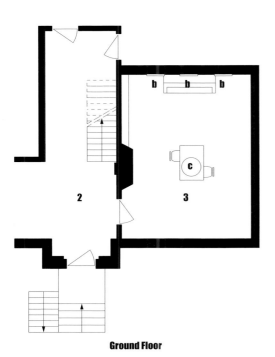

Ground Floor

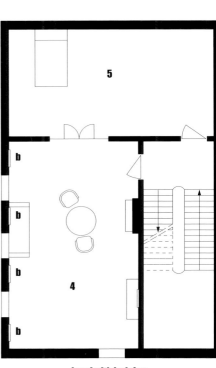

Level with Lodging

The Bunting house is the setting for *The Lodger*, the first film Hitchcock shot in England after making two pictures in a Munich studio and various European locations. Hitchcock himself presented the film as the one that inaugurated his authorship. "It was the first time I exercised my style," the director said in his interview with François Truffaut. "You might say *The Lodger* was my first picture."[1] The film not only contains the Hitchcockian theme of an innocent man wrongly accused of a crime, it also comprises many motifs that would recur frequently throughout Hitchcock's œuvre: blonde female protagonists, sinister staircases, handcuffs, painted portraits, and so forth. According to William Rothman, *The Lodger* is "not an apprentice work but a thesis, definitively establishing Hitchcock's identity as an artist. (…) Every shot, every framing, reframing, and cut is significant."[2] For many years, Hitchcock spoke of *The Lodger* as one of his favorite films and in the 1940s, he flirted with the idea of a remake in color.[3]

Loosely based on the story of Jack the Ripper, *The Lodger* was adapted from a bestselling 1913 novel by Marie Belloc-Lowndes about a serial killer who stalks and slashes his female victims in foggy London. It tells the story of a mysterious man with the mannerisms of a dandy, 'the lodger' (Ivor Novello), who rents a room in the house of the Bunting family at "two pounds ten a week." This middle-class family consists of Mr. Bunting (Arthur Chesney), his wife (Marie Ault), and their blond daughter Daisy (June), who is a fashion model. Both the Buntings and Joe (Malcolm Keen), a detective wooing Daisy, begin to suspect that the mysterious dandy cannot be but the so-called Avenger, who terrorizes the entire city by murdering young, blond women on Tuesday nights. In the end, the lodger turns out to be the brother of the Avenger's first victim, who swore at his mother's deathbed to bring the Avenger to justice.

As indicated by the subtitle of the film, the Bunting house is situated in London. In the Avenger's range of action, the house is localized on the city map, by both the police and the lodger, in the area where Vauxhall Bridge Road becomes Bessborough Gardens, just before Vauxhall Bridge. As Gary Giblin has demonstrated, this location in Pimlico refutes the claim, repeated by several commentators and Hitchcock himself in a 1970 interview, that the cinematic Buntings lived in Bloomsbury.[4]

A typical London terrace house constructed on a narrow and long building lot (probably situated on a street corner, as the reconstructed floor plan indicates), Bunting house answers to a highly urban architectural typology. The house is also unmistakably part of the modern metropolis, which Hitchcock evokes by shots of its traffic, flashing illuminated advertisings, newspapers, radio, crowds, revues, nocturnal pubs, hospitals,

1 Truffaut, *Hitchcock*, 44.
2 Rothman, *Hitchcock: The Murderous Gaze*, 7.
3 McGilligan, *Alfred Hitchcock*, 268-70. Maurice Elvey had already made a sound version in 1932, also starring Ivor Novello. The film was ultimately also remade by John Brahm in 1944 and by Hugo Fregnese as *Man in the Attic* in 1953.

4 Giblin, *Alfred Hitchcock's London*, 131. Giblin (98) further notes that in the Marie Belloc Lowndes source novel, the Buntings live on Marleybone Road.
5 Orr, *Hitchcock and 20th Century Cinema*, 30.
6 Schlör, *Nights in the Big City*.

and sophisticated fashion shows. Moreover, the story exists largely by the grace of the chaos and unpredictability of the crowd in modern city life.[5] The film brings to the fore the contrast between isolated individuals (the lodger, the Avenger's victims) and unparticularized crowds. It opposes the anonymity of the urban masses against the seclusion and security of the house. Furthermore, the context of the story is not the city as such. It is first and foremost the nocturnal metropolis, which combines the age-old fear of darkness with modern anxieties that have resulted from urbanization and its anonymity, its alienation, and its many new dangers. Scholars such as Joachim Schlör have pointed out that the development of both urban night culture and the imagery of a nocturnal urban landscape of expressionist *Angst* or *noir* paranoia were closely linked with modernizing processes such as urbanization, industrialization, and rationalization.[6]

The Bunting house contributes largely to the picture, which can be considered as a *Kammerspielfilm* that is constructed by means of architectural and domestic close-ups: the bottom part of an opening door, a hand on a doorhandle, a foot on a step of the stairs, a cuckoo clock, a mysteriously dimming wall lamp, a fire place, money on a mantelpiece, paintings and reproductions on the wall, a swinging ceiling lamp, to name but some. Furthermore, the film's title and protagonist indicate the importance of domestic settings, furnished rooms, and interiors. According to Donald Spoto, Hitchcock had "a three-sided house constructed, with narrow walls and low ceilings in the exact dimensions of a middle-class home. The difficulties of lighting such a set were considerable, but with [photographer Baron Gaetano] Ventimiglia's genial patience and Hitchcock's knowledge of how the Germans had moved cameras up and down a staircase (suspended,

I Kitchen (Digital Frame)
II Hall (Digital Frame)

if necessary, from tracking or scaffolding overhead), the complex and sinuously evocative shots were all achieved with surprising economy."[7]

Regardless of Hitchcock's preference for close-ups and the fact that the Bunting house is sizable, one continually gets a sense of spaciousness, three-dimensionality, and roominess on the screen. Hitchcock opens the space of the house by means of striking camera placements and swooping camera movements, which betray his collaborations with German technicians and his acute observations of German directors during the previous years. Apart from its handling of the camera, which glides restlessly up staircases and into bathrooms and which hovers from the rafters, *The Lodger* is also indebted to German expressionist cinema because of its lighting. In several scenes, such as the one situated in Mrs. Bunting bedroom, shadowy menacing shots create Caligaresque effects. In addition, references to light and darkness and to lamps run through the entire film: gloved hands switching off the lights, blackouts, the Avenger's crimes in the darkness of Tuesday nights, dimming wall lamps, blinking neon signs, and so forth.

Both Belloc-Lowndes and Hitchcock have emphasized the importance of a lower-middle-class household as the locus of the story. "Had the Buntings been in a class lower than their own, had they belonged to that great company of human beings technically known as the poor, there would have been friendly neighbours ready to help them, and the same would have been the case had they belonged to the class of smug, well meaning, if unimaginative, folk whom they had spent so much of their lives in serving," Belloc-Lowndes stated.[8]

In Hitchcock's interpretation as well, the home of the Buntings is pervaded with a kind of modesty that contrasts sharply with Daisy's world of a mannequin modeling high fashions. The modest Bunting house also stands out in contrast to the lodger's own aristocratic mansion, which is the setting for the final scene of the film. As late as 1937, more than ten years after the release of *The Lodger*, Hitchcock himself would criticize openly British cinema for its pronounced predilection for the higher strata of the British social scale, where "the veneer of civilization is so thick that individual qualities are killed." The director argued in favor of stories set among the middle classes in order to shatter the illusion of "other audiences that the English live either in cottages or cocktail cabinets, and speak with their lips twisted or with a plum in their throats."[9]

According to Lesley Brill, Hitchcock's art is characterized by "a clear sense of physical geography and an equally clear sense of social geography, class consciousness."[10] This is definitely the case in the Bunting House and its vertical structure, although a careful

7 Spoto, *The Dark Side of Genius*, 95. the Level," 4.

8 Marie Belloc-Lowndes quoted in Haeffner, *Alfred Hitchcock*, 20.

9 Hitchcock, "More Cabbages, Fewer Kings: A Believer in the Little Man," 177.

10 Brill, "Hitchcock's *The Lodger*," 75.

11 Zirnite, "Hitchcock on

I   II

reconstruction of its floor plan reveals several spatial inconsistencies. The floor level of the lodger's room, for instance, is unclear since sometimes he climbs only one, on other occasions two flights of stairs. In addition, the Bunting's living room is situated on the wrong side of the axis formed by the front door and stairwell. As a result, the direct vertical relation between the Bunting living room and the lodging, which is evoked in the famous scene with the glass ceiling, is completely disturbed. Other architectural inconsistencies or uncertainties include the relation between the Bunting bedroom and the street, and the position of the bathroom. However, in spite of these spatial incongruities or obscurities, Hitchcock took advantage of cinema's "creative geography" in order to build a house that forms the proper stage of a sinister domestic drama.

Moreover, the vertical organization of the Bunting house perfectly meets a dual spatial scheme that, according to Dennis Zirnite, recurs in many Hitchcock films. On the one hand, there is the main level, which is "generally characterized by banality, complacency and a shallow vigilance." This "earth-bound plane is personified by those who are impelled by a precarious sense of decency." On the other hand, there is the upper level, which "is the oppressive dominion of a malignant force, of human destructiveness; the 'overseeing' catalyst of moral instability. Typified by deceptive charm, a repressed misogyny, and an exuding seductiveness, this ascendant domain is incarnated by those who unleash the darkest human impulses."[II]

Zirnite's model applies perfectly to *The Lodger*, in which the Buntings live downstairs, even on a subterranean level. The viewer enters the house for the first time when Mr. Bunting descends an outdoor staircase and turns into the kitchen, which is situated half a floor under street level. Strikingly, the Buntings live in the kitchen. Many domestic

I Hall (Digital Frame)
II Stairs (Digital Frame)

scenes that include Daisy and her parents occur here. Joe as well, who acts as if he owns the house, enters via the kitchen exterior staircase. The Buntings seem uneasy in the upper floors of the house. Only Daisy appears to be a comfortable and welcome visitor to the second floor.

The both seductive and seemingly sinister lodger, by contrast, lives upstairs. Attracted by the sign "room to let," he enters the house by the front door. His remarkable arrival is theatrically heralded by the flickering and diminishing gas light in the inside of the house, followed by his foreboding shadow that slowly approaches and looms outside the Bunting door. The forward tracking movement of the camera (the first camera movement of the film) implies the lodger's point of view. Subsequently, his eerie entrance into the house is, in the words of Marc Raymond Strauss, "overly melodramatic, yet effectively noirish and expressionistic."[12] Immediately, the presence of the lodger turns the house, the most parts of which are unknown to the viewer until so far, into an uncanny and sinister environment. As soon as the lodger enters the house of the Buntings, who, of course, live at number 13, the rooms are filled with spooky shadows. As in *Rebecca, Suspicion, Shadow of a Doubt, Notorious*, and *Dial M for Murder*, a young woman has to live under the same roof as a man who falls under suspicion of being a murderer of even a serial killer. Daisy is a typical heroine of Hitchcock, who made several dramas about the appearance, as if by magic, of a mysterious man who may have the power to make a young woman's romantic dreams come true but who also may be a monster. In these dramas, the family home invariably becomes a site of fear, anxiety, betrayal, madness, and murder. In several Hitchcock films (*The Farmer's Wife, Rich and Strange, Number 17, Rebecca, Suspicion, Shadow of a Doubt, Notorious, The Paradine Case, Rope*,

72

12 Strauss, *Alfred Hitch-cock's Silent Films*, 30.
13 See Barr, *English Hitchcock*, 33.
14 Yacowar, "Hitchcock's Imagery and Art," 18.
15 Walker, *Hitchcock's Motifs*, 350-72. See also Strauss, *Alfred Hitchcock's Silent Films*, 34.

Under Capricorn, Dial M for Murder, Psycho, The Birds, Marnie), the house becomes a trap, the family a means of confinement. In *The Lodger*, this is also expressed by Joe's handcuffs, which, foreshadowing the famous handcuff episodes in *The 39 Steps* and *Saboteur*, implicitly connects marriage to bondage. The film also connects the house as a confinement with an Oedipal dimension in the narrative: both Daisy and the lodger are moving away from the bond with their other-sex parent to form a new heterosexual bond.[13]

The architectural junctions and connections between the spatial and social levels in the Bunting house are also important visual motifs and they mark significant moments in the narrative. The most important vertical connection between the different levels is, of course, the staircase, which Maurice Yacowar once labeled a "quintessential Hitchcock image."[14] Foreshadowing similar scenes in *Blackmail*, *Notorious*, *Shadow of a Doubt*, *Vertigo*, *Psycho*, and *Frenzy*, *The Lodger* contains an interesting early example of Hitchcock's many "sinister staircases."[15] One of the most memorable images of the film is a vertical shot down through the stairwell, which includes several flights of stairs, as the gloved hand of the lodger makes a circuit of the banisters. The furtive, disembodied hand, gliding down the banister, appears almost ghost-like. Furthermore, the stairwell itself is presented as an oppressive and haunting structure. In an overhead composition that looks vertiginously down the stairwell, Hitchcock presents the stairs so that the banister rails descend away from the camera in a spiral, drawing the eye down and creating a slightly giddy effect. Prefiguring the famous zoom in and dolly out in the mission tower scene in *Vertigo*, this top shot makes it seem as if the staircase itself has a malignant power. In addition, the visualization of the staircase creates other striking visual effects. The par-

73

I, II Bunting Living Room (Digital Frame)
III, IV Lodging (Digital Frame)

allel vertical lines of the banister constitute what William Rothman described as the //// motif, which functions as a kind of Hitchcock signature: on the one hand, it is his mark on the frame, akin to his ritual cameo appearances. On the other hand, it signifies the atmosphere of confinement that characterizes the Bunting house.[16]

Another connection between the two levels in the Bunting house is an aural one, which, in a silent movie, had to be evoked visually. This is achieved in the famous scene with the glass ceiling. Joe, Daisy, and her mother hear the lodger pacing about in the room above them − something which casts further suspicion on him. Hitchcock translated the perception of the lodger's footsteps into a shot of a moving chandelier and, subsequently, into a shot taken through a glass ceiling, so that the sound of his pacing is, as it were, visualized. The shot is striking, all the more so because it is taken from a tilted, oblique angle so that the lodger's body is visible foreshortened almost beyond recognition from his shoes upwards. Apart from the spatial incongruity that, as the floor plan reconstruction demonstrates, the Bunting's living room cannot be situated under the lodger's room, the glass ceiling emphasizes its opposite: the fact that the Bunting house is a typical nineteenth-century bourgeois dwelling, which secludes itself from the metropolis and which consists of separate rooms, all concealing their own identities and stories. Hitchcock's dramas usually take place in bourgeois interiors that box private life, together with its secrets, inside a barricade of walls, floors, and ceilings. The archetypal Hitchcockian house is completely at odds with the concept of the glass house that runs like a thread through the utopian aspirations of architectural modernism from Joseph Paxton to Paul Scheerbart, from the Bauhaus to Pierre Chareau, and from Ludwig Mies van der Rohe to Philip Johnson. Strikingly, prominent critics and theorists of the modern movement such as Siegfried Giedion interpreted modern glass architecture as a contribution to the rise of a new space conception and a new optical paradigm, which both were often compared with the medium of cinema. A result of modern technology, the new glass architecture was not only linked to new means of mechanical reproduction such as cinema, but also to a dynamic and 'cinematic' perception of space.[17] Strikingly, in the same year that *The Lodger* was released, Sergei Eisenstein scribbled down some notes for a film scenario that would become known as the *Glass House* project, which he would rake up a few times later in his career.[18] In this project for a drama on the conditions of living in transparency, Eistenstein explicitly noted the possibilities of using steep angles seen through transparent floors and ceilings − exactly what Hitchcock exceptionally did in *The Lodger*. In the cruel voyeurism of Eisenstein's glass universe, neighbors become rapt spectators of suicides and murders. In *Rear Window*, much later

74

16 Rothman, *Hitchcock: The Murderous Gaze*, 33.
17 See Öhner & Ries, "Bildbau," 31-36.
18 See Bulgakowa (ed.), *Eisenstein und Deutschland*, 17-38; and Goodwin, *Eisenstein, Cinema, and History*, 122.
19 Benjamin, "Erfahrung und Armut," *Gesammelte Schriften* II, 1, 217.

20 Benjamin, "Der Surrealismus: Die letzte Momentaufname der europäischen Intelligenz," *Gesammelte Schriften* II, 1, 298.

in his career, Hitchcock would deal with the new configurations of social existence and sexual desire produced by urban density and architectural transparency.

Walter Benjamin interpreted the glass building as the architecture of the future because it could destroy the excessively furnished bourgeois interior, in which everything was veiled, wrapped, cloaked, draped, and concealed. Glass objects, by contrast, Benjamin notes, "have no aura. Glass is the enemy of secrets. It is also the enemy of property."[19] In his 1929 essay on Surrealism, Benjamin extols the "revolutionary virtues" of living in a glass house.[20] The Bunting living room and the two adjacent rooms of the lodger do not answer to this revolutionary concept of habitation at all. On the contrary, the interior is closed and full of objects that have an aura. In the lodger's point-of-view panning shot of his new accommodation, we see that the room is full of painted portraits, which also play an important part in several other Hitchcock films (*Easy Virtue*, *Rebecca*, *Suspicion*, *The Paradine Case*, *Vertigo*, *The Birds*). Most of the paintings represent blonde women, another one depicts a scene of rape. The artworks show similarities with Pre-Raphaelite paintings; on the mantle, we even see a reproduction of the *Perseus Series: The Rock of Doom* (1885), a painting by Edward Burne-Jones. Strikingly, the lodger turns the paintings toward the wall. "I am afraid I don't like these pictures. Can't they be put somewhere else?" he asks. When Mrs. Bunting and Daisy have removed the paintings, empty spots mar the walls. "I know it looks ugly, but they got on my nerves," he explains. Later in the film, the portraits reappear on the walls of the Bunting's living room. Hitchcock emphasizes their symbolic dimension by a point-of-view shot of Mrs. Bunting when she starts to suspect the lodger of being the Avenger.

The attention that Hitchcock draws to these portraits is telling. They not only fore-

I Glass Ceiling (Digital Frame)
II Bunting Bedroom (Digital Frame)

shadow Hitchcock's lifelong cinematic fascination for blondes, these portraits are also symptomatic of a kind of shot that Hitchcock will often use in his vision of women, which are often influenced by pictorial precedents.[21] In addition, the portraits elicit a very attentive gaze from the characters – a kind of gaze that characterizes Hitchcock's cinema in general and his modernist masterpieces of the 1950s and early 1960s in particular (*Rear Window*, *Vertigo*, *Psycho*, *Marnie*). In the scene in which the lodger sees the paintings, the game of glances and gazes is even complicated by reflections in a mirror. A frame that includes both the lodger and a female portrait initially suggests that the painting is behind him, but when the lodger begins to move, it becomes clear that he is moving toward the portrait, and that the mirror behind him reflects both. Already in this 1926 film, Hitchcock creates a kind of dizzying relation between painting and reality that would mark films such as *Vertigo*.

Finally, because of Hitchcock's fascination for private and confined spaces, another important part of the Bunting house is the bathroom, which is situated on one of the intermediate floors at the back of the house. *The Lodger* contains one of the few Hitchcock scenes in which a bathroom is used for conventional purposes, such as taking a bath. Moreover, the bathroom scene is also one of the few that is situated in a domestic setting – remarkably, since most of Hitchcock's bathroom and washroom scenes are set in hotels, workplaces, at stations or in public transport vehicles.[22] In Hitchcock's universe, of course, bathrooms are linked with the notion of voyeurism and they are often presented as a site for the return of the repressed. The bathroom scene in *The Lodger* emphasizes Daisy's vulnerability. Anticipating by more than thirty years the shower scene in *Psycho*,

76

21 Tanski, "The Symbolist Woman in Hitchcock's Films," 149. For Hitchcock's cinematic and photographic fascination with blondes, see also Conrad, *The Hitchcock Murders*, 149-50.
22 Walker, *Hitchcock's Motifs*, 112-14.
23 Conrad, *The Hitchcock Murders*, 343.

the lodger creeps downstairs and stealthily tries the door handle of the bathroom. In addition, the scene, which is situated in the most private part of the house, has been invaded by the atmosphere that mystifies the city outside. As Peter Conrad noted, the warm vapors that condense into mist in the bathroom evoke the gloomy London fog in which the serial killer operates.[23] In the Bunting house, the dangers of the modern metropolis have penetrated the domestic safety of the interior.

I Mirrors and Paintings (Digital Frame)
II Paintings (Digital Frame)
III Bathroom (Digital Frame)

The Old Dark House: House Number 17

Drawings by Annelies Staessen

17 Anderson Road,
Amhurst Park,
London, England

Number Seventeen

Black-and-white
British International Pictures
1932

ART DIRECTION:
C. Wilfred Arnold

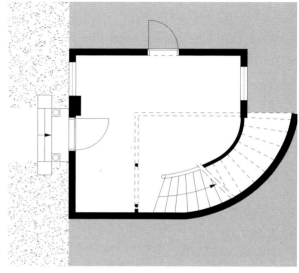

Ground Floor

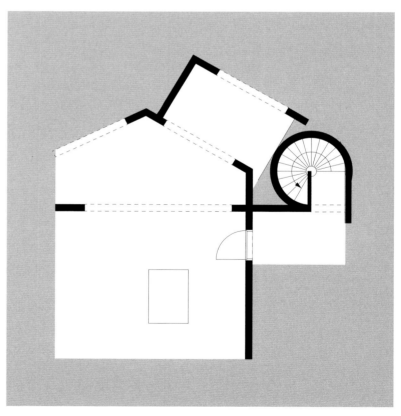

Basement

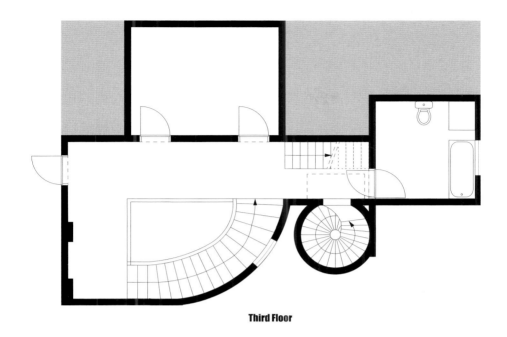

Third Floor

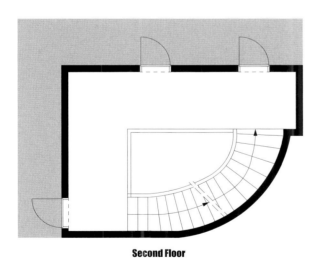

Second Floor

1m

The importance of this building is indicated by the fact that its house number is the title of the film – the entire address can be detected from a telegram addressed to the neighbor living next door at number 15. About three quarters of this 65 minutes' film are taking place within the confines of an old dark house. As such, Hitchcock already explores the possibilities of his later single-set pictures such as *Lifeboat*, *Rope*, *Dial M for Murder*, and *Rear Window*, which play with the boundaries of cinematic space. Strikingly, the last part of *Number Seventeen* consists of an extended and spectacular chase involving trains, buses, and boats, which opens up the space but also emphasizes the claustrophobic atmosphere of the first part.

The opening sequence immediately sets the tone of the film: scurrying down the nocturnal street, moved along by a gust of wind along with a flurry of leaves and his hat, a man, followed by a mobile, prowling camera, forces open the door of a deserted, uncanny house. Here, the man, who later turns out to be a detective, meets a series of mysterious characters who have entered the house at cross-purposes but who are all trying to get their hands on a diamond necklace. This precious piece of jewelry can be considered the first example of the Hitchcockian 'MacGuffin,' which is an item, the details of which are unimportant, that motivates and structures the thriller plot, such as the secret formula in *The 39 Steps*, the diplomatic message in *The Lady Vanishes*, the uranium in wine bottles in *Notorious*, or the microfilm in *North by Northwest*. The thin plot of *Number Seventeen*, which Charles Barr has called "a sophisticated deconstruction of the mechanics of the thriller" with characters "almost as if they were Luigi Pirandello's six characters in search of an author," seems just an excuse for a series of scenic effects with lights and shadows.[1] Within the boundaries of the set of the dark house designed by Wilfred Arnold, Hitchcock experiments with light effects in abundance, casting lurid shadows by means of matches, candles, or passing trains. Apart from its shadows, the house that bears the number 17 over its door contains a true catalogue of other Gothic elements: shadows, mysterious lights, cobwebs, banging doors, a creaking staircase, broken windows, howling wind, a clock striking at midnight, vanishing corpses, surprise intruders, a hand on the doorknob, a gloved hand appearing through the slit of the letterbox, a close-up of a foot, creepy music, and, as one of the characters says, "footsteps with no feet." Somewhat similar to *The Old Dark House* that James Whale directed in Hollywood in the same year, *Number Seventeen* can be considered a Grand Guignol parody of the source novel and play written by J. Jefferson Farjeon, of which Hitchcock exaggerated all the coincidences and contrivances.

The spatial restrictions Hitchcock used in the film are even more confined than the

1 Barr, *English Hitchcock*, 123. See also Yacowar, *Hitchcock's British Films*, 155.

I   Entrance (Digital Frame)
II, III, IV, V, VI   Stairwell (Digital Frame)

dimensions of the house since practically the entire film is situated in the hall and, particularly, at the impressive stairwell and its landing. In the end, practically no rooms constitute the cinematic space. On the contrary, it even turns out that the house contains more stairs, such as a spiral back staircase. In addition, the transition to the chase at the end of the film is marked by yet another impressive stair, which, as another horror cliché, leads to a subterranean exit to the nearby railway tracks. In short, the house is reduced to a series of winding staircases, which Hitchcock visualizes by means of his hyperkinetic camerawork and a series of impressive overhead shots and worm's eye views. Staircases enable Hitchcock to create depth in the single set and to mobilize the cinematic space. In addition, the stairwell, which invokes the use of changing viewpoints, contributes to the creation of a fragmented space, already splintered by the play

82

2 Walker, *Hitchcock's Motifs*, 365.

I Back Staircase (Digital Frame)
II Basement (Digital Frame)
III Stairs to railway (Digital Frame)

of light and shadow and the many close-ups of terrified faces and unidentified body parts. Furthermore, as in many of his other works, Hitchcock associates ascending or descending a staircase with unknown dangers or with terrible experiences. Although Hitchcock plays with the idea of a spooky staircase in a deserted house in an overtly parodic way, it is on the stairs that one of the protagonists gets shot in the arm and where two characters are tied together and trussed to a rickety banister.[2] Apart from being a place of dangerous and vertiginous heights, a Hitchcockian staircase also leads to a secret and forbidden space. As a result, stairs seem to enforce both the uncanny nature of the dark house and the fear of the characters.

Living Behind the Screen: Verloc House & Bijou Cinema

Plouthorp Road,
London, England

Sabotage

Black-and-white
Gaumont-British
1936

ART DIRECTION:
Oscar Werndorff
SET DIRECTION:
Albert Jullion

1 Shopfront Greengrocery
2 Interior Greengrocery
3 Dressing
4 Courtyard
5 Cinema Porch
6 Cinema Ticket Booth
7 Cinema Auditorium
8 Interspace behind Cinema Screen
9 Verloc Living Room
10 Hall
11 Kitchen
12 Stairs to Bedroom
13 Stairs to Balcony

Drawings by David Claus

Section

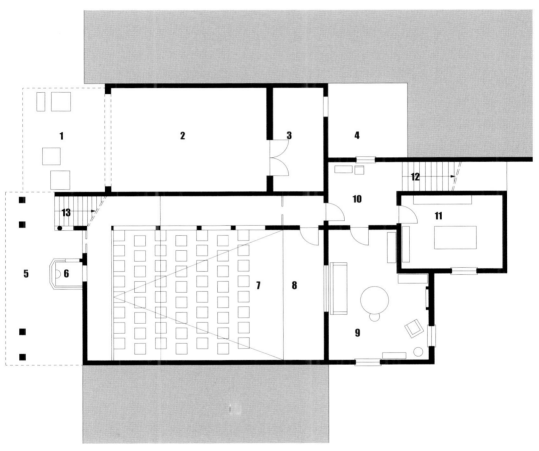

Ground Floor

1m

Producer Michael Balcon announced that *Sabotage* would "feature more of the real London than any film yet made."[1] Indeed, the film amply shows London places, landmarks, and institutions. The opening sequence, for instance, consists of shots of Oxford Street, the Houses of Parliament, Nelson's column at Trafalgar Square, and the Eros statue at Piccadilly Circus – all affected by a power blackout caused by sabotage at the Battersea Power Station. What's more, important scenes take place at Simpson's restaurant, the Zoo Aquarium, New Scotland Yard, the Lord Mayor Show Day parade, on buses and trams, and the busy streets and intersections of the metropolis. Hitchcock took many shots on location, which was not always easy since police and other authorities rarely gave permission to film in London's streets – a fact Hitchcock discusses in a 1937 article in the *London News Chronicle*.[2] For *Sabotage*, however, Hitchcock recreated London in the studio as well. To convey 'London' to American audiences, Hitchcock spent £ 3,000 to construct a facsimile tram line for only a single day of shooting and less than a minute of screen time. In collaboration with art directors Oscar Werndorff and Albert Jullion (uncredited), Hitchcock also had a replica of a London street made, complete with fully equipped shops, trams, buses, traffic lights, beacons, overhead railway, and hundreds of pedestrians on a remote site that Balcon used for exteriors on several occasions.[3] This full-sized street mock-up was built to enable the director to film dialogue scenes with traffic moving noiselessly in the background. "I have a penchant for including scenes of London in my films and in the old silent days we made endless excursions into the capital, shooting where and when we liked," Hitchcock wrote in the *New York Times*. "Today the extra equipment of sound hampers such maneuvers. It is impossible to record dialogue scenes in a crowded thoroughfare with the roar of traffic and clatter of passersby drowning the words of the stars. That is why in the recent case of *Sabotage* I had to build 'London' in a field. True, I still had my traffic and pedestrians, but I could control them by building the roadway slightly on the slant. Then I could have buses and vehicles coasting silently by while my artists conducted their conversation on the pavement. Proper traffic sounds were carefully blended in later."[4]

The street, for which also location shots in the environs of the studio doubled, is the fictitious Plouthorp Road, which, according to the SE5 postcode on a letterhead, should be situated in the South London district of Camberwell. Plouthorp Road is the location of the Bijou Cinema managed by Karl Verloc (Oscar Homolka), who is part of a gang of secret agents and saboteurs. Verloc practices his shady business secretly – even without the knowledge of his American wife (Sylvia Sydney) and her young brother Stevie (Desmond Tester), both of whom he lives with in rooms behind the cinema auditorium.

1 Krohn, *Hitchcock at Work*, 24.
2 Hitchcock, "Life Among Stars," 38.
3 McGilligan, *Alfred Hitchcock*, 190; Giblin, *Alfred Hitchcock's London*, 229.
4 Hitchcock, "Search for the Sun," 251.

Ted Spencer (John Loder), a Scotland Yard detective trying to track down the saboteurs, pretends to be an employee of a greengrocer shop adjacent to the Bijou Cinema.

The architecture of the Bijou cinema and the Verloc apartment can be considered a series of physical and social screens concealing one another. The building's façade is based on the model of a classical temple – a kind of Potemkin architecture that does not even refer explicitly to antiquity or high culture but rather attempts at evoking the luxury and dream world of the grand Art Deco picture palaces in a blue-collar neighborhood. The fake architecture is, of course, related to the fake world of the movies – so there is a Ruskinian truthfulness after all. The cinema, strikingly, does not appear in

Plouthorp Road with Bijou Cinema created in the Gaumont studios
(Set Photograph, British Film Institute)

Joseph Conrad's 1907 source novel *The Secret Agent*. Through Hitchcock's and screen-writer Charles Bennet's interpretations, Verloc's pornographic bookshop has become a movie theater. This enabled the director to reflect on the nature of film-watching itself, as many commentators have noted.[5] Not only does most of the action occur in a movie theater, Hitchcock also associates cinema and sabotage on more than one occasion. The blackout curtails the city's nocturnal entertainment including the Bijou Cinema itself and Verloc uses the cinema as a cover-up for his illegal activities. Furthermore, a bomb, which unintentionally kills Stevie among many others on a crowded city bus, is carried in a canister of film – inflammable material itself and actually prohibited on public transport.

Behind the screen of the picture palace's white temple façade there is another screen: the white movie screen. Ted is literally eager to see what's behind the screen, to see "where the sound comes from." He persuades Stevie to show him a corridor beyond the screen, situated between the semi-public space of the auditorium and the private sphere of the Verloc living room. Tellingly, in the wall that separates this interspace from the living room there is a fanlight – a kind of 'rear window' that can be interpreted as yet another screen. In keeping with the voyeurist connotations of Hitchcock's windows, the detective uses it to spy on the saboteurs. However, he is caught and is drawn through it – his own cover-up as a grocer is shattered when he breaks from the world of cinema into the 'real' world of the saboteurs. In short, Ted's quest through the building almost becomes a *rite de passage* in which, at every stage, a space has to be transgressed and screens mark the transfer to another reality. The Bijou Cinema's temple façade becomes appropriate: in a grocer's smock that looks like a wrapped film screen catching projected images, Ted enters the secret depths of a dark building in which auratic light is celebrated.

Earlier in the film, the fanlight cracks open during Ted's visit to the Verlocs. The sound resembles a woman's scream and Ted says that he thought "someone was committing murder!" "Someone probably is … up on the movie screen there," replies Verloc with a smile while pointing to the wall with the window. The distinction Verloc draws will soon prove illusory, however, since he will soon be murdered in the living room. Furthermore, living literally behind the movie screen, the Verlocs are an illusion themselves, a kind of Potemkin family concealing Mr. Verloc's heinous activities. In addition, of course, they live between two movie screens: the one of the Bijou Cinema and the one that we, as audience, are gazing at.

As a result of Verloc's urge to be inconspicuous, there's the mundane reality of domestic life behind the dream world of the movies. Everyday family life exudes through the fea-

5 See, for instance, Barr, *English Hitchcock*, 169-75; Cohen, *Hitchcock's Cryptonymies*, I, 145-62; Cohen, *Alfred Hitchcock: The Legacy of Victorianism*, 29-49; and Smith, "Disruption, Destruction, Denial," 45-58.

I Front (Digital Frame)
II,III Cinema auditorium (Digital Frame)
IV Interspace behind the screen (Digital Frame)
V Falling through the fanlight (Digital Frame)
VI Verloc living room (Digital Frame)

tures of middle-class conformist interior design: wallpaper, stucco mouldings above the door, prints and portraits on the walls, a clock and statuettes on the mantlepiece. The idyll of family life and its destruction is further dealt with by the domestic motif of the family dinner. Typical of Hitchcock, the image of the house as a place of conviviality where meals are taken together is disrupted. Three meal sequences are each more ominously marked by the potentially dangerous gestures accompanying the carving of meat – a ritual eventually leading to one of the most famous sequences in Hitchcock's œuvre, in which Mrs. Verloc murders her husband with a kitchen knife after she found out that her brother died as a result of Verloc's sabotage activities. So, as in many other Hitchcock films, the family, marriage, and the home are institutions or places of tension and entrapment – something the director, long before *Psycho* and *The Birds*, emphasizes by the recurrent motif of the bird cage. The maker of the bombs, the so-called Professor (William Dewhurst) who also operates in a mundane family setting, runs a pet shop that specializes in birds. In addition, the bomb is brought to Verloc in a bird cage with a coded message stating that "the birds will sing at 1:45," and the Bijou Cinema screens the Disney cartoon *Who Killed Cock Robin?* featuring birds. To protagonists such as Verloc, his wife, and the Professor, the home has become a cage – the first shot of the Verloc living room shows Verloc framed by the spindles of a chair.

90

I, II Verloc living room (Digital Frame)
III Hall (Digital Frame)
IV, V Verloc living room (Still, Royal Film Archive, Brussels)

I II
III IV

V

91

66-63

Bad Dream House: Newton House

Santa Rosa, California

Shadow of a Doubt

Black-and-white
Universal
1943

ART DIRECTION:
John B. Goodman
Robert Boyle
SET DECORATION:
R.A. Gausman
E.R. Robinson

1 Garden
2 Porch
3 Hall
4 Living Room
5 Dining Room
6 Kitchen
7 Garage
8 Landing
9 Bedroom Mr. & Mrs. Newton

10 Bedroom Ann & Roger
11 Bedroom Charlie
12 Dressing
13 Balcony
14 Backstairs

Drawings by David Claus

Back

Side

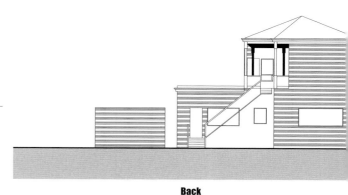

1m

Front

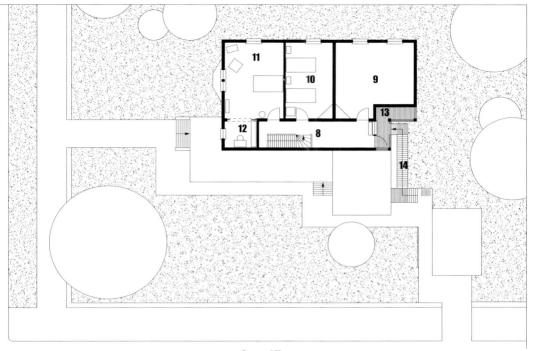

Second Floor

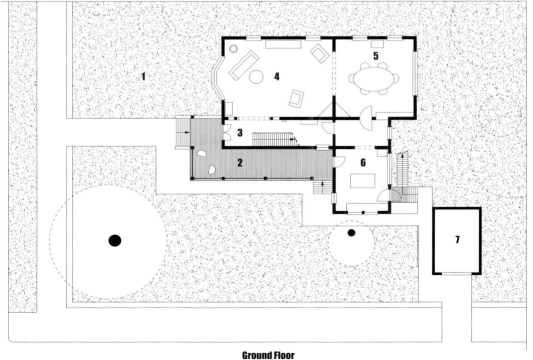

Ground Floor

Shadow of a Doubt tells the story of a debonair serial killer in small-town America. The famous playwright and novelist Thornton Wilder, who earlier had depicted small-town life in his Pulitzer Prize-winning play *Our Town* (1938), wrote the screenplay. The script was finished by Sally Benson, the author of *Meet Me in St. Louis*, another tale full of domestic scenes that originated as a series of *New Yorker* short stories in 1942. Together with the film versions of *Our Town* (Sam Wood, 1940) and *Meet Me in St. Louis* (Vincente Minnelli, 1944), *Shadow of a Doubt* is one of the many interesting depictions of small-town life made by the Hollywood studios in the 1940s.

Since the War Production Board had imposed restrictions on set construction, Hitchcock decided to shoot many scenes on location in Santa Rosa, a picturesque, Californian small town with a postcard-like local library, train station, telegraph office, and bank office. This location angle was quite a novelty in the early 1940s and it was elaborately discussed in the press – *Life* magazine even sent a team of photographers to record the filming. Characterized by an old-fashioned sense of law and decency, Santa Rosa is presented as a place where everybody seems to know everyone and where smiling police officers direct traffic. Although the town seems invaded by the paraphernalia of urban modernity, such as movies, radios, jukeboxes, and neon signs, the inertia of mundane family living in small-town suburbia is even the subject of a dialogue at the beginning of the film.

One of the protagonists, the demonic Uncle Charlie (Joseph Cotton), describes Santa Rosa as a place of "hospitality and kindness and homes…homes." Consequently, the main part of the film is situated in a suburban house in a lovely tree-lined street, which contrasts sharply with the industrial wasteland of New Jersey (standing in for the outskirts of Philadelphia) depicted in the opening sequence of the film. The house is owned by Joe Newton (Henry Travers), who works in the local bank, and his wife Emma Oakley (Patricia Collinge). They have three children: Charlie (Teresa Wright), Ann (Edna May Wonacott), and Roger (Charles Bates). In the film, they are visited by 'Uncle Charlie,' Emma's brother, who turns out to be a widow murderer and who attempts to hide his criminal identity by becoming part of the Newton family. As the title suggests, doubt enters the domestic sphere, which is usually associated with peace and security. In so doing, the film is critical of or at least ambivalent about the American Dream and the dominant culture of small-town life – a stance that can be found in several other 1940s films such as *The Magnificent Ambersons* (Orson Welles, 1942), *Kings Row* (Sam Wood, 1942), and *The Stranger* (Orson Welles, 1946).[1]

The Newton residence is a white wood house built in an eclectic style that combines

1 Levy, *Small-Town America in Film*, 71-108. See also MacKinnon, *Hollywood's Small Towns*, 114-16.

I, II   Santa Rosa, California (Digital Frame)

III, IV, V   Front (Digital Frame)

VI   Living room (Digital Frame)

some Colonial Revival elements with characteristics of what Virginia and Lee McAlester have called the "Free Classic" subtype of the Queen Anne style. This type of building became very common after 1890, especially in California and the South.[2] With its bay window, shallow rectangular windows, and a one-storey porch that extends along a side wall with classical columns raised on a pedestal to the level of the porch railing, Newton house perfectly answers to the descriptions of that type of vernacular architecture. Apart from a detached garage, it contains two floors. The ground floor consists of a living room with a bay window, a dining room, a laundry, a kitchen, and a porch. Once beyond the façade, these interior spaces are open to the visitor at a glance. The transparent structure of the plan intensifies the domesticity of the rooms, which are accessible to all the members of the family. Their interconnection is also emphasized by the fact people are calling to each other from one room to the next, or between floors. Behind the front door is a hall with a staircase, the lower part of which is clearly visible from the living room. As a result, this staircase functions as a kind of catwalk. In the scene in which the camera speeds into close-up of young Charlie's ring as she descends the stairs, the staircase guides the gaze of the people sitting in the living room and Hitchcock's bravura camera. Another external stairway is situated at the back of the house. Both staircases lead to the second floor containing three bedrooms. Typical of Hitchcock, both stairs and some of the bedrooms play an important part in the narrative. After some Santa Rosa establishing shots, we first enter the house through the front window on the second floor. We end up in young Charlie's bedroom, she is lying on her bed, daydreaming in a position similar to that of her uncle in the East Coast opening sequence. Her bedroom is temporarily at her uncle's disposal. During his stay, young Charlie sleeps in the adjacent room that belongs to her younger sister. Strikingly, the bedroom of the parents is never shown and no information is given about the place where Roger sleeps.

Several scenes at the house were also shot on location in Santa Rosa. Hitchcock himself discovered this private residence at McDonald Avenue. Thornton Wilder, however, "felt that it was too big for a bank clerk. Upon investigation it turned out that the man who lived there was in the same financial bracket as our character, so Wilder agreed to use it. But when we came back, two weeks prior to the shooting, the owner was so pleased that his house was going to be in a picture that he had it completely repainted. So we had to go in and get his permission to paint it dirty again. And when we were through, naturally, we had it done all over again with bright, new colors."[3] This urge to present the house as an impeccable showcase to outsiders is typical of the 'conspicuous consumption' and moral values of the suburban middle-class. Also the residents in the film clean the house to make a good impression on visitors.

2 Virginia & Lee McAlester, *A Field Guide to American Houses*, 264 and 326.

3 Truffaut, *Hitchcock*, 153.

I, II Dining room (Digital Frame)

III Kitchen (Digital Frame)

IV, V, VI Stairs (Digital Frame)

VII, VIII Landing (Digital Frame)

However, the house depicted in the movie differed in some ways from the real McDonald Avenue house.[4] It had no external stairway, for instance. Consequently, the scenes on the back stairs were filmed on a Universal sound stage, as where the interior scenes. Although Hitchcock originally wanted to film in the interior of the actual house, it was not big enough to allow for film equipment. Replicated from photographs and Robert Boyle's sketches, the sets were described as "quite a phenomenon" by the *New York Times*, who thought it "the most flexible thing ever built for a motion picture…(with) an amazing adaptability to camera angles." "As the camera moves into, out of, and through the house to record the action, windows come apart, the porch stands aside, the roof bends over, the kitchen walks away."[5] The sets had breakaway walls and several prop dinner tables of different sizes that split down the middle, allowing the camera to exploit unlikely angles in the family scenes. For the first dinner scene, Robert Boyle constructed an egg-shaped table, large at one end and tapering at the other, in order to have a viewpoint shot with most of the family members in it.[6]

"The house owns us," Mrs. Newton states, who is one of the rare mother figures represented positively in Hitchcock's œuvre.[7] With its floral wallpaper, white gauze curtains, solid oak chairs and side-boards, ceramic animals, and curio cabinets, the house represents the stolid middle-class values of the 1940s. The Newtons, moreover, are presented as a typical family – so typical, in fact, that detectives are posing as 'pollsters' sent by the National Public Survey to interview 'the representative American family.'

Produced during the war, at the eve of the massive suburbanization of the white middle-classes, the film explores the horrors and instabilities lurking just behind the

4 Kraft & Leventhal, *Footsteps in the Fog*, 34.
5 Quoted in Krohn, *Hitchcock at Work*, 63.
6 Ibid., 66. See also Turner, "Hitchcock's Mastery is Beyond Doubt," 62-67.
7 See Michie, "Unveiling Maternal Desires," 29-53.
8 Cohen, *Alfred Hitchcock: The Legacy of Victorianism*, 71-72.

9 See, for instance, McLaughlin, "All in the Family," 143-46; and Sterritt, *The Films of Alfred Hitchcock*, 59-62.

III IV

charming façade of a suburban house that is so closely connected with the notion of the nuclear family. As Paula Marantz Cohen has noted, the idea of the family unit is a central visual motif in the film. "A key scene features the usurpation of young Charlie's father, as Uncle Charlie takes his brother-in-law's place at the head of the table. (…) During the dinner, Uncle Charlie singles out young Charlie for special recognition and, later in the kitchen, seals their bond with a ring."[8]

This unsettling scene, which evokes romantic rhetoric but also incestuous boundary crossing and vampirist voraciousness, demonstrates perfectly that, in Hitchcock, the family is never innocent. *Shadow of a Doubt* presents the American home as a locus of idealized fantasies but also fears about safety. Besieged by malevolent forces from without and engendering murderous feelings within, the family and the house often produce the most oppressive of tensions. Long before the horror genre came to prefer the suburban house as its favorite setting in the 1970s and long before David Lynch explored the uncanny realm behind suburban white picket fences, Hitchcock presented the suburban dwelling as the true horror of the film – another house in the same street features in Wes Craven's horror movie *Scream* (1996). We should keep at the back of our minds, moreover, that *Shadow of a Doubt* is a production of Universal, the studio that became so successful with some seminal horror movies in the early 1930s. Several critics have also connected some of Uncle Charlie's characteristics (always in shadows, having telepathic powers and an aversion to cameras, charged with sexual aggression) to the vampire tradition.[9]

In order to present the suburban house as a trap, if not a tomb, Hitchcock used some expressive camera work including oblique angles and noirish *chiaroscuro* lighting. How-

99

I, II Charlie's bedroom (Digital Frame)
III Ann's and Roger's bedroom (Digital Frame)
IV Backstairs (Digital Frame)

ever, the house as a locus of dark secrets, tensions, and dangers is also made explicit on repeated occasions in the plot or dialogue. Suspicious of and irritated by the impending visit of the detectives, Uncle Charlie asks his sister why she lets "strangers into your house. Why exposing the family to a couple of snoopers?" Moreover, he asks the Newtons if they "know if you ripped the fronts off houses, you'd find swine." Tellingly, in order to whisk away a compromising article, he makes a paper house with a newspaper for the children. It's a typical Hitchcock house. Made of newsprint, it is walled with stories and it expresses the fragility of the architectural embodiment of the family.[10] Last but not least, architectural components of the suburban house are used as potential murder weapons: the external stairway at the back and the squeezing garage door are instruments that Uncle Charlie uses in order to get rid of his niece, who is discovering the truth about him. *Shadow of a Doubt*, in short, perfectly illustrates the statement Hitchcock made in 1955 when he presented his television show as something that would bring "murder into the American home, where it has always belonged."[11]

10 Conrad, *The Hitchcock Murders*, 331; McLaughlin, "All in the Family," 145.
11 Hitchcock quoted in Naremore, "Hitchcock and Humor," 31.

Studio replica (Set Photograph, Gjon Mili, Getty Images)

A Comfortable Little Place: Wendice Apartment

61A Charington Gardens,
Maida Vale, London, England

Dial M for Murder

Color
Warner Brothers
1954

ART DIRECTION:
Edward Carrere
SET DECORATION:
George James Hopkins

Drawing by Wesley Aelbrecht

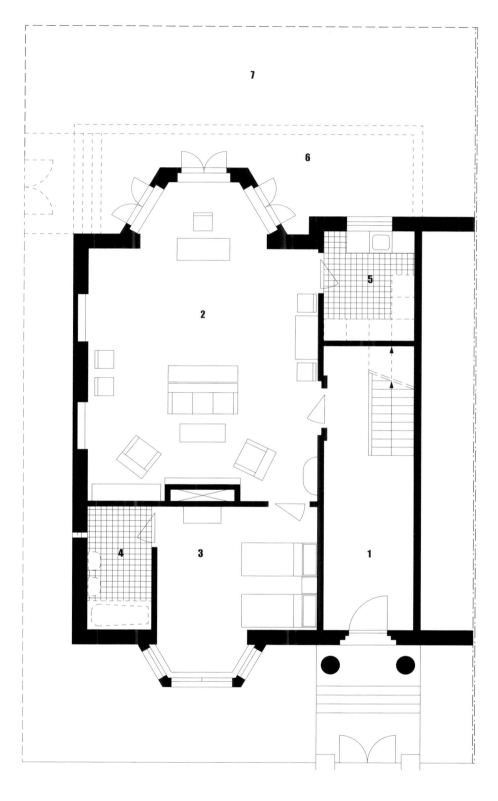

1m

I   II

Inhabited by Tony Wendice (Ray Milland) and his wife Margot (Grace Kelly), this apartment is the setting for a story about somebody trying to kill another resident of his own house – a theme Hitchcock also deals with in *The Lodger*, *Rebecca*, *Suspicion*, *Notorious*, *The Paradine Case*, *Under Capricorn*, *Strangers on a Train*, and *Rear Window*. Upon discovering his wife's affair with the visiting American mystery writer Mark Halliday (Robert Cummings), Tony decides to stage her perfect murder in order to benefit from his inheritance more quickly. Margot is lured to the telephone where Lesgate (Anthony Dawson), Tony's crooked ex-classmate blackmailed into handling the murder, awaits her. Margot, however, fights back and reaches for a pair of scissors and lethally stabs the intruder. Subsequently, Tony Wendice organizes the clues to fool the police, suggesting that Margot killed Lesgate (a.k.a. Swann) because he blackmailed her with an incriminating letter. However, Halliday and police inspector Hubbard (John Williams) refuse to accept the evidence provided and manage to expose the real killer.

According to the address he gives Lesgate, Tony Wendice and his wife live at 61A Charington Gardens in Maida Vale, a residential and affluent London district consisting of many large Edwardian Mansion Houses.[1] Wendice apartment is located on the ground floor of such a typical mansion showing a white stucco façade with decorative trimmings. The sets were constructed in the Warner Brothers studio by unit director Edward Carrere, who also had designed the imaginative modernist sets for King Vidor's *The Fountainhead* (1949), classical Hollywood's seminal film on modern architecture. However, Hitchcock originally had hoped to shoot *Dial M for Murder* in London on location and in the Elstree Studios but the Warner Brothers managers

1 There is no such street as Charington Gardens in Maida Vale. Gary Giblin has noted that there is a Warrington Crescent, which may have been what playwright Frederick Knott had in mind. Hitchcock intended to shoot exteriors in Randolph Crescent, one street over from Warrington Crescent, but this

street does not match the one in the film. See Giblin, *Hitchcock's London*, 95. A letter (May 13, 1953) in the Warner Bros. Archives contains a "list of Leica Kodachrome shots of possible locations." However, the addresses mentioned in the document (17 Randolph Avenue, 2 Carlton Avenue, 104 and 106 Sutherland

Avenue, and 70 and 72 Hamilton Terrace) do not match the shots used in the film.
2 McGilligan, *Alfred Hitchcock*, 469.
3 Truffaut, *Hitchcock*, 212.
4 Warner Brothers Inter-Office Communication note, dated October 28, 1953. Alfred Hitchcock Collection, Folder 132 *Dial*

M for Murder. Margaret Herrick Library, Academy of Motion Pictures Arts and Sciences, Los Angeles.

III IV

opposed that idea. "One cannot show modern London exteriors on the back lot," Hitchcock wrote, yet Warner's front office "could see no difference between the Brownstone New York street and Randolph Crescent, Maida Vale!" Furthermore, Hitchcock had to be on faux-English alert on the interiors and he had a fight with the studio hierarchy over the "shocking taste of the set-dresser."[2] Nonetheless, as usual, Hitchcock exerted an almost total control over the production design, carefully taking into account the tiniest details. "I even had the floor made of real tiles so as to get the sound of footsteps," Hitchcock said.[3] In a film almost entirely set in a single interior, the director carefully selected even the city sounds. A Warner Brothers inter-office communication note states that "Mr Hitchcock also feels that it would be very valuable if we could get a sound track of London traffic, to be used in the duping of the picture whenever we have street scenes. He feels that English traffic noises are different from the American ones. He would also like a few English auto horns."[4]

Although Tony Wendice can be classified in a large category of Hitchcock debonair villains, which also includes Professor Jordan (*The 39 Steps*), Maxim De Winter (*Rebecca*), Johnnie Aysgarth (*Suspicion*), Alex Sebastian (*Notorious*), Bruno Anthony (*Strangers on a Train*), or Philip Vandamm (*North by Northwest*), his apartment is definitely smaller and more modest than the interiors of these. Nonetheless, Lesgate is impressed by the sophisticated interior of the Wendice apartment. "I can see you managed to run a very comfortable little place," he ironically states.

In a November 1953 story outline by Ted Sherdeman, Wendice apartment is extensively described as a flat with a "small entrance hall with doors on either side, one of

I Charington Gardens (Digital Frame)
II View on Charington Gardens (Digital Frame)
III Hall (Digital Frame)
IV Living room with door to kitchen (Digital Frame)

which leads to the kitchen, the other to a bathroom. To one side of the entrance door are coat pegs. An arched opening leads to the living room which is well-groomed and very tidy. To one side is a wall filled with French windows which look out onto Charington Gardens. Those windows have fold-back shutters and heavy, full-length curtains. They open out onto a paved terrace beyond which is a small private garden enclosed by a tall iron fence. In the wall opposite the windows is a fireplace. On its mantlepiece is a clock and an impressive display of silver cups and tennis trophies, visually doubled in number by the wall mirror behind them. In this same wall is the door leading to the bedroom. Against another wall is a cupboard surmounted by book-shelves, with part of a shelf reserved for holding liquors and glasses. Also on this wall are a number of framed photographs, all pertaining to tennis. Above these hangs a tennis-racket. Furnishings include a flat table-desk on which there is a telephone, an address book, and a desk diary. The desk and its chair are located to gain advantageous light from the French windows. There is a sofa, and behind it an oblong table on which an ornate silver cigarette box, and a collection of magazines and newspapers. There is a low coffee table in front of the sofa. At an angle to the sofa is a small armchair and, beside it, a large raffia sewing basket with a lid. When we are inside the flat and the hall entrance door is open, we see the narrow passage which leads to the street door. The floor of this passage is tiled and footsteps outside the flat are easily heard. Against the far wall of the passage is a staircase leading to flats on upper floors. The stairs ascend past the doorway at such an angle that we can only see the legs of the people who use them. When the hall door is open, the door of the stair cupboard is also visible."[5]

In the film, clearly, some details have been changed but all of the important ingre-dients have been maintained. The sober and elegant classical decorations of the exterior also turn up in the living room with its eggshell colored walls. Classical refinement deter-mines the door cases with little architraves, the volutes and egg-and-tongue moulding on the chimneypiece, the garlands on the bookcases, and the little cornice of fretwork with a Greek key that runs over the walls. The Wendice living room, all four walls of which are visible to the viewer, is richly furnished: seats, armchairs, side-tables, and a writing desk fill the space that is beautifully rendered by Robert Burks' swank Warner-color photography, which also evokes an increasingly claustrophobic setting. In the beginning of the film, a breakfast table occupies the space near the kitchen door – in the latter part, this table has disappeared and the Wendices are never shown having lunch or dinner. Between the kitchen door and the main entrance, there are two antique chairs that bear a striking resemblance to the chairs Lisa McLaidlaw received as a wedding

5 Ted Sherdeman, *Story Outline for Dial M for Murder* (November 4, 1953), Warner Bros. Archives.
6 *Dial M for Murder*, Press Releases, Warner Bros. Archives. The Warner archives also indicate that for the preparation of the set also a drawing by Augustus John and books on Sickert were requested.

present from her father in *Suspicion* – did Tony Wendice buy them at a bargain from Johnnie Aysgarth?

In addition, the apartment is richly decorated and the sophistication of its residents is expressed by the presence of some artworks. A fauve landscape is atop of the mantle piece, which is adorned with vases and tennis cups. Tony Wendice's past as a tennis champion is also evoked by framed black and white photographs of tennis players that decorate another wall alongside a class reunion picture, which includes Hitchcock's infamous cameo appearance. The room also contains a classical landscape painting, a fauve painting of a church façade, a postimpressionist flower piece, an engraved portrait, and some pieces of china. In the adjacent bedroom, a Fragonard-like painting adorns the wall to which against two twin beds and a little nightstand are placed. In short, the Wendices love the arts, something which is also illustrated by the art books on the table where Margot puts her purse. Leonardo da Vinci, Giovanni Bellini, and French Impressionism seem to be the subjects that interested Tony or his wife shortly before the attempted murder. A Warner Brothers press release states that "because he is a man of taste and culture, Hitchcock hand-picked many of the props, including an original Rosa Bonheur oil painting, long hidden in Warners' property gallery, and a pair of valuable Wedgewood vases."[6]

Dial M for Murder is the third of Hitchcock's four one-set films (the others being *Lifeboat*, *Rope*, and *Rear Window*). Based on a play by Frederick Knott, which originally opened in London in June 1952, Hitchcock emphasizes in several ways the confines of the apartment. The boundaries of the space, for instance, are marked by a series of high angle shots in the scene in which Tony instructs Lesgate how to execute the murder. In so doing, the high angle shots suggest a floor plan employed in the context of plotting the murder. Similar top shots reappear the morning after Lesgate's death, when the police inspects the crime scene. Subsequently, Tony Wendice gives inspector Hubbard (and, consequently, the viewer) a little guided tour through the hall and the apartment, showing all its rooms – living room, kitchen, bedroom, and bathroom – and assuring that there are no other entrances or exits than the doors leading to the hall and the garden respectively. Moreover, in this film about a murder executed by means of domestic utensils, the confines of the apartment are also underlined by the motifs of the door and the latchkey – the hiding and switching of keys is reminiscent of *Notorious*. In addition, there are various close-ups of architectural details: the shadow of Margot and Mark kissing on the door opened by Tony, the steps of the staircase, the doorknob, the light under bedroom door, to name some instances.

Strikingly, Hitchcock chose not to open the play by situating scenes outside the apartment. In a 1963 interview, Hitchcock admitted that he almost slavishly respected the theatrical origins of the narrative: "They say 'Will you make a film of *Dial M for Murder?*' I say O.K., all right. But I refuse to open it up like they do in the movies. I said it's nonsense. What do you do? When you take a stage play, I said. What do you call opening it up? The taxi arrives, we have a long shot of the street. The taxi stops at the front door of the apartment house. The characters get out, cross the sidewalk, go into the lobby, get into an elevator, go upstairs, walk along the corridor, open the door, and they go into a room. And there they are, on the stage again. So, you might just as well dispense with all that, and be honest and say it's a photographed stage play and all we can do is to take the audience out of the orchestra and put them on the stage with players."[7]

Nonetheless, Hitchcock remains a dyed-in-the-wool film director and transcends theatrical conventions and the confines of the single set. The sheer fixity of the place is both endorsed and undermined by several overhead views and a series of fluid camera movements. As John Orr noted, "perceptually we know where we are, but cinematically we are shifted, decentred to an extreme degree. In this way, Hitchcock adapts a stage play by notionally retaining its set but in fact liquidating its proscenium arch theatricality. We are, metaphorically speaking, watching not only from the wings but also from the centre stage, from backstage, from the footlights, the curtains, the rafters and the balcony and at times we are everything at once."[8] Orr calls the film "the most underrated of the *Kammerspielfilms.*"

This spatial ambivalence is further elaborated by the 3-D process, the short-lived system of stereoscopic photography of the early 1950s that simulated a three-dimensional effect. Although Hitchcock refused to capitulate to the outrageous eccentricities of 3-D gimmickry (no objects are thrown in the face of the viewer), he favored compositions that place lamps, knick-knacks, and pieces of furniture in the foreground, walls well in the background, and human subjects in a middle-ground. In addition, a subtle depth of field is created by the camera, favoring low positions and gliding fluently around the furniture. In so doing, Hitchcock used the 3-D process to create dramatic effects, emphasizing the ways in which the apartment serves as a trap for the characters.[9]

108

7 Hitchcock, "On Style," 293.

8 Orr, *Hitchcock and 20th Century Cinema*, 59.

9 Leitch, *Find the Director and Other Hitchcock Games*, 163-64.

I Living room with antique chairs (Digital Frame)

II Living room (Digital Frame)

III, IV Living room with door to hall (Digital Frame)

V Living room (Digital Frame)

VI, VII Living room with door to bedroom (Digital Frame)

VIII Living room, facing garden (Digital Frame)

I　II
III　IV

V　VI
VII　VIII

Kitchen Sink Claustrophobia: Balestrero House

4024 78th Street,
Jackson Heights,
Queens, New York

The Wrong Man

Black-and-white
Warner Brothers
1956

ART DIRECTION:
Paul Sylbert
SET DECORATION:
William L. Kuehl

This humble dwelling is inhabited by Christopher Emmanuel – a.k.a. Manny – Balestrero (Henry Fonda), his wife Rose (Vera Miles), and their two young children. A jazz bassist at New York's Stork Club, Manny is arrested when office workers at an insurance company testified to having seen him commit an armed robbery. Taken through the neighborhood by police detectives, he is also subjected to the judgments of local merchants who have also were robbed. The similarity of Manny's appearance and handwriting to those of the thief leads to his arrest and imprisonment. In the end, when a look-alike is caught and arrested, Manny turns out to be innocent and he is released. However, the damage had already been done. Family life has been disrupted and the strain causes Rose to have a mental breakdown. As the narrative develops, the emphasis shifts from Manny's terrifying confrontation with the law to Rose's withdrawal from the world and her placement in a mental institution.

Based on a true story, this 'neorealist' subject matter benefited from a documentary approach and a journalistic look quite unusual for Hitchcock.[1] The special character of the film was even announced by the director himself, who exchanged his usual cameo appearance for a prologue reminiscent of his TV episodes, in which he enters a light beam in a huge, dark, and empty studio, ominously preceded by a shadow that elongates his body. Although restrained by the conventions of classical Hollywood cinema, vintage Hitchcockian suspense, and the stylized *noirish* photography of Robert Burks, the documentary approach categorized the picture under a series of contemporary films characterized by their remarkably fresh New York location shooting: films such as *On the Waterfront* (Elia Kazan, 1953), *The Sweet Smell of Success* (Alexander Mackendrick, 1957), *Marty* (Delbert Mann, 1955) and other so-called 'kitchen-sink' dramas. These films focused on the lives and struggles of working class people, emphasized the city's diversity, and sought a darker, more complex ambiguity over the clear-cut optimism of Hollywood.[2] The production of *The Wrong Man* implied careful attention to locations, which Hitchcock himself had scouted together with screenwriter Angus MacPhail and assistant-producer Herbert Coleman in February 1956.[3] Thanks to so-called Garnelites, a new type of portable light,[4] some scenes were even staged in the actual locales in Manhattan and Queens and the credits state that the picture was "made with the cooperation of the department of Commerce and Public Events, City of New York." Two *New York Times* articles paid attention to the location shooting, noting that Hitchcock was a "stickler for fidelity to detail."[5]

111   The Balestreros live in the residential neighborhood of Jackson Heights in Queens.

1 See Deutelbaum, "Finding the Right Man in *The Wrong Man*."
2 See Sanders, *Celluloid Skyline*, 339.
3 McGilligan, *Alfred Hitchcock*, 533.
4 See Foster, "Hitch Didn't Want it Arty." The new portable lights were also extensively discussed in Warner press releases.

5 See "Court is Turned into a Movie Set," *New York Times* (9 April 1956), and "All Around the Town with *The Wrong Man*: Hitchcock Troupe Shoots New Thriller at Surface and Underground Sites," *New York Times* (29 April 1956).

The precise address, 4024 78th Street, is mentioned twice: during the bureaucratic procedures when Manny is taken into custody and when he tells his story to his lawyer. A June 1955 story treatment further indicates that the Balestrero home is only two short blocks away from the subway stop in the Victor Moore Arcade Building at Roosevelt Avenue and 74th Street.[6] By the late 1950s, the area of Jackson Heights had been transformed from an idealistic real estate development into just another neighborhood. The open spaces, which had characterized the garden apartments area before the War, were replaced by block upon block of mediocre apartment buildings and rowhouses.[7]

The fact that Manny Balestro's house is not particularly a perfect haven is already announced in the Ford advertisement that he notices in a newspaper when traveling on the nocturnal subway train that brings him home from work. Cynically entitled "Family Fun," the ad shows a brand new car in front of a brand new suburban house, the dream of the post-war American middle classes to which Manny and his family aspire to belong in spite of their financial difficulties. The detail of the ad at the beginning of the film is telling because, as Paula Marantz Cohen has noted, "America's devotion to conformity, its drive for material success, and its support for rigid stereotypes and conventions appear as central themes in Hitchcock's films of the 1950s, but only in *The Wrong Man* do they emerge as overriding, destructive forces."[8] Manny's neighborhood, clearly, does not meet the Ford standard of suburban haven. The streets are anything but spacious – something which is perfectly evoked when Manny is arrested on the doorstep of his home just before entering and in the point-of-view shot when he looks at the other side of the street when released on bail. In addition, the front yards are tiny and the backyards, as indicated by the views through the kitchen windows, are very narrow. Furthermore, the Balestrero house is situated in the midst of the infrastructure and noise of the metropolis. The nearby elevated railway on Roosevelt Avenue can often be heard inside the house.

One enters the small detached Balestrero house by climbing a little exterior staircase (so probably there's a basement) leading to the front door, which opens on a narrow corridor. At the end of this corridor is the kitchen, which is situated at the backside of the house. On the right side of the corridor there are three doors. The first two are French doors leading into the living room that contains a wall cabinet, a couch, an upright piano, and a small writing desk. At night, this same room serves as a bedroom for the two children. The third door is the entrance to the bedroom of Manny and his wife. Strikingly, even before Manny's arrest, the bedroom is immediately associated with pain: when Manny gets home in the early hours, he finds that his wife has been

6 Herbert Brean, *A Case of Identity: the Balestrero Story* (June 6, 1955), 3 in the Warner Bros. Archives. This document also mentions that the real Balestrero family lived at 41-30 73rd Street, Woodside, New York.
7 Stern, Mellins & Fishman, *New York 1960*, 993.

8 Cohen, *Alfred Hitchcock: The Legacy of Victorianism*, 131.

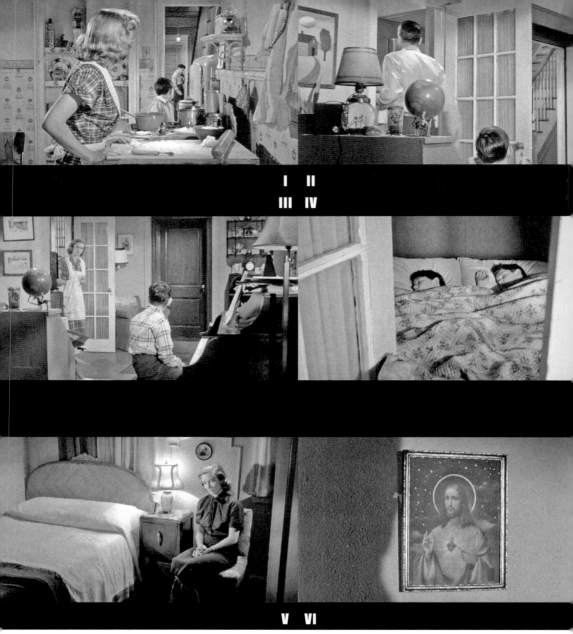

unable to sleep because of tootache.[9] It is also in this room that Rose will have a nervous breakdown, which make her hit and wound Manny with a hairbrush and splinter the mirror on the wall. Another prominent piece of wall decoration is a painting representing Christ as savior. Although paintings frequently play an important part in the films of this Catholic director, *The Wrong Man* contains one of the few occasions when Hitchcock makes significant use of a religious painting. In his video-essay *Histoire(s) du cinéma*, Jean-Luc Godard describes Hitchcock as "the only one, apart from Dreyer, who knew how to film a miracle."[10] Godard refers to the scene in which Manny prays to the painting and to the fact that his prayer seems to be answered: Hitchcock superimposes over Manny's face that of the real robber who is caught and arrested. Immediately before this superimposition, however, Hitchcock shows the painting by means of one of his characteristic forward tracking shots. As a result, the painting becomes invested with a strong sense of psychic closeness similar to the portraits in *Rebecca*, *Suspicion*, *The Paradine Case*, or *Vertigo*.

Other crucial scenes occur in the corridor itself, where there is a little writing desk with a telephone, right in front of the staircase, which is shown prominently although it is never used. No information is given about the spaces and functions on the upper level. The Balestrero house, clearly, is small and Hitchcock emphasizes its spatial delimitations. When Manny gets home and looks in on his sleeping children, their bed seem to fill the entire room. When he enters the house, the camera stays slightly under eye level, reducing the space and making it psychologically confining. Using the cinemascope aspect ratio, Hitchcock and cameraman Robert Burks fill the compact interior with the inhabitants and their family members.

Furthermore, Manny Balestrero is constantly framed and visually incarcerated by architecture: not only in his own house but also in the subway, in the corridor of the insurance company, at its barred office window, in the corridors of houses of possible witnesses, and in the robbed liquor shops and grocery stores. Even the city as a whole seems to have been barred. When a police car takes Manny from Queens to Manhattan, we see the city's skyline through the cables and pillars of a suspension bridge – the visual pattern of a series of vertical lines, which William Rothman termed Hitchcock's premier signature akin to his cameo appearances, is omnipresent in *The Wrong Man*.[11] Released on bail, Manny Balestrero finds that the city to which he returns is an extension of prison. But even before his arrest, as Paula Marantz Cohen has noted, "the 'outside' world, the symbolic site of action and variety within the lexicon of narrative film, is not really available to Manny. It exists only as a passage back to a domestic space. The image of the subway train and of the tunnel that Hitchcock films stretching in front of

9 See Walker, *Hitchcock's Motifs*, 61.
10 See Volume 4A, entitled "Le contrôle de l'univers," of the book version of Jean-Luc Godard's *Histoire(s) du cinéma*, 86-87.
11 Rothman, *Hitchcock: The Murderous Gaze*, 33.

the train expresses the idea vividly, as does the image of the house whose door Manny must unlock to enter."[12]

Obviously, this imagery of confinement and claustrophobia is central to the sequences dealing with the police procedures and the incarceration themselves: the interrogations, the line up, the taking of fingerprints, the penitentiary nicknamed "The Tombs," the patrol wagon, and so forth. Hitchcock stresses the subjective experience of space by his characteristic forward tracking shots in corridors and an impressive series of point-of-view shots of architectural details of Manny's prison cell – having reviewed the script of *The Wrong Man*, the censor made Hitchcock to eliminate the toilet fixture. In addition, the cell scenes contain some bravura camerawork: the camera, for instance, literally breaks through the small peephole of the prison door – this shot required an 18mm lens and in order to counter its perspectival distortions, production designer Paul Sylbert constructed an even smaller cell in which Henry Fonda had to take very little steps.[13] At another moment, facing Manny's face, the camera starts spinning. Clearly, we move from the physical world of enclosure of prison to a world of mental enclosure, which seem to threaten all characters: the secretaries in the insurance office shown in extreme close-ups, Hitchcock himself in the light beam in the prologue, and Manny's family members packed around the telephone down the staircase in the narrow corridor of the Balestrero house. For Rose, the house as a place of confinement still means safety: "We're gonna lock the door and stay in the house," she says. The only way to conquer this nightmare is to "lock all the doors and windows, and shut everyone out. We won't ever let anyone in. No one will ever be able to find us." Eventually, she is locked up literally, in a mental institution. According to her doctor, she is in a "maze of terror" and she lives "in another world from ours, a frightening landscape that could be on the dark side of the moon." Despite its documentary approach, *The Wrong Man* has been called Hitchcock's "most expressionistic film" since "the audience feels trapped along with the man falsely accused."[14] The Balestrero house is no longer a place of safety and domestic bliss but rather an ultimate example of Hitchcockian space of confinement, exuding a sense of claustrophobia similar to prisons and psychiatric hospitals.

116

12 Cohen, *Alfred Hitchcock: The Legacy of Victorianism*, 130.
13 Paul Sylbert, quoted in LoBrutto, *By Design*, 84.
14 Hurley, *Soul in Suspense*, 172.

Plan: Preliminary sketch (Academy of Motion Picture Arts and Sciences)

BALESTRORO HOME

FATHER IN LAWS.

BATH

Kitchen
TABLE
R
STOVE
SINK

TELL

LIVING ROOM
CASTRO

BED
BEDROOM

DOWNSTAIRS

Schizoid Architecture: Bates House & Motel

15 miles from Fairvale, California

Psycho

Black-and-white
Paramount
1960

ART DIRECTION:
Joseph Hurley
Robert Clatworthy
SET DECORATION:
George Milo

Site Plan

1 Motel
2 House
3 Neon Sign
4 Stone Staircase
5 Overgrown Path
6 Car Wreck
7 Rubbish

Bates Motel

1 Office
2 Office Parlor
3 Room No. 1
4 Room No. 10
5 Porch
a Mirror
b Counter
c Room Keys
d Linen Closet
e Bookcase
f Safe
g Painting of *Susanna and
   the Elders*
h Prints of Birds
i Nightstand with
   Newspaper
j Norman's Line of Sight

Drawings by David Claus

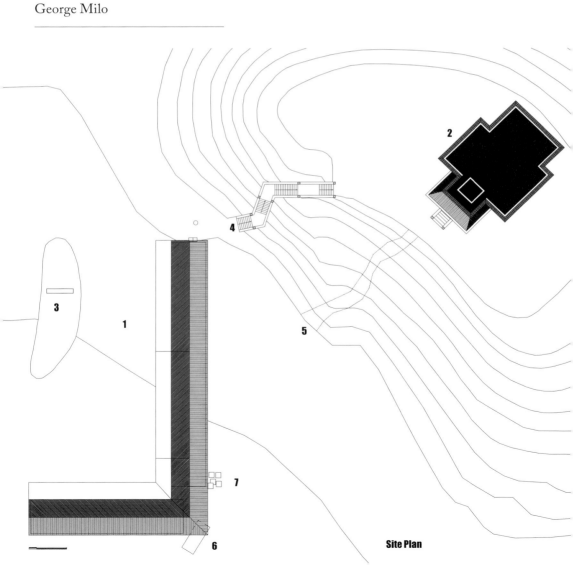

Site Plan

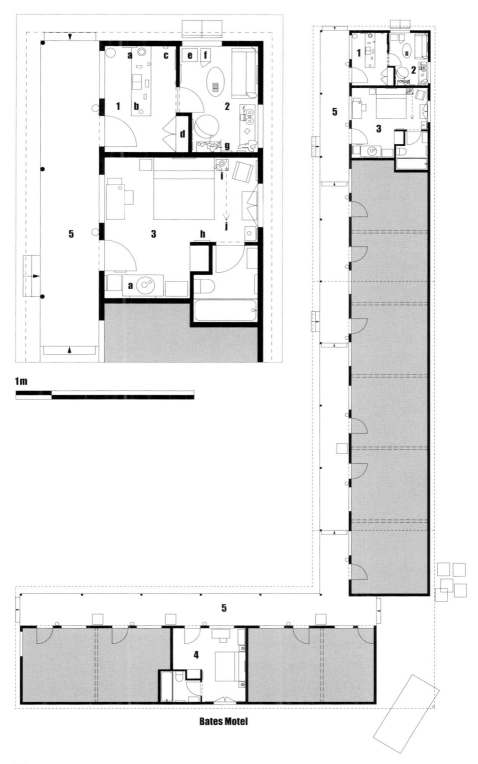

1m

1m

Bates Motel

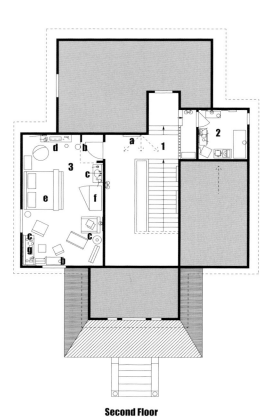

Second Floor

Drawings by David Claus

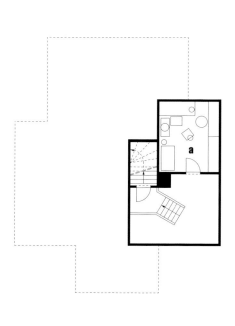

Basement

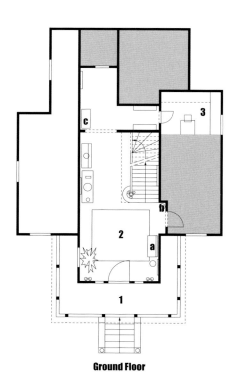

Ground Floor

1m

Made at a time when the tensions and dissatisfactions within the nuclear family – much celebrated in the American cinema of the 1950s – were increasingly discussed in both the social sciences and the popular media, *Psycho* is another Hitchcock meditation on the home and the house.[1] In addition, in film history, *Psycho* is considered the moment horror moved inside the home and the family. Consequently, its architecture is of primary importance and its sets became one of the most famous ever. The Bates estate is situated along a highway that connects Phoenix to California – the route Marion Crane (Janet Leigh) takes after having stolen forty thousand dollars from her employer. Marion's journey features the icons of the new American vernacular landscape of the 1950s and 1960s, which found its cinematic expression in the genre of the road movie: highway patrol cops, car dealers, roadside billboards, neon signs, and motels. Leland Poague has already noted the film's connection between money, cars, and madness and obsession: "only in a culture obsessed with automobiles would a Bates motel be built. Only in a culture obsessed with speed and volume of traffic would a main road be moved."[2] In order to represent this drab, diluted, suburbanized landscape, Hitchcock documented himself extensively on the topography of Route 99 (including names, locations, and room rates of every motel).[3] Assistant director Hilton Green later recalled that Hitchcock traced the route a woman might take to go from Phoenix to central California and he had pictures taken of every area along the way. On roadmaps hung on his office walls, Hitchcock traced with pushpins the heroine's exact route.[4]

During a heavy rainstorm – one of the many over-obvious horror clichés despite the fact that there are neither thunder nor lighting, only near-silence, rain, headlights, and windshield wipers – Marion is attracted by a neon sign showing "Bates Motel – Vacancy." The motel office is deserted, so she walks around the corner where she finds an old, grey, Victorian house at the top of a rise. She also notices the silhouette of a woman passing behind a bedroom window. Supposedly, this woman is the tyrannical mother of Norman Bates (Anthony Perkins), the shy owner of the lonely and run-down motel. Marion's coming up to the Bates house in the rain recalls the second Mrs. De Winter's approach to Manderley in *Rebecca*.[5] Both homes loom large and, as it turns out, are filled with the presence of an assasinated female/maternal figure since the woman in the window is Norman Bates himself.

The isolated and contrasting positions of both the horizontal motel and the vertical Gothic house are striking and make them seem quite menacing. Both buildings are disconnected from each other – something which was not the case in early versions of the screenplay[6] – and from the rest of the world. Arbogast (Martin Balsam), the private investigator tracing Marion, states that "the past two days I have been in so many hotels

1 Cohen, *Alfred Hitchcock: The Legacy of Victorianism*, 144-45.
2 Poague, "Links in a Chain: *Psycho* and Film Classicism," 344.
3 Rebello, *Alfred Hitchcock and the Making of Psycho*, 42.
4 Ibid., 56.
5 Samuels, "Epilogue: *Psycho* and the Horror of the Bi-Textual Unconscious," 156.
6 Rebello, *Alfred Hitchcock and the Making of Psycho*, 35.

that my eyes are bleary with neon but this is the first place that looks like it's hiding from the world." Even the motel seems 'left behind' when the highway moved. This isolation, which seem to banish the Bates Motel to the past, is a product of the spatial organization of modern society, however. Since the 1940s, the new interstate highways had bypassed the older, more local, networks of roads, and the small rural towns they served. As a result, not only the Victorian house but also the modern motel has this feel of the once familiar that has been extracted from the flow of life – both the house and the motel, the ancient setting and contemporary road culture, breathe the atmosphere of an uncanny ruin. "This fella lives like a hermit," sheriff Chambers (John McIntire) tells us about Norman Bates."

Moreover, the motel punctuates the isolation and loneliness of the main characters because, as a building type, it is inherently linked with the boring and the ordinary and because it presents itself as an impossible substitute for the home. Originated in the tourist campsite and the motor court, motels developed into rows of functional cabins, which give a minimal impression of homey lived-in domesticity. In his classic on American roadside architecture, Chester Liebs demonstrated that motels, although little more than a bedroom with a bathroom attached, place considerable emphasis on symbolic furnishings: heavy chenille bedspreads, an oak writing desk with a blotter, wall-to-wall carpeting, prints hung on the walls, closets lined with quilted satin paper, soap and shampoo, etc.[7] Precisely because the emphasis is on an adequate set of functional articles charged with symbolic meaning, motels are particularly interesting architectural items in cinema.

Hitchcock was unmistakably interested in the banality of the building type. The Bates motel bears the same grey drabness of Marion's lower middle-class secretarial life with its crushed dreams. Its desolation and disconsolate character are unmistakably important to the mood of the entire picture, which was certainly emphasized by the canny production design by Joseph Hurley and Robert Clatworthy.[8] Hurley was a production illustrator who had no previous credits in art direction whereas Clatworthy had assisted Robert Boyle on *Saboteur* and *Shadow of a Doubt*. Clatworthy had also been the art director of Orson Welles' *Touch of Evil* (1958), another picture featuring Janet Leigh in a seedy motel with a loony night man. Hurley and Clatworthy constructed the famous sets in the Universal studio: both buildings were erected on a hill off 'Laramie' Street, named for a western series, whereas the interiors were constructed on the sound stage.

The layout of the motel is characterized by an L-shaped floor plan that consists of a tiny office with a parlor and a linear succession of twelve rooms – "twelve cabins, twelve

7 Liebs, *Main Street to Miracle Mile*.
8 Heisner, *Hollywood Art*, 301-302.

I Bathroom of Room No. 1 (Digital Frame)
II, III, IV, V Motel office (Digital Frame)
VI Painting of *Susanna and the Elders* (Digital Frame)

vacancies," Norman says both to Marion and Arbogast. In a way, the motel can be interpreted as a graphic scheme of the entire film, which Raymond Bellour described as a story determined by a succession of bedrooms – the Phoenix hotel room, Marion's room in the Bates motel, Norman's room, and the mother's room.[9] All bedrooms are linked to the film's theme of voyeurism: the penetration of the panoptic camera into the Phoenix hotel room after the couple's love-making, Norman spying on Marion undressing in her room bordering the office parlor, and the intrusion of the bedrooms in the house under the discovering look of Lila (Vera Miles), Marion's sister. The succession of bedrooms, each linked with a form of voyeurism, answers to what Barbara Klinger called the "move from a scenographic space to an obscenographic space" that marks the structure of the film.[10] In addition, the series of cubicles also represent the spatial compactness and even compression that characterize the entire film, which opens with Saul Bass' abstract design concept of verticals and horizontals.[11] In *Psycho*, everything seems to engender entrapment – something that is also emphasized by the film's bird imagery (which cannot be found in Robert Bloch's source novel) and Norman's statement that "we're all in our private traps, clamped in them, and none of us can ever get out. We scratch and claw but only at the air, only at each other. And for all of it, we never budge an inch." The themes of voyeurism and entrapment are further connected by the imagery of (architectural) details structuring or blocking the view: opaque windows, closed Venetian blinds, shower curtains, dark reflecting glasses, windshields blurred by heavy rain, mirrors, peep holes, and swinging light bulbs.

Two of the twelve motel rooms are shown in the film: room number 1, the one Marion is allotted to, and number 10, which, much later in the film, is occupied by Sam Loomis (John Gavin) and Lila Crane, Marion's lover and sister, who register as man and wife in order to look for clues of the disappeared Marion. Both rooms contain undistinguished hotel furniture – a bed, a nightstand with a lamp, a wardrobe, a mirror, a little writing desk and a chair, curtains with a stripe pattern. The walls of room number 1 are decorated with floral wallpaper, a mirror framing Marion in several shots, and prints of birds – Norman sees Marion undressing in the proximity of these birds and one of the framed prints falls to the floor when the shocked Norman discovers the lifeless body of Marion in the bathroom. Strikingly, when Norman showed Marion the room, he was unable to say "bathroom," he simply points at the room that is one of the most important of the film. As in some of his earlier films, Hitchcock presents the bathroom as a place of revelation or menace. In his screenplay, Joseph Stefano writes that its "white brightness…is almost blinding."[12] Strikingly, the scene of the greatest horror of the film inverts the usual darkness of the haunted house. Hitchcock even

9 Bellour, "Psychosis, Neurosis, Perversion (on *Psycho*)," 252.
10 Klinger, "*Psycho*: The Institutionalization of Female Sexuality," 335.
11 Kolker, "The Form, Structure, and Influence of *Psycho*," 211.
12 Rebello, *Alfred Hitchcock and the Making of Psycho*, 70.

incited set decorator George Milo to make certain that the bathroom fixtures gleamed and created an eerily disorienting brightness – a partiality that harked back to bathroom scenes in *Murder* and *Spellbound*.[13] Its bright, clean, and aseptic character is even more highlighted through Norman's careful cleaning after the bloody murder. Hitchcock's camera does not only show the shower, which supports the film's interlinked motifs of enclosure and voyeurism, but also the toilet. Marion tears up a piece of paper and flushes it down the toilet – something which had never been seen on-screen before. After Marion's stabbing, itself rendered in a famous sequence of hyperfragmented editing, Hitchcock explores the entire space by means of a single sweeping camera move. Opening on a screen-filling close-up of Marion's lifeless eye, the dolly glides low along the bathroom floor past the toilet, then into the motel room to end on the night table and, atop it, the newspaper in which the stolen money is hidden. As the camera holds the shot, the open window (actually a screen with projection) discloses Norman running down the stairs from the house toward the motel. Strikingly, the camera remains in a room that is temporarily deprived of any human presence. According to George Toles, its purpose in doing so is "to tranquilize this setting by invoking an aesthetic response to it. The fearful disarrangement of the bathroom space that horror has just visited is not simply curtailed, it is denied."[14]

In addition, in Hitchcockian topography, the bathroom is the stage of the voyeur and a site for the return of the repressed.[15] Room number 1, after all, borders on the tiny motel office, containing a mirror that frames Marion immediately when she enters this room, and an adjacent parlor where Norman has made a peephole in the wall. When Marion retires to her room and prepares to take a shower, Norman takes a picture off its hook revealing this peephole. Strikingly, the picture Norman removes from the wall doubles the events of the narrative since it depicts Susanna and the Elders, the apocryphal story of three old men who spied on a naked woman as she prepared for her bath. Serving as a screen of sorts covering Norman's peephole, the story depicted in the painting also refers to themes central to *Psycho*: voyeurism, wrongful accusation, corrupted innocence, secrets, lust, and dead.[16] In addition, the painting is part of the decoration of the parlor, which is filled with stuffed birds, one of them an enormous owl that seems to look down on Norman and Marion. Also the pictures on the walls are all of birds or winged angels. In his screenplay, Stefano describes the parlor as "a room of birds…The birds are of many varieties, beautiful, grand, horrible, preying."[17] As a result, the parlor looks like a piece of the dark, Victorian mansion transferred to the motel. This also applies for the other side of the peephole. Raymond Durgnat has noted that in a shot cut out of the film, the camera tracks very slowly in one of the rosebuds in the

13 Ibid., 102.
14 Toles, "If Thine Eye Offended Thee," 127.
15 Walker, *Hitchcock's Motifs*, 113.
16 See Lunde & Noverr, "Saying It With Pictures," 101; and Peucker, "The Cut of Representation,"148.
17 Rebello, *Alfred Hitchcock and the Making of Psycho*, 69.
18 Durgnat, *A Long Hard Look at 'Psycho'*, 107.
19 Heisner, *Hollywood Art*, 301-302.
20 Rebello, *Alfred Hitchcock and the Making of Psycho*, 68.
21 Kraft & Leventhal, *Footsteps in the Fog*, 238-40.

I   II

old-fashioned floral wallpaper to show that it camouflages Norman's peephole.[18] Evoking the Victorian mansion, a patch of this wallpaper with a heavy, tight pattern of darkish blooms can be spotted in the mirror behind Marion.

Contrary to information in sources that state that it was an existing building, the Gothic Bates mansion was also a new set designed by Joseph Hurley and Robert Clatworthy. Apart from utilizing cannibalized stock unit sections – parts of the rooftop were borrowed from the house built for *Harvey* (Henry Koster, 1950) and the impressive doors originally belonged to the Crocker House of San Francisco – Hurley and Clatworthy constructed an original house, which unmistakably referred to a rich tradition of Folk Victorian houses and their associations in art and popular culture.[19] Several plausible sources have been mentioned. According to novelist James Michener, the Bates Mansion was based on a haunted house built in the early 1800s in Kent, Ohio. Other possible sources of inspiration that have been suggested are the eerie Addams Family residence familiar from the celebrated Charles Addams cartoons in the *New Yorker* and Edward Hopper's famous 1925 painting *House by the Railroad* showing a melancholy mansard-roofed house with cornices, pilasters, and an oculus window.[20] Jeff Kraft and Aaron Leventhal state that the Gothic Bates house was inspired by a dilapidated Santa Cruz hotel[21] – an opinion in line with statements by Hitchcock himself. In his interview with François Truffaut, Hitchcock stated that "the actual locale of the events is in northern California, where that type of house is very common. They're either called 'California Gothic,' or, when they're particularly awful, they're called 'California Gingerbread.' I

127

I Bates house (Still, Royal Film Archive, Brussels)
II Bates house (Academy of Motion Picture Arts and Sciences)

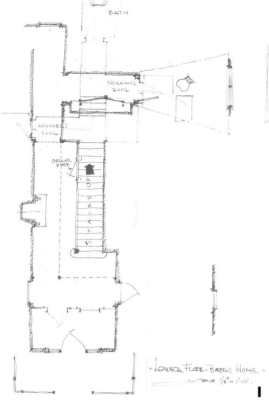

- LOWER FLOOR · BATES HOME ·
    SCALE 1/4"=1'-0"

did not set out to reconstruct an old-fashioned Universal horror-picture atmosphere. I simply wanted to be accurate, and there is no question but that both the house and the motel are authentic reproductions of the real thing. I chose that house and motel because I realized that if I had taken an ordinary low bungalow the effect wouldn't have been the same. I felt that type of architecture would help the atmosphere of the yarn."[22]

With its symmetrical façade, cornice-line brackets, simple window surrounds, and a porch with spindlework detailing, the Bates house is a good example of the Folk Victorian architecture that was popular in the late nineteenth and early twentieth centuries in the entire United States.[23] The ocular window in the high-pitched roof is perfectly in line with the film's voyeurist theme. In contrast with the ordinariness of the motel, the ornate Gothic Revival mansion is one of the long series of 'haunted houses' from Uni-

22 Truffaut, *Hitchcock*, 269.
23 Virginia & Lee McAlester, *A Field Guide to American Houses*, 309-310.
24 David Stove, quoted in Wilson, "Monsters and Monstrosities," 145.
25 Toles, "If Thine Eye Offended Thee," 144.
26 Rebello, *Alfred Hitchcock and the Making of Psycho*, 69.
27 Benjamin, "Erfahrung und Armut," in *Gesammelte Schriften*, II, I, 217; and "Das Passagen-Werk: Aufzeichnungen und Materialien," in *Gesammelte Schriften*, V, I, 291-92.

I Plan Bates house: preliminary sketch
(Academy of Motion Picture Arts and Sciences)
II Bates house foyer: sketch
(Academy of Motion Picture Arts and Sciences)
III Bates house landing: sketch
(Academy of Motion Picture Arts and Sciences)

versal horror films, most of whose exteriors had only been seen in mattes. Norman Bates and his mother would certainly have felt at home in James Whale's *The Old Dark House* (1932) – Hitchcock himself corroborated this association with the horror tradition in the film's funny trailer, in which he poses as a veritable House of Horrors tour-guide stating that "even in daylight, this place looks a bit sinister." The ample porch leads unto an impressive foyer, which connects to a corridor showing the way to the kitchen. The foyer is dominated by a large stairway complete with intricate carved newels and stained-glass windows. The staircase leads to the upper floors with the bedrooms of Norman and his mother. Victorian paintings in ornate frames adorn the walls of the landing, which reveals the several levels of the large house. Hitchcock explores this space by means of impressive dolly shots ending in vertical top shots on the stairway.

The uncanny interior of the Bates mansion is a perfect example of what David Stove has called *Victorianarum*: "that horror which even nowadays is felt, at least to a slight degree, by almost anyone who visits a display of stuffed birds under glass, for example, or of Victorian dolls and doll's clothes."[24] The plush rooms contain conspicuous carpets that contribute to the hushed, smothering atmosphere of the house, which is crammed with furniture and objects. These are often emphatically displayed. George Toles even claimed that "in no other Hitchcock film does the camera close in on so many objects that refuse to disclose their significance."[25] Production designer Robert Clatworthy recalls Hitchcock being far more finicky about odd, unsettling details of décor – such as the kitschy sculpture of the hands folded in prayer in Mother's room – than about the general architectural structure.[26] The crammed house full of charged objects answers perfectly to Walter Benjamin's observations of the packed, plush, Victorian bourgeois interior, in which everything is covered by drapes and upholsters.[27] According to Benjamin, the bourgeois interior does not only present itself as a mirror image of man's sojourn in the mother's womb, it also dazes its inhabitants. In the crammed interior, residents are turned into fossils whereas every object bears the traces of the inhabitants. The Bates house, like the houses in the stories of Edgar Allan Poe, is a reflection of its inhabitant's mind, its rooms carefully preserved. Norman's room, which has to be reached by ascending another flight of stairs, is that of a child with a record player and fluffy childhood toys, which are obviously still played with. Norman's room is never seen as a visual whole, just a succession of thight details, in contrast with his mother's room, which is visualized by wide shots. The bedroom of Mrs. Bates is crowded with Victorian furniture and artifacts: a cold white marble fireplace, a sumptuous armoire with old-fashioned dresses, the aforementioned sculpture of hands, black statues of winged

I   II
III   IV

angels that mirror the stuffed birds in the motel parlor. This sepulchral room even retains a bed which still bears the imprint of the body of Norman's mother. Another striking piece of furniture are the mirrors, which are omnipresent in *Psycho* – "Let's have lots of mirrors, old boy," Hitchcock told set decorator George Milo.[28] In mother's room, just before discovering the terrible secret, Lila is trapped between two facing mirrors. Conventional markers of both the need for introspection and the haunted double,[29] mirrors are also suitable props for the representation of a split personality.

    This uncanny atmosphere is not only the result of the production design but also of John L. Russell's camerawork. Camera positions make the mammoth interior dwarf the characters. This is the case, for instance, in the hallway perspective of Norman seated at the kitchen table directly before the shower scene – as if the only spaces that he feels

130

28 Rebello, "Psycho," 57.
29 Rosenblatt, "Doubles and Doubt in Hitchcock," 37-63.
30 Toles, "If Thine Eye Offended Thee," 136.
31 Ringel, "Blackmail," 22.
32 Durgnat, *A Long Hard Look at 'Psycho'*, 171.

V VI
VII VIII

free to occupy in his own person are peripheral rooms behind the main living area.[30] Twisted dolly shots are not only used for narrative purposes (such as in the scene in which mother kills Arbogast or the one in which Norman's carries his mother down the stairs) but also function as visual extensions of Norman Bates' trapdoor spider view of life.[31] Camera movements enforce the feeling that the house is haunted, the space sentient, and that objects are charged. To keep the intruding Arbogast in view, for example, the camera pulls backwards up the stairs or, as Raymond Durgnat has noted, it seems more like a zoom lens on a camera outside diegetic space. The 'flattened-out' perspective then characteristic of zooms makes conspicious the hallway below him (into which he will indeed fall).[32]

131

I, II Foyer with stairs (Digital Frame)
III Foyer (Digital Frame)
IV Stairs (Digital Frame)
V Landing (Digital Frame)
VI, VII, VIII Mother's bedroom (Digital Frame)

I Sculpture, mother's bedroom (Digital Frame)
II Bed, mother's bedroom (Digital Frame)
III Stairs to Norman's room (Digital Frame)
IV Norman's room (Digital Frame)
V Stairs to basement (Digital Frame)
VI Basement (Digital Frame)
VII Hitchcock in mother's bedroom (Academy of Motion Picture Arts and Sciences)

Psycho does not only deal with an uncanny house but also with what's underneath. The climax, after all, is situated in the basement of the Bates house where the mommy/mummy is discovered. The uncanny house is literally connected with death and functions as a funerary monument. The discovery in the basement makes clear that the entire house, and the mother's room in particular, make up a tomb. Like an Egyptian pharaoh, mother has been mummified and buried with her household belongings. Given this perspective, the crammed Bates house incarnates the womb/tomb rhyme that preoccupies house-building in many cultures. The Bates mansion is such a powerful image since it is reminiscent of archetypal forms of early neolithic domestic architecture, in which the dead are buried under the floors or their bones incorporated into the substructure of the houses.[33]

The scene situated in the cellar – a dark space where, according to Gaston Bachelard, fears are difficult to rationalize[34] – adds a third level to the house as a result of which Slavoj Zizek, in his *Pervert's Guide to Cinema* (2006), is able to read the tripartite structure of the Bates house as a representation of (Nor)man's mind: on the ground floor lives the ego; the second floor is the space of the (maternal) superego; whereas the *id* dwells in the basement. However, more important than the tripartite structure of the Victorian house is its juxtaposition to the motel. Zizek even goes so far as to trace Norman Bates' psychotic split to his inability to locate himself between the anonymous modernist box of the motel and his mother's Gothic house on the hill.[35] According to Zizek, it would take a deconstructivist architect such as Frank Gehry to mediate between such two opposites, which are often obfuscated in the postmodern architecture of *New Urbanism* characterized by a staging of the cosy atmosphere of small-town family life. "If the Bates Motel were to be built by Gehry," Zizek writes, "directly combining the old mother's house and the flat modern motel into a new hybrid entity, there would have been no need for Norman to kill his victims, since he would have been relieved of the unbearable tension that compels him to run between the two places – he would have a third place of mediation between the two extremes."[36]

33 Rykwert, "One Way of Thinking About a House," 85-87.
34 Bachelard, *La poétique de l'espace*, 35-36.
35 Zizek, "In His Bold Gaze My Ruin is Writ Large," 231-32.
36 Zizek, "Is There a Proper Way to Remake a Hitchcock Film?," 273.

Mother's chair (Academy of Motion Picture Arts
and Sciences)

Living in a Cage: Brenner House

Bodega Bay, California

The Birds

Color
Universal
1963

PRODUCTION DESIGN:
Robert Boyle
SET DECORATION:
George Milo

Drawings by Linde Vertriest

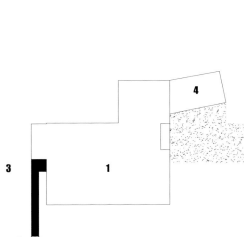

Site Plan

1m

Ground Floor

1m

The Brenner house is situated at Bodega Bay, a large protected small-boat anchorage on the picturesque Sonoma Coast in Northern California. It is inhabited by Mrs. Lydia Brenner (Jessica Tandy) and her young daughter Cathy (Veronica Cartwright). In addition, her son Mitch (Rod Taylor), a young San Francisco lawyer, often stays in the house. In the film, the Brenners are visited by Melanie Daniels (Tippi Hedren), who had met Mitch lately in San Francisco and who followed him in order to give a couple of love birds to Cathy as a birthday present. As soon as Melanie arrives in Bodega Bay, the town is plagued by a series of mysterious and ever more dangerous attacks of birds, who also wreak havoc to the Brenner house.

Characteristically, even before screenwriter Evan Hunter started on the job, Hitchcock had decided that he would exchange the coast of Cornwall, where the original Daphne du Maurier novella is situated, for Northern California.[1] According to Hitchcock, the area's geographical condition was perfectly appropriate for a story with aerial protagonists: "In order to get the photography of the birds in the air, we needed an area with low land, not high mountains or a lot of trees. In a pictorial sense, it was vital to have nothing on the ground but sand so that we had the entire sky to play with. Bodega Bay had all of that," Hitchcock later told.[2] Conversely, the local topography inspired some specific scenes. "Many filmmakers," Hitchcock stated, "forget how important geography is to a story. I chose Bodega Bay because I wanted an isolated group of people who lived near an articulate community. Bodega Bay is a place where sophisticated San Franciscans drive to spend the weekend. The location provided the combination we wanted."[3] "The whole thing was based on the geography," Hitchcock concluded.[4]

The small-town setting is important to the narrative. Melanie is clearly seen as an outsider, not only by Mrs. Brenner but also by several inhabitants of the town – something which is clearly dealt with in the scene set in restaurant *The Tides*. In their studies of small-towns in cinema, Kenneth MacKinnon and Emanuel Levy compare Bodega Bay with the settings of contemporary science fiction films such as *Invasion of the Body Snatchers* (Don Siegel, 1955), in which a peaceful place is imperceptibly taken over by an alien force and normality, ordinariness, and orderliness are disrupted. The small-town community blames Melanie, a product of decadent San Francisco, for the strange behavior of the birds and seems to be as ready to lapse into witch-hunting and pseudo-rationalization as was Salem.[5] The ideological message of *The Birds* is similar to that of Hitchcock's other small-town film, *Shadow of a Doubt*, set in nearby Santa Rosa: the fragility of our supposedly orderly world. Paying close attention to the area's geography, business, and flavor, Hitchcock combined various locations around the Bodega Bay

1 Hunter, *Me and Hitch*, 10 and 23.
2 Counts, "The Making of Alfred Hitchcock's *The Birds*," 16.
3 Alfred Hitchcock quoted in Kraft & Leventhal, *Footsteps in the Fog*, 181.
4 "Hitchcock on Style," 35.
5 MacKinnon, *Hollywood's Small Towns*, 100-102; Levy, *Small-Town America in Film*, 160-64.

I Bodega Bay (Digital Frame)
II The Brenner house at the bay (Digital Frame)
III Garden (Digital Frame)
IV The Brenner house from the bay (Digital Frame)
V House and barn (Digital Frame)
VI Living room (with dining room in the back) (Digital Frame)
VII Living room (Digital Frame)
VIII Dining room (Digital Frame)

I II
III IV

V VI
VII VIII

region with studio footage into a single compressed 'downtown' Bodega Bay, which did not actually exist.[6] In order to construct this cinematic town in which surreal and apocalyptic incidents occur, Hitchcock employed his characteristic documentary naturalism. "I had every inhabitant of Bodega Bay – man, woman, and child – photographed for the costume department. The restaurant is an exact copy of the one up there," Hitchcock told François Truffaut.[7] The interior of Dan Fawcett's farmhouse is an "exact replica" of one near Bodega Bay: "the same entrance, the same halls, the same kitchen. Even the scenery of the mountain that is shown outside the window of the corridor is completely accurate."

This accuracy, however, was violated to a large extent since Hitchcock was looking for a peculiar mood. Production designer Robert Boyle and matte painter Albert Whitlock toured the Bodega Bay locations to make sketches. The mattes not only created a town center when there was none but also changed the clear marine sky to cloudy – "to give it mood," as Whitlock put it.[8] Undoubtedly, Whitlock, who had worked with Hitchcock in England before the war and would continue to be responsible for the 'pictorial designs' and 'special photographic effects' of all of Hitchcock's Universal films, contributed significantly to the imagery of the Bodega scenery. Tying the multiple locations together, he kept the look of the picture constantly ominous. "I wanted it to be gloomy," Hitchcock remarked. "It was necessary to subdue the color of many of the scenes in the film lab to get the proper effect." Robert Boyle later recalled that "some of the reviews criticized us for not playing up the beauty of Bodega Bay, but we didn't want it to be colorful. We weren't making a 'a Bright Day at Malibu' type picture."[9]

140

6 Kraft & Leventhal,
Footsteps in the Fog, 168-88.
7 Truffaut, *Hitchcock*,
253-54.
8 Counts, "The Making of
Alfred Hitchcock's *The
Birds*," 17.
9 Ibid.
10 Ibid.

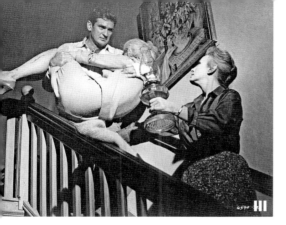

These subdued colors also recur in the exteriors and the interior of the Brenner estate, which is not situated in (the partly fictitious) downtown Bodega but on a remote part of the bay. According to Robert Boyle, finding a suitable property to represent the Brenner farm was the most difficult of all locations. The ideal building turned out to be on Bodega Head, where senior citizen Rose Gaffney had recently made headlines by battling the local power company's plans to build a power plant on her land. "The house was nothing but a shack when I first saw it," Boyle said. "Rose used it as extra property and hadn't kept it up very well over the years. We had to literally make a new house out of it by building over it. Additionally, the out buildings and barn in the back were considered too far from the house for filming purposes, so an extra barn was put up to group the reconstructed structures closer together. A small pier was added to the front of the property, a gazebo built for the party sequence and the overgrown grounds and trees generously trimmed."[10]

As indicated by the reconstructed site plan, the Brenner estate comprises a white house, a garden with a white picket fence and gazebo, a garage, and a red barn. By means of a little pier, the Brenner house is accessible by boat. Of the house itself, only about half of its ground floor is visible in the film: a living room gives direct access to a dining room, which connects to a kitchen, and a narrow corridor situated between two non-descript and unexplored spaces. The corridor also connects to a staircase, which leads to an upper-floor containing at least three bedrooms: that of Mrs. Lydia Brenner, a guest room where Melanie is staying, and Cathy's room, where a climactic bird attack occurs at the end of the film. There are no indications as to where Mitch's sleeping place is located.

I Living room after bird attack (Still, Royal Film Archive, Brussels)
II Living room (Still, Royal Film Archive, Brussels)
III Stairs to Cathy's room (Still, Royal Film Archive, Brussels)

As in *Easy Virtue, Number 17, Rebecca, Suspicion, Shadow of a Doubt, Notorious,* and *Psycho*, the house is not presented as a realm of safety but rather as a suffocating place, which is the upshot of a series of repressions. Given this perspective, it is interesting to note that Hitchcock insisted that the birds be "domestic birds" and not "vultures" or raptors.[11] Slavoj Zizek even noted that the picture is perfectly imaginable as a story without flying creatures: a typical American family drama, such as the many that were made during the 1950s, both in cinema and the theater, about a son unable to commit to one woman because he is unable to free himself from the pressure exerted by a possessive mother.[12] In light of this, the birds embody a kind of maternal superego and their attacks function primarily as extensions of the mother's hysterical fear of losing her son. In Lee Edelman's queer analysis, the birds mark an intrusion of a sexuality without reserve, a sexuality which threatens to destroy the home as a spatial manifestation of the heterosexual ideology of reproductive necessity.[13]

No matter how, the Brenner house could not hold out in the face of the intruders. It is intruded by the birds, but primarily by Melanie. Strikingly, when the viewer sees the Brenner interior for the first time, he or she accompanies the tiptoeing Melanie, who behaves like a trespasser or even a burglar. Melanie is clearly out-of-place here. Camille Paglia, in her monograph on *The Birds*, notes that "she glamorously cuts through the modest, stuffy, early American interior like the lord of the manor at a serf's cottage."[14] The idea of intruding or trespassing a private realm is further emphasized in the *mise-en-scène* and the editing. In his famous shot-by-shot analysis of the sequence, Raymond Bellour has demonstrated that the principle of alternation between 'Melanie seeing' and 'what Melanie sees' marks the previous series of shots that show Melanie's approach of the house. However, this continuity is broken in the shots where she moves in the hallway and enters the dining room. According to Bellour, "Melanie ceases to be the seer and becomes the seen, explicitly so, although not by a character but by the camera and the cameraman."[15]

Caught by the viewer, Melanie becomes an element of discord in the interior. Consequently, the assaulting birds epitomize a disturbance of the relations within the domestic realm of the detached house. Beaks unstoppably splintering the doors and window shutters, gulls dive-bombing the front door, and sparrows sliding down the chimney, *The Birds* emphasizes the vulnerability of the home in many ways. Both in Dan Fawcett's farm and in the Brenner house, the vulnerability of domestic space is further visualized by broken teacups, which Robin Wood calls a "leitmotif" in the film symbolizing human fragility.[16] Moreover, the Brenner house itself exposes its vulnerability: cut off from the world and unprotected, it is no more than a wooden shelter situ-

11 Bogdanovich, *The Cinema of Alfred Hitchcock*, 45.

12 Zizek, "The Hitchcockian Blot," 123-40. See also Horowitz, "*The Birds*," 279.

13 Edelman, "Hitchcock's Future," 239-58.

14 Paglia, *The Birds*, 34.

15 Bellour, *The Analysis of Film*, 51. Bellour's text was originally published as "*Les oiseaux*: Analyse d'une séquence," in *Cahiers du cinéma* 216 (October 1969).

16 Wood, *Hitchcock's Films Revisited*, 165.

17 Hunter, *Me and Hitch*, 48-49.

18 Paglia, *The Birds*, 7-8.

19 Ibid., 76.

I II

ated amidst the endless expanses of water and sky. In a deleted scene, which was filmed but never used according to screenwriter Evan Hunter, Melanie says that she is frightened and confused and that she wants "to go back to San Francisco where there are buildings and… and concrete."[17]

The wooden walls are not strong and solid enough to keep the hostile and aggressive birds outside; yet, they are too thick and inflexible for the human inhabitants. "With profound feeling for architecture," Paglia notes, "Hitchcock sees the house in historical terms as both safe haven and female trap. Ten thousand years ago, when man the nomad took root in one place, he brought animals with him into human service. But domestication was to be his fate too, as he fell under architecturally reinforced female control."[18] In several ways, the film uses the imagery of the house as a claustrophobic space of confinement. During her first visit to the house, Melanie is seen walking down a Hitchcockian corridor. In addition, the assaults on Melanie, both the one in the phone booth in downtown Bodega Bay and the one in Cathy's attic room, are reminiscent of the famous shower scene in *Psycho*. Moreover, the Brenner house is completely boarded up to keep out the hostile flying intruders: the dwelling is transformed into a cage and even into a dark box. After Mitch has boarded up the windows with jagged, weathered planks, Lydia asks what will happen when they run out of wood. "We'll break up the furniture," he says. Eventually, he does. When the front door gives way to pecking beaks, Mitch moves a heavy furniture piece with a glass mirror and nails it in place. "Architecture is devolving," Paglia wrote. "Mitch has evidently torn apart a barn to turn the house into a blind bunker. It's back to cave-man days."[19] Raymond Durgnat

43

I Stairs to Cathy's room (Digital Frame)
II Cathy's room (Digital Frame)

compared the besieged Brenner house to the 'log cabin' of America's fabled past, which is invaded here by the terrible "beak-tomahawks" of bloodthirsty Indians.[20] Not coincidentally, during their first attack, the birds enter the house through the hearth – in many cultures the ritual center of family gatherings and domestic contemplation. Frank Lloyd Wright, who could have felt at ease in the rustic Brenner house, often referred to the fireplace as the 'heart' of the house, meaning the spiritual center that visualizes and symbolizes the sanctity of the household.[21]

However, not only the birds attack the house, the house itself seems to threaten its inhabitants. As in a classic horror movie like *The Haunting* (Robert Wise, 1963) or in Roman Polanski's *Repulsion* (1965), it's as if the house itself were aggressively haunted. By means of carefully selected camera positions, the ceilings seem to weigh down on the besieged inhabitants, who press themselves anxiously against the walls and furniture. During the last attack, Melanie is shown from overhead and then from an oddly low angle. She retreats to a sofa in a corner. Embodying a spatial paranoia, she raises her legs as if the sofa might enclose and protect her. As is often the case in Hitchcock's work, confined spaces are both a refuge and a trap.

"Though there is no Gothic manor house, the story's bleak atmosphere and ferocious weather resemble those of the great Brontë novels, which are the literary ancestors of *Rebecca*," Camille Paglia noted.[22] Apart from the notion of the house as a trap, the architectural implications of such a theme are further visualized by another motif borrowed from the Gothic plot: the concealed or forbidden room. After climbing the stairs, Melanie enters the secluded attic room, in which the birds make their last vicious attack. The room, clearly, belongs to Cathy – as if Melanie transgresses the safe psychological space of childhood. Cathy's room, however, has already been invaded by birds, which made a ragged hole in the roof. Through the hole shines a radiant blue sky, which, in contrast with the light beam from the sky in science fiction films, seems to promise no salvation. After disrupting Cathy's birthday party and attacking the school, the birds, by invading Cathy's room, repeat their unconstrained aggression against children and the sacralization of childhood – as if they want to damage the house at its most vulnerable place.

In order to construct the interior of the Brenner house on a Hollywood sound stage, Hitchcock wrote a fascinating memorandum, which was sent to assistant producer Peggy Robertson, production designer Robert Boyle, and set decorator George Milo in January 1962.[23] The memorandum convincingly demonstrates that each component of

144

20 Durgnat, *The Strange Case of Alfred Hitchcock*, 340.
21 Twombly, *Frank Lloyd Wright*, 39-42.
22 Paglia, *The Birds*, 8.
23 *Memorandum Indicating Set Dressing: Requirements for "The Birds"*, 24 January 1962, Folder 111, Alfred Hitchcock Collection, Margaret Herrick Library, Academy of Motion Pictures Arts and Sciences, Los Angeles. A card attached to the memo, mentions Bob Boyle, George Milo, Doc Wiley, Norman Deming, Peggy R(obertson), and "file" as addressees.

I   II

III   IV

the set is significant. Pieces of furniture and objects reflect the financial possibilities and social position of the inhabitants. Inaccuracies and hybrid combinations are not the result of a negligence on part of the set designers but a well-considered interpretation of contrasting patterns of taste of different inhabitants. Other strange arrangements indicate that the interior is constructed by means of objects coming from other places (such as a San Francisco apartment), which played a role in the off-screen life of certain characters. In the film, the chairs, for instance, seem too big and too robust for the table, as is suggested in the memorandum:

The first set we are concerned with is the Brenner home which is out on the far side of Bodega Bay.

145

I Spatial paranoia (Digital Frame)
II Kitchen (Digital Frame)
III Corridor (Digital Frame)
IV Boarding up the house (Digital Frame)

As the script indicates, Mrs. Brenner is a widow who now lives at this farm with her 11-year-old daughter. Her son, Mitch, has a small apartment in San Francisco (he is a criminal lawyer) and comes to the farm every Friday night and stays until early Monday morning. Mrs. Brenner's 11-year-old daughter lives with here all week and goes to the local Bodega school.

Mrs. Brenner has been living this way since her husband died 4 or 5 years ago. At present, the script does not provide for the nature of the late Mr. Brenner's profession or economic status. I think it is fair to assume, however, that whatever their business was, the elder Brenners were well off enough to have an apartment in San Francisco and the farm at Bodega Bay as a weekend retreat. We can obviously infer that, after Mr. Brenner's death, the two places were more than sufficient for Mrs. Brenner's needs so she gave up the apartment and came to live permanently at the small farm at Bodega Bay.

Now, we come to the thought as to how the main downstairs interior of the Brenner farm should be dressed. The first consideration should be that the Brenners are reasonably educated and literate people. Whether they had any taste in paintings, for example, would depend largely upon their economic status. We could assume though, however, that she might possess a couple of small gouaches by perhaps, Utrillo or Vlaminck, but they should be quite small and not at all pretentious. The furnishings, in fact, would be divided between the original farm furnishings and choice pieces that she would have brought from San Francisco after closing the apartment. Perhaps, the rest of the pieces were taken by Mitch himself, although one could assume he had already been in possession of his own apartment, if this change-over had taken place as recently as 4 years ago, because he is already a practicing lawyer. There is a piano. Depending upon our research, we have to decide whether this is a small boudoir grand or a small upright. The boudoir grand would obviously have been brought from the apartment at San Francisco. On the other hand, if the piano had already been there, even when it was a weekend home, it would obviously be an upright.

The general atmosphere of taste and character would be, it would seem, to combine that of the mother and her son. It could be assumed that many of their possessions were at the weekend home, especially in view of the fact that, so far as we know, Mitch Brenner is never going to be free enough of his mother to have all his possessions in an apartment and away from her. So it would indicate that the books on the shelves, the hi-fi, the records and, maybe a gun or two, would belong to Mitch Brenner. The evidence around the room of Mrs. Brenner would be whatever we decide (after discussion) what her main interests were.

Naturally, if the elder Brenners did like paintings, the place of honor could be a portrait of the deceased Mr. Brenner. This could have been a presentation made by the fellow directors of his company at some time. There would be a writing desk in the room which would absorb

24 Krohn, "Le musée secret de M. Hitch-cock;" see also Nathalie Bondil-Poupard, "Alfred Hitchcock: An Artist in Spite of Himself," 179-88.

most of the memorabilia of both Mitch and his mother. And, perhaps, on the walls around the desk would be the college pictures belonging to Mitch. (Was he on the football team?) There should be other effects on the walls, perhaps, some relative pictures, and one nice touch would be a blown up picture of Cathy, Mrs. Brenner's 11-year-old daughter. It could be one of those blown up and hand tinted photographs. One interesting effect of the furnishings might be that the dining chairs came from the apartment in San Francisco but the oval table belonged originally to the farm setting.

Now, for the rest of the touches, I think we should rely on the following research: photographs should be taken of a number of interiors around Bodega Bay. These should range from the house of such a character as Rose Gaffney. Her complete interior may not be suitable but it may contain touches of dressing that we could use. We should also look into the Chancellor home, there might be something of interest there. As I understand it, neither of these two homes are very elegant, or even attractive, so we should also look around for some better class interiors into the Bodega Bay area. Shouldn't we look, for example, for the home of perhaps the most well off of all the residents in the area.

For the father's portrait it will be necessary to research who is the best portrait painter in San Francisco. I think also, we should look out for some water colors done by such an artist as Don Kingman (who is a well known San Francisco water colorist).

SPECIAL NOTE: In regard to Mrs. Brenner's personal interest we might take some inspiration from the collection hobby of Rose Gaffney.

It should be very carefully born in mind that the dressing of this set should take for many of its touches just perhaps one item from the many photographs of interiors we hope to get. In other words, we are not trying to get our inspiration for dressing the set from one particular interior, it is to be a combination of ideas.

The role artworks play in the interior is striking. In the first place, they have to support the profile of the characters, which, in the memorandum, are described as "reasonably educated and literate people." The presence of modern art in this interior is taken for granted. In contrast with many Hollywood movies of the 1940s and 1950s (cf. the police inspector and the cubist painting in Hitchcock's *Suspicion*), nowhere is the presence of modern art in the living room ridiculed. Besides an obligatory piano, the memorandum speaks of small gouaches by Maurice Utrillo and Maurice de Vlaminck – every one of them artists being part of Hitchcock's own art collection, which also included works by Georges Braque, Chaim Soutine, Raoul Dufy, Paul Klee, Georges Rouault, Henri Gaudier-Brzeska, Jacob Epstein, and Amadeo Modigliani.[24]

Several landscapes and flower pieces painted in a postimpressionist style clearly

render a strong colorful accent to most of the rooms. Strikingly, in the artworks on the walls in the room where Melanie stays, a more traditional taste dominates. Passionate colors seem to mismatch in the bedrooms of the Brenner house since Lydia's bedroom as well is characterized by subdued colors. According to Camille Paglia, an ormolu clock, London city prints, and a heavy gilt mirror suggest that Lydia or her parents were not natively Californian or even American.[25] Apart from these two bedrooms, the style of most of the artworks in the Brenner house can be defined as a decorative or domestic modernism – the kind of art created by Sam Marlowe, the protagonist painter in *The Trouble With Harry*.

One artwork in particular, however, strikes another key: the portrait of the deceased husband/father that hangs over a piano adorned with pastoral rococo porcelain figurines. The fauve palette and the usually somewhat naive style of watercolorist Don Kingman (who is explicitly mentioned in the memo) is completely absent in the bourgeois realist portrait of Mr. Brenner. According to Camille Paglia, the portrait is even a photograph, "a convincingly typical, American small-town studio shot in the Rotary Club, civic-pride style."[26] As is often the case with painted portraits in literature and cinema, Mr. Brenner's portrait functions as a *memento mori* and invokes a restless sense of fate. As is true of the painted portraits of Caroline de Winter in *Rebecca*, General MacLaidlaw in *Suspicion*, Colonel Paradine in *The Paradine Case*, and Carlotta Valdez in *Vertigo*, the image of Mr. Brenner embodies the mysterious presence of an important absentee. Furthermore, there is a close relationship between the portrayed person and the characters looking at the portrait. In Hitchcock's cinema, which repeatedly has been interpreted as a complex system of reflecting gazes, the portrayed person is looking

25 Paglia, *The Birds*, 64.
26 Ibid., 44.
27 Wood, *Hitchcock's Films Revisited*, 163.

Portrait of Mr. Brenner (Digital Frame)

back. Strikingly, as a result of the camera positions or the framing, initially, the portrait is hardly noticeable although Melanie looks at it emphatically ("Is that your father?") while Mrs. Brenner talks into the telephone. While playing the piano, she sits right in front of it. Only after the first bird attack, when the portrait hangs crooked, the spectator gets a clear view of the picture. When Mrs. Brenner tries to put the portrait straight, a dead bird falls from behind the picture frame. In the scene in which the inhabitants anxiously wait for the second attack, the portrait even dominates the space. This confirms the psychoanalytical interpretations of the film: patriarchal order is restored when the mother, who has taken a seat beside the portrait of her deceased husband, accepts Melanie as a member of the family. In light of this, the portrait supports the general atmosphere of the interior that Robin Wood described as "heavy masculine."[27] It indicates Mrs. Brenner's attachment to the past and her emotional connection to the house and its furniture.

Behind the Jungle Gym: Hayworth House

Bodega Bay, California

The Birds

Color
Universal
1963

PRODUCTION DESIGN:
Robert Boyle
SET DECORATION:
George Milo

Drawing by Linde Vertriest

150

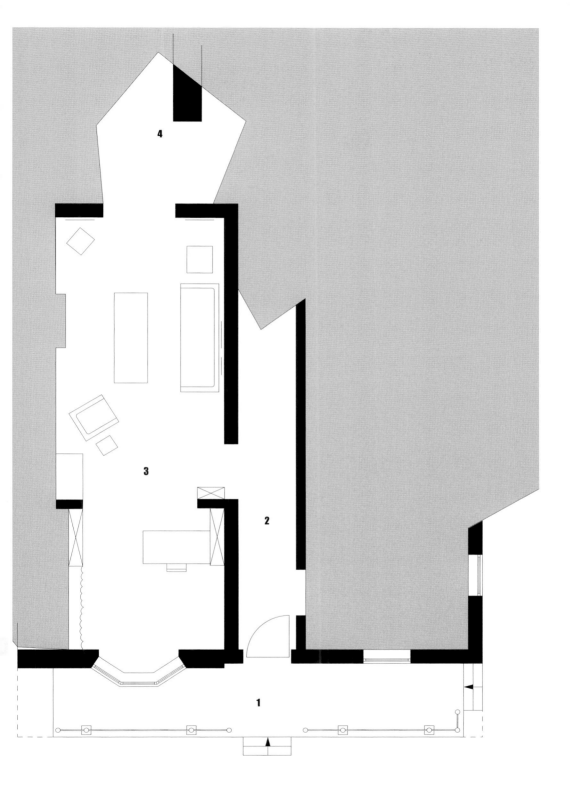

1m

A tourist guide of California states that "in the town of Bodega (65mi N of San Francisco), you will find the building (17110 Bodega Lane) that served as the schoolhouse in Alfred Hitchcock's film *The Birds* (1963). Originally the Potter School (1873), the Italianate structure has been converted into a bed-and-breakfast inn."[1] Production designer Robert Boyle had found this Victorian schoolhouse, which, in Camille Paglia's words, "looms up like a spooky Bates mansion in *Psycho*."[2] "The schoolhouse was boarded up and had long been condemned as an unsafe structure," Boyle told. "A crew repaired it and added a fence and playground equipment, which would figure later in the crow attack."[3] The jungle gym in particular would grow into one of Hitchcock's iconic objects since it becomes a base of operation for the hostile birds that terrorize Bodega Bay and its population including the schoolchildren. "The iron frame itself resembles the unfurling Bauhaus grid of Saul Bass' great title sequence for *North by Northwest*," Camille Paglia notes. "It represents social structure and, in *The Birds*, fate or Necessity. The jungle gym is where children clamber like monkeys as they practise for adulthood – learning the ropes, as it were, on the webbed rigging of life's voyage."[4]

The school itself will be one of the targets of the mysterious and apocalyptic birds attacks. In this attack, the teacher, Annie Hayworth (Suzanne Pleshette), loses her life when she fails to reach her house, situated next to the school, in time. As production designer Robert Boyle later told, Annie's Hayworth's house was specially built for the movie. At a short distance from the schoolhouse, "a façade was erected to serve as Annie Hayworth's home, and was dismantled once filming was complete."[5] The exterior of her modest dwelling, which is surrounded by white picket fences, shows some characteristics of the colonial style, such as a protruding gable and classical elements such as a pediment above the entrance and a porch supported by slender columns. In the window, a 'Room for Rent' sign is displayed – just like the sign that attracts *The Lodger* to the Bunting house.

The interior of the house is modest, as is the character of Annie Hayworth. Screenwriter Evan Hunter wrote that "Hitch dressed this beautiful woman like a grocer's wife, lighted her badly, and shot her from the most unflattering angles. Three minutes after we'd been introduced on the set, the first words Suzanne said to me were, 'The blonde, he gives a mink coat. Me, he gives wedgies and a house dress.'"[6] Annie Hayworth, however, seems to have reconciled herself to her situation although, at some point, when Melanie returns after her dinner at the Brenners, she even seems trapped in her own narrow living room.

1 *California*, 173.
2 Paglia, *The Birds*, 31.
3 Counts, "The Making of Alfred Hitchcock's *The Birds*," 17.
4 Paglia, *The Birds*, 66.
5 Counts, "The Making of Alfred Hitchcock's *The Birds*," 17. See also Kraft & Leventhal, *Footsteps in the Fog*, 194.
6 Hunter, *Me and Hitch*, 27.

As is the case with the interior of the Brenner house, the interior and the occupant of the Hayworth house are elaborately described in a memorandum addressed to production designer Robert Boyle and set decorator George Milo among others:

Annie Hayworth is about 27, or at the most 28. She taught when she was somewhat younger, at a private school in San Francisco. For emotional reasons, she has moved into Bodega Bay and has secured the job of teaching at the local school. Again, we have a literate person in a modest setting. Her one story home would contain a large number of (a) books that she had from home and school, (b) recently acquired paper backs, the reason for the latter is that economically she might not be able to afford to buy hard cover books in any great quantity. She has one or two prints on the walls of her living room. They would be Braque, maybe something

I School (Digital Frame)
II Jungle gym (Digital Frame)
III Hayworth house (Digital Frame)
IV Hayworth house and school (Digital Frame)

Mexican from the Museum of Modern Art, and perhaps even, she might be catholic enough in her taste as to have a Grant Wood print. She might have on the mantel shelf some pre-Columbian pieces. Her furnishings would be quite modest but very tasteful, perhaps a little chintzy. There ought to be a photograph on the wall of Annie and her parents when she was much younger. Then, perhaps, also in the room are again college pictures. Perhaps, even a picture of herself with the children at the private school in San Francisco.

The research for Annie's interior should be sought:

(a) at the school teacher's house in Bodega Bay,

(b) a slightly up-graded teacher's home in San Francisco, and perhaps,

(c) a female professor's room at Berkeley or Stanford

and the settings should take advantage of the combination of these backgrounds. One should add, of course, that there is a television set in both the Brenner home and in Annie Hayworth's home.

Some thought should be given to music in Annie's house. This should consist of a player and piles of records.[7]

As in the interior of the Brenner house, artworks illustrate the personality and social position of the occupant. Hitchcock explicitly mentions something Mexican from the Museum of Modern Art, a Grant Wood print, some pre-Columbian pieces, and Georges Braque, an artist works of which were also part of Hitchcock's own art collection. A Modigliani print, which is not mentioned in the memorandum, can clearly be recognized in the living room. A Cézannesque still life is echoed by the fruit bowl on the table in the adjoining room. Hayworth's modest living spaces contain several reproductions of modern masters, which attract much attention by their powerful contrasts of colors. Camille Paglia noted that "Annie's sensibility is embodied in her avant-garde sculpted lamp and modernistic wall prints. (…) Her family could be native New Yorkers (we later hear of 'her sister in the East'), but Annie comes from bohemian San Francisco, then a center of Beat culture. Yet she's romantic at heart, as evidenced by the prominent album of Wagner's Tristan and Isolde, with its theme of self-immolation through doomed love."[8]

7 *Memorandum Indicating Set Dressing: Requirements for "The Birds"*, 24 January 1962, Folder iii, Alfred Hitchcock Collection, Margaret Herrick Library, Academy of Motion Pictures Arts and Sciences, Los Angeles. See also Truffaut, *Hitchcock*, 254.

8 Paglia, *The Birds*, 46.

55

I Front garden (Digital Frame)
II, III Living room (Digital Frame)
IV Hitchcock and Tippi Hedren in front of the screen façade of the Hayworth house
(Set Photograph, Royal Film Archive, Brussels)

Childhood Memories:
Edgar House

116 Van Buren Street, Baltimore

Marnie

Color
Universal
1964

PRODUCTION DESIGN:
Robert Boyle
SET DECORATION:
George Milo

This terraced house situated in the Baltimore harbor is the home of Bernice Edgar (Louise Latham), the mother of Margaret 'Marnie' Edgar (Tippi Hedren). A compulsive thief, Marnie moves from job to job, changing her name and appearance. So *Marnie* is a story of homelessness, in which the heroine is continually traveling, by train, car, taxi, ship, on horseback, moving from one place to another but getting nowhere – a point that, according to Robin Wood, "the dream-like quality given by the back-projection to the horse-riding sequence epitomizes."[1] The no-man's land of train stations and offices, which recalls the austere settings of Bresson and Antonioni, encompasses all of America, its lonely geography characterized by hotels and roadside Howard Johnsons. According to Michele Piso, "placelessness is crucial to *Marnie*, identifying woman as wanderer, the one who, crossing borders and thresholds, merely expands a territory of desolation. To be without place is to be without identity; Marnie has had several, none sufficient."[2]

One day, Marnie is caught and exposed by Philadelphia businessman Mark Rutland (Sean Connery), who blackmails her into marriage. Following the rules of Hitchcockian logic, the house of the newlyweds is presented as a trap. In the case of *Marnie*, the golden cage is Wykwyn, the grand Rutland Colonial Revival house with an irregular stone façade, dormers on the side-gabled roof, and a classical white porch. With its grand staircase, ornate furnishings, and wainscotted rooms, Wykwyn is the perfect locale for the Gothic plot, the most important themes of which recur in *Marnie*. In a film that uses frequently keys as visual motif, Wykwyn is perceived as a prison. "Come on, Marnie, it's not exactly a house of correction, you know," Mark says when Marnie hesitates to enter their private rooms after returning from honeymoon. Subsequently, Marnie's bedroom is shown extensively through a series of point-of-view shots. When descending the staircase the following morning, Mark sarcastically instructs Marnie: "This is the drill, dear. Wife follows husband to front door. Gives and or gets a kiss. Stands pensively as he drives away. Oh, a wistful little wave is optional." Other obligatory ingredients of the Gothic plot are also present but modified. For instance, the pre-Columbian art collection of Mark's deceased first wife passes for ancestral paraphernalia but they are not kept at Wykwyn but displayed in Mark's wainscotted room in the Rutland office building. Moreover, the requisite troubled past lies outside Wykwyn since it is not part of the life of the husband but the female protagonist. Mark soon finds out, as textbook Freud tells us, that larceny is related to sexual pathology; Marnie is not only a thief but also pathologically frigid. Obviously, Mark discovers that Marnie's neurosis has something to do with a repressed childhood experience.

1 Wood, *Hitchcock's Films Revisited*, 192.
2 Piso, "Mark's Marnie," 298.

I   II

To enable her to reenter and reexperience the past in memory, Mark brings Marnie to the house of her mother, the existence of which she had kept secret to her husband. As in *Psycho* and *The Birds*, the mother's home becomes the most important stage of the conflict. Its address – 116 Van Buren Street, Baltimore – is reported to Mark by an off-screen private detective who turns out to be a Mr. Boyle – a little acknowledgement by Hitchcock to the production designer who also had collaborated on *Saboteur*, *Shadow of a Doubt*, *North by Northwest*, and *The Birds*. At the Edgar house, in a final confrontation between mother and daughter, it emerges that Bernice was a prostitute who took the blame for Marnie's childhood killing of a sailor (Bruce Dern) she thought was attacking her mother. The mental breakdowns Marnie suffers when confronted with red surfaces – visualized by red suffusions filling the screen – refer to the repressed memory of the sailor's bloodstained T-shirt.

The contrast between Bernice Edgar's humble house and working-class neighborhood and the elegant Rutland mansion is striking. In a typed-out preparatory conversation with screenwriter Evan Hunter, production assistant Peggy Robertson, and production designer Robert Boyle, Hitchcock evoked the Bernice Edgar house and its neighborhood as follows: "Her mother is going to live in Baltimore. In one of those streets where they have all those steps – you know – the whitewash steps? This again, is a tremendous contrast 'cause you see, we've practically shown, we've done all this cinematically – we've told the mystery of this girl in a series of images of pictures and settings and backgrounds. That's why they're important because they do make statements all the time. Now we get this cheesy, long Baltimore residential street. It's almost like a – you haven't been to Baltimore, have you? Well, it's like the north of England street – just the same – oh yes,

3 *Story Outline for Production Design* (February 4, 1963), 10. In this 54 pages transcription of a production conference, Hitchcock, Evan Hunter, Robert Boyle, and Peggy Robertson discuss the settings of *Marnie*. See Folder 490 *Marnie*, Hitchcock Collection, Margaret Herrick Library, Los Angeles. Parts

of this transcription have been published as "Hitchcock at Work," *Take One* 5, 2 (May 1976): 31-35.
4 Ibid., 11.
5 Wood, *Hitchcock's Films Revisited*, 214.
6 *Story Outline for Production Design* (February 4, 1963), 11.
7 Taylor, *Hitch*, 272.
8 Robert Boyle, quoted in

Stein, "Filmographies of Art Directors and Production Designers," 199.

I Wykwyn (Digital Frame)
II Wykwyn, hall (Digital Frame)

just like the north of England. Rows of houses and chimneys but the one feature of Baltimore is that people take great pride in their steps 'cause all the houses have one step up from the sidewalk. And they're always done with pumice stone or whitewashed or painted white. You get this vista of all these steps, you see, and she drives down this street, maybe in a taxi."[3] Hitchcock also stated that it "would be nice if at the end of the street we could see masts of ships 'cause this is very important later on. And they do have them, there're probably streets around there with this terribly sordid atmosphere – the saloon at the corner and the ships down at the bottom."[4] In the film, eventually, a ship looms up at the end of the street. Apart from referring to the sailor, the ship blocks the exit and contributes to the sense of imprisonment and claustrophobia created by the unbroken rows of brick houses. The street is characterized by a corridor pattern of converging, receding lines, that, earlier in the film, also marked the edges of a station platform, a hotel corridor, and a honeymoon ship. According to Robin Wood, this pattern has an "immediately expressive impact with its suggestion of a trajectory, introducing the 'journey' motif on which the film is built."[5]

In addition, Hitchcock describes the house as "a dowdy place" and "quite small."[6] Eventually, Robert Boyle and George Milo created a small living room decorated with grey floral wallpaper. A kitschy painting of a dog and a puppy adorns the wall at the base of the staircase leading to the bedrooms upstairs. The living room contains a television set with a plaster sculpture, a china cabinet, a grey chair, and a green couch. French doors with lace curtains lead to the green-tiled kitchen where a table stands in the middle.

Although Hitchcock, Boyle, and Milo emphasized the humble and mundane qualities of the Edgar house, the setting of the cathartic scene is also an emotional landscape. A kind of dreamscape referring to childhood memories is created. The chant of children outdoors contributes to this effect as does the ship at the end of the street. Hitchcock wanted to recreate the unreal, dreamlike effect he had seen two or three times in his life, in Southampton, and again in Wellington, New Zealand, of ships looming surrealistically above the roofs of houses, with no evidence of water to explain them or give perspective.[7] Furthermore, together with the horse-riding scenes, the shot of the street and the ship is a clear example of Hitchcock's blatant disregard for realism. *Marnie* was heavily criticized for its 'amateurish' special effects or 'obvious' back-projections and painted backdrops. Critics found the sets distracting and phony. However, according to Robert Boyle, the artificiality of the set was intended: "We were aware of the impact of that matte shot and the diminished perspectives of the Baltimore Street and it was a conscious decision to leave it that way."[8] Some critics have interpreted the artificial backdrops as the result of an intense expressionism, a modernist self-reflection, or as masterly examples of fetishism made visually manifest.[9] Robin Wood argues that "the constrictedness of Marnie's life belongs essentially to the world of unreality, the trap she is caught in is irrational and her prison will be finally shattered by true memory."[10] In this perspective, the false backdrops are a concise image of Marnie's predicament: she is dislocated from her surroundings and from her own past. The false backgrounds provide a physical expression of the disjunction in her mind.[11] According to Robert Boyle, Hitchcock was trying to get at something you couldn't see. He was trying to tell a story of things that are not at all overt… He was trying desperately to really dig into the psyche of this woman."[12] Marnie's world is a world of surfaces: not only of red flashes filling the screen but also of false identities, constructed appearances, empty spaces, looks, ritualistic hand movements, and emphatic close-ups – features that characterize the postwar modernist European art cinema of the period, the innovations of which Hitchcock desired to incorporate into his own films. As Joe McElhaney has noted, the film in particular shows some resemblances with Michelangelo Antonioni's *Il deserto rosso*, which was released in the same year.[13] Antonioni's first color film too features a heroine whose mental instability is denoted by the arresting use of color. With its subdued colors, the Edgar house would not be out of place in the bleached postindustrial landscape of Antonioni's film. In Marnie's mother's living room, grey hues determine the interior – making the vase with red gladioluses, in the scene early in the film when Marnie visits her mother to 'buy' her affection with expensive presents, all the more striking and disturbing.

Expressionist spatial distortions also dominate in the flashback of the murder itself. Comparable with the famous tower sequence in *Vertigo*, the flashback starts with a reverse tracking shot and a simultaneous forward zoom. The result is a vertiginous effect; the room seems to almost expand and shrink at the same time. Together with the similar effect of the crude backward and forward zooms when she tries to steal money from the Rutland safe, the 'folding' Edgar room is part of a mental state which is blocked and unable to process. Although, according to some commentators, the scene is conceived as a continuity, as if Marnie sees the murder happen in the same room, there is no direct relation between the layout of the rooms and their furnishings in the flashback and those in the 'present' interior.

9 Leitch, *The Encyclopedia of Alfred Hitchcock*, 201.
10 Wood, *Hitchcock's Films Revisited*, 214.
11 Yacowar, "Hitchcock's Imagery and Art," 22.
12 Robert Boyle, quoted in Kapsis, *Hitchcock*, 129.
13 McElhaney, "Touching the Surface," 87-105.

I, II Van Buren Street, Baltimore (Digital Frame)
III Living room with front door (Digital Frame)
IV Living room and kitchen (Digital Frame)
V Living room in flashback (Digital Frame)
VI Living room (Still, Royal Film Archive, Brussels)
VII Kitchen (Still, Royal Film Archive, Brussels)

I   II

III   IV

V   VI

VII

Simple Family Life:
Moat House

Peveril, England

Easy Virtue

Black-and-white
Gainsborough Pictures
1927

ART DIRECTION:
Clifford Pember

Moat house is the palatial country estate of the Whittaker family, a wealthy, class-conscious English family. It is the home of Colonel Whittaker (Frank Elliott), his wife (Violet Farebrother), their son, John Whittaker (Robert Irvine), and two daughters (Dacia Deane and Dorothy Boyd). At the French Riviera coast, John meets and marries Larita (Isabel Jeans), who was once the notorious Mrs. Filton, the defendant in an ugly divorce case. The divorce petition was granted to Larita Filton when the jury accepted the evidence of her adultery with the artist who painted her portrait. In reality, no act of adultery ever took place. The plot of this bitter picture of the English upper-class family enabled Hitchcock to deal with a series of themes and motifs that would later reappear frequently in his films: a concern with guilt and innocence, betrayal and revelation; the courtroom as location; the painted portrait (here reproduced in a newspaper) as a sign of doom; and the family, home, and house as sites of psychological tensions.

When John Whittaker, a handsome but rather weak young man, brings his newly wedded wife Larita home, the family, and his mother in particular, fail to accept her. The very moment she meets Larita, Mrs. Whittaker's whole demeanor signals hostility and repressiveness. In addition, Larita's new mother-in-law learns that Larita was (unfairly, as we know) accused of impropriety in the earlier divorce case, but the very idea of scandal is unacceptable to the family, and John is unwilling and unable to stand by his wife against his mother's moral outrage.

Easy Virtue, an adaptation by Eliot Stannard of a controversial Noel Coward play, anticipates *Rebecca*, *Notorious*, and *Marnie* through its story of a new bride brought back to the family mansion where she encounters hostility. Hitchcock also introduces the figure of the malevolent mother, which would recur frequently in his entire filmography.[1] Mrs. Whittaker can be considered a prototype of the bossy aunt Margaret (*Young and Innocent*), Mrs. Danvers (*Rebecca*), Mme. Sebastian (*Notorious*), Mrs. Bates (*Psycho*), Lydia Brenner (in the first sequences of *The Birds*), or Marnie's mother (*Marnie*). In the Whittaker family as well, there are Freudian overtones of the mother-son relationship and the mother figure acts as a snob (*Notorious*, *The Skin Game*, *The Manxman*, *The Birds*), who defends the home, the family position, and the family tradition against the intruding woman. In particular the narrative scheme of *The Birds* becomes apparent in *Easy Virtue*: the fallen woman brought by her new husband to his country home receives a cool welcome.

Strikingly, Hitchcock's hostile mothers are invariably linked to the home and, consequently, to domestic architecture. In addition, *Easy Virtue* contains another typical Hitchcock pattern that relates to the tensions within the family and the house: after an

1 The figure of the dominant mother and the Oedipus complex are recurrent themes in Hitchcock criticism. See, for instance, Modleski, *The Women Who Knew Too Much*; Bellour, *The Analysis of Film*; and Walker, *Hitchcock's Motifs*, 307-18.

elided honeymoon sequence, there is a post-honeymoon scene that shows things are beginning to go wrong, as in *Downhill*, *Rebecca*, and *Suspicion*.[2]

The sacrosanct home, house, and (in her own words) "simple family life" that Mrs. Whittaker defends against intruders took shape in Moat house, one of the first impressive, aristocratic country estates that pervade in Hitchcock's *œuvre*. It heads the list of a series of similar mansions in England or Scotland, such as the Hillcrest Mansion (*The Skin Game*), Jordan Mansion (*The 39 Steps*), Pengallan House (*Jamaica Inn*), Manderley (*Rebecca*), Aysgarth House (*Suspicion*), McLaidlaw House (*Suspicion*), and Hindley Hall (*The Paradine Case*). In addition, similar 'English' country estates turn up in New England, such as Green Manors (*Spellbound*), the Glen Cove Townsend Mansion (*North by Northwest*), and Wykwyn (*Marnie*); on Cuba, such as the estate of Juanita de Cordoba (*Topaz*); and in Australia, such as Minyago Yugilla (*Under Capricorn*). As many of these palatial country houses, Moat house – its name emphasizing the family's insular values – is a secluded place. Mrs. Whittaker rules the house with the arrogance and exclusiveness of a defended fortress.[3] A label on a traveling trunk indicates it is situated at Peveril and, clearly, one has to travel along long and empty country roads in order to get to it. Its architectural style can be described as 'Shavian Manorial' – as the mansions built by Richard Norman Shaw in the 1860s and 1870s, Moat house shows a picturesque combination of vernacular elements, articulated entrances, and tall window-walls. Although only parts of its exterior can be seen in the film, the building consists of an asymmetrical combination of volumes that constitute what Henry-Russell Hitchcock has called the "agglutinative plan."[4] In fact, the exteriors are location shots of Langley Court in Liss, Hampshire, which doubles as the fictitious Moat house in Peveril.[5] As many Victorian country houses, Langley Court began as a hunting lodge during the reign of Elizabeth I and was expanded in the nineteenth century to its present picturesque configuration. Expressing the upper-class status of the family, which is so important to the narrative, the architecture is meant to make an impression on the visitors and on newcomers such as Larita. Successfully, as it turns out, since Larita eventually states that "this place is getting on (her) nerves."

Although, in her statement, "this place" stands undoubtedly as a metonymy for the inhabitants of Moat house, the building's interior can be called, without exaggeration, nerve-racking. Some spaces in particular are worth mentioning, such as the great hall that, unmistakably, bears medieval associations. Such great medieval halls were built throughout the nineteenth century in English country houses. The baronial hall was

2 Walker, *Hitchcock's Motifs*, 63.
3 Yacowar, *Hitchcock's British Films*, 57.
4 Henry-Russell Hitchcock, *Architecture*, 294 and 360.
5 Giblin, *Alfred Hitchcock's London*, 288.
6 Girouard, *The Victorian Country House*, 77.
7 Girouard, *Life in the English Country House*, 292.
8 Barr, *English Hitchcock*, 50.
9 Walker, *Hitchcock's Motifs*, 167 and 353. See also Strauss, *Alfred Hitchcock's Silent Films*, 2004), 84.

first, rather modestly, revived by Augustus Welby Pugin, at Scarisbrick for instance, but it returned at full scale as an obligatory component of the Shavian style. Several of Shaw's medieval style Great Halls were used more as a sitting room than an entrance or dining room.[6] They acquired a multi-purpose role, part living room, part meeting place, a venue for games and parties, and a setting for afternoon tea. As is the case in Moat House, such halls "came especially into their own with big house-parties," Mark Girouard noted. "Once the rest of the house was stratified into areas for men and women, they made a useful common meeting-place. In some houses the family and guests assembled in the hall before dinner rather than in the drawing room."[7]

The Moat house hall with huge, bare wall surfaces is dominated by an asymmetrical stairwell under which seatings are arranged. Like Norman Shaw's staircase at Flete (1878) in Devon for instance, the Moat house staircase creates inglenooks, changes of height and level, and adds to variety. Halls with staircases leading into them became especially popular in the late nineteenth and early twentieth century, perhaps because they were nicely adapted for evening gatherings. The descent of the ladies in their evening splendor could be watched by the party assembled below. The staircase, unmistakably, lends a theatrical effect to the Moat house hall, which is much more castle-like than the exterior. Hitchcock emphasizes the theatricality of the space by a frontal camera set-up – earlier in the film, in the French Riviera sequence, both the hotel lobby and the hallway of Larita's room resemble theater stages as well. In addition, similar theatrical framings are used in the scenes situated in Larita's Moat house bedroom, which is dominated by an enormous canopy bed.

Typical of Hitchcock, the staircase plays an important role and key scenes are enacted out upon it. The rivalry between Mrs. Whittaker and Larita is perfectly visualized by a repeated high-angle set-up from the top of the stairs, giving first the mother's point-of-view at their first meeting, then Larita's as she makes an unwelcome revenge appearance at the party.[8] Strikingly, in both scenes, we initially see some characters below the empty but expectant staircase and banister, which dominate the upper half of the frame. Both Mrs. Whittaker's and Larita's exhibition staircase descents prefigure similar scenes in *Rebecca*, *Shadow of a Doubt*, and *Under Capricorn*. By using the stairs in such a way, *Easy Virtue* establishes the general pattern of female exhibitionism in Hitchcock's films. As Michael Walker noted, moments of humiliation when the heroine is forced against her will to be "on exhibition" are followed by "a short-lived moment of triumph when she succeeds in displaying herself on her own terms."[9]

Using the stairs as a kind of catwalk with women who are looking and who are being looked at, Hitchcock breaks the theatricality of the space. By combining the stairs with striking point-of-view shots, and by using alternating close-ups, long shots, reverse angles, and camera set-ups from different directions, Hitchcock creates a strong sense of three-dimensionality.

Also note-worthy is the design of the Whittaker baronial dining hall. According to Donald Spoto, "it's a curious anomaly, a formal room over which loom enormous painted icons of saints and patriarchs – clearly more expressionistic than realistic, more apt for a Byzantine cathedral than an English country house."[10] Indeed, the all-over effect seems more appropriate to Hearst Castle or *Citizen Kane*'s Xanadu than to the dining room of an English upper-class family honoring age-old traditions. Bill Krohn noted that the sets of *Easy Virtue* "would not be out of place in a silent version of Dracula" – a statement that, no doubt, applies best to this part of the house.[11] Hitchcock emphasizes the representative character of the room and the ceremonious customs of its inhabitants by photographing the household dining table theatrically in a proscenium arch perspective via a Last Supper motif, a huge chandelier splitting images of Christ-like figures that tower presidingly over the affair above a mantel.[12] Sitting down to dine beneath a mural of gaunt-looking saints, the characters find themselves in a sepulchral realm where the dead hand of the past weighs oppressively.

Finally, another Moat house room of interest is the Colonel's study, the French windows of which connect directly to the garden. Strikingly, it is in this rather casual space that Larita is confronted twice with her troubled past. Here, Mrs. Whittaker shows her the newspaper reproduction of her painted portrait that exposes Larita as the notorious Mrs. Filton. In addition, sitting on a diagonally placed couch, Larita notices a box camera on a wall cabinet aiming right at her. A typically Hitchcockian charged object, this camera, a similar one of which was shown under the opening credits, reminds Larita of her unpleasant confrontation with the press and the public when she divorced from Mr. Filton. In addition, it heralds a new painful confrontation with press photographers because John Whittaker will abandon Larita in order to keep up appearances. In the last scene of the film, Larita exits the courthouse and, facing the camera, she states: "Shoot! There's nothing left to kill." Although Hitchcock later claimed it was the worst single moment of dialogue he ever had in a movie,[13] the statement and the presence of the camera introduce the theme of the oppressive male gaze and that of the murderous camera eye, which both would recur frequently in Hitchcock's cinema.

166

10 Spoto, *The Art of Alfred Hitchcock*, 13.
11 Krohn, *Hitchcock at Work*, 251.
12 Strauss, *Alfred Hitchcock's Silent Films*, 72.
13 Truffaut, *Hitchcock/Truffaut*, 51.

I Langley Court in Liss, Hampshire, doubling as Moat house
(Location Photograph, British Film Institute)
II Garden façade (Digital Frame)
III Hall (Still, British Film Institute)
IV Dining room (Digital Frame)
V Larita's bedroom (Still, British Film Institute)

Vitrivius Britannicus: Pengallan House

Cornwall, England

Jamaica Inn

Black-and-white
Mayflower Pictures
1939

SETTINGS:
Thomas N. Morahan
ASSISTANT ART DIRECTOR:
John Hoesli (uncredited)

Loosely based on a 1936 novel by Daphne Du Maurier, *Jamaica Inn*, Hitchcock's last British film, is one of his rare period pieces. Set in 1819 on the Cornish coast, in a "lawless corner of England, before the British Coastguard Service came into being," the film tells the story of Mary Yellan (Maureen O'Hara) who, after the death of her mother in Ireland, comes to stay with her Aunt Patience (Marie Ney) and Uncle Joss Merlyn (Leslie Banks). They run the remote Jamaica Inn, which turns out to be a den of cutthroats who wreck and plunder ships under Merlyn's direction. The figure of authority Mary confides her knowledge to is Sir Humphrey Pengallan (Charles Laughton), the local squire and justice of the peace. Pengallan agrees to help but soon it becomes clear that he himself directs the looting operations.

Despite the Regency adventure story hoopla, the film contains some recognizable Hitchcockian elements. Thomas Leitch has noted that *Jamaica Inn* is the first of Hitchcock films to take homelessness as its subject[1] – as *Rebecca*, Hitchcock's subsequent and first American film, it is based on a Daphne Du Maurier novel about a homeless heroine. Especially in his American films of the 1940s, Hitchcock focuses on homeless principals or homebodies whose homes become become traps and prisons: *Rebecca*, *Mr. and Mrs. Smith*, *Suspicion*, *Shadow of a Doubt*, *Notorious*, *The Paradine Case*, and *Under Capricorn* are sceptical about the values associated with a stable home. This series is inaugurated by *Jamaica Inn* that touches upon the theme of homelessness by the perversion of hospitality, which is picked up in the two homes shown in the film: Merlyn's rough tavern on the one hand and Pengallan's estate on the other. In a way, the film can be interpreted as a story of these two ominous houses. To a large extent, the film's first half is claustrophobic since it is shot within the confines of these buildings that in many ways are each

169

1 Leitch, *Find the Director and Other Hitchcock Games*, 109.

Jamaica Inn (Digital Frame)

I II

III IV

V VII

VI

other's opposites. Whereas Merlyn's tavern is rough, dark, noisy, crowded and disordered, Pengallan's opulent mansion is polished, bright, quiet, and well-ordered. Whereas the inn is reminiscent of a Piranesian dungeon full of oddly beamed ceilings, shadows, and capricious perspectives, Pengallan house is characterized by the clarity of neoclassicism. Nonetheless, as Merlyn and Pengallan are part of the same gang, the inn and the mansion are two areas of the same spiritual estate and both are locales of moral decay. Hitchcock will elaborate such a schizoid architectural scheme of evil, of course, in *Psycho*. As owner of both the Victorian house and the modern motel, Norman Bates combines the Merlyn and Pengallan characters in his split personality. In *Jamaica Inn*, both houses also enable Hitchcock to ridicule both the torpid aristocracy and the petty, self-concerned lower class.

Pengallan house belongs to the colorful collection of fascinatingly luxurious houses inhabited by Hitchcock villains – other exquisite real estate jewels being part of that collection are the mansion of Professor Jordan (*The 39 Steps*), Sutton house (*Saboteur*), Sebastian house (*Notorious*), the penthouse of Phillip and Brandon (*Rope*), Anthony house (*Strangers on a Train*), Wendice apartment (*Dial M for Murder*), and Vandamm house (*North by Northwest*). According to Maurice Yacowar, Pengallan, like Fry, Bates, and Uncle Charlie, "is a Hitchcock villain to whose 'case' psychological explanations are shallow tangents. (…) Pengalan has simply devoted himself to the energies, style, and morality normally considered evil. He lives it through, unrepentant to the end."[2] From early on, Pengallan is presented as a bloated dandy who cares more for objects than people. During a sumptuous dinner party with as decadent sycophants in an opulent candlelit dining room, Pengallan orders his butler to bring a figurine since he needs inspiration to toast on beauty. Art objects do not uplift but are powerful weapons that enable Pengallan to impress and humiliate his guests. When one of the table companions objects that the figurine is not alive, he states that it is "more alive than half the people here." His next – and living – example of beauty is Nancy, who turns out to be his favorite horse that he leads through the dining room like a true Calligula.

Pengallan's entire mansion is part of his superficial veneer of culture. The architectural design of Pengallan house emanates wealth and luxury. However, it does not have the flamboyant and grotesque qualities of its owner but looks surprisingly austere. As a result of that, Sir Humphrey's decadence and extravagance are emphasized – in a way, the white neoclassicism of the interior exposes the plumpness of his figure. In its simple refinement, the house seems more related to eighteenth-century Palladianism than early-nineteenth century neoclassicist tendencies. One can perfectly imagine the young Pengallan or his father finding inspiration for a house during a Grand Tour. The Pen-

2 Yacowar, *Hitchcock's British Films*, 254.

I Pengallan house (Digital Frame)
II Dining room (Still, British Film Institute)
III Dining room (Still, Royal Film Archive, Brussels)
IV Hall (Still, Royal Film Archive, Brussels)
V, VI Hall (Digital Frame)
VII Hall (Still, Royal Film Archive, Brussels)

gallan library could include copies of Lord Burlington's edition of Palladio's drawings (1730) or Colen Campbell's *Vitrivius Britannicus* (1715-25), books that marked the classical revival in English eighteenth-century architecture. With its white, symmetrical, classical façade containing a central portico with two double columns carrying a pediment, the house can be considered a simplified version of Campbell's Wanstead house near London (1720), which influenced a series of mansions and country houses up until the early years of the nineteenth century. The interior too is luxurious and expensive but the studied elegance and the white, shining marble surfaces are more reminiscent of the solemnity of Palladian architects such as Campbell, John Carr, or Robert Taylor than of the variety and gaiety propagated by other neoclassical architects such as Robert Adam, James Wyatt, or John Soane, their style, nonetheless, being more popular in the early nineteenth century in which the story of *Jamaica Inn* is set.

Apart from its dining room, the film particularly shows Pengallan house's impressive front hall. Here, classical refinement recurs in the white marble surfaces: the walls contain niches with statues, there is a Roman bust on a pedestal, and the floor is decorated with a compass rose – how appropriate for a leader of ship wreckers. In front of an elegant staircase there is an impressive chimneypiece, which is the sole example of baroque excess in the decorative scheme of the hall. Some paintings adorn the walls. The hall also contains a large table at which Pengallan receives his tenants as a capricious despot.

The sets were designed by Thomas Morahan, who also would provide other Georgian or classically inspired settings for *The Paradine Case* and *Under Capricorn*. According to Edward Carrick, *Jamaica Inn* is a "film well suited to Morahan's lively imagination and vigorous approach. His drawings were very personal in style, and at the time were extensively reproduced and much talked of."[3]

3 Carrick, *Art and Design in the British Film*, 88.

173

I Colin Campbell, Wanstead house (1720)
II John Carr, Harewood house, Yorkshire (1755)

Bluebeard's Castle: Manderley

Cornwall, England

Rebecca

Black-and-white
Selznick International Pictures
1940

ART DIRECTION:
Lyle Wheeler
INTERIOR DESIGN:
Joseph B. Platt
INTERIOR DECORATION:
Howard Bristol

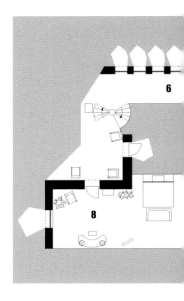

1 Entry
2 Great Hall
3 Library
4 Dining Room
5 Morning Room
6 East Wing
7 West Wing
8 The Second
   Mrs. De Winter's Room
9 Rebecca's Room
10 Dressing
11 Bathroom

Drawings by Linde Vertriest

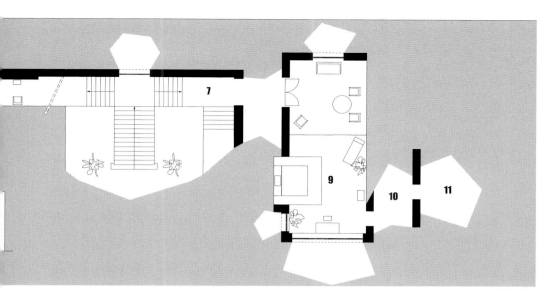

Second Floor

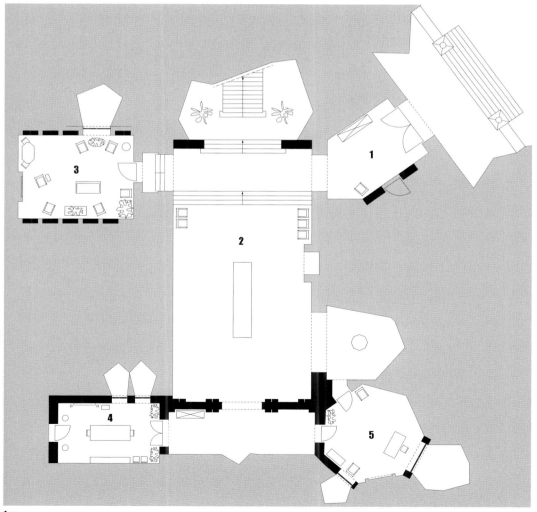

1m

Ground Floor

The opening scene of *Rebecca* immediately shows the prominent part that architecture takes up in this film. While the camera glides softly through a foggy landscape, a voice-over states the famous opening sentence of Daphne Du Maurier's novel with the same name: "Last night I dreamed I went to Manderley again…" Manderley appears to be the ruin of the once splendid castle situated at the Cornwall coast, owned by the tormented widower Maxim De Winter (Laurence Olivier). After remarrying the young, shy, and nameless protagonist of the film (Joan Fontaine) in the South of France, he took his new bride to Manderley, when it was still existent in all its glory. The entire story and every component of the *mise-en-scène* emphasize the importance of the first view of the building. Before you arrive at the place itself, Manderley is constantly referred to in the Monte Carlo sequence of the film. To enter the castle, first you have to pass a stately gateway and then drive a long and winding road in order to reach the main building. Both in the opening scene, in which the building is presented to the viewer as a ruin sitting in moonlight, and in the scene in which the female protagonist sees it for the first time through the windshield of a car driving through the rain, Manderley appears gradually as a castle from a fairy tale. Hitchcock even highlighted the phantasmatic quality of Manderley by having a windshield wiper clearing the heroin's field of vision. The new bride's first view of Manderley is explicitly framed, as though this were her own private film screen.[1]

From the beginning, Manderley is not only presented as a house but also as a symbol of domesticity as such, not only to the female protagonist but to the viewers too. Both the novel and the film were quite popular, consequently, the name 'Manderley' became extremely popular even for ordinary houses. At one time it was even the most common house name in the United Kingdom. In his a slightly differently spelled *Manderlay* (2005), Lars von Trier, undoubtedly, referred to this idea of domestic bliss to construct his dark and dystopic view of a closed community of masters and servants.

Since the architecture of Manderley was completely interwoven with the narrative, producer David O. Selznick, who assigned *Rebecca* to Hitchcock as his first Hollywood film, was convinced that the success of the movie depended on the way in which the building could bear its mark on the film.[2] Selznick, who was known for his women's pictures, undoubtedly steered Hitchcock toward strong 'domestic' narratives. As a result, Hitchcock himself stated that "in a sense the picture is the story of a house. The house was one of the three characters of the picture."[3] It features prominently in the publicity campaign of the film. Posters and lobby cards show the lead players with the outlines of a grand mansion. In addition, the importance of a luxurious interior to

1 Bronfen, *Home In Hollywood*, 36.
2 Affron & Affron, *Sets in Motion*, 15 and 40. For a detailed discussion of *Rebecca*'s set construction, see also Turner, "Du Maurier + Selznick + Hitchcock = *Rebecca*."
3 Truffaut, *Hitchcock*, 131.

I Manderley through the windshield (Digital Frame)
II, III, IV, V Exterior (Digital Frame)
VI Advertisement *New Yorker* 1940

I
II
III
IV
V
VI

the narrative was emphasized by a merchandising campaign that included prestigious commercial tie-ups such as wallpaper patterns and an expensive furniture line. An advertisement of W & J Sloane in the *New Yorker* in January 1940 is accompanied by a drawing of a luxurious interior with a quote from Daphne Du Maurier's source novel: "This was a woman's room, graceful, fragile, the room of someone who had chosen every particle of furniture with great care, so that each chair, each vase, each small, infinitesimal thing should be in harmony with one another, and with their own personality… There was no intermingling of style, no confusing of period, and the result was perfection in a strange and startling way…vividly alive, having something of the same glow and brilliance that the rhododendrons…had been permitted to the room itself. Their great warm faces looked down upon me from the mantelpiece, they floated in a bowl upon the table by the sofa, they stood, lean and graceful, on the writing desk beside the golden candlesticks."

"It's the morning room at Manderley," the Sloane advertisement clarifies. "Echoing still of the tragic *Rebecca*…crystallizing the first mistress of that fabulous country seat. Daphne Du Maurier does it with singing words. Sloane translates it here into a design for the actual room. You don't have to have the facile pen of a Du Maurier to picture your room to Sloane decorators. They will read between the lines… put your individuality into colors, woods, fabrics. And they can do it… as no one else can…because theirs are the imaginations of artists; theirs a world of treasures to draw on." "Watch for the Selznick-International Film of *Rebecca*," the advertisement concludes.[4]

Right from the start, Hitchcock knew what he wanted the great house to look like. According to the Brussels *Selznick Journal*, a post-war European leaflet to promote *Rebecca* published by the Selznick studio, Hitchcock had in person prospected historic mansions in Surrey for months and sent notes, sketches, and photographs to the studio. In addition, he had several other historic English mansions photographed. Among the English estates photographed by a second-unit crew in 1939 was Milton Hall in Peterborough, Cambridgeshire. This mansion, which combined Tudor and Wren stylistic elements with eighteenth-century Georgian alterations, had impressed the young Daphne du Maurier on several visits during World War I. When she wrote *Rebecca* some twenty years later, the interior of Manderley was based on her recollection of the rooms of Milton Hall.[5] However, neither Hitchcock nor Selznick were impressed with the results. According to Hollywood legend, Selznick's staff also scoured the U.S. and Canada for the perfect manor house to represent Manderley in the same tradition of publicity as the search for Scarlett in *Gone with the Wind* (Victor Fleming, 1939), which Selznick

4 *New Yorker* (January 20, 1940), 11. See also Edwards, "Brand-Name Literature."
5 See the CAMUS Project, *Five Parishes, Their People, and Places*, 227-38. See also Giblin, *Alfred Hitchcock's London*, 281.
6 Mandelbaum & Myers, *Forties Screen Style*, 41.
7 Raymond Klune, interview by John Dorr, 1969, *An Oral History of the Motion Picture in America*, 102-103.
8 Heisner, *Hollywood Art*, 111.
9 Folder 628 *Rebecca (prod.)* in the Hitchcock Archive in the Margaret Herrick Library contains a "Rebecca Set List" mentioning the following Manderley spaces: Int. Upper gallery, passage, anteroom, double bedroom; Int. passage, Rebecca's former room – West wing; Int. Main hall, staircase, landing; Int. Small Morning Room; Int. Dining Room; Int. Library; and Ext. Ruined early Tudor House.

was producing as well.[6] This location scouting, however, yielded nothing that fit the many prerequisites. Furthermore, Selznick's art department objected to location shooting: the war in Europe had begun and it was necessary to show the house both intact and in ruin.[7] As a result, the creation of the impressive sets for the epitome of Gothic romance was left to art director Lyle Wheeler, who had been responsible for the highly stylized sets for several Selznick color productions such as *The Garden of Allah* (Richard Boleslawski, 1936), *A Star is Born* (William A. Wellman, 1937), *Nothing Sacred* (William A. Wellman, 1937), and, most notably, *Gone with the Wind*. The sets for Selznick's epic film on the civil war were even still in use when construction began on the forty settings Wheeler designed for Hitchcock's American debut. As soon as a *Gone with the Wind* set was struck, a *Rebecca* set grew in its place. "I remember we couldn't wait to strike the Twelve Oaks hallway to make room for Manderley," Wheeler recalled later.[8] Twenty-five sets for interiors were constructed, including those of the boathouse, the coroner's courtroom, the doctor's office, and an inn but most sets gave shape to Manderley with its main hall, ornate rooms, gigantic fireplaces, towering staircases, high doors, and massive chandeliers.[9]

However, to a large extent, Manderley was also created by the special effect department of the Selznick studio, which ingeniously combined sets, miniatures, and mattes made by Albert Simpson, Clarence W.D. Slifer, and Jack Cosgrove. Hitchcock had used scale model shots throughout his early days. For *Rebecca*, together with Lyle Wheeler and Raymond Klune of the Selznick production department, he decided to build several different-sized miniatures of Manderley. The first miniature, Manderley with adjacent landscaping and a sky backing, was probably the largest-scale miniature that had ever been built. It almost filled an entire de-soundproofed stage and it was used for close views, such as when a light is seen moving through the rooms and during the climactic fire. Since there was not enough room on the stage to take full shots of the building, a second mansion half the size but surrounded by forest and including the winding road through the woods was built on another stage. There, matte artist Cosgrove filmed the visually stunning opening sequence of the film. In addition, matching portions of the exterior – the entrance, for instance – were built full-scale. According to Wheeler, every single camera movement was outlined in the sketches, which indicated where the real set ended and a painted matte began. In doing so, many upper walls, ceilings and chandeliers were introduced into interiors, and architectural features were added to partial exterior sets. Some of the flames in the film's climax were composed from shots made by Clarence Slifer during the burning of 'Atlanta' in *Gone with the Wind*. Thanks to these elaborate special photographic effects, Manderley could be perceived variously according to the action and mood of the moment. It is shown by day, by night, in rain, mist, and in flames. Alternatively, the mansion is perceived as warm and friendly, cold and forbidding, lively and in ruins.

Furthermore, the studio creation of Manderley contributed to its abstract and isolated character. "The location of the house is never specified in a geographical sense; it's completely isolated," Hitchcock later told. "That's also true of the house in *The Birds*. I felt instinctively that the fear would be greater if the house was so isolated that the people in it would have no one to turn to. In *Rebecca* the mansion is so far away from anything that you don't even know what town it's near. Now, it's entirely possible that this abstraction (…) is partly accidental and to some extent due to the fact that the picture was made in the United States. Let us assume that we'd made *Rebecca* in England. The house would not have been so isolated because we'd have been tempted to show the countryside and the lanes leading to the house. But if the scene had been more realistic, and the place of arrival geographically situated, we would have lost the sense of isolation."[10]

In addition, in the film, Manderley's exterior is hardly visible, which adds to the building's general atmosphere of mystery. Its proximity to the coast – with Californian locations doubling for Cornwall[11] – is only created by skillful editing. The film contains only a few exterior establishing shots (of miniatures) of the building, most of them obscured by a cloudy night, rain, or flames. The long panning shot of the building when Maxim and his second wife arrive evokes the breathtaking experience of a person's first encounter with the imposing mansion. As Moat House (*Easy Virtue*), Jordan House (*The 39 Steps*), MacLaidlaw House (*Suspicion*) or Hindley Hall (*The Paradine Case*) do, Manderley shows many similarities with Victorian country houses built in the middle of the nineteenth century. However, of all the English country houses that pervade in Hitchcock's œuvre, Manderley, which Donald Spoto once called "ridiculously mammoth,"[12] is undoubtedly the most impressive. Its architecture overwhelms the young heroine, not only at her first arrival but also during her entire stay at the estate. The sheerly massive size of the building also modified Hitchcock's film style, which earlier relied on the use of montage. In an interview with Peter Bogdanovich, Hitchcock admitted that his experiments with a tracking camera, which would characterize several of his subsequent films of the 1940s and 1950s, were prompted by the fact that he was "going around a big house."[13]

Although some parts of Manderley could pass for remnants from an older, medieval, or early Tudor structure – after all, the De Winter family is presented as *old* aristocracy –

10 Truffaut, *Hitchcock*, 131-32.
11 *Rebecca* contains location footage of the Californian coast shot at Point Lobos and Catalina Island. See Kraft & Leventhal, *Footsteps in the Fog*, 224-33.
12 Spoto, *The Art of Alfred Hitchcock*, 84.
13 Bogdanovich, *Who the Devil Made It*, 507.
14 Girouard, *The Victorian Country House*, 55.
15 Ibid. 216.

the general atmosphere of the building as well as some architectural details such as bay windows are undoubtedly Victorian. With its architectural elephantiasis, Manderley is an exaggerated example of the most spectacular Victorian country houses, such as Anthony Salvin's Scotney Castle (1835-43) in Kent, John L. Pearson's Treberfydd (1848-52) in Breconshire, George Devey's Betteshanger (1856-82) near Deal in Kent, William White's Humblewood Castle (1866-70) in County Wicklow, or Cragside (1869-84) in Northumberland designed by Richard Norman Shaw. Like these mansions, Manderley is characterized by massive walls, which express the kind of 'muscular' or 'vigorous' effects praised by critics of the time.[14] In addition, these buildings display a variety of windows and, in the first place, an irregular jigsaw of diagonal roofs and gables resulting in vivid skylines. Similarly, Hitchcock's panning camera movement exposes a somewhat strange and endless concatenation of architectural volumes, gable roofs, turrets, chimneys, solid stone walls, mullioned bays with window-walls, merlons, and a dungeon. As is evident in the country house designs by prominent Victorian architects such as Augustus Welby Pugin, George Devey, or Richard Norman Shaw, Manderley looks like a mansion that had grown up over the years and had become a patchwork of different dates and styles, and of different materials all jumbled up together, with wings at odd angles to each other.[15] This is also noticeable internally: one gets often the impression of going through a sequence of different units rather than subdivisions of one large whole. This kind of spatial planning, which shows an inherent 'cinematic' quality, is just right for a cinematic mansion as Manderley. Strikingly, it is hardly possible to connect spatially its exterior views with those of the interior. In collaboration with production designers, interior decorators, and matte artists, Hitchcock made full use of cinema's power to practice a kind of 'creative geography' in order to link the different spaces of the narrative.

The hybrid and whimsical shapes of the Victorian country house's exterior are mirrored in its irregular and 'additive' plan, which is, undoubtedly, its most interesting architectural aspect. These buildings, which accommodated a huge indoor staff and a large number of people who had to be carefully stratified and subdivided, can be considered as complicated and highly articulated machines typical of a specific way of life. Households were divided into family, guests and servants; the servants were divided into lower and upper servants; the family into children and grown-ups, and all groups were marked by a sex division. It was considered undesirable for children, servants, and parents to see, hear, and smell each other except at certain recognized times and places. As a result, half of the architect's skill lay in the correct analysis and disposition of lines of communication in the form of corridors and staircases. Food had to go to the dining room,

I   II

III

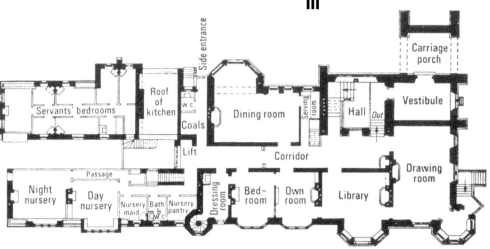

housemaids to the bedrooms, and the butler to the front door without disturbing the privacy of the family, or even meeting them in the corridors. Furthermore, these mansions had to accommodate a various number of visitors at specific times. The country house weekend was an important ritual in Victorian culture. Hordes of guests descended suddenly by rail on Friday evenings, and vanished as suddenly on Monday. As Mark Girouard has noticed, "the additive plan was exactly suited to deal with this violent fluctuation in a country house population. The sequence of different towers, staircases and wings combined to form a series of different bedroom suites which could be filled up for house parties and conveniently forgotten in the intervals, without the

16 Ibid., 77-78.

17 Gilbert & Gubar, *The Madwoman in the Attic*, 337.

I William White, Humblewood Castle (1866-70)

II Richard Norman Shaw, Cragside (1869-84)

III William White, Humblewood Castle (1866-70)

house seeming empty; and the inglenooks, bay windows, galleries and changes in level provided a series of different focuses, of recesses for different groups to retire to, which gave scope for a complex and sophisticated social life."[16]

This irregular plan of the Victorian country house suits perfectly *Rebecca*'s Gothic plot. In the late eighteenth and early nineteenth centuries, the Gothic novel was literally founded on the rambling, disorienting, and claustrophobic architecture of medieval castles, dungeons, and ruins. Everywhere, the whimsical and labyrinthine qualities of this architecture were stressed. Characters were confronted with a confusing built environment reflecting the mysterious and inscrutable structure of the story. The ultimate romantic interpretation of this motif was realized, no doubt, in Charlotte Brontë's *Jane Eyre*, a film version of which was made by Robert Stevenson in 1944 with *Rebecca*'s star Joan Fontaine in the leading role. In their seminal study on nineteenth century women writers, Gilbert and Gubar describe this novel as "the archetypical scenario for all those mildly thrilling romantic encounters between a scowling Byronic hero (who owns a gloomy mansion) and a trembling heroine (who can't quite figure out the mansion's floor plan)."[17] Indeed, especially the women protagonists of the Gothic novel and their descendants in romantic literature lose their bearings in a maze of rooms and corridors. This mental, psychological and often also physical inability to discern the structure of the house can be attributed, to a certain extent, to a spatial determinism: the irregular layout of the architecture encourages a disorientation of the kind. Often a literal labyrinth to the characters, the architecture is also presented as a mentally disrupting construction.

This is also the case in a Gothic romance film such as *Rebecca*. On the one hand, the heroine is intimidated by the sheer size of the house and its luxurious and opulent interior decoration. On the other hand, she loses her bearings in the mansion that always seems to have yet another hidden room, corridor, and corner. With its almost endless succession of corridors, rooms, halls, stairs and towers, Manderley is a hyperbolic application of the highly irregular floor plans, which developed during the Gothic Revival in the eighteenth century but which remained important throughout nineteenth century Anglo-Saxon domestic culture, reaching its apogee in the Victorian country house. In architectural theories of the late nineteenth and early twentieth centuries, this whimsical and indiscernible structure of the floor plan was precisely associated with the modern notion of domesticity. Asymmetrical floor plans and the tendency to individualize every room are exactly characteristics of the English Victorian home that was documented and celebrated extensively by Hermann Muthesius in his influential

1904 book *Das englische Haus*. Ironically, in the Gothic novel and Gothic romance film, this spatial disorientation causes fear and an uncanny restlessness rather than domestic safety.

The irregular and additive plan of the Victorian country house also characterizes Manderley. The reconstruction drawing of its floor plan demonstrates that Manderley is first and foremost conceived as a concatenation of different volumes. On the ground floor, the main entrance is connected to one of the corners of the great hall, which seems to occupy the center of Manderley. It is a large room decorated with Gothic mouldings and high, wooden wainscottings. Partly constructed by means of a matte shot, the baronial hall is the place where Maxim De Winter and his second wife are awaited and greeted by the entire staff of servants. Among them are Frith (Edward Fielding), the butler, and Mrs. Danvers (Judith Anderson), who cherishes Manderley as a shrine to the late Rebecca, Mr. De Winter's first wife. In the middle of the hall, there's a big table with an impressive bouquet of flowers – flowers seem to be present in most of Manderley's rooms and, in one of the dialogues, we are told that the flower arrangements are inevitably Rebecca's. "This was the banquet hall in the old days," Frith informs the second Mrs. De Winter. "It's still used on great occasions such as a big dinner or a ball. And the public is admitted here, you know, once a week." Such great halls were an important feature of Victorian country houses. In particular, the 1830s and 1840s saw a true revival of medieval or Elizabethan halls and the feature was taken up again by architects such as Nesfield and Shaw in the 1870s. Pugin, who built a great hall at Alton Towers in Staffordshire in 1836, advocated the medieval hall for both social and romantic reasons in his *True Principles of Pointed or Christian Architecture* (1841). In his Catholic paternalism, Pugin saw these halls as expressions of the organic community of ancient times, when the gentry had constant residence on their estates and exercised "the rights of hospitality to their fullest extent," also favoring the humbler classes.[18] Pugin's own Lismore Castle, in 1850 restored in collaboration with J.G. Grace, contains a hall that shows some similarities with that of Manderley.

On one side, Manderley's great hall is dominated by an impressive staircase leading to a landing with a vast, Gothic, mullioned window-wall. These windows were typical of Victorian country houses, which took advantage of new techniques of manufacturing sheet and plate glass and the abolition of the window tax in 1851.[19] From this impressive window-wall, the staircase splits into two stairs, each leading to one of the wings on the first floor. The staircase, its banister decorated with pinnacles, plays an important role in

184

18 Girouard, *The Victorian Country House*, 45.
19 Ibid., 21.

I, II Hall (Digital Frame)
III Augustus Welbin Pugin, Hall at Lismore Castle (1850)
IV Hall and staircase (Digital Frame)
V Landing with window-wall (Digital Frame)
VI Hall with door to library (Digital Frame)
VII, VIII Library (Digital Frame)

I II
III IV
V VI
VII VIII

two climactic scenes in particular. It is used dramatically when the heroine ascends to Rebecca's bedroom and in the costume ball scene, in which she descends the stairs wearing a gown copied from a painted portrait of Caroline De Winter, one of Maxim's ancestors. It turns out, however, that the deceased Rebecca had worn a similar dress and the humiliated second Mrs. De Winter has to climb the stairs again. The scene, a vintage Hitchcock sequence constructed by means of point-of-view shots, is a perfect example of the use of staircases in Hollywood melodramas as discussed by Thomas Elsaesser. Elsaesser refers to the sudden succession of emotional extremes in melodramas that are almost invariably played out against the vertical axis of staircases.[20]

The rooms directly connected to the great hall are, markedly, situated at its four corners. Apart from the entry, there is a library, a dining room, and a morning room. The library, situated across the entry, is actually the only comfortable room in the house. As Dan Auiler has noted, it is the only room where we see Max and his second wife enjoy some warmth together.[21] The walls are covered with bookcases. Seats, little side tables, and a globe are informally arranged all over the room. There's a grand fireplace – the butler, however, draws the heroine's attention to the fact that "usually, the fire in the library is not lit until in the afternoon."

On the other side of the great hall, there's the dining room, which is as austere and intimidating as the great hall itself. The room is dominated by an enormous, white chimney with classical mouldings, which is flanked by vases on pedestals. The high doors, their handles practically at the heroine's eye level, are framed by classical mouldings as well – the classical, Georgian decorative scheme seems a bit at odds in Manderley's overall Gothic atmosphere. On both sides of the door, tables carry impressive flower arrangements. Painted portraits decorate the white walls. A carpet, a big table, and a crystal chandelier occupy the center of the dining room.

Opposite the dining room is the morning room. Morning rooms first appeared in the early nineteenth century in country houses when drawing rooms had become more than ever formal rooms. Usually, informal life tended to go on the morning room – in particular for women.[22] Manderley's morning room, however, rather than a sitting room, is a private working space for women. This room, too, has a fireplace with a chimney bearing classical decorations such as double Doric columns. China statuettes are placed on the mantelpiece and in a fragile display case against the wall. In front of the window, there is a writing desk, on top of which are lavishly decorated candleholders, baroque statuettes, and a white telephone – a token of affluence in the 1930s, such as demonstrated by the contemporary Italian comedies and melodramas set

20 Elsaesser, "Tales of Sound and Fury," 60-61.
21 Auiler, *Hitchcock's Notebooks*, 304.
22 Girouard, *Life in the English Country House*, 293-94.

I, II Dining room (Digital Frame)
III, IV Morning room (Digital Frame)
V East wing corridor (Digital Frame)
VI East wing corridor with portrait of Lady Caroline De Winter (Digital Frame)
VII East wing (Digital Frame)
VIII The second Mrs. De Winter's bedroom (Digital Frame)

among the upper classes, which were nicknamed 'white telephone films.'[23] Also on the desk is a china cupid – "one of our treasures," which the second Mrs. De Winter accidentally breaks into brittle pieces. To the young heroine, this feels like an act of sacrilege. The morning room, after all, is suffused with the memories of Rebecca, who worked in this room every day. Her books with menus, addresses, and guests, each one of them provided with an embroidered letter 'R' on its cover, are symmetrically arranged on the desk. The morning room also contributes to the labyrinthine structure of Manderley – initially, the heroine is unable to find the room and she has to ask the butler for directions. Moreover, the room, probably heptagonal in shape, is confusing in itself.

The second floor is organized around an axis that, strikingly, is perpendicular to that of the ground floor, formed by the great hall. Going to the left, when ascending the stairs, one enters Manderley's east wing. This wing consists of a memorable long upper-passage decorated with ancestral painted portraits, among them that of Lady Caroline De Winter. This corridor leads to the second Mrs. De Winter's room, the white walls of which are decorated with wainscottings and painted portraits. As Mrs. Danvers tells the young heroine, the room, which contains a dressing table and a canopy bed, was redecorated on the basis of Mr. De Winter's instructions. Before his second wife's arrival to Manderley, the room "had an old paper and different hangings, it was never used much, except for occasional visitors." Furthermore, according to Mrs. Danvers, the entire east wing was hardly used before since "there's no view of the sea from here." There is only a good view of the sea from the west wing, where Rebecca's room is situated. Strikingly, there are no indications of the position of Maxim's bedroom. Furthermore, Maxim is even absent from all the female spaces in Manderley, including the bedrooms of Rebecca and his second wife. This indicates not only the gender division in the plan of the Victorian country house but also the non-sexual nature of Maxim's marriages.[24]

The west wing, clearly, has a different architectural layout than the east wing. From the landing of the stairs coming from the great hall, a short corridor leads to Rebecca's rooms. These comprise a kind of antechamber with seating and high walls decorated with wallpaper and some painted portraits. A wall-to-wall transparent curtain leads to the proper bedroom, which contains a bed, placed on a little platform, and a dressing table with Maxim's framed photograph. A dressing room with a big mirror-fronted wardrobe and a bathroom lie behind the bedroom. "Nothing has been altered since that last night," Mrs. Danvers states. "It's not used now. It's the most beautiful room in the

188

23 Liehm, *Passion and Defiance*, 21-23. Liehm notes that there were almost no white telephones in Italian films. The nickname probably originated because of the presence of white telephones in American movies, which became the symbol of upper-class affluence in Italy.

24 See Walker, *Hitchcock's Motifs*, 37.

I West wing with door to Rebecca's bedroom (Digital Frame)
II Antechamber (Digital Frame)
III Entering Rebecca's bedroom (Digital Frame)
IV, V, VI Rebecca's bedroom (Digital Frame)
VII Rebecca's bedroom and bathroom (Digital Frame)
VIII Rebecca's dressing table (Digital Frame)

I Rebecca's bed and nightgown (Digital Frame)

II Rebecca's bedroom (Digital Frame)

III, IV Sketch of Rebecca's bedroom (Academy of Motion Picture Arts and Sciences)

V Rebecca's bedroom: exterior view (Digital Frame)

house; the only one that looks down across the lawns to the sea." Through the window, however, we never get to see the sea because of the fog. Urged by Mrs. Danvers to commit suicide, the young heroine leans over the windowsill and she sees the fog clouds covering the tiles of the terrace beneath the window. The veils of mist are reminiscent of the whirlpool of waves that beat against the Monte Carlo cliffs in an earlier scene of the film. Moreover, this window plays an important role in the exploration of this room by the young heroine. It is the view from the morning room (something which looks impossible on the plan reconstruction), of Mrs. Danvers closing one of the windows of Rebecca's room that entices her exploration of the closed wing in the first place.

"You've always wanted to see this room, haven't you Madam?" Mrs. Danvers says when she catches the second Mrs. De Winter in the room. To both Mrs. Danvers and the second Mrs. De Winter herself, entering Rebecca's bedroom feels like trespassing. Everything in Hitchcock's *mise-en-scène* emphasizes that an entire series of spatial and psychological thresholds have to be crossed in order to enter the room: the forward tracking shot of the closed door with the faithful dog lying in front of it, the entire corridor blanketed in a mysterious veil of the shifting shades of the rain on the windows, the slow ascend of the staircase by the heroine, her point-of-view shots of the door, the close shot of her hand on the door handle, the passing of the curtain between the rooms, the opening of the drapes covering the high Gothic window, Franz Waxman's Debussy-esque score, and so forth. The still and mysterious atmosphere of an aquarium, which Mario Praz perceived in fifteenth-century Flemish paintings of interiors, is perfectly evoked here.[25] In the end, the entire film appears constructed around this scene of the gradual and slow intrusion into Rebecca's room.[26]

This intrusion in the forbidden room – the so-called Bluebeard motif – is typical of the Gothic plot discussed in chapter one. What is hidden behind the closed doors of these forbidden rooms seems always to contain an explanation for the strange behavior of the owner of the house. In *Rebecca*, however, surprisingly, the doors to the west wing do not hide some horrible secret. On the contrary, Mrs. Danvers is only celebrating a rite of memory. However, the forbidden room is full of sexual undertones. The room is a bedroom, the site of the 'primal scene' and, consequently, connected to a kind of voyeuristic pleasure.[27] Although it turns out that Rebecca had most of her sexual escapades in London or in Manderley's beach house, which also has to be trespassed, it is in the intruded bedroom that the second Mrs. De Winter is completely overshadowed by Rebecca's sexual power, evoked by the sensuality and tactility of her furs, silk lingerie,

25 Praz, *An Illustrated History of Interior Decoration*, 49.
26 Cogeval, "What Brings You to the Museum, Mr. Hitchcock?," 29.
27 Fletcher, "Primal Scenes and the Female Gothic," 341-70.

and ivory-handled hairbrushes. This intrusion of the bedroom is all the more striking since it is situated in an English Victorian house, where the bedroom was rarely seen by others than the ones who sleep in it. French novelist Balzac noted that the bedroom in England was so sacred that even servants could not enter it. Other preeminent nineteenth-century French observers, such as architectural theorist César Daly, reacted with amazement and laughter to the atmosphere of secrecy and privacy that surrounded the English bedroom.[28]

This spatial organization based on a division between open and closed rooms, transforms Manderley into a threatening environment subjected to an invisible system of control and surveillance. The massive halls and corridors dwarf the heroine. The house crushes the characters and it imprisons them – Hitchcock continuously stages the heroine's subjection to the architectural design by means of specific lighting techniques, viewpoints, and camera movements. Luis Buñuel caricatured skilfully this aspect in his surrealist masterpiece *El ángel exterminador* (1962), in which a group of worthies are invited in a splendid house and, as a result of an inexplicable cause, are no longer capable of leaving the drawing room. Hitchcock, similarly, presents Manderley as a psychological prison. This is both the case for the new Mrs. De Winter and for Mrs. Danvers, who eventually dies in the flames of the burning Manderley. To the second Mrs. De Winter, Manderley even becomes claustrophobic and suffocating. Shadows loom all over her face. Constantly, she presses herself against the walls and the furniture as if she is looking for shelter. By turning the home into a prison, the Gothic romance film exposes one of the essential characteristics of the house, which has been understood as a mechanism for the domestication of women since antiquity.[29] Reflecting the power structures of patriarchal society, the house becomes a spatial structure that is maintained by both a controlling eye and a system of locks, bars, bolts, and shutters, which seal all openings. In Manderley, the house has become a spatial system of surveillance. Rebecca's castle perfectly illustrates Beatriz Colomina's thesis that "architecture is a viewing mechanism that produces the subject. It precedes and frames its occupant."[30] In the Victorian mansion, this viewing mechanism and this system of surveillance were even emphasized since it was conceived as a stage on which to play out a set of bourgeois social conventions. According to Lynn Spigel, "since the Victorian period, the theatre served as a central organizing principle of domestic architecture. 'Upstage' and 'backstage' spaces (such as the front and the back parlour) served to make the home a kind of stage where family members and visitors knew what kind of roles to assume depending on which spaces of the home they inhabited. Archways between rooms

28 See Olsen, *The City as a Work of Art*, 146.
29 See Wigley, "Untitled: The Housing of Gender," 332-38.
30 Colomina, "The Split Wall, 83.
31 Spigel, "From Theatre to Space Ship," 219.
32 See Cohen, *Alfred Hitchcock: The Legacy of Victorianism*, 52. Cohen

further notices that "as the woman is granted a psychological presence, she is also fetishized, as if to counter what otherwise promises to upset the traditional gender hierarchy" (88).

approximated a sense of proscenium space, while the late Victorian penchant for ornate trim and excessive decor provided an aura of public grandeur to private rooms."[31]

Manderley also answers to the conventions of the Gothic plot because it seems to come alive. Not coincidentally, the story is situated in a building with a long history. Manderley is not only the place where Maxim was born and where he has lived all his life, it is also an ancestral mansion: a place where domesticity is connected to nostalgia and the burden of bizarre family histories. Painted portraits of ancestors, such as that of Lady Caroline De Winter, dominate the walls of the rooms, halls, and corridors. In the Gothic romance film, this interest in ancestors not only responds to all kinds of spiritistic associations but brings out the loneliness of the character as well. Rather than embodying the family values of bourgeois society, the atavism refers to the fact that modern bourgeois society seems no longer capable of substituting the languishing aristocratic and feudal structure by new organic social bonds. However, first and foremost, as the title of the film indicates, the entire mansion is haunted by a deceased person. Maxim's family members and the servants constantly speak of her. Every room seems to show the traces of her bygone presence. Napkins, writing paper, blankets, notebooks, handkerchiefs, and nightgown cases carry Rebecca's monogram. Manderley, in short, is a tomb, a crypt, or a mausoleum.

Furthermore, Mandereley's interiors are not only abundantly provided with ancestral memorabilia, it is also literally transformed into a cabinet of curiosities or a museum. Manderley adorns postcards and, once a week, its great hall is open to the public. The bedroom of the deceased Rebecca is the *sanctum sanctorum* of the building, which is, of course, *not* open to the public, not even to the inhabitants. The room seems to be magically transformed into a shrine where only initiates can and even dare touch the objects. When Mrs. Danvers catches the new Mrs. De Winter unawares in Rebecca's bedroom, she gives her a guided tour pointing out the luxury in which the deceased bride was living. Rebecca's mirror, brush, and nightgown are each ritualistically displayed and handled. In the process, they become fetishes and so charged with meaning that they intimidate the heroine to the extent that she contemplates suicide.[32]

Design Before the Fact: Aysgarth House

Wickstead, England

Suspicion

Black-and-white
RKO
1941

ART DIRECTION:
Van Nest Polglase
ASSOCIATE ART DIRECTION:
Carroll Clark
SET DECORATION:
Darrell Silvera

Ground Floor

1 Entry
2 Hall
3 Dining Room
4 Drawing Room
5 Study
6 Garden Terrace
a General McLaidlaw's Portrait
b Cubist Painting

Drawing by Anna Barborini

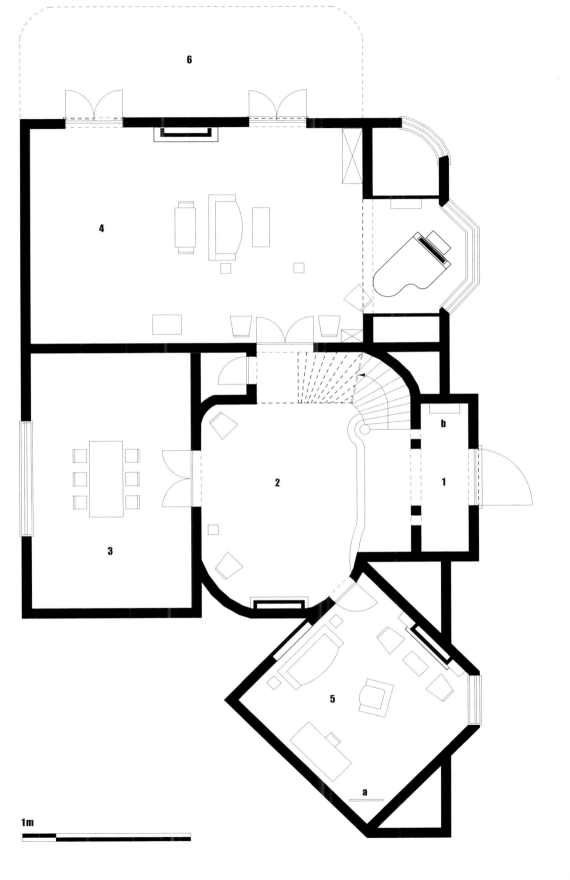

6

4

b

1

2

3

5

a

1m

This elegant house is inhabited by the irresponsible but dashing spendthrift Johnnie Aysgarth (Cary Grant) and his wife Lina McLaidlaw (Joan Fontaine), a somewhat dowdy daughter of the rigidly proper and wealthy General McLaidlaw. An address label on a traveling trunk used while honeymooning indicates that the house is situated in Wickstead, England. The house forms the background of a narrative that answers to the conventions of the 'female Gothic' or the 'Gothic romance film,' in which a woman falls in love with or marries a man she subsequently starts to fear.[1] Hitchcock contributed to the development of this genre with other pictures as well, such as *Rebecca* and *Notorious*. In addition, *Spellbound* and *Shadow of a Doubt* are also pictures that Hitchcock made during the 1940s which involve women whose lives appear to be endangered by the men they love.

With its impressive and determining architectural setting, its English atmosphere, a glossy photography, a fragile wife cringing in dread of her husband's secrets, a suicide-murder twist ending, and Joan Fontaine in the leading role, *Suspicion* seems almost a remake of *Rebecca*. The film is based on Anthony Berkeley's novel *Before the Fact*, in which a woman gradually comes to realize that she has married a murderer. She is so in love, however, that, eventually, she allows herself to be killed by her playboy husband. Forced by the Hollywood Production Code and the producers, who could not accept the idea that Cary Grant play a murderer, the film tells quite another story. *Suspicion* is about a woman who, discovering that her husband is a liar and squanderer, starts to imagine that he also attempts to kill her. Wrongfully, as it eventually turns out. In contrast with *Rear Window*, the lethal signs prove to be deceptive and they are retroactively transformed into a series of coincidences.[2] At first sight, this version of the story is much weaker, especially the ridiculously happy ending is less than convincing. However, the less dramatic plot generated an increased psychological tension. As the title indicates, suspicion, not murder is the main subject of the film. The drama has been interiorized and answers more to a typical Hitchcockian formula based on the distortions of subjective vision.

At any rate, the story is conceived as a domestic drama in which all parts of the house play an important part in the *mise-en-scène*. The tensions within the marriage are visualized and spatialized by means of tensions within the house. In one of his typical sardonic articles, Hitchcock wrote that, in England, people are not only renowned for their reserve but also for their inordinate regard of personal privacy. Hitchcock speaks of a typical English kind of murder that lurks behind the façades of houses.[3] Aysgarth House even hides its secrets behind a distinctively representative front provided with a protruding central bay with a classical pediment. Beaky Thwaite (Nigel Bruce), a friend

1 See chapter 1.
2 Dolar, "A Father Who is Not Quite Dead," 144.
3 Hitchcock, "Murder – With English on It," 134.

I Front façade (Digital Frame)
II Garden façade (Digital Frame)
III, IV Hall (Digital Frame)
V, VI Drawing room (Digital Frame)
VII, VIII Dining room (Digital Frame)

I   II

III   IV

V   VI

VII VIII

of Johnnie's, describes the place as a redecorated old Georgian house. In this case, however, the alterations involved clearly much more than a redecoration. The horizontally proportioned big windows at the sides indicate that, at least partially, the house is a modern building. This is even better visible at the side (or back) façade, the brickwork of which is undoubtedly modernist and there's even a curved glass corner. Nonetheless, the usual classical or Georgian scheme combining a representative front with a more rustic back is respected in this building, which makes it an apt setting for a story about secrets and suspicions.

However, the classical symmetry of the front, which contrasts strongly with the irregular and traditional mansion of Lina's parents, is not entirely respected in the layout of the interior spaces. A reconstruction of the floor plan reveals a remarkable deviation from classical symmetry. The door between the central hall with its impressive stairway and the study is not situated on the axis of the entrance leading to the drawing room but is placed asymmetrically, at a spot almost invisible when entering the house – this can be detected in the scene in which the police inspectors enter the study. The study, clearly, is situated in the left part of the house but its relation to the other rooms remains unclear.

Notwithstanding the irregular plan, the neo-Georgian style reveals itself clearly in the interior, most of all in the luxuriant hall. Here, the bright and white surfaces and classical elements, such as double Tuscan columns, architraves, pediments, cornices, and mouldings, give the house an even palatial grandeur. The white walls and classical scheme, which also contrast sharply with the darker interior of General McLaidlaw's house, can also be found in the rooms both downstairs and upstairs as well. Here, however, the classical decorative elements are made use of on a much more moderate scale – especially in the drawing room, which contains elegant but rather unpretentious pieces of furniture and some unmistakably modern paintings. Nonetheless, the entire interior is lavishly decorated and testifies to the wealth that Johnnie Aysgarth in reality never has. Having arrived at the house shortly after the honeymoon, Lina herself states that she never dreamed she would have "such a gorgeous place" and she asks her husband if he is sure he can afford it. When she finds out that Johnnie is broke, she asks him what made him to buy such "an extravagant house."

The importance of the house, its architecture, and its decoration are emphasized by the minor character of the interior designer Mr. Bailey (Rex Evans, uncredited). He welcomes the couple when they arrive at their new home after their honeymoon and Johnnie introduces him to his wife as the man who "decorated the place." Hitchcock himself was not very enthusiastic about Mr. Bailey's exploits. The director complained

---

4 Truffaut, *Hitchcock*, 143.

about RKO's *faux* British production design. "The elegant sitting rooms, the grand stair-cases, the lavish bedrooms, and so forth, those were the elements that displeased me."[4] In relation to other films, such as *Rebecca* and *The Paradine Case*, he uttered similar remarks in relation to Hollywood interpretations of English interiors. Instead of a redecorated old Georgian house, the Aysgarth residence rather seems right up the alley of Van Nest Polglase, a practicing architect and decorator who was the head of the RKO art department throughout the 1930s and early 1940s. Since Polglase's name appeared on the credits as a representative of the art department as a whole, it is difficult to determine to what degree he was involved in the set design of the Aysgarth house. Especially his later work during the 1940s must be attributed to other studio employees, such as

 Carroll Clark in the case of *Suspicion*. Nonetheless, the Aysgarth House, and its hall in

I, II, III Study (Digital Frame)
IV Mr. Bailey, interior designer (Digital Frame)

particular, show some vague reminiscences to the distinctive visual style Polglase and Clark developed throughout the 1930s in some memorable, lavish art deco sets for musicals such as *Swing Time*, *Top Hat*, *The Gay Divorcee*, and *Flying Down to Rio*.[5] The Aysgarth house answers to the same total, smooth environment that gives a feeling of stark elegance. As the so-called *Big White Sets* of the Astaire-Rogers films, the Aysgarth house is characterized by a tension between curved surfaces and sinuous lines on the one hand, and angular mouldings and pronounced vertical elements on the other.[6]

In the hall, all attention is drawn to the curved staircase, which is both an obligatory set piece in musicals but also a "quintessential Hitchcock image."[7] Staircases pervade in Hitchcock's œuvre. Conveying ordeal and moral change, they punctuate crucial narrative elements in films such as *The Lodger*, *Number Seventeen*, *Rebecca*, *Shadow of a Doubt*, *Notorious*, *Strangers on a Train*, *Vertigo*, *Psycho*, *The Birds*, and *Frenzy*. In *Suspicious*, strikingly, the first view the spectator gets of the house is not an exterior establishing shot but an image of the curved central stairway. Following the montage-sequence of the honeymoon, a trunk covered with hotel stickers is carried up the stairs while Johnnie Aysgarth, accompanied by the interior designer Mr. Bailey, shows his bride round the house. The stairs are also the locale of one of the most famous sequences of the film, which is beautifully photographed by Harry Stradling. It is the scene in which Johnnie brings Lina a glass of milk and both she and the spectator suspect that the glass contains poison. First, a top shot shows a light beam from the kitchen that falls into the dark hall, projecting Johnnie's shadow on the floor. Then, Johnnie crosses the hall and climbs the stairs, each step heightening the suspense, while the glass is lit from within by the special effect department, almost literally highlighting its vile contents. This visual accent is accompanied by the sinister shadows that a skylight with web-patterned windows – never visible itself – casts over the stairs and the entire hall, especially in the second half of the picture. The characters seem caught in a 'spider's web' of shadows, which expresses both Lina's fear of her husband and his (imaginary) predatory murderous designs on her.[8] Furthermore, the organic shapes of the shadows provide the classically inspired architecture with a kind of spatial and optical ambiance reminiscent of *art nouveau* or *Jugendstil*. With its elegant curvilinear patterns and soft light, the hall of the Aysgarth house evokes the dreamy atmosphere of an aquarium – think of the combination of dim backlight and slowly moving animal shapes in the tanks in *Sabotage* or in the San Francisco Aquarium in Orson Welles' *The Lady from Shanghai* (1948). Art Nouveau architects transformed the dwelling into a submarine realm. The French writer Paul Morand described Art Nouveau as "le style pieuvre" (octopus style).[9] The undulation of Jugend-

5 Ramirez, *Architecture for the Screen*, 39.
6 See Stein, "Filmography of Art Directors and Production Designers," 234.
7 Yacowar, "Hitchcock's Imagery and Art," 18. See also Funck, "Fonctions et significations de l'escalier dans le cinéma d'Alfred Hitchcock."
8 The spider metaphor has been noted by many others. See, for instance, Spoto, *The Art of Alfred Hitchcock*, 106; Richard Allen, "Hitchcock, or the Pleasures of Metaskepticism," 226; and Walker, *Hitchcock's Motifs*, 265.
9 Paul Morand, quoted in Walter Benjamin, "Das Passagen-Werk," *Gesammelte Schriften* v, 2, 681.

I Stairs (Digital Frame)
II Landing (Digital Frame)
III Sinister staircase (Digital Frame)
IV Caught in a spider's web (Digital Frame)
V, VI Bedroom (Digital Frame)
VII "Father's most precious possessions" (Digital Frame)

I   II
III IV
V   VI
VII

stil ornaments is the one of water plants and the colors invoke a dreamy aquatic world. As in some prominent Art Nouveau interiors, the Aysgarth house is transformed into an organism.

The vertical spine of the house, the curved stairway also provides a vista of the entire entrance hall. Its grandness undoubtedly expresses Lina's loneliness and vulnerability. The stairs, of course, lead to the bedroom, where several crucial steps occur in the development of Lina's increasing suspicion. The white walls, the classical mouldings, cornices, and columns of the Georgian interior design reoccur but the more baroque decorations and draperies predominate. Instead of the last refuge, the bedroom becomes a suffocating trap where daylight is shut out by heavy curtains. Lina is in bed when she receives the ominous glass of radiating milk.

Finally, some household objects in the Aysgarth house receive specific attention. This is the case with the chairs that Lina gets as a wedding present from her father. Their tight and uncomfortably structure, whimsical decorations, and dark color in no way fit into the bright and elegant Aysgarth interior. The chairs are a *pars pro toto* hinting at the incompatibility of Johnnie Aysgarth's lifestyle with that of Lina's parents. As a result, the pair of identical chairs articulates the differences between both spouses – Lesley Brill has pointed out that the symbolism of the connubial chairs goes back in Hitchcock's movies at least as far as *The Farmer's Wife*.[10] Furthermore, being "father's most precious possessions," the chairs bring an alien atavistic dimension in the slick, newly designed Aysgarth house: "we had them in the family before I was born," and "they really belong in a museum," Lina states. Johnnie, undoubtedly, tries to fob them off not only because of the money they can yield but also because of the patriarchal associations they engender.

The presence of the father in the house of the daughter is also guaranteed, of course, by General McLaidlaw's portrait, the function of which is similar to the patriarchal portraits in the Paradine House (*The Paradine Case*) and the Brenner House (*The Birds*). The painting, made by "the distinguished artist Sir Joshua Netllewood," is the sole object that Lisa, to Johnnie's disillusionment, inherits from her father. It plays an important part in an earlier sequence in the film, which is situated in the interior of the McLaidlaw House. When it is transferred to the Aysgarth House, it operates like a superego to Lina.[11]

The portrait and its bourgeois realist style contrast sharply with some other paintings in the interior, in particular the post-cubist still-life in the hall, which draws the focused attention of police inspector Benson (Vernon Downing, uncredited). His fascination

10 Brill, *The Hitchcock Romance*. Brill discusses examples of this motif throughout his book.
11 Dolar, "A Father Who is Not Quite Dead," 147; Walker, *Hitchcock's Motifs*, 322.
12 In his influential "Narrative Space," Stephen Heath used the scene to begin an argument about the inextricable links in classical style among screen space, narrative, and the spectator's psychological identification. See also Worland, "Before and After the Fact," 3-26.
13 Waldman, "The Childish, the Insane, and the Ugly," 55; Peucker, "The Cut of Representation," 142; Walker, *Hitchcock's Motifs*, 329.

with the painting is striking, certainly because it is 'useless' from the point of view of narrative motivation.[12] The still life, the *nature morte*, even halts the action for a while. The attention to the painting, however, must be seen in relation to General McLaid-law's portrait, which dominates the scene. As the chairs, both paintings emphasize the differences between the traditional values of the MclLaidlaws and the recklessness and snobbery of Johnnie Aysgarth.[13] In addition, Benson's fascination with the painting and the supposed humor of the sequence answer to a predominantly hostile attitude towards modern art in Hollywood in the 1940s. Modern art is presented as incomprehensible to a layperson such as a police detective and is often equated with decadent or criminal characters. In Hitchcock's œuvre, houses of rather suspect figures, such as Philip and Brandon (*Rope*) or Jonathan Cooper (*Stage Fright*), contain modernist paintings.

I General McLaidlaw's portrait (Digital Frame)
II Cubist painting (Digital Frame)
III *Top Hat* (Mark Sandrich, 1935)
Art direction by Van Nest Polglase and Carroll Clark (Digital Frame)

Building Above All Suspicion: McLaidlaw House

Hillside, Hazledene,
Sussex, England

Suspicion

Black-and-white
RKO
1941

ART DIRECTION:
Van Nest Polglase
ASSOCIATE ART DIRECTION:
Carroll Clark
SET DECORATION:
Darrell Silvera

One of the many English country houses that pervade Hitchcock's œuvre: Moat House (*Easy Virtue*), Hillcrist House (*The Skin Game*), Jordan House (*The 39 Steps*), Pengallan House (*Jamaica Inn*), Manderley (*Rebecca*), or Hindley Hall (*The Paradine Case*). This mansion belongs to General McLaidlaw (Sir Cedrick Hardwicke) and his wife Martha (Dame May Whitty). It is situated, as stated on a telegram, in Hillside, Hazledene, Sussex.

The McLaidlaws have a daughter Lina (Joan Fontaine), who leaves the house, without asking her parents' permission, to marry the charming playboy Johnnie Aysgarth (Cary Grant). Consequently, in a film that entirely deals with domestic tensions, the architecture and the decoration of the McLaidlaw house must be seen in relation to that of the Aysgarth House, with which it contrasts sharply in several ways. Averse to the urbane elegance and the cosmopolitan classicism of the Aysgarth House, the McLaid-law House radiates English tradition in every respect. The house, the exterior of which is only partly visible, is almost designed to look like a segment of a medieval village. Based on the image of the traditional English house with wooden trusses visible on the exterior, it is characterized by an irregular and asymmetric disposition of volumes, which Hermann Muthesius documented and celebrated in his seminal book on *Das englische Haus* (1904). In contrast with the Victorian country houses in the grand manner such as Manderley or Hindley Hall, the McLaidlaw house is evidence of a more organic approach to the country house, which had first begun to appear in the mid nineteenth century. This approach was developed by architects such as George Devey, who was the first Victorian architect to work out a way of building derived from the local vernacular. McLaidlaw house can be compared with Devey's many-gabled Hammerfield at Pen-

205

ı Exterior view (Digital Frame)
ıı Front yard (Digital Frame)

hurst or his Ascott Lodge in Buckinghamshire, which became prototypes of what contemporaries called his 'cottages.' Such half-timbered houses became very successful in the 1890s when cultivated upper middle-class families who read their Ruskin and Morris expressed their artistic tastes in their houses, which were often modified versions of the so-called Old English style of Shaw and Nesfield.[1] Propagated, from the late 1890s onwards, in the pages of *Country Life*, this vernacular style remained admired and imitated up until the 1930s in England and it also became a dominant style of domestic suburban building in the United States in the 1920s and early 1930s.[2]

The McLaidlaw interior too evokes solidity. In the hall, there is a robust wooden staircase that contrasts with the elegant, white, and curved stairway in the Aysgarth House. Solid beams support the doorways to the adjacent rooms, such as the dining room that is decorated with wooden wainscotting. Another room connected to the hall is the vast living room, in which the underside of a wooden load-bearing structure of the roof is visible. The walls of this room are paneled in wood up to the chest and there seems to be an abundance of pieces for sitting. Bouquets of flowers dominate both the central table and a side table. The solidity of the room evokes calm and repose, which is confirmed by the fact that this room is the background for scenes in which solitary individuals sit quietly self-engaged: Lina reading a book on the sofa in front of a bay window, General McLaidlaw reading the newspaper and smoking his pipe, and his wife practicing embroidery. It is also in this room that the mourning family gathers to listen to the reading of General McLaidlaw's testament.

The presence of General McLaidlaw is manifested more explicitly in the study dominated by his portrait painted by "the distinguished artist Sir Joshua Netllewood." After escaping the Hunt ball, Lina and Johnnie Aygarth end up here talking to the portrait. "He doesn't like me, he doesn't trust me," Johnnie claims, although he asks the painting (instead of the general himself) the hand of his daughter. On the wall, there is another reference to their marriage: there is a picture of the Rialto Bridge in Venice, one of the destinations of their honeymoon in a succeeding montage sequence. Later in the film, Johnnie addresses the portrait again as it turns out to be the sole piece that he inherets from the general. "You win, old boy," Johnnie states. These scenes, in which the characters speak to, almost interact with the painting, employ the portrait as a kind of externalized emblem of the internalized father.[3] By inhereting the portrait, Lina takes the paternal law, which found its expression in the solidity of the McLaidlaw mansion, to her own house.

20

1 Girouard, *The Victorian Country House*, 83 and 375.
2 See Girouard, *Life in the English Contry House*, 300-307; and Virginia and Lee McAlester, *A Field Guide to American Houses*, 358.
3 Felleman, *Art in the Cinematic Imagination*, 16-17.

I Hall (Digital Frame)
II Landing (Digital Frame)
III Living room (Digital Frame)
IV A conversation piece in the living room (Digital Frame)
V Living room (Digital Frame)
VI, VII Dining room (Digital Frame)
VIII General McLaidlaw's portrait (Digital Frame)

Manhattan Manners: Sutton House

Manhattan, New York

Saboteur

Black-and-white
Universal
1942

ART DIRECTION:
Jack Otterson
ASSOCIATE ART DIRECTION:
Robert Boyle
SET DECORATION:
Russell A. Gausman

Sutton house is the Manhattan mansion of Mrs. Henrietta Sutton (Alma Kruger), who belongs to a gang of Nazi fifth columnists. In this perspective, this swanky mansion is one of many interesting Hitchcock residences belonging to sophisticated villains such as Professor Jordan (*The 39 Steps*), Sir Humphrey Pengallan (*Jamaica Inn*), Alexander Sebastian (*Notorious*), Brandon and Philip (*Rope*), Charlotte Inwood (*Stage Fright*), Bruno Anthony (*Strangers on a Train*), Phillip Vandamm (*North by Northwest*), and Norman Bates (*Psycho*). Usually, Hitchcock's evil characters seem to have more interesting and sophisticated domestic tastes than his heroes, the dwellings of which we often do not get to see.

This is also the case in *Saboteur*. Its hero, the aircraft factory worker Barry Kane (Robert Cummings), is constantly on the road since he was wrongfully accused of having commited arson at a factory in which his best friend perished. Featuring a journey through the entire country, from West Coast to East Coast, and an amiably roguish hero, *Saboteur* unmistakably refers to a picaresque tradition, which favors a quick succession of changing imposing locations: an aircraft factory, a modest suburban house, a ranch, a log cabin in the woods, desert roads, a circus caravan, a deserted city, a Manhattan mansion, a skyscraper office, shipyards, a large movie theatre, and, last but not least, the Statue of Liberty. The film, consequently, required a large number of impressive sets, which were designed by Robert Boyle under the guidance of Universal supervising art director Jack Otterson. Having collaborated on the Empire State Building as an architect in the early 1930s before entering the movie industry, Otterson must have felt at home on the sets of the midtown and downtown Manhattan locations. Boyle, who had joined Universal only in 1941 and had *Saboteur* as one of his first assignments, would later also design sets for *Shadow of a Doubt*, *North by Northwest*, *The Birds*, and *Marnie*. Boyle also drew the storyboards for *Saboteur*, which he described as "the hardest job I ever had." "I had more of a theatrical background than a lot of art directors, and I also had done storyboards at Paramount. I guess I worked more like a director in that sense, and that's what Hitchcock wanted," Boyle stated.[1]

According to Boyle, during the production process, Universal studio officials grew "alarmed at the 50-odd sets Hitchcock ordered, especially a vast stage 12 desert, a reconstruction of a part of the turbulent Kern River including a waterfall, and the grand ballroom of a Park Avenue Mansion."[2] Boyle said that everything had to be done through "short cuts: we made airplane hangars out of storage bins on the lot. We used mattes, we used miniatures, scenic backings. All of those things which I knew about, but which I had never put all together in one film."[3]

1 Robert Boyle, quoted in LoBrutto, *By Design*, 7-8.
2 Robert Boyle, quoted in Turner, "*Saboteur*," 88. Boyle also notes that the sets were completed only days before the government had set a strict ceiling of $2,500 for new materials to be used in building sets because of America's intervention in the Second World War.
3 Robert Boyle, quoted in Turner, "*Saboteur*," 88-93.

Such "short cuts" were also used for the construction of Sutton house, the "Park Avenue Mansion" – a production file containing a list of studio interiors mentions a "house on Madison Avenue."[4] Together with Otterson and set decorator Russell Gausman, Hitchcock and Boyle managed to evoke the grandness of the mansion by showing only parts of the building. Of the exterior, definitely not situated at the much broader Park Avenue itself but possibly at one of its sidestreets, only a small fraction is visible. However, the rusticated façade and the coupled fluted columns on both sides of the entrance suggest a big and monumental building that could have been built in the 'Modern Renaissance' style, which was very popular in the area of Fifth Avenue and Park Avenue around 1900.[5] Sutton house is a typical example of the urban, domestic architecture of the nineteenth-century American millionaire who favored an architecture 'rich in historical association' and which could be built in a style varying from Gothic Revival to Queen Anne to Richardsonian Picturesque to Renaissance Classicism. Furthermore, its decorated façade demarcates the symbolic boundaries of social exclusion. An elegant princely mansion of the wealthy elite, Sutton house is a display case for consumption and possession. As M. Christine Boyer has demonstrated, late nineteenth-century Manhattan architecture presented itself as a "scenographic arrangement of luxury."[6]

Saboteur's protagonists, however, disrupt this scenographic and architectural disposition of bourgeois respectability. Strikingly, the exterior view only comes at the end of the entire Sutton house sequence since Kane does not enter the mansion through the main entrance but through the kitchen after passing a backroom of a drugstore and a dark alleyway. However, when he actually ends up in the mansion interior, the set of which was built at a cost of $45,000 and furnished with antiques insured over $200,000,[7] Kane is surprised and impressed by the grandeur of the richly decorated corridors and the grand ballroom. He even asks if they brought him to a hotel.

First, Kane is lead into one of the rooms upstairs where he is introduced to the mistress of the house, Mrs. Henrietta Sutton, who hosts a charity ball that night. In this room, Kane also sees Pat (Priscilla Lane) again, who is now taken captive by the gang of spies. It is a stylish study decorated in a manner appropriate of the urban palaces built in the late nineteenth or early twentieth centuries. The walls are decorated with loud wallpaper and painted portraits in gilded frames. A mantelpiece is ornamented by a precious clock, statuettes, and candlestands. Drapes cover the windows and the corners of the room, which contains refined side-tables, elegant chairs, Chinese vases, impressive candleholders, table-lamps, and statuettes. On one side of the room there is a writing desk, behind it a bookcase covering an entire wall. Every detail in the room oozes wealth and cultural sophistication but also power and bourgeois ostentation. In this

210

4 See Folder 637 *Saboteur* (Production) of the Hitchcock Collection in the Margaret Herrick Library, Academy of Motion Pictures Arts and Sciences, Los Angeles.
5 See Stern, Gilmartin, and Massengale, *New York 1900*, 307-59.
6 Boyer, *Manhattan Manners*, 130-92.

7 Robert Boyle, quoted in Turner, "*Saboteur*," 89.

I, II   Exterior view (Digital Frame)
III, IV   Corridor (Digital Frame)
V, VI   Study (Digital Frame)

perspective, the Sutton house contrasts sharply with the modest Californian suburban dwelling of Kane's friend, who was killed in the fire caused by the sabotage, and the log cabin of the blind man, who sheltered and helped the fugitive Kane.

Later, Kane is also brought into another upstairs room with similar frivolous decorations. In this drawing room, Kane confronts Charles Tobin (Otto Kruger), another leading member of the gang of Nazi spies, who unmasks Kane as an infiltrator. Kane had met Tobin earlier in the latter's Deep Spring Ranch, near Springville, where he was playing in the large backyard swimming pool with his toddler grandchild. Tobin orders one of the butlers to knock Kane out, who is subsequently locked up in the mansion's pantry. As frequently happens in a Hitchcock movie, the house becomes a trap and a place of confinement. Kane, however, manages to escape the nest of spies by raising a match to a sprinkler system, thus setting off an alarm.

However, not only the small basement pantry but the biggest room of the mansion too becomes a trap for the main characters. They fail to escape from the most impressive part of the Sutton house, which is the grand ballroom. This room is dominated by an impressive, double, curved staircase, which was a typical feature of the awe-inspiring homes built by American capitalist entrepeneurs in the late nineteenth and early twentieth centuries. Nearly every stately mansion had such a grand, representative staircase that attempted to outdo palatial European models.[8] Graphically, the Sutton staircase also answers to an abstract pattern of lines radiating from a central hub, which recurs a few times in the film.[9] The closed contours of the prominent ballustrade, for instance, are echoed by the curve and closely-spaced openings of the viewing ports inside the diadem of the Statue of Liberty.

The grand staircase in the Sutton ballroom would not be out of place on a musical set – in fact, the Sutton house set, Robert Boyle later told, "was built onto a set that was already there. The stairway was left from a Deanna Durbin picture, so I just added on to that. We had to get a very big long shot that required a matte, and since the old Deana Durbin set didn't have a matte, I had a hard time putting a ceiling on it."[10] The combination of set pieces and matte paintings resulted in a room marked by a superpostion of two neo-renaissance arches: those on the ground floor are separated by Corinthian pilasters, those above are decorated with a balcony and drapes. Corynthian pilasters also adorn the corners of the room, which is topped by a richly decorated ceiling with crystal chandeliers.

When Kane arrives at the Sutton house, the ballroom is the locale of a ritzy party. Susan Smith has noted that, in Hitchcock's œuvre, parties often serve as the occasions

8 Ramirez, *Architecture for the Screen*, 206-207.
9 Deutelbaum, "Seeing in *Saboteur*," 63.
10 Robert Boyle, quoted in Turner, "*Saboteur*," 89.

I Drawing room (Digital Frame)

II, III, IV Ball room (Digital Frame)

V, VI Ball room and stairs (Digital Frame)

for key suspense sequences, such as in *The 39 Steps*, *Young and Innocent*, *Rebecca*, *Notorious*, *Rope*, *Under Capricorn*, *The Man Who Knew Too Much*, *The Birds*, or *Marnie*. Also the figures of the hostile host and the unwelcome or uninvited guest often play an important part in Hitchcock films. According to Smith, these characters "help to dramatize the closeness of the interrelationship between setting and tone in Hitchcock's work. Indeed, it is quite striking how many unsettling moments often arise from the violation or rupture of a seemingly autonomous, clearly demarcated sphere."[11] Parties, of course, turn the private sphere of the house into a semi-public realm and Hitchcock's cinema often deals with the deceptiveness of appearances, even often in ways that provide implied critique of upper-class respectability. Art director Robert Boyle emphasized that "the opulence of the ballroom underlines the irony that a fabulously wealthy society matron could be a ringleader of a plot to overthrow her country."[12] However, surrounded by scores of people in evening dress but not knowing friend from foe, Kane and Pat find themselves helpless to escape. When Kane tries to tell an unsuspecting senior guest that the mansion is no more than a hide-out of Nazi spies, he is coldly informed, "You're not even dressed!" Even his costume does not tally with the architecture of the Sutton house. In this perspective, the pompous architecture of the Sutton ballroom is part of what Slavoj Zizek has called the "third gaze" or "the Other" that often plays an important role in Hitchcock's interaction of gazes.[13] Since Kane and Pat try to escape from the Nazis in the representative architecture of the great hall filled with hundreds of guests, both sides have to observe the rules of etiquette. The duel of two gazes takes place against the background of a third. Kane and Pat, so it seems, are not only watched by the Nazi spies and the ignorant upper-class guests but also by the architecture itself.

11 Smith, *Hitchcock*, 78.
12 Robert Boyle, quoted in Turner, "*Saboteur*," 89.
13 Zizek, "In His Bold Gaze My Ruin Is Writ Large," 215.

I Robert Cummings on the same staircase, with Deanna Durbin in
It Started With Eve (Henry Koster, 1941)
Art direction by Jack Otterson, set decoration by Russell A. Gausman (Digital Frame)
II Hall and ball room (Digital Frame)
III Hall (Digital Frame)
IV Pantry (Digital Frame)

Psycho-Building:
Green Manors

Vermont

Spellbound

Black-and-white
Selznick International Pictures
1945

ART DIRECTION:
James Basevi
ASSOCIATE ART DIRECTION:
John Ewing
INTERIOR DECORATION:
Emile Kuri

Green Manors is a psychiatric institute and the location of the first sequences and the penultimate scene of *Spellbound*, which Hitchcock, somewhat disapprovingly, called "just another manhunt story wrapped up in pseudo-psychanalysis."[1] A precursor of *Vertigo*, *Psycho*, and *Marnie*, *Spellbound* is Hitchcock's first film to deal with a pathological mental case and, much more explicitly than in any other of his films, with psychoanalysis.[2] When producer David O. Selznick asked for a theme about "the healing potential of psychiatry," Hitchcock and screenwriter Ben Hecht came up with an adaptation of *The House of Dr. Edwardes*, a Francis Beeding novel, which John Orr simply calls a "Gothic novel" and which Patrick McGilligan describes as "almost a country house mystery."[3] Green Manors, indeed, can be considered a Gothic country house comparable to Manderley (*Rebecca*) or Hindley Hall (*The Paradine Case*). It is the place where Dr. Constance Petersen (Ingrid Bergman) falls in love with the new superintendent of the mental institution, Dr. Anthony Edwardes (Gregory Peck), who comes to replace Dr. Murchison (Leo G. Carroll). When the troubled Edwardes starts to act strangely, Petersen discovers that he is an imposter suffering from amnesia. However, Edwardes, whose real name turns out to be John Ballantine, is also tormented by a dark secret in his past. With the help of her former teacher Dr. Brulov (Michael Chekov), Petersen manages to heal Ballantine. In addition, she discovers that Dr. Murchison murdered the real Dr. Edwardes to save his own position.

Although Hitchcock and Hecht went trawling for verisimilitude in mental hospitals and psychiatric wards in Connecticut and New York,[4] Green Manors, comfirming its pastoral name, is situated in Vermont – as the letterhead of a note by Ballantine to Petersen reveals. The film opens with a Shakespeare quote printed on an establishing shot of the building's exterior. It is a long and symmetrical building with a central portico with four Ionic columns carrying a pediment. On both sides, slightly projecting wings are topped by pediments as well. The roof is punctuated by dormers and a central turret. The style of the building, which shows a vague similarity to the Culver City colonnaded studio façade in Selznick's trademark, answers perfectly to the typology of the Georgian hospitals and asylums, which were built in America in the early nineteenth century. With their long fronts, with or without projecting wings, with or without porticoes, and with or without cupola, they were much like country houses.[5]

The general view of the building is immediately followed by an establishing shot of Green Manors' main entrance. This shot is the background for a text that introduces the 1945 audience to psychoanalysis, "the method by which modern science treats the

1 Truffaut, *Hitchcock*, 165.
2 See Jonathan Freedman, "From *Spellbound* to *Vertigo*," 77-98; and Hyde, "The Moral Universe of Hitchcock's *Spellbound*," 153-61.
3 Orr, *Hitchcock and 20th Century Cinema*, 98; McGilligan, *Alfred Hitchcock*, 348.
4 McGilligan, *Alfred Hitchcock*, 354.
5 Pevsner, *A History of Building Types*, 149. At the level of the narrative as well, John Orr states that "Green Manors may be Hitchcock's cryptic version of Selznick International Pictures."

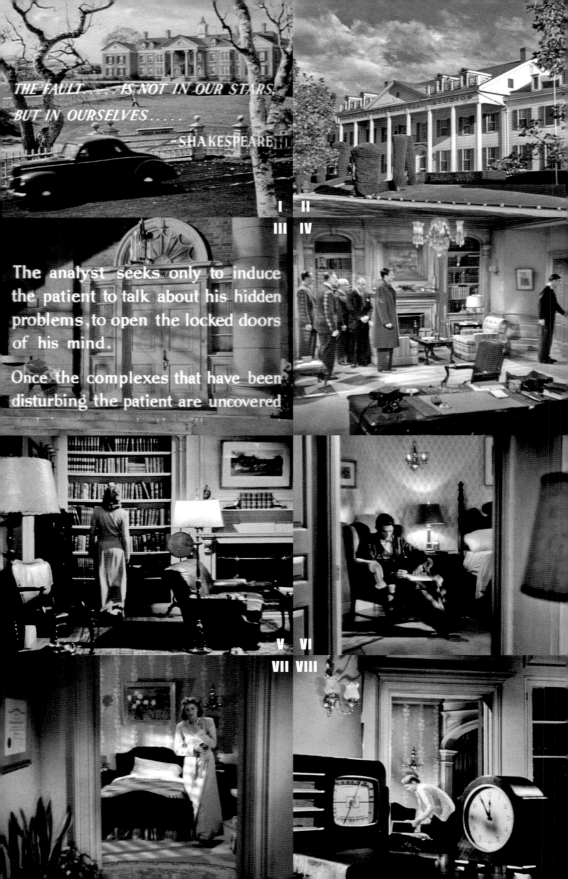

THE FAULT..... IS NOT IN OUR STARS,
BUT IN OURSELVES.....
—SHAKESPEARE

The analyst seeks only to induce
the patient to talk about his hidden
problems, to open the locked doors
of his mind.

Once the complexes that have been
disturbing the patient are uncovered

I   II

III   IV

V   VI

VII   VIII

emotional problems of the sane." In addition, the introduction tells us that "the analyst seeks only to induce the patient to talk about his hidden problems, to open the locked doors of his mind." Strikingly, the text attempts to explain psychoanalysis by means of the metaphor of the locked door while it rolls over the image of a closed door – an image that recurs a few times at important moments throughout the film. This image is only one of several architectural metaphors used in a film, which revolves around the disappearance of the real Dr. Edwardes, who is, tellingly, author of *The Labyrinth of the Guilt Complex.*

A mental institution, Green Manors is a maverick in a chapter dealing with Hitchcock's domestic architecture. However, its exterior does not only look like a country house, both patients and doctors actually live there. Furthermore, the library and the rooms of both Dr. Murchison and Dr. Petersen are decorated as homely, bourgeois interiors. Of the superintendent's quarters, the alleged Dr. Edwardes remarks that "they are very festive for an institution."

In his memoirs, set decorator Emile Kuri, who had joined Selznick to work on the small-town sets of William Dieterle's *I'll Be Seeing You* (1942), discusses extensively the furnishing of the interior of the "well-to-do sanatorium, somewhere in New England." Dr. Peterson's quarters "consisted of her sitting room, study, bedroom and bath. I had to find a psychiatrist, interview him, look over his offices and library and ask a lot of questions. (…) I visited the psychiatrist. He was very cooperative and after looking at his medical library I asked him if it were possible to rent such a library. He told me that the company from which he purchased his books also had a rental service to doctors and that their service included newly published volumes that would keep the library up to date."

In addition, Kuri mentions in his memoirs that he "wanted to go to a furniture store and buy good quality 'Grand Rapids' furniture in eighteenth-century English style." "The best I found," Kuri wrote, "was at the J.W. Robinson Company, a department store in downtown Los Angeles. There I bought a Georgian library desk and chair, a typewriter table, Chippendale sofa and coffee table, wing chairs, lamps, and complete bedroom furnishings. The set that was being built had built-in book cases and through-out the set I tried to introduce a certain masculinity to go with the way the script described the doctor's character, which Ingrid Bergman was to portray. I had asked the still department to make five-by-seven and eight-by-ten pictures in black and white of Miss Bergman, which I had selected from a large group, and to superimpose the figure of a woman standing by her, supposedly her mother, and others of a man, her father, a

I Exterior view (Digital Frame)
II Selznick Studio (Digital Frame)
III Entrance (Digital Frame)
IV Dr. Murchison's room (Digital Frame)
V Library (Digital Frame)
VI Dr. Edwardes' room (Digital Frame)
VII, VIII Dr. Petersen's room (Digital Frame)

medical school graduation picture, medical diplomas with her name and other such personal effects."[6]

The homely, bourgeois interiors of the doctors' quarters contrast sharply with the clean, clear, and white corridors and operating rooms. Strikingly, Edwardes/Ballantine is frightened by white, the color not only of aseptic hospitals but also of architectural modernism. Table-linen, an operating table in the surgery, a bedspread, and a bathroom induce nervous breakdowns. Dr. Brulov, Petersen's mentor, assumes that Ballantine is frightened by light, and diagnoses photophobia – eventually, snow turns out to be the reason of Ballantine's mental distress since he witnessed the real Dr. Edwardes' murder on the ski slopes.

Green Manors' bourgeois interiors also enable Hitchcock and cinematographer George Barnes to create all kinds of *noirish* effects. Camera positions lend a tension to the furnished quarters of the doctors. For instance, when Dr. Petersen packs her suitcase to follow Ballantine to New York, a clock and a radio dominate the foreground of the frame. Both the quarters of Dr. Petersen and Dr. Murchison are steeped in a threatening atmosphere of contrasting lights and shadows. The rooms themselves seem to evoke the feelings of Green Manors' residents who are basically haunted by delusions of neurotic guilt caused by traumas. When she enters the guest room in Dr. Brulov's house in Rochester, Dr. Petersen herself lectures bookishly on the psychological dimension of architecture: "You know, this room does look changed. But it isn't. It is I who am changed. It's called transfer of affects. (…) The fact that everything seems so wonderful in this room." Petersen explicitly emphasizes that the beholder transforms and sculpts the space – a fact which Hitchcock in *Spellbound* endorses not only by using some of his trademark point-of-view shots, but also by combining some of these point-of-view shots with impressive optical distortions. Examples of this are the glass of drugged milk at Dr. Brulov's house (we look through the glass of which Peck is drinking) and, situated at the superintendent's quarters at Green Manors, the gun (in fact, a huge, wooden hand holding a prop gun so that Bergman could be kept in clear focus beyond) that kills Dr. Murchison.

Of course, the famous dream sequence, designed by art directors James Basevi and William Cameron Menzies and set decorator Emile Kuri based on sketches by Salvador Dali, should also be considered in this perspective. Avoiding the usual montage *à la* Vorkapich and the obligatory blurs or swirling smoke for Hollywood dream sequences, Dali provided the architectural effects Hitchcock wanted. "I wanted Dali because of the

6 Kuri, *Memoirs*, 28-29.
7 Truffaut, *Hitchcock*, 165.
8 Leff, *Hitchcock and Selznick*, 158.

architectural sharpness of his work," Hitchcock stated. "Chirico has the same quality, you know, the long shadows, the infinity of distance, and the converging lines of perspective."[7] Leonard Leff noted how Dali's universe perfectly tailored Hitchcockian space: "Dali placed distinct 'things' in aspatial or atemporal contexts, much as Hitchcock often placed his characters among 'things' in an alienating environment."[8] The dream sequence also illustrates that Hitchcock associated mental disturbance with spatial distortions. Demanding "long shadows, infinity of distance, and covering lines of perspective," Hitchcock and Dali created an uncanny landscape that foreshadows the terrifying empty space that characterizes the crop dusting sequence or the shot on top of Mount Rushmore in *North by Northwest*. Although it mixes locations (Edwardes' New York club, the ski slopes among others) and lacks spatial consistency, as dreams are

I, II, III Dream sequence (Digital Frame)
Art Direction by William Cameron Menzies and James Basevi based on sketches by Salvador Dali

considered to do, parts of Ballantine's dream are situated at Green Manors. "He dreamed he was in a gambling house," Dr. Petersen summarizes. "It was full of odd people playing with blank cards. (…) One of the people in the place went around cutting the drapes in half. Another was a scantily dressed girl who was kissing everybody. (…) There were eyes painted on the curtains around the walls." Both Petersen and Murchison conclude that "with a little effort, one could almost imagine them in the midst of Green Manors." At Green Manors, after all, patients play bridge (as shown in the opening scene) and one of the inmates, the nymphomaniac Miss Carmichael (Rhonda Fleming), could pass for the scantily dressed girl in the dream. Dr. Murchison interprets the eyes on the walls as Green Manors' guards. The dream image of a man cutting painted eyes in half with giant scissors is an explicit reference to *Un chien andalou* (1929), Luis Buñuel's early surrealist masterpiece to which Dali contributed as co-screenwriter. In addition, walls decorated with giant eyes evoke the notions of the omnipotent gaze and panoptic control, which Hitchcock later elaborated in films such as *Rear Window* and *Vertigo*.

Spatial distortions and *noirish* effects also occur in two scenes, mirroring one another, in which Constance Petersen climbs the stairs in order to enter Dr. Murchison's room. Twice, Hitchcock combines the image of a staircase with that of a locked door – a combination also used in climactic scenes in *Rebecca* and *The Birds*. Petersen leaves her quarters downstairs, climbs the nocturnal staircase and notices the light coming from the chink at the door of the superintendent's room. In both scenes incorporating subjective camera shots, the stairs and the closed door evoke desire – the erotic desire for the handsome alleged Dr. Edwardes in the first scene, and the longing to unlock the mystery of Ballantine's illness and dream in the second. In the first scene, the metaphor of the closed door is further elaborated in one of Hitchcock's most famous kissing scenes. To evoke the hypnotic attraction between Petersen and Ballantine, Hitchcock not only uses sensuous, gliding camera moves and gorgeous lingering close-ups but also a cross-fade to an image of a series of opening doors, which give way and disclose a crucible of ardent sunlight in the innermost room. The opening of these doors, which suggest the release of a long repressed love, is later in the film mirrored by the image of swinging prison bars over a close-up of Bergman's face. Although it is an extreme example, the door sequence illustrates perfectly how Hitchcock created a site of abstraction in the country asylum of Green Manors, as he had done with *Rebecca*'s Manderley.

Finally, one should note another of Green Manors' architectural details. At dinner, after

the alleged Dr. Edwardes' arrival, Constance Petersen discusses the construction of a new swimming pool at the estate. Convinced of the benefits of open-air amusement for the patients, Petersen notes that there's a perfect spot for the swimming pool in the elms grove on Green Manors' grounds. She advises against (for therapeutic reasons?) the construction of an oblong pool and she argues in favor of an irregular one. "Something like this," she says while drawing with her fork an organically shaped form in the table-cloth and, in so doing, introducing the pattern of parallel lines on a white surface that causes Ballantine's mental disturbances.

23

Nazi Hominess: Sebastian House

Rio de Janeiro, Brazil

Notorious

Black-and-white
RKO
1946

ART DIRECTION:
Carroll Clark
Albert S. D'Agostino
SET DIRECTION:
Darrell Silvera
Claude Carpenter

This Italianate villa, situated at the curving coastline in the outskirts of Rio de Janeiro, consists of a long two-story volume with a low-pitched hipped roof covered with ceramic tiles. It is marked by an impressive entry porch topped with a semicircular pediment and supported by two columns. According to Hitchcock, a house in Beverly Hills stood for this Rio mansion.[1] This indicates that in the early twentieth century, European beaux-arts eclecticism was not only popular among Hollywood film stars but also among the Brazilian upper-classes – something that is also demonstrated by the famous Teatro Municipal shown in one of the film's establishing shots of Rio de Janeiro.

The house belongs to Alex Sebastian (Claude Rains) and his mother (Leopoldine Konstantin), who harbor a group of Nazi refugees. Alex falls in love with Alicia Huberman (Ingrid Bergman), the daughter of a sentenced Nazi agent. However, Alicia was

1 Truffaut, *Hitchcock*, 172.

I Teatro municipal, Rio de Janeiro (Digital Frame)
II, III Exterior view (Digital Frame)
IV Entrance (Digital Frame)

never involved in her father's activities. After leading a fast life in Miami, she accepted the request of American government agent T.R. Devlin (Cary Grant) to infiltrate the gang of Nazi exiles in Rio. In order to spy on them, Alicia even marries Alex and becomes the mistress of the Sebastian mansion, that evokes the atmosphere of a castle of a fairy tale, in which the heroine is trapped and turned into a sleeping beauty.[2] Having passed the impressive doorway, the visitor ends up in a stately hall with a grandiose curving stairway, which would not be out of place in an opera house. The hall, as well as most rooms of the house, is richly furnished. Set decorator Darrell Silvera, head of the RKO prop department, could give free vent to his talents: crystal chandeliers, numerous paintings, antique furniture, ornate mantlepieces, doors with classical moldings, clocks, and vases adorn the interiors of the mansion. Several stately rooms are visible in the film: the living room, the dining room, the library, and a garden terrace are the locales of scenes situated on the ground floor. Upstairs, Hitchcock offers us a view into the bedroom of Sebastian's mother and that of Alicia.

The latter, as well as the hall and the cellar are very important to the narrative. Newly wed, Alicia, accompanied by the butler, unlocks all the doors. Eventually, Hitchcock shows us an extreme close-up of the wine cellar lock. Being told that Mr. Sebastian always carries the key that gives access to the cellar with him, Alicia and her American employers suspect that the basement hides an important secret – given this perspective, *Notorious* is, after *Rebecca* and *Suspicion*, another Hitchcockian variation of the female Gothic plot with a trembling heroine in a castle that contains a dangerous husband and a forbidden room. Alicia steals the key and with Devlin she explores the cellar during a party and they discover uranium ore concealed in wine bottles. The transgression of the forbidden space of the cellar is masterly introduced in the grand hall by one of Hitchcock's famous camera movements: a breathtaking crane shot in which the camera descends without a cut from a vast overview of the foyer to a close-up of the key clutched in Bergman's hand. This shot is not only an imposing instance of Ted Tetzlaff's daring cinematography, it also enables the director to combine two levels of reality in a single image.[3] The crane shot suggests that something dangerous lies within this impressive and sophisticated setting; one spatial continuum contains the double reality of bourgeois respectability and Nazi ideology. As in the Sutton house in *Saboteur*, a swank party in an eclectic mansion is a red herring for Nazi activities.

When Alex Sebastian finds out that his wife is an American agent, the Nazi safe house is transformed from a site of adventurous espionage into a claustrophobic trap, in which the characters move over the tiled floor as pawns in a game. Leaving the cellar, first his shadow, then Alex himself crosses the main hall and goes upstairs to his mother's

2 Abel, "Notorious," 162-69.
3 Spoto, The Art of Alfred Hitchcock, 152.

I Hall (Digital Frame)
II Hall and stairs (Digital Frame)
III Crane shot of the hall (Digital Frame)
IV, V Drawing room (Digital Frame)
VI Drawing room (Still, Royal Film Archive, Brussels)
VII Dining room (Still, Royal Film Archive, Brussels)
VIII Dining room (Digital Frame)

I II

III IV

V VI

VII VIII

I II
III IV

V VI
VII VIII

bedroom. From then onwards, Mrs. Sebastian rules the house and controls the phallic imagery – the keys, the embroidery needles, the aggressive cigarette-smoking posture.[4] Alicia is slowly poisoned with arsenic, her senses become distorted. She ends up weakened in her bedroom, where she is eventually liberated by Devlin. The climax is a genuine Hitchockian staircase scene, in which the tensions between the characters are translated into spatial affect: Devlin guides the poisoned Alicia down the stairs out of the mansion, whilst Alex and his mother walk impotently besides them since they want to conceal the blunder of having married an American agent from their Nazi entourage. In the end, the house becomes a sepulchral prison for Sebastian himself: when Devlin and Alicia drive away, he fearfully has to face the circle of suspicious Nazis in the final fade-out. *Notorious* is a film about doors and thresholds, which suggest undecidable interiors.[5] As a transition between two doors – the door to Alicia's bedroom and the front door – the stairway highlights the temporary and relative nature of the many enclosed interiors through which the characters have passed in this film: the opening shot of the doors of a Miami courtroom, Devlin standing in Alicia's Miami doorway, the balcony connected to her Copacabana apartment, and the Sebastian mansion in which the Nazi machinations are figured *behind closed doors*, such as the locked wine cellar, the closed door of Mrs. Sebastian's bedroom, or the library where the fate of one of their 'weaker' members is sealed. Hitchcock, however, intensifies the claustrophobic character of the mansion by 'closing' it cinematically: the visualization of the Sebastian house is characterized by an emphatic attention to charged domestic objects (wine bottle, key, Unica lock, coffee cup), blurred images evoking the distorted vision of the poisoned Alicia, oppressive framings, and the strikingly abundant use of close-ups and extreme close-ups, sometimes supported by the use of overscaled props, such as a coffee cup containing poison.[6] In a 1948 review of the film, Eric Rohmer observed that the originality of *Notorious* consisted in the creation of the mobile close-up.[7] As the claustrophobic character of the mansion is strengthened, Hitchcock moves from farther away to closer up, as in the famous crane shot on the cellar key. The combination of architectural grandeur and claustrophobia, however, is unmistakably also the result of the art direction by Albert D'Agostino, who introduced a *noirish* style characterized by odd angles and striking lighting effects at RKO. *Notorious* clearly displays the characteristics of the influential style of D'Agostino, who, in the 1940s, also created the designs for other films with uncanny interiors such as *Stranger on the Third Floor* (Boris Ingster, 1940), *Cat People* (Jacques Tourneur, 1942), *The Body Snatcher* (Robert Wise, 1945), or *The Spiral Staircase* (Robert Siodmak, 1946).

4 Renov, "From Identification to Ideology," 108.
5 Morris, *The Hanging Figure*, 155-58.
6 According to McElhaney, the 101-minute film *Notorious* contains 119 close-ups and 72 extreme close-ups. See McElhaney, "The Object and the Face," 66.

7 See Bonitzer, "Notorious," 153.

I Door to mother's room (Digital Frame)
II Mother's room (Digital Frame)
III Door to Alicia's room (Digital Frame)
IV Alicia's room (Digital Frame)
V Door to wine cellar (Digital Frame)
VI Wine cellar lock (Digital Frame)
VII Wine cellar (Digital Frame)
VIII Charged domestic objects (Digital Frame)

Unfathomable Plans:
Paradine House

33 Wilton Crescent,
Belgravia, London, England

The Paradine Case

Black-and-white
Selznick International Pictures
1947

PRODUCTION DESIGN:
J. McMillan Johnson
ART DIRECTION:
Thomas Morahan
SET DECORATION:
Joseph B. Platt (interiors)
Emile Kuri

Drawing by Bruno Poelaert

230

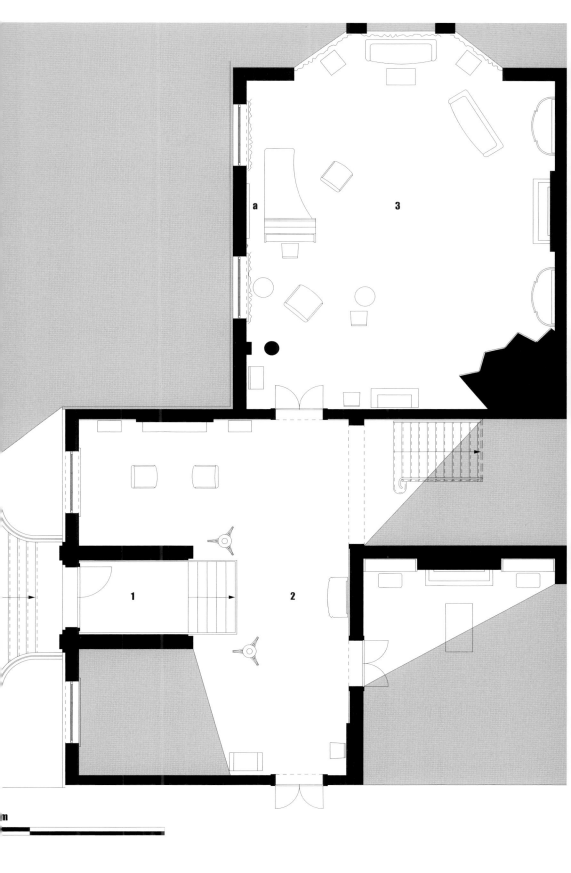

a

3

1

2

m

This house belongs to Mrs. Maddalena Paradine (Alida Valli) who is accused of having murdered her blind husband, Colonel Richard Patrick Irving Paradine. It only features in the opening sequence of the film, which Hitchcock described as "a love story embedded in the emotional quicksand of a murder trial."[1] The Paradine house is situated in Wilton Crescent in London, where a second unit made some location shots in half light.[2] The exact location is indicated by the street sign attached to the façade of the mansion, which is situated in the district of Belgravia, a typical example of the continuation of the Georgian tradition in most large British towns in the early nineteenth century. Belgravia was developed in the 1820s by Thomas Cubbitt, one of the largest of all Victorian spec-ulative builders who was responsible for building large areas of London, in particular almost the whole of Belgravia. Highly successful, widely respected in his day, and able to live in high style, he employed leading architects such as George Basevi (1794-1845), a pupil of John Soane. In Belgravia, Basevi followed the Georgian tradition of uniform Classical terraces built of brick faced with stucco. Like Georgian terrace houses, they have kitchens and service rooms in the basement that look on to an area, which is railed off in front. The ground floor has a Classical porch sheltering the front door, which leads to the entrance hall and staircase. The living rooms are on the ground and first floors. Bedrooms for the family occupy the upper floors and attics provide bedrooms for the servants.[3]

The first shot of the film pans across Wilton Crescent to No. 33, the then Cuban embassy, which Hitchcock and unit manager Fred Ahern selected on a location trip to London in April 1946.[4] Subsequently, the camera moves through the foyer of this elegant man-

1 Hitchcock, "Let'Em Play God," 114.
2 This location is men-tioned in a 16-page docu-ment entitled "London & Cumberland Locations," dated 18 May, 1946. See Folder 558 *The Paradine Case* (misc.) in the Hitch-cock Collection in the Margaret Herrick Library.
3 See Dixon & Muthesius, *Victorian Architecture*, 56-59.
4 See Giblin, *Alfred Hitch-cock's London*, 23.
5 Leff, *Hitchcock and Selznick*, 227; McGilligan, *Alfred Hitchcock*, 390.

sion, following the butler who enters the study on the left. In this room, he finds Mrs. Paradine playing a romantic nocturne on the piano in front of the full-length portrait of her late husband. In this parlor, she also receives the police officers who come to arrest her. Answering perfectly to the glamor photography, the chic wardrobe, and the elegant sets, the camera circles around her in fluid motions and sculpturally defines the spatial boundaries of the scene. Both the camera movements and the high key light, which renders Mrs. Paradine's features almost mask-like, are perfectly tailored to the white walls and the elegant Regency classicism of the interior, which is designed by Joseph McMillan Johnson and Thomas Morahan and decorated by Joseph B. Platt and Emile Kuri – all names that recur in Hitchcock's filmography. Furthermore, Hitchcock presents the architecture of this high-class *milieu* as a mental and physical straitjacket for the characters – in particular for Mrs. Paradine, who is called a "woman of unattractive past" and who disgraced herself by an *amour fou* since she has been passionately attached to a servant.

As in many other Hitchcock films, bourgeois 'normality' and its spatial embodiment, the house, are empty and unsatisfying. Everything beyond or within it is terrifying. Although only the Paradine house is the location of a murder, tension and oppression characterize all the domestic settings of the film, for which Hitchcock himself did some extensive location scouting:[5] the Paradine Mansion in the Lake District, the opulent mansion of the judge Lord Horfield, and the house of Anthony Keane, Mrs. Paradine's lawyer. These interiors, every one of them, are tellingly juxtaposed to the spaces of criminal justice: the Bow Street Police Station, the Holloway Prison, and the Central Criminal Court, known as the Old Bailey. According to Susan Smith, the entire film is

I Façade (Digital Frame)
II Foyer (Digital Frame)
III Foyer with door to study (Digital Frame)
IV Study with portrait of Mr. Paradine (Digital Frame)

characterized by a "spatial dialectic between the masculine domain of the court and the feminine world of domesticity."[6] The Paradine house, consequently, plays an important part in the process that Smith described as the "patriarchal invalidation and denial of the female voice."[7] Patriarchal order is also symbolized by the dominant portrait of Colonel Paradine during Mrs. Paradine's arrest – she even points it out to the police officers.

In the famous interview with François Truffaut, Hitchcock stated that he did not really grasp how the murder was committed since everything was complicated by people walking from one room to another, up and down the corridors. He never understood "the geography of that house or how she managed the killing."[8] Although many of his films are set in grand mansions (cf. Moat House, Pengallan House, Manderley, Aysgarth House), Hitchcock stated in more than one interview that he felt lost and disoriented in such surroundings. He couldn't figure out where the people went to the bathroom in such mansions.[9] The floor plan, consequently, plays an important part in the murder plot and the prosecuting attorney uses blueprints of the floor plan as an exhibit in his indictment.

6 Smith, *Hitchcock*, 79.
7 Ibid., 37.
8 Truffaut, *Hitchcock*, 174.
9 McGilligan, *Alfred Hitchcock*, 389.

I Study (Digital Frame)
II The prosecutor holding the floor plan (Digital Frame)
III Mrs. Paradine and her late husband's portrait (Still, Royal Film Archive, Brussels)
IV Foyer (Still, Royal Film Archive, Brussels)

Bedroom of the Picturesque:
Hindley Hall

Lake District,
Cumberland, England

The Paradine Case

Black-and-white
Selznick International Pictures
1947

PRODUCTION DESIGN:
Joseph McMillan Johnson
ART DIRECTION:
Thomas Morahan
SET DECORATION:
Joseph B. Platt (interiors)
Emile Kuri

Hindley Hall is the remote Paradine country estate situated in the Lake District, of which a second unit made location shots based on the instructions Hitchcock compiled in a memo on the "London and Cumberland locations."[1] Hitchcock, who did a lot of research and coordinated the second-unit work in England between May and late August 1946,[2] gave specific guidelines for the shots of landscapes indicating that the mansion is a remote and secluded building. The memo asked for a series of views, among them one of the "railway station at Braithwaite outside Keswick," a shot of Hindley village, a view of the famous and often depicted "Jaws of Borrowdale," and a shot "looking across from round hill just outside Ambleside going North, with Grasmere and Rydal lakes and mountains in the background." By means of what Lev Kuleshov had called the "creative geography" of cinema, Hitchcock convincingly edited the shots, which were taken sometimes more than 50 miles apart, into the continuity.[3]

In addition, the memo demanded a "beautiful view of a lake with lawns and cultivated gardens in the foreground – make sure mountains in background (sic) with strong cross light." "This should be the most beautiful shot in the whole of the picture," the memo states. "Strong moonlight effect of gorgeous lakeland scenery. Silhouetted, contemplative figure walking along edge of lake strongly back-lit. It should have moon-lit effect. This need not necessarily be near the house but can be in an entirely independent setting. Would like to have feeling in this particular spot that weather is going to be pretty dirty later on – in other words, a foreboding mood created by heavy clouds." In the film, eventually, this results in a view through a window that is a veritable black-and-white version of a Caspar David Friedrich landscape painting.

Of the mansion itself, to which the memo and a line in the dialogue in the film refer as Hindley Hall, an exterior long shot was taken. The building that doubled for the fictitious Hindley Hall is the Langdale Chase Hotel in Windermere, which was built in 1890 as a private home and transformed into a hotel in 1930.[4] "Blessed with so many architectural and decorative examples of our heritage, not to mention hidden treasures, such as the original mosaic floors in the porch, laid by craftsman brought over from Italy, the house is listed as one of national and historic interest. The hotel's outstanding interior and location, made it a natural choice for the classic English country house in Alfred Hitchcock's production of *The Paradine Case*," so the hotel website and tourist brochure tell us. Hitchcock incorporated a shot of the building's entrance, as well as a shot of Lake Windermere in the finished film. Some interiors, such as the entrance hall with staircase, were faithfully recreated in Hollywood, through a combination of studio sets and matte paintings by Jack Cosgrove along with Jack Shaw and Spencer Bagdatopoulos.

1 See Folder 558 *The Paradine Case (misc.)* in the Hitchcock Collection, Margaret Herrick Library, Los Angeles. The document is dated 18 May, 1946. See pages 6-12 in particular.
2 McGilligan, *Alfred Hitchcock*, 390-92.
3 See Giblin, *Alfred Hitchcock's London*, 284-87.
4 Ibid., 287.

The exterior shot of Hindley Hall shows only a part of the building that is approached by a horse and a carriage bringing the lawyer Anthony Keane (Gregory Peck), who defends Mrs. Paradine (Alida Valli), who is accused of murdering her husband. In contrast with the Palladian reminiscences of the London Paradine house, the Cumberland mansion of the Paradines is, in the words of set decorator Emile Kuri, "a large manor house of Gothic design, surrounded by acres and acres of beautiful gardens."[5]

Although some parts of the estate may be remnants of a Tudor or Elizabethan country house, the entire mansion gives the impression of being a Victorian manor built in the picturesque vernacular style, which came to be known as 'Old English' and which was popularized by architects such as Richard Norman Shaw during the 1860s and 1870s. With its irregular floor plan, asymmetrical fenestration, high ceilings, prolific wooden wainscotting, ornate furniture, stained glass windows, and dark shadows, Hindley Hall is also reminiscent of Manderley (*Rebecca*). Both become a virtual character symbolizing a mixture of patriarchal oppression and passionate romance. In addition, both strongly affect the modern-day people who inhabit or visit them.[6] Pretending to be interested in renting the estate, Keane is given a guided tour by a woman servant. She shows him around the huge hall and several of the impressive rooms.

The tour ends in the very large bedroom of Mrs. Paradine, which set decorator Emile

5 Kuri, *Memoirs*, 42.
6 Naremore, "Hitchcock at the Margins of Noir," 275.

I, II Langdale Chase Hotel (Tourist Brochure)
III Exterior (Digital Frame)
IV View of the lake (Digital Frame)
V, VI Hall (Digital Frame)
VII Drawing room (Digital Frame)
VIII Corridor (Digital Frame)
IX Mrs. Paradine's bedroom (Digital Frame)
X Bed (Digital Frame)

III   IV

V   VI

VII   VIII

IX   X

Kuri called "pure stone Gothic. The décor became a blend of very feminine softness. Hitch suggested that the floor covering might be done with some sort of soft white animal skins and luckily, I was able to get long haired, white sheep skins."[7]

In the ornate bedroom, Keane lingers over everything. Hitchcock juxtaposes this room to the bedroom in Keane's own house: both bedrooms link the two women in Keane's life: Mrs. Paradine, with whom he is in love, and Gay, his wife. The *mise-en-scène* puts the emphasis on the bed, which, as often in Hitchcock's œuvre, is a site of disturbance. A generic place of amorous encounters, the bed and the bedroom denote Keane's unfulfilled desire for Mrs. Paradine, who he only can meet in the surveyed and sterile environment of the prison. The room and every object in it seem sexual solicitations: the bed, the filmy nightclothes on it, the brace of fox tails on a gaping trunk, and the bathroom that rather looks as a set piece of a Cecil B. DeMille picture set in ancient Rome or Babylon. The proper place for the strategic *deshabillé* of an actress, bathrooms are often dramatically significant architectural elements in Hollywood cinema.[8] DeMille's sybaritic bathtubs, in which movie stars exposed their corporal divinity, intensified the connection between baths and (unfulfilled) desire.

Keane's unanswered longing is further enhanced by the oval portrait of Mrs. Paradine. According to a 'campaign manual' of *The Paradine Case* published by the Selznick company, both this portrait of Mrs. Paradine at Hindley Hall and that of Colonel Paradine at their London house were created by Audubon Tyler, "grandson of the famous bird painter James Audubon." Strikingly, Mrs. Paradine's portrait is embedded in the headboard of her bed. As in some seminal examples of contemporary film noir, such as Otto Preminger's *Laura* (1944) or Fritz Lang's *Woman in the Window* (1945), the painted

7 Kuri, *Memoirs*, 42. Kuri mentions that Peck was allergic to animal skins.
8 Ramirez, *Architecture for the Screen*, 208-10.
9 Walker, *Hitchcock's Motifs*, 321-326.
10 Elsaeser, "Mirror, Muse, Medusa," 148.

portrait of the *femme fatale* is associated with the desire of the male beholder. In the Paradine bedroom scene, Hitchcock places great emphasis on the looks: that of Keane himself, gazing repeatedly at the portrait, and that of Mrs. Paradine in the portrait, whose eyes, looking straight out at the viewer, seem to follow Keane across the room.[9] Simultaneously, as in many other Hollywood movies of the era, painted portraits are associated with a violent or morbid death: Colonel Paradine, whose portrait dominates the study of the London residence, was poisoned whereas Mrs. Paradine faces capital punishment. Furthermore, portraits of women often connote a surrealist ghost story – such as the picture representing Carlotta Valdez in *Vertigo* or the painting in William Dieterle's *Portrait of Jennie* (1948), which Selznick produced while still working on *The Paradine Case*. According to Thomas Elsaesser, painted portraits in cinema almost invariably invoke the genres of the fantastic, the uncanny, the gothic, since they cast "a radical uncertainty around what is alive and what is dead," they install "at the heart of the filmic representation a *memento mori*."[10] In the Paradine bedroom scene, this dimension of the portrait is confirmed by the architecture and the interior decoration of the entire mansion.

In addition, Keane's visit to Hindley Hall contains another characteristic component of the Gothic plot: the forbidden or mysterious room connected with secret passions. When leaving Mrs. Paradine's bedroom, Keane notices, supported by a point-of-view shot, a closed door transected by the shadow lines of a Gothic window. It turns out to be the room of André Latour (Louis Jourdan), Mrs. Paradine's lover who will commit suicide during the period of the trial.

i Portrait of Mrs. Paradine (Digital Frame)
ii Bathroom (Digital Frame)
iii Door to Latour's Room (Digital Frame)

Warm, Cozy, and Protective: Keane House

Portland Place,
Marylebone, London, England

The Paradine Case

Black-and-white
Selznick International Pictures
1947

PRODUCTION DESIGN:
J. McMillan Johnson
ART DIRECTION:
Thomas Morahan
SET DECORATION:
Joseph B. Platt (interiors)
Emile Kuri

1 Hall
2 Drawing Room
3 Dining Room
4 Mrs. Keane's Bedroom
5 Mr. Keane's Bedroom

Drawings by Bruno Poelaert

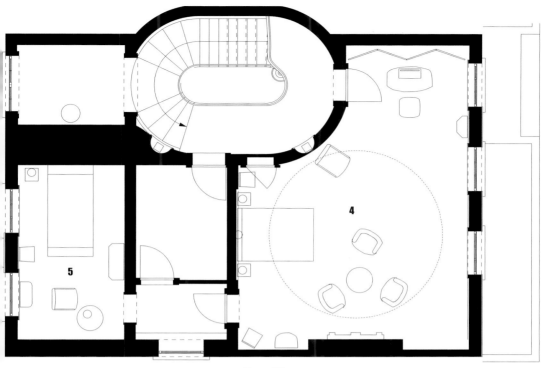

Second Floor

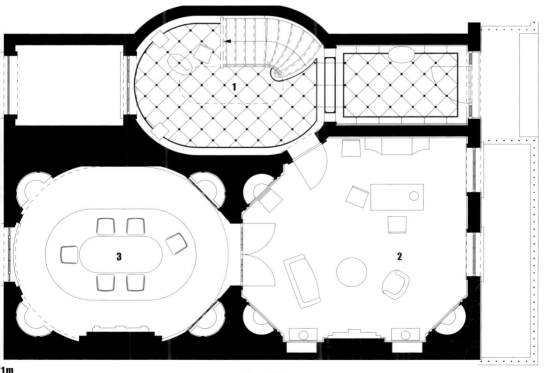

1m

Ground Floor

This elegant London residence is situated in Portland Place, a street in the Marylebone district that was laid out by the brothers Robert and James Adam for the Duke of Portland in the late eighteenth century. In an exterior establishing shot filmed by a second unit, the equestrian statue of field marshal Sir George Stuart White (John Tweed, 1922) is clearly recognizable.[1] The house, which is inhabited by lawyer Anthony Keane (Gregory Peck) and his wife Gay (Ann Todd), has a classical façade and a bright interior characterized by Palladian elements such as classical door cases and cornices, architraves above doors, curved pediments and shellwork in the wall cabinets. A 'Campaign Manual' accompanying the film's re-release in the late 1950s proudly stipulates that "the drawing room in the Keane house is a charming, intimate room, Georgian architecture, with interesting corner cupboards filled with Chinese objects and books. It is furnished with a pair of Queen Anne settees, fine walnut desk, plain carpet, and many books." The dining room is "late Georgian in character, with Adam consoles and chimney piece, and lovely Sheraton chairs, contemporary paintings, and silver."

Facing the front entrance, an elegant, curved, central staircase leads to the bedrooms upstairs, in which several important scenes are situated. According to the same promotion leaflet, the bedroom of Mrs. Keane is "also late Georgian, with a modern tufted headboard, sumptuously draped in damask; the delicacy of the Sheraton marquetry night table is suitable with this." The staircase itself features prominently in the film. In the opening scene, Anthony and Gay meet on the stairs, which Hitchcock also uses to evoke the strain on the marriage brought about by Anthony's obsession with Mrs. Paradine.

The stairwell is visualized by means of a series of long takes and breathtakingly fluid camera movements, two elements of 1940s Hollywood glamor photography that Hitchcock undoubtedly adopted from producer David O. Selznick. While the probing camera followed the actors through long and arduous takes, grips frantically pulled away furniture to make a path.[2] In Selznick's view, however, Hitchcock carried this new aesthetic too far and the producer ordered more conventional retakes or broke up the takes during the editing process. The director would further elaborate the long-take technique in his subsequent pictures *Rope* and *Under Capricorn* made for Transatlantic.

Hitchcock's mobile camera not only cherished the vertical space of the stairwell but also several of the rooms, showing all sides of them, including the ceilings. Selznick International had always matted in its on-screen ceilings through special effects, but for *The Paradine Case* Hitchcock asked that they be constructed. Robert Boyle, the production designer who worked on *Saboteur*, *Shadow of a Doubt*, *North by Northwest*, *The Birds*, and *Marnie*, stated that "cameramen hate ceilings" but that Hitchcock and himself liked to work with them. "I like ceilings," Boyle stated, because that's another dimension to

1 A document entitled "London & Cumberland Locations" (dated 18 May, 1946), containing guidelines for a second unit making location shots, indicates "Backing through Keane's front door on to Portland Place with horse statue in b.g." See Folder 558 *The Paradine Case (misc.)* in the Hitchcock Collection in the Margaret Herrick Library. See also Giblin, *Alfred Hitchcock's London*, 101.

2 Leff, *Hitchcock and Selznick:*, 250. Some of the long takes were shot with the help of "Rosie's Dolly," a new kind of dolly invented by Morris Rosen, head grip for Selznick. See Sheridan, "Three And A Half Minute Take," 305-314.

I   Portland Place (Digital Frame)
II Front door (Digital Frame)
III Hall (Digital Frame)
IV Staircase (Digital Frame)
V   Hall and staircase (Digital Frame)
VI Landing (Digital Frame)

any room. Ceilings are terribly important. Michelangelo recognized that and so did the Pope."[3]

The bill for the scene design of *The Paradine Case*, consequently, exceeded that of Selznick's magnum opus, *Gone with the Wind*, for which Paradine production designer Joseph McMillan Johnson had made sketches as well.[4] For *The Paradine Case*, McMillan Johnson, who would later also design sets for *Rear Window* and *To Catch a Thief*, collaborated with Tom Morahan, who also worked on Hitchcock's *Jamaica Inn* and *Under Capricorn*. In addition, the Keane house sets were decorated by Joseph Platt, who had also been involved in the set design of *Gone with the Wind* and *Rebecca*, and Emile Kuri, whose credits include *Spellbound* and *The Trouble with Harry*. The lavish sets even inspired the publicity department since the already mentioned 'Campaign Manual' states that "the theme of the promotion could be to show how period elements can be artistically imposed in a modern apartment or home background – with the succesful combination of both antique or period furniture and a modern décor. Of course, the displays, etc., would be inspired by the beautiful sets for the $4,000,000 David O. Selznick motion picture production *The Paradine Case*."

In addition, Hitchcock's mobile camera transforms the grand and transparent structure of the house into a space of tension and oppression. As in some other of Hitchcock's 1940s films – *Rebecca, Suspicion, Shadow of a Doubt, Notorious* – the idyll of domestic bliss is shattered.[5] In spite of the white walls, the director managed to create a *noirish* atmosphere by means of *chiaroscuro* lighting. Although Keane says to his wife that "this is a place for you, warm, cozy, protective," the house turns into a place of confinement. By means of various editing and visual strategies, the director invites the viewer to draw parallels, not just contrasts, between the scenes at the Keane home and those at the prison, where Mrs. Paradine is kept in detention.[6] This is developed through the extensive use of imprisonment motifs within the *mise-en-scène* of the Keane home – most notably, the prominent bedroom ceiling, the prison-like bars of a door window, and the shadows of the banisters creating an enveloping cage effect.

3 Robert Boyle in LoBrutto, *By Design*, 14.
4 Leff, *Hitchcock and Selznick*, 236.
5 See Michie, "Unveiling Maternal Desires," 29-54. Michie refers to *Shadow of a Doubt, The Man Who Knew too Much* and *The Paradine Case*.
6 Smith, *Hitchcock*, 80.

I Landing (Digital Frame)
II Drawing room (Digital Frame)
III Drawing room (Still, Royal Film Archive, Brussels)
IV Hall and dining room (Digital Frame)
V Dining room (Digital Frame)
VI Mrs. Keane's bedroom (Digital Frame)
VII Mrs. Keane's bedroom (Still, Royal Film Archive, Brussels)

I II
III IV
V VI
VII

Tropical Classicism:
Minyago Yugilla

Near Sydney,
New South Wales, Australia

Under Capricorn

Color
Transatlantic Pictures
1949

PRODUCTION DESIGN:
Thomas Morahan
SET DRESSER:
Philip Stockford

Ground Floor

1 Hall
2 Dining Room
3 Kitchen
4 Antechamber
5 Drawing Room
6 Porch

Drawing by Linde Vertriest

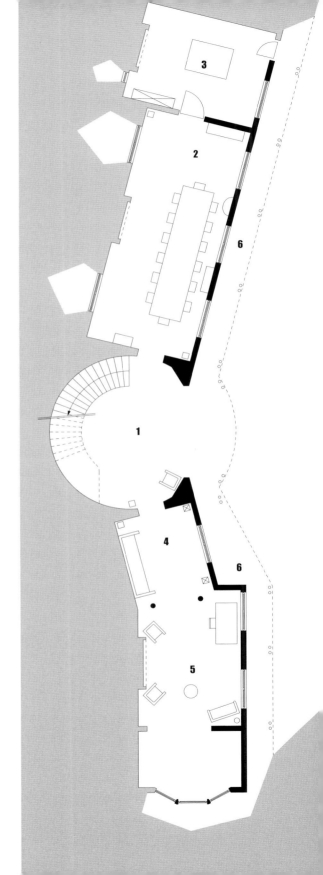

1m

With *Waltzes from Vienna* and *Jamaica Inn*, *Under Capricorn* is one of Hitchcock's rare historical costume dramas. Taking place in New South Wales in 1831, the story required sets that evoke a specific historic context. Two sets in particular should be mentioned. The first one is that of the Sydney palace of the new governor (Cecil Parker): a white neoclassical building marked by a central portico with six Ionic columns carrying a pediment – the pillared front of the Canoga Park Highschool in Los Angeles was used in one of the exterior shots showing the central section of the building.[1] The palace's elegant interior, created in the studio, is extensively explored by the camera in one of the film's impressive long takes. Charles Adare (Michael Wilding), the governor's nephew, visits his uncle. After Charles has crossed the main hall and ascended the staircase, the camera follows him along a second-story corridor, striding through several rooms until he finally reaches a chamber where the governor is sitting in a hip-bath. The camera's movement through an interior reminiscent of John Soane or Robert Adam demonstrates that neoclassicism was the predominant style in the early decades of the new colony. As a matter of fact, the governor of New South Wales owned such a fashionably neo-classical villa in that era.[2] It was designed by Henry Kitchen, a London architect newly arrived in the colony in 1820. It had two large domed rooms and one of these was used as a ball room – in the film, a ball at the governor's palace provides the context for an important scene.

The second impressive set piece of the film is that of Minyago Yugilla, the mansion of Sam Flusky (Joseph Cotton), a so-called 'emancipist,' an ex-convict who is described as a "financial genius" and someone "who made most profitable investments." Back in Ireland, Flusky was the groom of Lady Henrietta 'Hattie' Considine (Ingrid Bergman).

250

1 The Warner Bros. Archives contain a correspondence dated October/November 1948 between the studio and the Los Angeles City Board of Education on that matter.
2 Irwin, *Neoclassicism*, 351-54.
3 Morrison, "Hitchcock's Ireland," 203.

III IV

They fell in love, eloped, and married but were caught up by Hattie's brother, who was about to kill them both. Hattie shot her brother but Flusky took the blame and was convicted. Apart from pointing to the typically Hitchcock theme of the transference of guilt, *Under Capricorn* also deals with tensions in a marriage and its spatial expression, the home, which is also an important theme in *The Manxman*, *Rich and Strange*, *Sabotage*, *Rebecca*, *Mr. and Mrs. Smith*, *Suspicion*, *Notorious*, *The Paradine Case*, *Dial M for Murder*, *The Man Who Knew Too Much*, *The Wrong Man*, and *Marnie*.

In *Under Capricorn*, the domestic drama occurs in Minyago Yugilla, which Charles Adare calls "a handsome establishment" during his first visit. The coachman, however, does not agree and states that there is "something queer about that place." Adhering to the romantic Gothic convention of named houses (as Manderley), the place is already ominous by its name, which means "Why Weepest Thou" in the aboriginal language. Strikingly, although evoking the 'primitive' and pagan Australia, the name refers to the New Testament story of Christ's resurrection, in which an angel appears at Christ's tomb and asks Mary Magdalene "Woman, why weepest thou?" (John: 20:12-13)[3] The architecture too seems a hybrid construction borrowing from a strange combination of sources – something which is typical of idiosyncratic houses built in the colonies. An elongated mansion with a central rounded hall, the Flusky house evokes the Anglo-Palladian tradition, which was very popular in the British Empire and the United States in the early nineteenth century. The exotic portico, the ample use of open loggias, fragile columns, and French doors are also reminiscent of Samuel Sloan's serial production of country houses built in the United States in the 1850s and 1860s. Sloan's houses, based on a central circular or octagonal volume with rectangular extensions, often included

251

I Governor's palace (Digital Frame)
II Governor's palace, hall (Digital Frame)
III, IV Minyago Yugilla, exterior (Digital Frame)

exotic forms drawn from sources as remote as Persia and China.[4] More evidently, Minyago Yugilla also shows vague similarities with early Australian architectural design forms, the first sources of which were the English Georgian farmhouse and the Indian bungalow as interpreted by the British.[5] With its extended portico, Minyago Yugilla acquired one of the key features of British colonial architecture: a verandah, which often extends round three, sometimes all four sides of the house. Taken to Australia from India via England or, more directly, by British army officers in Sydney who had served in India, verandahs supported at their edges by thin wooden columns characterized the homesteads in New South Wales from the 1820s. Minyago Yugilla can be interpreted as a fictitious example of the Australian bungalow, which "achieved a level of sophistication never seen in India."[6]

However, since it is built for a "financial genius," Minyago Yugilla exceeds the bungalow and only combines some of its features with the British Georgian country house. A release campaign leaflet of *Under Capricorn* claims that "it is right to state that the English made their colonial towns as living reflections of their own metropolitan cities. Maybe this is one of the reasons why the director thought it was not necessary to take his entire crew to Australia. However, it is in England and not in the United States that he shot his film, using two properties in the County of Suffolk and surveying with painstaking attention the authenticity of the costumes and props."[7] Minyago Yugilla denotes a kind of 'Britishness' by its unmistakable references to the picturesque country houses designed by John Nash between 1790 and 1815. As some of Nash' buildings, Minyago Yugilla seems to be inspired by an Italianate style based on vernacular buildings in the backgrounds of paintings by Claude – a source recommended by theoreticians of the picturesque such as Richard Payne Knight.[8] Actually, the exterior views of Minyago Yugilla look like Claude paintings themselves: the exteriors are only represented by means of matte shots (and not by miniatures as several authors claim) that show, through the pictorial convention of framing trees, the building bathing in Claudean twilight or a nocturnal blue. Unmistakably, these pictorial light effects have to conceal the artificiality of the matte but, at the same time, they contribute to both the exotic and uncanny atmosphere of the house. At any rate, the picturesque and Anglo-Palladian associations of the architecture are emphatically British – the colonial setting unmistakably serves to emphasize the complex web of British class and gender categories important to the narrative: man versus woman, Irish versus English, white versus aboriginal, aristocracy versus lower class, emancipists versus new colonists, rich versus poor, et cetera.[9]

Several of these social and cultural antagonisms are also dealt with against the backdrop

4 Handlin, *American Architecture*, 95.
5 King, *The Bungalow*, 231.
6 Hesketh, *Architecture of the British Empire*, 194-95.
7 Warner Brothers Belgian release leaflet for *Under Capricorn* in the French language in the Royal Film Archive, Brussels. (Author's translation).
8 Watkin, *English Architec-ture*, 146.
9 Morrison, "Hitchcock's Ireland," 193-210.
10 Walker, *Hitchcock's Motifs*, 272.

of Minyago Yugilla's splendid interiors. The Italianate, cylindrical middle part of the building marks the hall, which is accessible via an exotic porch. The colors that dominate the hall also prevail in the other interiors: light blue walls and white decorations such as fluted Tuscan columns and half columns, simple mouldings, and mantle pieces. On the left side of the hall, there is a small antechamber that contains a wall-sized tapestry. This room, or rather passageway, leads to the elegant semicircular drawing room, which contains a few chairs and a writing desk. Above the mantle piece, in front of which fireside chairs are placed, there's a Claudean landscape showing two dorsal figures before a mirroring lake – it is as if the picturesque setting of the house itself recurs in the paintings it contains.

On the other side of the hall, there is the elegant dining room with burgundy draperies on the windows. A long table occupies the center of the room – the site of the dinner party during which both Charles and the viewer meet the drunk and barefoot Hattie for the first time. Elegant tables and closets are placed along the walls, which are decorated with candleholders and several paintings such as a grisaille tondo showing nudes atop the mantle piece, a picture of a horse, a portrait of a horseman, and several landscapes (one containing a Watteau-esque scene). In short, the paintings show the combination of classical restraint and romantic and picturesque elements that also characterize the architecture – even a genuine Gainsborough landscape painting was used in the film. Pictures taken on the set show Hitchcock and art director Thomas Morahan showing it to visitors.

Across from the connection to the hall, the dining room has a door that leads to the kitchen, which is the site of an important scene that deals with the control over the household. Encouraged by Charles, Hattie reclaims her position as lady of the house from the housekeeper Milly (Margaret Leighton). She throws Milly's whip into the fire and takes command over the clumsy kitchen servants. However, Milly sabotages Hattie's attempts by humiliatingly displaying the signs of Hattie's alcoholism (empty bottles) to the kitchen staff. The power struggle between Hattie and Milly is further elaborated by means of another preeminent domestic and Hitchcockian symbol: the house keys. Milly's status as the figure who runs the Flusky household is explicitly visualized by the house keys, which she wears attached to her belt.[10]

The circular hall itself is dominated by a curved staircase which serves several narrative functions. The stairs are transformed into a catwalk when Hattie appears in her white dress to go to the governor's ball. The positive associations are endorsed by the fact that the staircase gives Hattie a feeling of safety instead of being a site of dramatic conflicts: she grabs "the good old balustrade" when she escapes to her bedroom on the

I · II
III · IV
V · VI
VII · VIII

I Cronkhill, Salop (John Nash, 1802)

II Sandrich Park, Devon (John Nash, 1805)

III Hall (Digital Frame)

IV Hall (Still, Royal Film Archive, Brussels)

V Antechamber (Digital Frame)

VI Antechamber and drawing room (Digital Frame)

VII, VIII, IX Drawing room (Digital Frame)

X, XI Dining room (Digital Frame)

XII Dining room (Still, Royal Film Archive, Brussels)

XIII Hall, stairs (Digital Frame)

XIV Hall, landing (Digital Frame)

second floor. However, as in many Hitchcock films, the staircase leads to an upper level, which is, according to Dennis Zirnite, "the oppressive dominion of a malignant force, of human destructiveness; the 'overseeing' catalyst of moral instability. Typified by deceptive charm, a repressed misogyny, and an exuding seductiveness, this ascendant domain is incarnated by those who unleash the darkest human impulses."[11] In *Under Capricorn*, the sole room on the second floor that is visible to the viewer is Hattie's elegant bedroom, which is the equivalent of the forbidden locked room in many other Gothic Hitchcock stories. Charles flamboyantly enters it through the window while Sam waits outside. Typical of Hitchcock, the bedroom is a site of disturbance: it is the place where Hattie is slowly poisoned by Milly, where she sees phantoms but also 'real' terrors such as a mummified aboriginal head.

Not only its over-all look but also Minyago Yugilla's floor plan shows some similarities with some of the picturesque country houses by John Nash. Varied, compact, with many ground floor windows reaching to floor level so as to make the most of the contact with the outside, Nash's planning anticipates the organic sophistication of Frank Lloyd Wright's so-called prairie houses.[12] Moreover, the integrated, open space also served Hitchcock's impressive long takes that sometimes move from floor to floor, through lengthy corridors and several rooms. In *Under Capricorn*, Hitchcock took the innovative single-take technique of *Rope* a step further and combined it with the dark psychology, Gothic romanticism, and huge mansions that were present in *Rebecca*, *Suspicion*, and *Notorious*. For that purpose, Hitchcock had the Flusky mansion built in the MGM British Studios, near London – some exteriors were shot on the Hollywood back lot of Warner Brothers, the company that distributed the film.[13] The set was designed by Thomas Morahan, who also collaborated on *Jamaica Inn* and *The Paradine Case*, in collaboration with Kenneth McCallum Tait (uncredited). Erected on a specially built studio floor of asphalt, layers of felt, and carpet, which was adapted to smooth and silent dollying in any direction, the set consisted of sections that could slide open electrically to allow giant camera cranes to float through doorways and walls. Cameraman Jack Cardiff, who had served as an operator on *The Skin Game* and had acquired a reputation for the sensual color photography on some Michael Powell & Emeric Pressburger films, attached lights to cranes, dollies, boom mikes, and even crew members to make them mobile enough to light a shot and then get out of the way of the ponderous crane that followed the actors. Cardiff wrote that Hitchcock himself drew every set-up on paper already prepared with frame lines. Another part of the careful preparation was the use of a "large model of the composite set, using scale actors, furniture, and even scale lights. With a perfect minia-

11 Zirnite, "Hitchcock on the Level," 355.
12 Middleton & Watkin, *Neoclassical and 19th Century Architecture*, 49.
13 Cardiff, *Magic Hour*, 108.

I, II, III Hattie's bedroom (Digital Frame)
IV Porch (Digital Frame)
V Jack Cardiff (left) on the set (Set Photograph, British Film Institute)

ture of our crane we mapped out every camera movement exactly, so that at least we knew what we were up against."[14]

The flexibility of the architecture also applied to the furniture. "Tables were slipped away by grips, chairs put into view just as the camera came near you, walls were whipped up in the air," Ingrid Bergman later recalled.[15] Long takes shot by the enormous Technicolorcamera required the dinner table to disintegrate in the middle of a meal. The large Regency table was cut into fourteen divisions laterally and vertically, which came apart when the camera had to pass through. "The start of the scene showed the guests sitting in their places and the table adorned with gastronomic delights," Cardiff later recalled. "Now the camera moved forward, seemingly on an inevitable collision course, but at the last moment, each of the guests fell back on to a mattress clutching his section of the table with all props stuck on it! To have the camera cleave its way through the collapsing guests, falling back like dominoes in rapid succession, was like a surrealistic dream, but it worked."[16] Another impressive set piece was the bed, which "had machinery that enabled it to tilt forward about 45 degrees." "We could thus affectively look 'down' on Bergman," Cardiff wrote, "without going high and tilting our Titan blimp. Miss Bergman performed a remarkable feat in acting and maintaining equipose on a bed which performed silent see-saws!"[17]

Strikingly, the mobile long takes do not exude the apprehension of real space and mobilization that long shot scales do to allow the spectator a greater freedom of observation – a freedom that André Bazin so applauded in the long-take aesthetics that Max Ophüls, William Wyler, and Orson Welles were developing in the 1940s. At times, Hitchcock's long takes do provide a sense of an unobstructed, holistic unity of space. Mostly, however, the long takes evoke spatial disorientation and do not situate the characters in their social context within an integrated space. On the contrary, in Hitchcock's photography of Minyago Yugilla, the characters are isolated and both socially and psychologically disconnected. Whereas Welles tracks in medium and long shots, Hitchcock tracks in medium shot and close-up. In contrast with Gregg Toland's deep focus in the films of Wyler and Welles, which permit the eye to wander within the shot, Cardiff's camera glides through cinematic space without disclosing it. The shallow depth of field, selective focus, and claustrophobic camera distance prevent the spectator's immediate understanding of the cinematic space of the single set. Rather than disclosing the space and its continuity, the camera conceals it. This is also the result of the fact that the mesmerizing long takes seem to serve no purpose. As John Belton noted, "unlike the elaborate cranes in *Young and Innocent* and *Notorious* which voyeuristically search for

14 Cardiff, "The Problems of Lighting and Photographing *Under Capricorn*." See also Hitchcock, "Production Methods Compared;" and Krohn, *Hitchcock at Work*, 108.
15 Ingrid Bergman, quoted in Spoto, *The Art of Alfred Hitchcock*, 176.
16 Cardiff, *Magic Hour*, 105.

17 Cardiff, "The Problems of Lighting and Photographing *Under Capricorn*," 359.
18 Belton, "Alfred Hitchcock's *Under Capricorn*," 373.

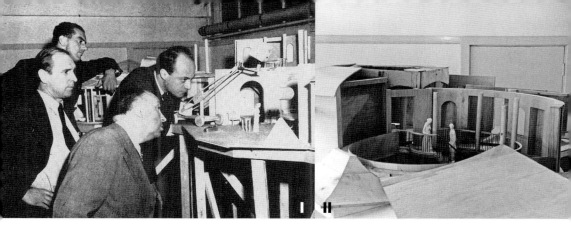

and descend upon crucial objects (the drummer's twitching eye, the key), the camera movements in *Under Capricorn* do not explore space or reveal secrets within it."[18] Indeed, in this *film chouchou* of French critics, the camera glides through space without charting it. However, these apparently aimless camera movements enhance the claustrophobic atmosphere and the feeling of voyeuristic intrusion that accompanies the entire visualization of the Flusky mansion. This is already clear in the way Hitchcock's long takes introduce the spectator, with Adare, to the house. The scene, in which Adare eavesdrops on the Flusky household before announcing himself, identifies Adare as a voyeuristic intruder. The angles and movements of the camera underscore his intrusiveness and convey a sense of violation of a private space. This feeling, however, continues to vibrate throughout all the other scenes set in Minyago Yugilla by the penetrating gaze of the omnipresent camera, which also draws attention to the unconcealed theatricality of the set design and the emphatic artificiality of the house's front.

I Thomas Morahan, Alfred Hitchcock, and Jack Cardiff inspecting a scale model of Minyago Yugilla (*American Cinematographer*, 1949)
II Scale model of Minyago Yugilla: Hall and landing (British Film Institute)

The Oedipal Bedroom: Anthony House

Washington DC Area

Strangers on a Train

Black-and-white
Warner Brothers
1951

ART DIRECTION:
Edward S. Haworth
SET DECORATION:
George James Hopkins

1 Hall
2 Living Room
3 Backroom
4 Landing
5 Corridor
6 Unidentified Room
7 Mr. Anthony's Bedroom

Drawings by
Thomas De Keyser

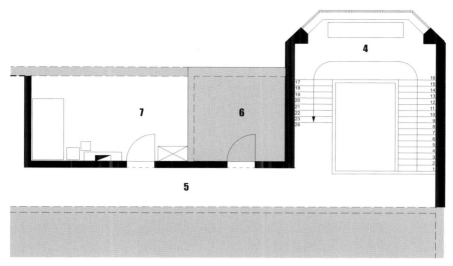

Second Floor

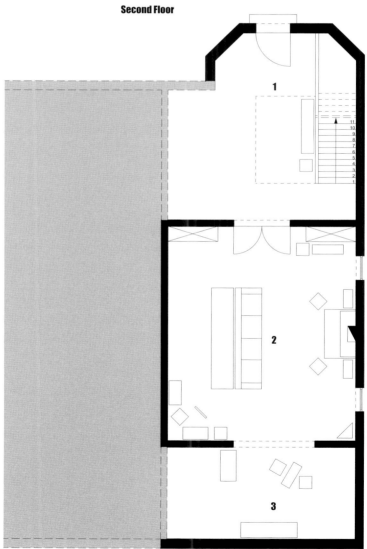

1m

Ground Floor

Filmed in black-and-white by Robert Burks and designed by Edward Hayworth, *Strangers on a Train* is a typical early 1950s Warner Brothers production in the sense that it combines claustrophobic noir sets with out-of-doors action.[1] The action moves restlessly from trains, to exteriors and interiors in Washington DC and Connecticut, to tennis courts and urban monuments, to an amusement park and a stately mansion. Situated in the environs of Washington DC,[2] the mansion belongs to Mr. Anthony (Jonathan Hale) and Mrs. Anthony (Marion Lorne). Typically Hitchcock, domestic space is turned into a site of tensions since their son, Bruno Anthony (Robert Walker), wants to kill his father. After meeting Guy Haines (Farley Granger), a famous tennis player with political aspirations, on the train, Bruno suggests the perfect scheme: They should exchange murders. Bruno is willing to murder Guy's ghastly wife whereas Guy, on his part, would then kill Bruno's father. Guy laughs Bruno off, but Bruno puts his part of the horrifying plan into effect. Then he expects Guy to honor his side of the bargain.

With its asymmetric arrangement of volumes, its mullioned window-walls, prominent chimney, and a steeply pitched, side-gabled roof punctuated by little piancles and dormers with flared eaves, Anthony house is one of the eclectic Tudor houses with stone wall cladding, which were very fashionable in the United States during the 1920s and 1930s.[3] Because this American Tudor style was only loosely based on a variety of early English building traditions, the house resembles the Victorian mansions that play such an important part in other Hitchcock films: Moat House (*Easy Virtue*), Manderley (*Rebecca*), McLaidlaw House (*Suspicion*), and Hindley Hall (*The Paradine Case*). Its stone walls partly covered with ivy and its backside overlooking a vast sloping lawn, which is shown only in moonlight, Anthony house expresses wealth, tradition but also a certain mysterious tension. In his first draft of the screenplay, Raymond Chandler describes it as a "very spacious and expensive looking place, standing in considerable grounds surrounded by a high wall."[4]

This same atmosphere exudes from the Victorian interior, which Chandler evokes as "enormous and loaded with heavy antique furniture, lamps, chairs, tables, what-nots, an enormous grand piano, pictures in gilt frames. It looks pretty nearly Gothic. There is so much dark furniture in the room that although it is a sunny day, the room is dark."[5] Chandler also states that "there is evidence of long established wealth in the heavy dark appointments in this room," which, in the film, comprises high walls covered with wooden wainscotting, a classical mantle-piece, a crystal chandelier, pieces of heavy furniture, large carpets and tapestries, paintings with gilded frames, and side tables with vases,

1 See Heisner, *Hollywood Art*, 146–47.

2 The exact location of the Anthony house is never shown or mentioned in the film. In a story treatment (dated June 20, 1950) by Whitfield Cook, Anthony house is situated on Long Island, whereas the revised treatment and a draft screenplay by Raymond

Chandler (July and August 1950 respectively) mention a series of establishing shots that situate the house in Arlington, Virginia, near Washington DC. See the *Stranger on a Train* production notes, Warner Bros. Archives, USC Cinema and Television Library, Los Angeles.

3 See Virginia & Lee

McAlester, *A Field Guide to American Houses*, 354–71.

4 Raymond Chandler, *Strangers on a Train* (First Draft Screenplay) (August 25, 1950), 18. Warner Brothers Archives.

5 Ibid.

I Bruno's plan (Digital Frame)

II Garden (Digital Frame)

III Garden façade (Digital Frame)

IV Front façade (Digital Frame)

V Living room (Digital Frame)

VI, VII Living room and hall (Digital Frame)

VIII Back room (Digital Frame)

I

II

III

IV

V VI

VII VIII

candlesticks, and table-lamps. In the middle of these paraphernalia of the bourgeois interior, the dandyesque Bruno Anthony has wrapped himself in a showy dressing gown.

As in several others of his film scenes situated in lavish interiors, Hitchcock pays attention to one artwork in particular. In the case of the Anthony house, it is the painting made by Mrs. Anthony, one of Hitchcock's many grotesque mother figures. Unmistakably, the painting, exhibited on an easel in the living room, signifies Mrs. Anthony's unworldliness and weirdness. It is an expressionist rendering of a human face – Hitchcock told Ted Haworth, who just had started his career as an art director, to model the painting on the work of the American expressionist Abraham Rattner.[6] Rattner's and, consequently, Mrs. Anthony's paintings are slightly reminiscent of the work of the French fauvist Georges Rouault. Paintings by this artist were part of Hitchcock's personal collection. Rouault's *La suaire*, which depicts the face of the Redeemer as imprinted in blood on Christ's burial shroud, dominated the foyer of Hitchcock's house on Bellagio Road.[7] When Mrs Anthony claims that it represents St Francis, her son roars with laughter. "That's father all right," Bruno remarks when he looks at the figure with a claw where the right hand would be. Because he sees the painting to represent his father as a king exerting despotic control over his wife and son, the portrait can be compared with other father portraits in Hitchcock's œuvre, which are representative of the patriarchal order, such as the portrait of General McLaidlaw (*Suspicion*) or that of Mr. Brenner (*The Birds*).[8]

The architecture of the Anthony house is also interesting because its floor plan advances the plot. Bruno has drawn a plan of the house and sent it, with the front door key, to Guy to enable him to enter the house and find his way to the room of Bruno's father. To get to Mr. Anthony's bedroom, Guy has to shine his flashlight on the drawing. Then, he has to climb the staircase, which is situated just besides the entrance. Photographed beautifully by Warner Brothers cameraman Robert Burks, who would provide the camerawork for most Hitchcock films of the 1950s and early 1960s, it is one of Hitchcock's most memorable staircase scenes. First, Guy has to confront a Great Dane on the landing. Only dangerous in appearance, the dog benignly licks his hand. Instead of leading to the bedroom of a mysterious and absent woman (*Rebecca*, *The Paradine Case*), the Anthony house staircase leads to the bedroom of the father. However, when Guy enters the room and switches on the light, he finds Bruno instead of his father in the bed. Although Bruno is still dressed in dinner jacket, the gay subtext is plain enough, as is the case in several other scenes in this film: the map Bruno provided has served to guide Guy, Bruno's object of desire, to Bruno himself, waiting in bed.[9]

6 Krohn, *Hitchcock at Work*, 119.
7 McGilligan, *Alfred Hitchcock*, 476.
8 See Peucker, "The Cut of Representation," 146.
9 See Walker, *Hitchcock's Motifs*, 62.

I Painting by Mrs. Anthony (Digital Frame)
II Hall and living room (Digital Frame)
III Landing (Digital Frame)
IV Landing (Still, Royal Film Archive, Brussels)
V Mr. Anthony's bedroom (Digital Frame)

Long-Take Architecture:
Brandon-Phillip Penthouse

54th Street/1st Avenue,
Manhattan, New York

Rope

Color
Transatlantic Pictures
1948

ART DIRECTION:
Perry Ferguson
SET DECORATION:
Emile Kuri
Howard Bristol

Drawing by Linde Vertriest

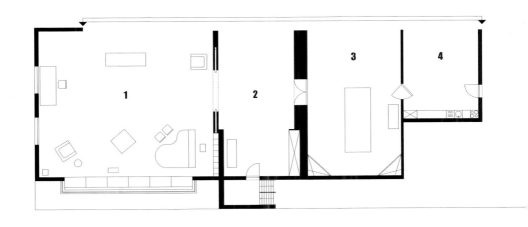

1m

This Midtown Manhattan penthouse is situated in an affluent neighborhood where, since the late 1920s, modern apartment houses were built for a metropolitan upper-class savoring low-key luxury.[1] Its inhabitants, Brandon (John Dall) and Phillip (Farley Granger), are two young bachelors who strangle a college friend, David Kentley (Dick Hogan), just for the thrill of it. The two Nietzschean dandies conceal their friend's body in a chest in their living room in which his father (Cedric Hardwicke) and Janet, his fiancée (Joan Chandler), are invited to a cocktail party. Also present at the party are Mrs. Atwater (Constance Collier), David's aunt, and Kenneth (Douglas Dick), Janet's ex-lover. From the chest's lid, Brandon and Phillip calmly serve a buffet dinner to the dissatisfaction of Mrs. Wilson (Edith Evanson), the talkative maid, who complains about their unsetting her dinner table. Eventually, David's body is discovered by another guest at the party, Rupert Cadell (James Stewart), the former college professor of both the victim and the murderers.

After an opening view of the street, the entire story is situated inside the apartment that consists of a living room dominated by a panoramic window, a hallway, a dining room, and a kitchen. There are no indications about the whereabouts of bathroom and bedrooms. This omission is telling since the viewer sees the other spaces of the apartment in meticulous detail. Undoubtedly, this is because Brandon and Phillip are probably gay lovers and the presence of a bedroom would dramatize their sexuality.[2] However, the presence of a bedroom is implied in the narrative but never actually shown: Mrs. Wilson points the way to the telephone to Mrs. Atwater as "down the hall to your left, dear, the first bedroom" – so, there is a second, we may assume. To make a telephone call, Mr. Kentley, Janet, and Mrs. Atwater go all to this bedroom, which must be situated opposite the entrance of the apartment.

Sharing a bedroom or not, Brandon and Phillip are eccentrics and the penthouse and its furnishings emphasize their sophisticated but eccentric taste. Unmistakably, they answer to the typical penthouse-dweller as depicted in Hollywood movies: wealthy, well educated, and unsentimental.[3] Since chic penthouses were associated with the rich and because they are inaccessible to most urbanites, movies were particularly attracted to penthouses – *Penthouse*, in fact, was even the title of a 1933 film directed by W.S. Van Dyke and starring Warner Baxter and Myrna Loy. From the early 1930s onwards, the building type developed into an obligatory component of Hollywood's 'modern mystique' that also included Art Deco executive offices, nightclubs, hotels, and ocean liners.[4] More than the mansion, the penthouse became the quintessential residence of the rich and powerful and it drew its mystique from the verticality that was New York's special trademark.[5] Both popular songs and films presented penthouses as

268

1 See Stern, Gilmartin, and Mellins, *New York 1930*, 367; and Willensky & White, *AIA Guide to New York City*, 258 and 286.
2 See Kehr, "Hitch's Riddle," 9-18.
3 Rosa, "Burning Down the House," 160-61.
4 See Albrecht, *Designing Dreams*.
5 Sanders, *Celluloid Skyline*, 245-46.

I Street view from the apartment (Digital Frame)

II, III, IV, V Living room (Still, Royal Film Archive, Brussels)

VI Neon sign (Digital Frame)

secluded love nests removed from the turmoil of the city or lofty retreats in which personal dream worlds could be created.[6] Penthouses became a standard for an elegant, modern, metropolitan way of life. A product of the skyscraper building boom, the penthouse also opened itself visually to the metropolis by means of great banks of windows. New building methods and the feasibility of glass panes allowed spectacular, uninterrupted views of the city such as the one visible through the panoramic window in the apartment of Phillip and Brandon. Their penthouse offers a breathtaking view of Manhattan including some of its landmarks such as the Empire State Building, St Patrick's Cathedral, the Waldorf Astoria Hotel, Radio City, the Chrysler Building, the City Bank Farmers Trust Building, and the Woolworth Building.

The eccentric and refined as well as decadent lifestyle of the penthouse's inhabitants is accentuated by depicting the apartment as a temple of fine arts. Phillip plays a grand piano, which is prominently placed near the panoramic window. Brandon collects paintings and, clearly, favors modern art – a conventional token of suspect figures in 1940s Hollywood that also recurs in the houses of other Hitchcock dandies such as Johnnie Aysgarth (*Suspicion*) and Jonathan Cooper (*Stage Fright*). Early versions of the script contained – eventually deleted – derogatory references to Mondrian's paintings. A post-Cubist painting of a seated woman adorns one of the walls of the dining room. A small painting in the living room is referred to as the work of "a young American primitive," whereas the painting in between the two windows on the opposite wall is a work by the Cuban modernist Fidelio Ponce de Léon. Hitchcock himself acquired this 1941 painting just before the film was shot, and had it displayed in his own living room.[7] However, the art foregrounded in *Rope* is literature: Rupert is a publisher of philosophy books, Janet writes for a magazine called *Allure*, and Mr. Kentley is a bibliophile who collects rare first editions. What's more, several walls of the apartment have bookshelves and books are also Phillip's and Brandon's pretext for their morbid party. Through their insistent association with crime, books become agents of death. In *Rope*, the pursuit of a sterile bookishness is associated with the act of murder.[8] Murder, however, both Brandon and Rupert admit, "can be an art too." Reminiscent of Thomas De Quincey's *Murder Considered as One of the Fine Arts*, Phillip's and Brandon's crime only comes out right amidst their music, painting, and literature.[9]

The presence of modern art and the striking modernity of the wall-sized window contrasts with the apartment's interior, which is decorated with heavy moldings around the doors. The dark wood panneling in the dining room, the painted balustrade motif

6 Stern, Gilmartin, and Mellins, *New York 1930*, 89.
7 Bondil-Poupard, "Alfred Hitchcock: An Artist in Spite of Himself," 181.
8 See Kehr, "Hitch's Riddle," 9–18; Cohen, *Alfred Hitchcock: The Legacy of Victorianism*, 91; and Spoto, *The Art of Alfred Hitchcock*, 168.
9 According to Peter Wollen, De Quincey's text was important to Hitchcock's work in general and a direct inspiration for films such as *Rope*. See Wollen, "*Rope*: Three Hypotheses," 83.

I Living room, view toward hall, dining room, and kitchen (Digital Frame)

II Hall (Digital Frame)

III Dining room (Digital Frame)

IV Dining room and kitchen (Digital Frame)

V Painting by "a young American primitive" (Digital Frame)

VI Painting by Fidelio Ponce de León (Digital Frame)

on the hallway's wall, the rather heavy imitation antique furniture, the numerous table lamps, statuettes, candelabra, and excessive flower arrangements indicate a rather conservative bourgeois taste. In a white and transparent modernist interior, the chest concealing the body of the murder victim would be too much out of place. Juhani Pallasmaa has noted that the chest is not only a neutral storage place but also a buffet table and that it functions, on a symbolical level, as a coffin, sacrificial altar, sarcophagus, stage of black magic, and table for the Last Supper.[10] Despite the glass wall, the penthouse is turned into a Hitchcockian claustrophobic interior. The window, in fact, provides the only escape to the public realm and it emphasizes both the intimacy and confinement of the interior. Presented as a public space that functions as a theatrical setting for a game of cat and mouse, Brandon and Phillip turn their home into a trap: first for David, their victim, then for themselves. In several ways, Hitchcock even sets their confining penthouse against another home: the Kentley home, which, although it is never shown, becomes more and more insistently present through Mr. Kentley's calls to his wife about David's failure to return home.[11]

This feeling of confinement and claustrophobia is also achieved through the spectacular use of a single set. Similar to *Dial M for Murder* and *Rear Window*, *Rope* is exclusively situated in a closed apartment recreated in the studio. However, *Rope*, no doubt, is the most remarkable of Hitchcock's single-set films because its spatial confinement is connected to a supposedly single take. Taking place roughly in real time between 7.30 and 9.15 in the evening, the film seems to be made without cutting with a continuously traveling camera – at least, that is the suggestion that Hitchcock created by means of ten-minute takes, the length of a film roll in a camera magazine, and by concealing the inescapable cuts by close-ups of dark surfaces (the back of a jacket, the lid of the chest), which enabled Hitchcock and his crew to change the reel. However, as many commentators have noted, only few of the takes last ten minutes and there are visible cuts in the film.[12] In addition, as André Bazin remarked and Hitchcock himself admitted, despite the use of long takes, the mobility of the camera and the movement of the players more or less closely followed conventional Hollywood cutting practice.[13] Hitchcock maintained the rule, for instance, of varying the size of the image in relation to its emotional importance. At any rate, the film's unbearable sense of claustrophobia unmistakably results from both its extended takes and the increasing restriction of the camera's movement – from free movement between the different apartment rooms, to restricted movement within the confines of the living room, and then the scarcely moving camera in the final minutes of the film.[14]

10 Pallasmaa, *The Architecture of the Image*, 57.
11 Leitch, *Find the Director and Other Hitchcock Games*, 140.
12 See, for instance, Bauso, "*Rope*: Hitchcock's Unkindest Cut;" Hemmeter, "Twisted Writing; and Wollen, "*Rope*: Three Hypotheses," 77-78.
13 Bazin, *What Is Cinema?*,

11, 76; Truffaut, *Hitchcock*, 180.
14 Perkins, "Rope," 12.

I Set Photograph (Royal Film Archive, Brussels)
II Set with wild walls (Royal Film Archive, Brussels)

In so doing, Hitchcock even entrapped the audience and made it complicit in the murder. Furthermore, by rejecting cross-cutting, Hitchcock tied the audience closer to the camera's perspective. As a result, he constructed a screen space that seemed to contain both the drama and the audience.[15] Hence, his self-imposed restrictions, which contradicted his earlier ideas on montage, had several implications for the film's cinematic space. In addition, both the unconventional cinematic space and complex camera movements required original procedures in the design and construction of the set.[16] This task was assigned to Perry Ferguson, who had been the principal art director for Orson Welles' *Citizen Kane* (1941) and had done sets for several Sam Goldwyn productions in the 1940s. The film was shot in the Warner Brothers studio where a special floor was constructed that consisted of tongue-and-groove lumber covered with layers of soundproof celotex, carpet, and felt. This extra floor assured that there would be no creaking as the heavy Technicolor camera, which was mounted on a special dolly invented by camera operator Morris Rosen, passed over free of any tracks. The intricate movements of both the actors and the camera were carefully planned out by Ferguson, editor William Ziegler, and cinematographers Edward Fitzgerald, Paul G. Hill, Richard Emmons, and Morris Rosen. For this purpose, Ziegler, who exceptionally had to edit the film before it was actually shot, rearranged the rooms of his daughter's doll house and used chess men as actors. Hitchcock worked out every movement of the camera and the actors on a blackboard "with a football skull practice."[17] On the set, the entire floor area was subdivided into one-foot squares, marked in chalk and numbered. In addition, numbered circles tacked to the floor indicated positions of actors and the camera so that in the event of retakes the filmmakers could go back to the exact spot.

In order to roll a camera back and forth in a four-room penthouse for ten minutes without a halt, Hitchcock needed what he called a "collapsible" apartment. The basic element was a series of wild walls hung from heavily greased overhead U-tracks so that grips could pull them silently out of the camera's way as it followed the actors through doors, then roll them back into position before they came back into camera range. All of the furniture was wild as well. Tables, chairs, and the massive wooden chest containing the corpse were on wheels and were pulled away by prop men as the camera swung through the apartment. Every plate, dish, and drinking glass had to be moved on cue as well. In a 1948 interview, Hitchcock emphasized the almost surreal situations resulting from the dynamic and ephemeral architecture: "Once, (…) Joan Chandler, who played the feminine lead, had to put her wine glass down on a table. But the table was gone. Joan merely put the glass down where the table should have been, one of the crouching prop men (unseen by the camera, of course) raised his hand and Joan's glass found a

15 See Kehr, "Hitch's Riddle," 10; and Hemmeter, "Twisted Writing," 263.
16 On the construction of the set of *Rope*, the most important sources are Hitchcock, "My Most Exciting Picture;" Yates, "*Rope* Sets a Precedent;" and Turner, "*Rope*: Something Different."
17 Hitchcock, "My Most Exciting Picture," 276.

I Building the Manhattan skyline (Warner Brothers Release Leaflet)
II Studying camera movements on blackboard and with a scale model of the set
(*American Cinematographer*, 1948)

resting place in it. Another time, an actor had to reach for a plate off the unseen table. Again, a prop man moved in, handed the actor a plate, and the action went on."[18]

From the outset, it was clear that such a complex and sophisticated set demanded more than the customary painted backdrop or process shots to show Manhattan as it appears through the window – particularly because the passage of time from late afternoon to night required changing light and cloud formations. Since the importance of this effect to a story being told in 'real time' was crucial, the penthouse was surrounded by a spectacular miniature New York skyline, laid out on an eighty-foot semicircle. The closer 'buildings' in this semicircular cyclorama where three-dimensional whereas most structures were photographs printed up to scale in forced perspective and mounted on shallow cut-outs, rendered on only two sides. Several buildings were equipped with steam pipes to feed 'smoke' through chimneys and stacks. To slow down the smoke that, at normal speed, would have instantly given away the reduced size of the buildings, dry ice was added to chill the vapor. To provide a convincing transition from day to night, each building was individually wired and connected to a 'light organ' that allowed for the gradual activation of the skyline's thousands of lights and hundreds of neon signs. Meanwhile, spun-glass clouds were shifted by technicians from left to right during moments when the camera turned away from the window.

Hitchcock attached a lot of importance to the atmospheric shifts in the cityscape seen through the penthouse's window. A Griffith Observatory meteorologist was called in to authenticate their resemblance to New York's actual cumulus clouds. In addition, Hitchcock sent photographers to three locations to photograph the setting sun at five minutes intervals after being displeased with a first version of the sunset, which was treated in conventional movie style with an abundance of red-orange light. As a result of this, *Rope* became Hitchcock's first color picture since color denoted the change in time of day from sunset to darkness which was of vital importance to the narrative. The gradual darkness not only increased the sense of isolation, confinement and claustrophobia, it also allowed Hitchcock, a decade prior to *Vertigo*, to experiment with the expressive possibilities of urban neon light. After sunset, unnatural colors intrude the apartment and the confines of the single set through a full scale neon sign spelling out 'Storage' in red, blue, and green near the windows in the side wall. The garish neon sign – its proximity to such an elegant penthouse, no doubt, violating New York's zoning laws – begins flashing just at the climax of the movie, when the murderers are revealed. In the end, the man at the light organ had played, in Hitchcock's words, "a nocturnal Manhattan symphony in light."[19]

18 Ibid., 281.
19 Ibid., 278.
20 Ibid., 275.
21 Pallasmaa, *The Architecture of the Image*, 54-55.
22 Kehr, "Hitch's Riddle," 11.

In short, *Rope*'s set was a virtuoso stage machine – Hitchcock said that shooting the film was "like unpuzzling a Rube Goldberg drawing."[20] Pallasmaa compares the sophisticated set to famous modern mechanized dwellings with dynamic and flexible components such as Pierre Chareau's *Maison de verre* (1929) with its mobile units, Angelo Invernizzi's and Ettore Fagiuli's *Girasole* (1935) that revolves on wheels along a circular railway tracks to follow the course of the sun, or the mechanized homes of Archigram in the 1960s.[21] In any case, the spatial set-up of *Rope* is that of a Chinese-box confinement: through the single-take, the audience is captivated in a cinematic space created in a sound studio, inside of which is a artificial cyclorama of the New York skyline, inside of which is an oppressively close apartment set, inside of which is a wooden chest, inside of which is a corpse.[22]

Architecture of the Gaze: Jeffries Apartment & Courtyard

West 10th Street,
Greenwich Village, New York

Rear Window

Color
Paramount
1954

ART DIRECTION:
Hal Pereira
Joseph MacMillan Johnson
SET DECORATION:
Sam Comer
Ray Moyer

1 Restaurant
2 Street
3 Alley
4 Courtyard
5 Apartment Miss Lonely-
  hearts
6 Corridor
7 Apartment Sculptress
8 Apartment Miss Torso
9 Thorwald Apartment

Drawings by David Claus

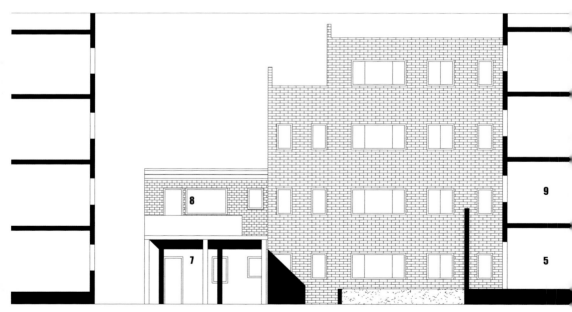

Section

1m

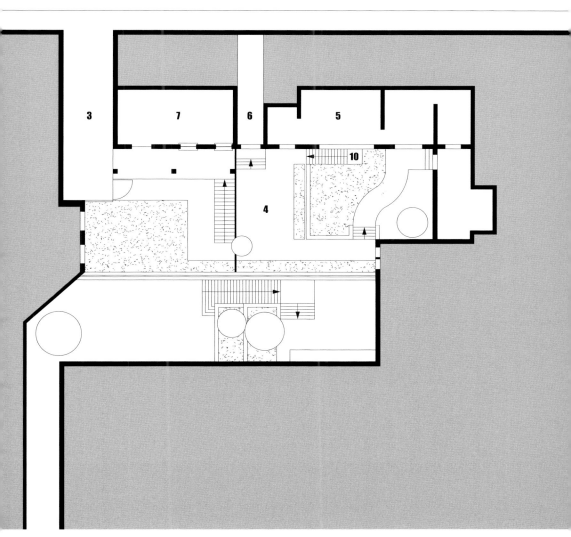

Ground Floor

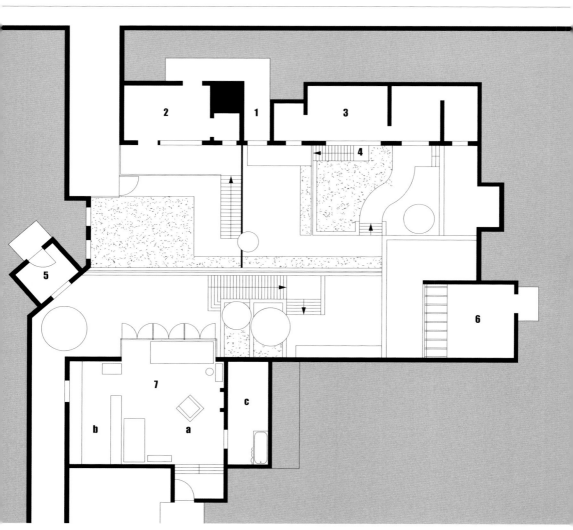

Second Floor

1 Corridor
2 Apartment Miss Torso
3 Thorwald Apartment
4 Balcony with Fire Escape
5 Apartment Newlyweds

6 Apartment Composer
7 Jeffries' Apartment
a Living Room
b Kitchen
c Bathroom

*Drawings and photo
montage by David Claus*

1m

This apartment is a smallish studio with the kitchen hidden from view by a bookshelf. The only interior door, apart from the entrance, is the one of the bathroom, of which the inside is never seen in detail. It is not clear whether there is a separate bedroom. The big window looks out unto a courtyard, enclosed by the rear walls of a three-story apartment building in a vernacular 'Federal Brick' style. Only one narrow alleyway leads to a parallel street. The apartment itself is situated on 10th Street, just east of Hudson Street, Manhattan. As Donald Spoto and Juhani Pallasmaa among other commentators have argued, its location can be deduced from the address mentioned of the apartment on the other side of the courtyard: 125 West 9th Street.[1] Because American law required that a film crime was not situated at an existing place, the address is fictitious: in reality, 9th Street changes into Christopher Street west from 6th Avenue. However, at 125 Christopher Street, the building was situated that inspired Hitchcock, who, according to a Paramount Advance Campaign document, "dispatched four photographers to that colorful section of New York with instructions to shoot the Village from all angles, in all weather and under all lighting conditions, from dawn to midnight."[2]

The 10th Street apartment is the residence of L.B. Jeffries (James Stewart), who is confined to his wheelchair due to a leg fracture. Killing time by watching his neighbors through a rear window, his attention is drawn in particular by Lars Thorwald (Raymond Burr), who murdered his wife – at least, this is Jeffries' interpretation of a series of incidents he witnessed: the disappearance of Thorwald's bedridden and nagging wife; Thorwald inspecting her personal belongings such as a purse and wedding ring that are still in the apartment; Thorwald cleaning a butcher knife and bathroom tiles; Thorwald leaving the apartment with a big suitcase in the middle of the night; etcetera.

The protagonist of *Rear Window*, a film dealing with voyeurism, is even a professional voyeur: a photojournalist accustomed to nosing into other people's affairs and owning an arsenal of professional viewing devices (binoculars, telephoto lens) he eagerly deploys to spy on his neighbors. Precisely because of its voyeuristic theme, its tension between watching and being watched, and its outspoken attention to optic instruments, *Rear Window* has been repeatedly seen as an allegory of the gaze and the cinematic apparatus.[3] Hitchcock himself described the film's plot as "the purest expression of a cinematic idea" and as a meditation on the famous Kuleshov effect.[4] The film's protagonist is almost a hybrid creature: half man half camera, he even comes with his own tracking apparatus[5] – a few years later, cameraman Raoul Coutard would famously use a wheelchair for the tracking shots in Jean-Luc Godard's *A bout de souffle* (1959).

Revealing himself in earlier films as a master of point-of-view editing, Hitchcock presented *Rear Window* as a film in which the subjective point of view dominates

1 Spoto, *The Art of Alfred Hitchcock*, 217; Pallasmaa, *The Architecture of the Image*, 145.
2 "Rear Window: Paramount Advance Campaign," document in the Royal Film Archive Brussels. See also the correspondence and documents in the Paramount Files 14 and 17 on *Rear Window*,

Margaret Merrick Library, Los Angeles. See also Curtis, "The Making of *Rear Window*," 29.
3 Douchet, "Hitch et son public;" Stam & Pearson, "Hitchcock's *Rear Window*;" Harris, "*Rear Window* and *Blow-Up*;" and Sharff, *The Art of Looking in Hitchcock's Rear Window*.

4 Truffaut, *Hitchcock*, 214-16.
5 Kehr, "Hitch's Riddle," 12.

1.11 Courtyard (Set Photograph, Royal Film Archive, Brussels)

10331-2/28

(though not to an absolute degree). This resulted in a very specific topography. Since distance is important to the plot, we seldom get close to the characters on the other side of the courtyard. Furthermore, the predominantly fixed viewpoint implies an important spatial restriction: the film takes place in a single, but gigantic and diversified set that represents a Greenwich Village block comprising 31 apartments. Based on the hundreds of photographs and sound recordings obtained by the party exploring the neighborhood, the $100,000 set was designed by Paramount unit art director Joseph MacMillan Johnson under the supervision of Hal Pereira, head of Paramount's art department. For months, Hitchcock, Pereira, and MacMillan Johnson did nothing but plan the design of what was to become the largest indoor set ever built at Paramount. Hitchcock himself superintended the huge and complex construction that took six weeks to set up. The entire set was fit with a sophisticated drainage system for the rain scene and with

6 Krohn, *Hitchcock at Work*, 141.
7 Ibid. See also Gavin, "Rear Window;" and Atkinson, "Hitchcock's Techniques Tell *Rear Window* Story."

Hitchcock and cameraman Robert Burks in Jeffries' apartment (Set Photograph, Royal Film Archive, Brussels)

an ingenious wiring mechanism for the highly complex lighting of day and night scenes in both the exterior of the courtyard and the interiors of the apartments. The earlier mentioned Paramount Advance Campaign document proudly displayed an impressive collection of statistical data: The set "consumed 25,000 man-hours. It used 175,000 board-feet of lumber, 200 sacks of plaster, 750 gallons of paint, and 12 tons of structural steel for flooring and for eye-beams from which to hang balconies. Steel was also used for roof vents, down-spouts, chimneys and fire-escapes, all of which were 'practical', which is the film term for usable, as opposed to plainly ornamental. More than 20,000 square feet of imitation brick was cast-staff, in a new method introduced solely for this film."

However, the set was not only a huge piece of machinery, it also contained numerous well-considered details. Since about a dozen of the apartments play a role in the story line and because the camera peeked into the interiors by means of giant booms, they were upholstered or furnished extensively by Sam Comer and Ray Moyer to match the character of their occupants. A publicity handout announced that New York designer Grace Sprague (uncredited) had been hired to work out "visualizations" of the apartments as well as sketching "the kind of costumes needed for the actors working in them."[6] An unsigned Paramount memo further states that "Hitchcock feels due to the fact that he will be jumping around in the various apartments so much that the color of the background walls within the apartments, as well as color of wardrobe, will help orient the audience quicker than anything."[7] Such a meticulous attention to details gave the set its realist but also its uncanny look: a feeling of threat and danger gradually penetrates into an everyday and familiar environment. "This movie could never have been accomplished on location with the same dramatic impact," Pereira assured.

The careful attention to details already characterizes the impressive camera movement that opens the film and immediately evokes the claustrophobic atmosphere of the courtyard. In the first place, this crane shot serves as a classical establishing shot that gives the spectator an understanding of the architectural organization of the situation and of the spatial relations between the different places important to the narrative. During the long take, the camera rises and descends, slows down and accelerates slightly: from the very beginning, specific areas of the set are emphasized. However, after plunging through the window into the courtyard, the camera returns to the interior of Jeffries' apartment and explores his belongings. It is a perfect illustration of Hitchcock's visual way of storytelling: gliding past a broken camera, a snapshot of a racecar accident, war pictures, all kinds of photographic equipment, and stacks of illustrated journals successively, the shot gives us a lot of information on the inhabitant without any dialogue or voice-over. In a general study on art direction, the opening scene of *Rear Window* is described as "a good example of production design which, with the help of art works and props, presents a story (narration) – not only supporting it, furthering and interpreting it but actually telling it."[8]

The theme of voyeurism combined with the spatial confinements of a single set turns the architectural construction of *Rear Window* into a magisterial viewing device. The architecture becomes an instrument of the gaze, a kind of *camera obscura* on an urban scale. First and foremost, Hitchcock's presents the architecture as a tool of the scopic drive by emphasizing the window, which, as the film's title suggests, is also the veritable subject of the film. Unmistakably, he presents the window as a metaphor for the film screen. In *Rear Window*, the window has become a cinematic equivalent of the old pictorial metaphor that dates back to the Renaissance, when the Italian architect and art theoretician Leone Battista Alberti defined painting, in his *De Pictura* (1435), as a window onto the world. Instead of a flat surface that is being looked *at*, the painting is a frame that is looked *through*. This concept, which is often visualized in the countless illustrations of so-called perspective machines of the fifteenth and sixteenth centuries, demonstrates that the visual understanding and the optical domination of the world is dependent on the construction of a frame situated between the world and its beholder.

Not coincidentally, the image of the window, which serves as the opening credits of *Rear Window*, is an important architectural motif in Hitchcock's entire œuvre. *The Lady Vanishes*, *Shadow of a Doubt*, *Rope*, *I Confess*, and *Psycho*, as well, start with the image of a window that marks the transition from an urban exterior to the seclusion of an interior. In contrast with these films, the trajectory in *Rear Window* is made from inside to outside: by means of an impressive dolly shot, we plunge through the window, then slide, from right to left, along the façades of the courtyard and, eventually, end up inside Jeffries' apartment back again.

Not only the window of Jeffries' flat functions as a film screen, each window on the other side of the courtyard does as well – the proportions of these windows even match perfectly the aspect ratio (1.66:1) of the film. Viewed across the courtyard, the characters seem just real enough, something half-remembered, like the images on a cinema screen.[9] The façade on the other side is like a movie library. Each window, each film, answers to specific generic conventions: a comedy of newly-weds during their turbulent honeymoon, a musical comedy with the eligible dancer Miss Torso, a melodrama of a woman nicknamed Miss Lonelyhearts, a biopic of a young composer of popular songs, and, of course, the Hitchcockian murder mystery in Thorwald's flat. In addition, the film offers a view of some other residents of the building, such as the couple with the little dog that

8 Lüdi & Lüdi, *Movie Worlds*, 20.

9 Brougher, "Hitch-Hiking in Dreamscapes," 8.

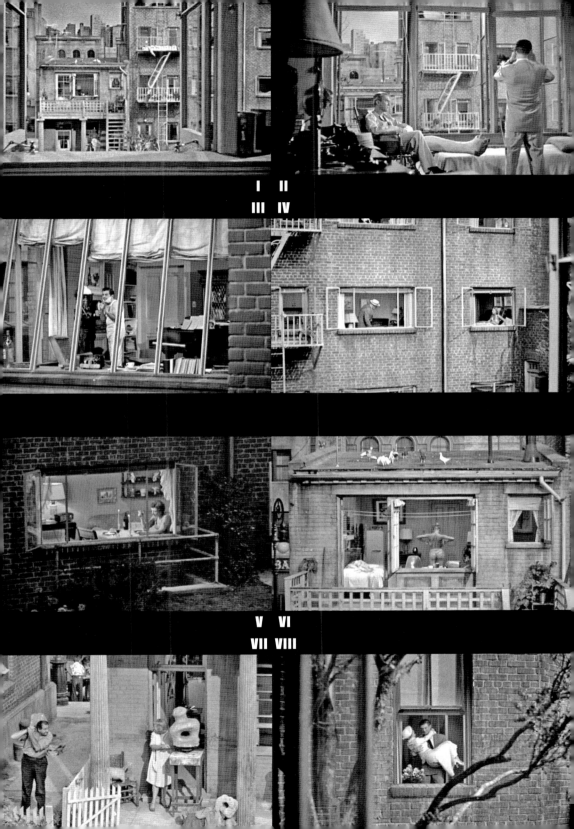

I   II
III   IV

V   VI
VII   VIII

sleeps on the escape ladder and the woman who makes abstract sculptures. This last character alludes, together with the composer, dancer, and photographer, to the different senses but also to the fact that the story is situated in a neighborhood that is a perfect biotope for the fine arts.

Given this perspective, *Rear Window* contains a series of films into one single film. Each window offers a view to a singular picture and the entire courtyard is a kind of urban equivalent of a cable television mosaic with Jeffries (as well as the spectator) zapping between channels. Strikingly, each film deals with love or marriage: the lonely woman waiting for prince to come, the newly-weds making love all the time, the dancer desired by many men, the childless couple that adore their little dog, the couple that quarrels until the wife gets murdered, and, last but not least, Jeffries who is unwilling to marry his ravishing fiancée Lisa Freemont (Grace Kelly). As critics such as Robin Wood have noted, all windows, in short, represent alternative scenarios for Jeffries' own life.[10] The windows on the other side of the courtyard are also cinematic screens of desire and the events become the gratification of the voyeuristic longings of both Jeffries and the spectator.

Since the windows on the other side of the courtyard function primarily as screens, the rooms behind them are squashed. The reconstruction drawing of the floor plan indicates that the flats across the courtyard are narrower than Jeffries' apartment. Thorwald's apartment and the one underneath (occupied by 'Miss Lonelyhearts') and above (by the couple with the dog) only connect to the hallway. They seem to be so-called 'railroad apartments' which are quite common in New York brownstone apartment buildings. Similar in design to a railway car, such an apartments comprise a series of rooms, connecting to each other in a line. Often, there is no adjacent hallway, such that in order to move from the first to the third room, one must cross the second. Of course, such one-sided apartments with flattened spaces posited linearly next to one another are perfectly suited to the plot. In so doing, the rooms are arranged parallel to the range of vision of both Jeffries and the spectator.

Because the architecture is subjected to the gaze, the entire building shows several similarities with building types that serve as perspectival machines such as the theater and the panopticon. The space of *Rear Window* can be considered a theatrical or scenographic device because the story depends on the repression of the fourth side of the city block. Although, as Michel Chion has noted, this fourth side is briefly exposed, the dominant point of view makes us forget that there may be on Jeffries' side of the block other apartments from which one can see just as well and perhaps even better what goes on in

28

10 Wood, *Hitchcock's Films Revisited*, 100-107.

I   Jeffries' broken camera (Digital Frame)
II View toward kitchen (Digital Frame)
III Lisa in Jeffries' flat (entrance door) (Digital Frame)
IV Jeffries' flat (door to bathroom on the right) (Digital Frame)
V   Lisa entering Jeffries' bathroom (Digital Frame)
VI "The show's over for tonight." (Digital Frame)

Thorwald's place.[11] Furthermore, the image Jeffries is watching from his theater seat resembles the archetypical stage set: Jeffries' rear window offers a view of the city, which was also the stage image of the earliest examples of modern theater architecture in the sixteenth century. The modern Renaissance theater building does not only incorporate all kinds of urban architectural fragments (windows, balconies, balustrades, stairs, etcetera) in its decorative scheme, the stage itself represented invariably an urban street in shortened perspective. With their perspectival vistas of the city, both Vincenzo Scamozzi's design for the permanent stage of Andrea Palladio's *Teatro Olympico* in Vicenza (1584) and Sebastiano Serlio's famous drawings of a tragic and comic scene illustrate that the origins of the modern theater coincides with those of modern urban

290

Margeret Merrick Library, Los Angeles. See also Curtis, "The Making of *Rear Window*," 29.

3 Douchet, "Hitch et son public;" Stam & Pearson, "Hitchcock's *Rear Window*;" Harris, "*Rear Window* and *Blow-Up*;" and Sharff, *The Art of Looking in Hitchcock's Rear Window.*

4 Truffaut, *Hitchcock*, 214-16.
5 Kehr, "Hitch's Riddle," 12.

6 Krohn, *Hitchcock at Work*, 141.
7 Ibid. See also Gavin, "Rear Window;" and Atkinson, "Hitchcock's Techniques Tell *Rear Window* Story."

Scena tragica, *Sette libri dell' architettura* (Sebastiano Serlio, 1545)

planning – both are disciplines subjecting space to the gaze and to the new logic of geometric perspective.

Since Hitchcock, as opposed to most other Hollywood directors, had a sound grasp of the optical aspects of filmmaking, he undoubtedly exploited skillfully the perspectival distortions of the camera. Already at the start of his career, Hitchcock knew perfectly how a set would look like in the film. It was a lesson that he learned in the early 1920s from German masters such as Murnau: "What you see on the set does not matter. All that matters is what you see on the screen."[12] In *Rear Window*, the viewpoint determines the space even more than usual since Jeffries watches the spectacle from a distance and from a fixed position. As a result, his apartment serves as a box in the theater. This tallies with Hitchcock's frequent use of the theatrical metaphor. Crucial scenes in several films (*The Pleasure Garden*, *Downhill*, *Murder*, *The 39 Steps*, *Stage Fright*, *I Confess*, *The Man Who Knew Too Much*, *Torn Curtain*) occur in theater and concert halls. In addition, Hitchcock frequently employs architectural or decorative elements referring to the theater. *Rear Window*, as *Stage Fright*, opens with the rise of a curtain. At the end of the film, the curtains in Jeffries' box are lowered. Midway the story, Lisa endorses the theatrical metaphor by literally closing the curtains while stating that "the show's over for tonight." Several authors have interpreted the presence of theatrical places and conventions in Hitchcock's *œuvre* as a Brechtian estrangement effect – a striking feature in the work of a director who presents cinema as almost the opposite of theater by means of fluent camera movements, dynamic editing, and the extensive use of point-of-view shots.[13] According to John Belton, *Rear Window* plays self-consciously "with the differences between theatrical and cinematic film space, relying on set design and certain kinds of camera movements to establish a concrete, unified theatrical space and on editing, framing, and camera movement to construct a more abstract, psychological, cinematic film space."[14] In the Paramount Advance Campaign document, production designer Pereira pointed out that the impressive single set reversed the usual rules. "It's ambition of every New York producer to acquire a property using a single set. The great properties of motion pictures have often resulted from the purchase of stage plays and then the movies have amplified these to create added scope and interest." Yet, the same document emphasizes, "*Rear Window* uses only a single set which never could have been duplicated on the stage. Hitchcock has reversed the time-worn rules by creating a one set movie which could only be done as a movie."

The subjection of the environment to the logic of the look gives the space of *Rear Window* not only qualities of the theater but also of the panopticon.[15] In the late eighteenth century, Jeremy Bentham presented this circular building with central surveillance unit as a building type perfectly fit for all institutions dealing with control. Whereas the theater directs the gaze of many onlookers to the single focal point of the stage, the panopticon inverts this logic by subjecting the space to a single point of view. The space of *Rear Window* adopts the imaginary form of a cone, whose apex is constituted by Jeffries' living room (or his head) and then extends out toward its base in the courtyard. Just as the panopticon combines spectacle with surveillance, Hitchcock subjects the space to an all-encompassing gaze that transforms the environment into spectacle. The spectator/voyeur himself is invisible. As Bentham' guard, who bases his absolute and demonic power on his own invisibility in the dark core of the building, *Rear Window*'s voyeurs hide themselves in the dark: Jeffries pulls back in the shade or extinguishes the light when Thorwald can notice him. Thorwald himself hides in the only non-lighted flat when the little dog of one of the neighbors has been found dead.

Nonetheless, the panoptic power is limited. As in every classical Hollywood film, *Rear Window* comprises many spatial ellipses and there are doors of which it is unclear where they are leading to. In *Rear Window*, however, these features have an added value because of the unusual cinematic space of the single set. In addition, not everything is exposed to the gaze of the protagonist. On the one hand, he is not able to perceive everything (because he sleeps, for instance). On the other, some areas, which can only be imagined by the viewer, are invisible because of the fixed viewpoint. Still other spaces are rendered invisible by characters such as the newlyweds closing the curtains. Moreover, Hitchcock rewardingly uses the border between visible and invisible spaces. The bare walls between the windows, for instance, play an important part in the scene of the quarrel between Thorwald and his wife or in the one in which Lisa intrudes the Thorwald apartment. Hitchcock, as it were, introduces, on screen, an off-screen space. Because of this, he rouses the spectator's curiosity and imagination and he maximizes suspense. Furthermore, in contrast with the logic of the panopticon, the gaze is mirrored at a climactic moment in the film: Thorwald looks back at Jeffries and, through him, at the camera, the director, and the spectator.

Michel Foucault, who presented Bentham's panopticon as an allegory of the processes of normalization and discipline of modernity, noted that in Bentham's building, "every cage is a small theater in which the actor is alone, perfectly individualized and permanently visible."[16] As in Bentham's panopticon, there seems to be no communication among the individual residential units. Foucault noted that, consequently, the visual logic of the spectacle is turned upside down. Instead of exposing some individual bodies to a community (as the architecture of the temple, theater, and circus in antiquity

16 Foucault, *Surveiller et punir*.

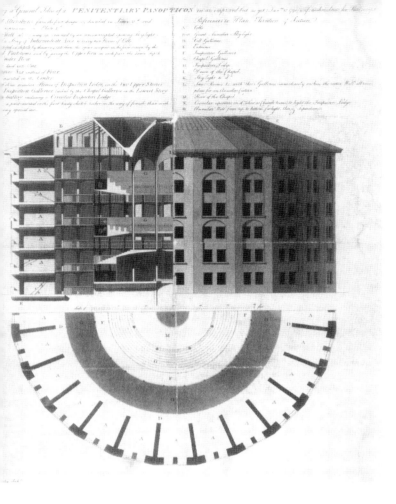

did), the panoptic courtyard of *Rear Window* provides the lonely surveyor with an overview of many separated individuals. As the panopticon, the urban courtyard belongs to a modern society without a ritual mediation between particular individuals and the abstract concepts of the state or the law. The voyeur sees a collection of anonymous metropolitans that are part of a *Gesellschaft* of autonomous individuals. The inhabitants rather live isolated from than *with* each other. Even the courtyard is not that of a single apartment block but consists of a number of individual back yards attached to distinct, architecturally different buildings on a single city block.

General Idea of a Penitentiary Panopticon (Jeremy Bentham, 1791)

Given this perspective, *Rear Window* is an interesting meditation on modern urban society. The film, as it were, offers a cross-section of an urban segment in a manner that resembles the popular nineteenth-century prints showing Paris apartment buildings. These prints, which show an unseen density and social diversity within a single architectural construction, illustrate the development of a new, modern and urban way of life in a metropolis radically transformed by Baron Haussmann. Hitchcock's evocation of Greenwich Village shows a colorful urban universe in which inhabitants live as strangers next to each other. Nonetheless, *Rear Window*'s characters are no monads existing only on themselves. Their dwellings have windows and they open up to the world. The characters exist as representations and as images. The dialectic between seeing and being seen touches not only on the essence of Hitchcock's *œuvre* but also, as authors such as Erving Goffman and Lyn Lofland have demonstrated, on that of the urban way of life. In light of this, *Rear Window* is a wonderful evocation of the way in which the spatial organization of the city determines the lives of its residents.[17] The behavior of some inhabitants is unmistakably connected to the fact that the story takes place in this kind of semi-public courtyard in the midst of a metropolis. Hitchcock, whose films comprise many hidden or impenetrable spaces, maximizes the voyeuristic pleasure by showing a space, which is usually invisible for most of us. The story develops not before a window but, tellingly, in front of a rear window. The set consists of an informal backside containing a capricious combination of terraces and little gardens and which undoubtedly sharply contrasts with the invisible front side. *Rear Window* clearly deals with the contrast between formal and representative facade and informal backside, which is one of the essential characteristics of urban architecture since early modernity – the set, moreover, contains little pieces of such representative front sides in the form of a protruding brownstone façade with a cornice and window mouldings on the other side of the street. Hitchcock realizes that some inhabitants would hesitate to perform the same acts behind a window on the front side or street side of the building. On the informal backside facing the courtyard, by contrast, nobody takes pain to hide or to close the windows with curtains or shutters. The urbanites perform their daily rituals without screening off their rooms. Jeffries too sits in front of the window in his pajamas and shaves. Instead of an absolute privacy behind doors and walls, the courtyard is characterized by a conditional or mediated form of privacy, which is based on the knowledge that others can watch but usually do not. It is a delicate social balance based on the collective use of spaces and on implicit rules of conduct between neighbors. Precisely the relative isolation and the lack of interference in the everyday life of others are the attractive elements of big city life. The story of *Rear Window* is unthinkable in a small

17 Sanders, *Celluloid Skyline*, 228-41.
18 Fawell, *Hitchcock's Rear Window*, 112.
19 See AlSayyad, *Cinematic Urbanism*, 147.

town or in suburbia since the balance between individualism and collectivity is completely different in such places.

Dealing with social representation and its dialectic between coded forms of voyeurism and exhibitionism, the film is much more than simply "a commentary on the alienation of urban life."[18] The film discusses the relation between urban alienation and visual power – something that has become much more important in an era when cameras and other systems of surveillance are ubiquitous in both public and private spaces.[19] *Rear Window* announces a postmodern urban space, the boundaries of wich are no longer defined by architectutral structures but by the screen and the lens.

Paris au travail (Magasin pittoresque, 1883)

The Machine in the Garden: Vandamm House

Nearby Mount Rushmore
Memorial, South Dakota

North by Northwest

Color

MGM

1959

PRODUCTION DESIGN:
Robert Boyle

ART DIRECTION:
William A. Horning
Merrill Pye

SET DECORATION:
Henry Grace
Frank McKelvey

Plan Level 0

1 Entrance
2 Covered Entrance
3 Road to Landing-Strip
4 Drive
5 Foyer
6 Kitchen
7 Dining Room
8 Living Room
9 Terrace
10 Valley
a Fireplace
b Statue with Microfilm
c Trees

Plan Level -1

a Trees
b Retaining Rubble Wall
c Steel Supports
d Girder

Drawings by David Claus

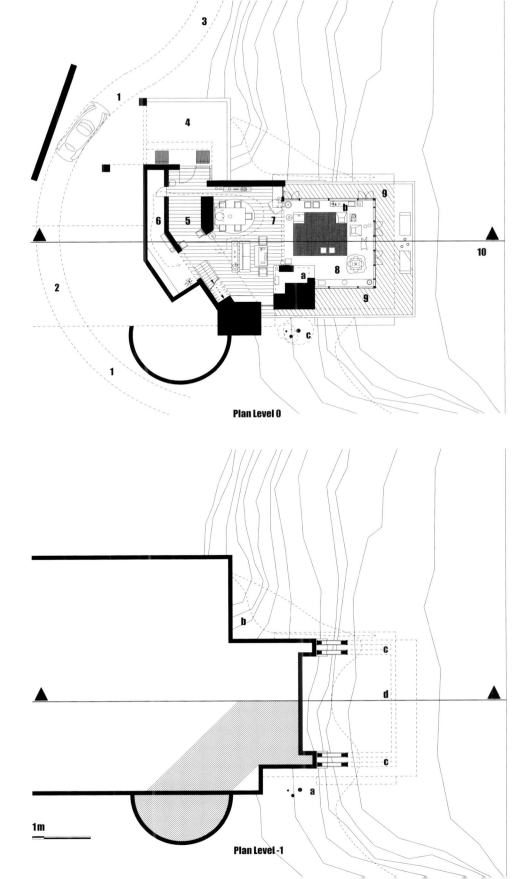

Plan Level 0

Plan Level -1

1m

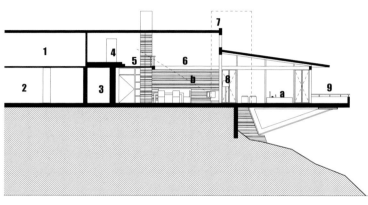

Section

1 Guest Rooms
2 Carport
3 Kitchen
4 Door to Eve's Room
5 Landing
6 Void
7 Outline of Chimney with Fireplace
8 French Doors to Terrace
9 Terrace
a Statue with Microfilm
b Thornhill's Reflection in Television

Section

Plan Level +1

1 Guest Rooms
2 Eve's Room
3 Terrace
4 Dressing
5 Landing
6 Void
7 Chimney
8 Sloping Roof

Drawings by David Claus

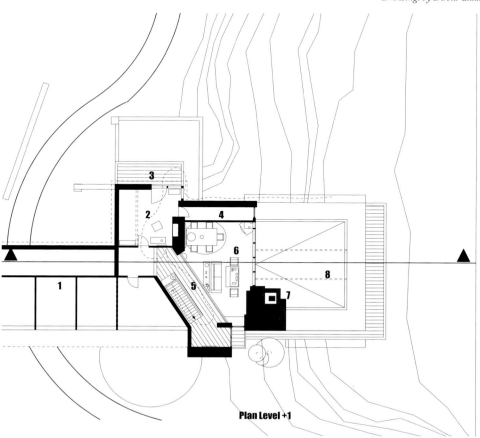

Plan Level +1

1m

I   II

In *North By Northwest*, Hitchcock's only production for MGM, the studio whose name has become synonymous with glamour, modern architecture plays the role of catalyst. The film's protagonist, the debonair bachelor Roger O. Thornhill (Cary Grant), becomes literally trapped by architectural design on several occasions. This is already announced by the famous opening credit sequence designed by Saul Bass, which shows an abstract play of lines on a green surface that gradually turns into the reflecting glass curtain wall of the C.I.T. Building, which was designed by Wallace K. Harrison and Max Abramovitz in 1957.[1] Mirroring the congested and hectic streets of the metropolis, the geometric grid of window panes shows the biotope of Madison Avenue advertising executive Thornhill. The film, after all, was made in an era that saw a generation of new, much talked-of Midtown Manhattan glass-walled skyscrapers such as Lever House (Skidmore, Owings & Merrill, 1952), the United Nations Headquarters (International Committee of Architects, 1953), and the Seagram Building (Ludwig Mies van der Rohe & Philip Johnson, 1958) — all have been identified erroneously as the office building in the opening shot by several authors. The film, in short, introduces us immediately to the urban space of modernity characterized by the diagrammatic and rectilinear structure of Mondrian's *Broadway Boogie-Woogie*. Moreover, the lines in the Bass credits not only delineate the fenestration pattern of these new high-rise buildings, they also evoke the vectors of the film's title. In addition, they allude to the emblematic spatial organization of the grid, which recurs throughout the film, such as in the famous scene at the deserted prairie crossroads, where Thornhill is attacked by a cropdusting plane. This set is quintessential Hitchcock: an endless, flat, and brown field under a huge expanse of blue sky that contrasts sharply with the confines of the train compartment in one of the

1 Harrison & Abramovitz' original eight-story Commercial Investment Trust Building was erected at 650 Madison Avenue, between 58th and 60th Street. In 1987, the building was reclad and a tower was added by Fox & Fowle. See Willensky & White, *AIA Guide to New York City*, 283.

I, II C.I.T. Building (Digital Frame)

previous sequences. At this point, the film has turned into an exploration of America's open spaces – a Hitchcockian Western or a Midwest version of Michelangelo Antonioni's *L'avventura*. According to Fredric Jameson, "the emptiness of the field constitutes a veritable hypostasis of space itself" and demonstrates that Midwestern nature has been colonized by the urban grid of industrial agriculture.[2] As a result, Hitchcock's high angle shot of the empty field does not only resonate with the vertiginous top shots of the United Nations Headquarters and Mount Rushmore elsewhere in the film, but also with a modern conception of space as such. The high angle shot that situates the small figure of Cary Grant on the x- and y-axes in the vastness of an empty field shows a remarkable similarity with a famous drawing by Oscar Niemeyer, one of modern architecture's heroes who contributed to the design of the United Nations Headquarters. Niemeyer's drawing shows two minuscule figures in a panorama of an endless plain transected only by two orthogonal axes. The sketch is something like a simplified representation of the urban plan of Brasilia, of all the cities that have been built undoubtedly the one that best corresponds to the modernist urban utopia, and which Niemeyer, in collaboration with Lucio Costa, was designing at the time of *North by Northwest*'s release. Combining geometric simplicity with endless vistas, both the drawing and Hitchcock's panoptic shot of the evacuated field evoke an emptiness that gives not only spatial but also socio-psychological shape to the modern city-dweller's condition. It is in such a space that Thornhill is situated. Constantly moving through horizontal and vertical grids, he finds himself in a series of pitfalls.

The first of these traps turns out to be the building of the previously mentioned United Nations Headquarters (1947-53), perhaps the prime example of postwar modern architecture because of its combination of two essential forms and techniques of modernism: the simple, geometric, and freestanding slab of the Secretariat tower with glass surfaces on the one hand, and the organic and sculptural shape of the concrete General Assembly hall on the other. Expressing a utopian new world order, the United Nations building was designed by an international committee of architects that included, among others, Le Corbusier and Oscar Niemeyer. Wallace K. Harrison, who also designed the office building of the film's opening shot, acted as chairman of the board of designers.[3] In *North by Northwest*, United Nations Headquarters' glass surfaces, sweeping plazas, marble masses, and elegant lobbies – or their cinematic simulations[4] – become the scene of a staged murder and the beginning of Thornhill's escape route in a *North-Westerly Direction*, as a working title for the film indicates.

During his adventurous journey, Thornhill finds himself trapped in another icon of twentieth-century modern design: Henry Dreyfuss' luxury 20th-Century Limited train.

2 Jameson, "Spatial Systems in *North by Northwest*," 61. See also Millington, "Hitchcock and American Character," 135-54.
3 See Newhouse, *Wallace K. Harrison, Architect*, 104-43.
4 After the location shooting of *The Glass Wall* (Maxwell Shane, 1953), Dag Hammarskjöld prohibited the shooting of feature films at the U.N. premises. For *North by Northwest*, location shots were filmed with a candid camera and the entire sequence was made with the help of set reconstructions and matte shots. See Truffaut, *Hitchcock*, 252.

I Prairie crossroad (Digital Frame)
II, III, IV United Nations Headquarters (Digital Frame)
V Sketch of Brasilia by Oscar Niemeyer

I II
III IV

Combining speed and claustrophobia, the Hitchcockian motif of the train provides the circumstance for the no-exit cat-and-mouse between Thornhill and the police but also for his encounter with the chilly blonde double agent Eve Kendall (Eva Marie Saint), who tellingly poses as an industrial designer. Last but not least, Thornhill gets caught in the impressive, cantilevered glass-and-redwood house of Philip Vandamm (James Mason) near Mount Rushmore.

This remarkable location of the Vandamm house is revealing in several ways. First, typical of Hitchcock, the film that was temporarily titled *The Man on Lincoln's Nose* originated as a set of ideas for scenes on places that seem definitely American such as the Mount Rushmore memorial.[5] Using a carved rock containing the gigantic granite portraits of George Washington, Thomas Jefferson, Theodor Roosevelt, and Abraham Lincoln as a backdrop, Hitchcock suggests that what happens there is of national importance.[6] Situated in a fictitious forested plateau atop the monument, the house, inhabited by a master criminal, dominates a devotional shrine of American democracy.

Second, its Midwestern location – in the Black Hills region, near Keystone, South Dakota – is of importance. The move toward the west, evoked by the film's title, brings the protagonists to the American heartland, the spine of the continent, and site of infamous "Indian wars." In addition, apart from its stylistic similarities with Frank Lloyd Wright's architecture, Vandamm house refers to Wright's notion of the 'prairie house' and his idea of a 'Usonian' architecture adapted to the vast territories and decentralized urbanization of the American West.[7] Evoking the clash between the pastoral idea of harmonious accommodation to nature and the progressive quest for power and wealth, Mount Rushmore and Vandamm house are typical products of American culture as interpreted by Leo Marx in his 1964 seminal study *The Machine in the Garden*. Combining the idyllic log cabin with the modern penthouse, Vandamm's eyrie blends nature and culture.

Third, this hybrid contamination of the natural and the artificial is significant in itself. Vandamm house is part of an anthropomorphized landscape. Sculpted between 1927 and 1941 by Gutzon Borglum, Mount Rushmore is a surreal landscape – René Magritte's renderings of gigantic granite birds, chairs, or letters come to mind. Whereas the mountain has become a head, Vandamm house can be interpreted, as Raymond Durgnat has written, as a "repressed libido" or "an alien, malign, disaffected intelligence."[8] The surrealist connotations of the Mount Rushmore sequence, furthermore, unmistakably refer to Hitchcock's earlier fascination with gigantic stone faces in *Blackmail* and *Saboteur*.

302

5 See Leff, "Hitchcock at Metro," 41-61; and Brady, "An Interview with Ernest Lehman," 186-88.
6 Cavell, "North by Northwest," 260.
7 See Twombly, *Frank Lloyd Wright*, 240-74.
8 Durgnat, *The Strange Case of Alfred Hitchcock*, 312.
9 Millington, "Hitchcock and American Character,"
148-49.
10 Jameson, "Spatial Systems in *North by Northwest*," 56.

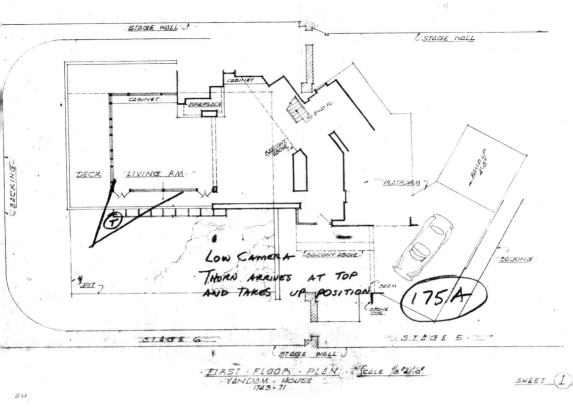

Plan with indication of camera set-ups (Academy of Motion Picture Arts and Sciences)

Fourth, Vandamm house is situated on top of a mountain. Consequently, it expresses visual domination and panoptic control. Moreover, its visualization evokes the high angle shots used earlier in the film. Thornhill's climb up the vectorlike buttresses and vertiginous stone walls unmistakably refer to the face of the skyscraper in the opening sequence.[9] In addition, the house has its private airport and, as Fredric Jameson has noted, "the twinkling rows of landing lights direct our attention off into the void; meanwhile this spatial structure is powerfully reinforced by the peculiar cantilevering of the house itself, which also juts out into empty space (and various spatial arrangements in the scenes themselves – Cary Grant looking down on the vast central living-room, for example – echo and mimic this phantasmic relationship to the edge and the void)."[10]

Situated on a spectacular site and exerting visual domination, the Vandamm house is the archetypal dwelling of a rogue. Like Professor Jordan (*The 39 Steps*), Sir Humphrey

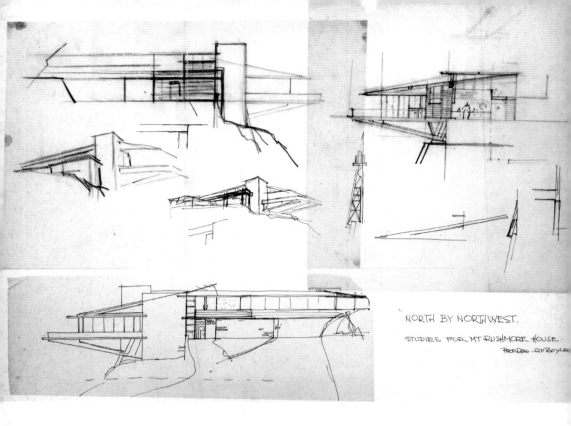

NORTH BY NORTHWEST.
STUDIES FOR MT RUSHMORE HOUSE.
PROD.DES. RF BOYLE

Pengallan (*Jamaica Inn*), Johnnie Aysgarth (*Suspicion*), Tobin (*Saboteur*), Uncle Charlie (*Shadow of a Doubt*), Alex Sebastian (*Notorious*), Phillip and Brandon (*Rope*), Bruno Anthony (*Strangers on a Train*), or Tony Wendice (*Dial M for Murder*), Philip Vandamm – damnation even resonates in his name – is a typical sophisticated Hitchcock villain. This goes for Leonard (Martin Landau) as well, Vandamm's loyal henchman, who is, unmistakably, sexually attracted to his employer and jealous of his mistress. Apart from his distinctly European touch and the high prestige rating of Vandamm's Dutch name, he is an art lover – in Hollywood cinema a conventional association with villains and spies.[11] The entire art auction scene establishes Vandamm's relation to high culture and simultaneously indicates, as Raymond Durgnat has noted, "the capture of the muses by the Mammon."[12] "I didn't realize you were an art collector," Thornhill jeers at Vandamm, "I thought you just collected corpses." Art, no doubt, denotes in the first place not *Bildung* but wealth and luxury. Vandamm's living room is furnished with

304

11 Walker, *Artists on Screen.*
See also Andrea Codring-
ton, "Modernist Malice."
12 Durgnat, *The Strange
Case of Alfred Hitchcock*, 301.

I Sketches by Robert Boyle (Academy of Motion Picture Arts and Sciences)
II, III, IV, V Exterior (Digital Frame)
VI Supporting beam structure (Digital Frame)
VII Climbing the beam structure (Digital Frame)

typical late 1950s furniture and art. Modern American armchairs and low-slung coffee tables are accompanied by geometric textiles with a modern Scandinavian touch – some of the pieces of furniture are reminiscent of the works of Edward Wormley, who designed 'contemporary' middle-class furniture with slight references to Scandinavian design. In addition, there are several pieces of non-Western art and a Pre-Colombian statue figures prominently in the action. The statue, as it turns out, carries microfilm, which is the so-called McGuffin that generates the story but also points, according to commentators as Stanley Cavell, to the "present film."[13]

In the first place, however, the house, which is resolutely modern, breathes wealth and extravagant luxury. Its flashing modernism contrasts sharply with the classical estate in Glen Cove, Long Island, where Thornhill had met Vandamm for the first time.[14] Moreover, apart from the moderate modernism of the penthouse of Phillip and Brandon (*Rope*) and Scottie's apartment (*Vertigo*), it is the sole "high-modernist" domestic building in Hitchcock's entire *œuvre*. Tellingly, this luxurious modernist eyrie is inhabited by a villain. Both love of the arts and a predilection for modern architecture are persistent Hollywood signifiers of menace and malice. In American popular culture since the 1930s, modern architecture was considered appropriate for the workplace though unsuitable for the middle-class home. Classical Hollywood reserved modern domestic settings for youthful singles, the unusually wealthy, easy women, terminal bachelors, and, most of all, "characters who are evil, selfish, obsessive, and driven by the pleasure of the flesh."[15] In spite of the utopian aspirations of architectural modernism, its walk-on parts in films are practically always associated with cruelty, control, and vanity – an aspect that is abundantly clear in the dwellings of the rich collection of extravagant villains in James Bond films. Depicting a chase through a succession of spectacular locations, *North by Northwest* has been considered a precursor of the James Bond series – this certainly applies to the Vandamm house as well. The Bond films, in which a master criminal with foreign accent inhabits remote and precariously sited ultramodern hideaways, confirmed the connection between modern design and dastardly doings. Undoubtedly, the Vandamm house could have been designed by Ken Adam, the production designer responsible for famous Bond set pieces such as the in-rock-carved ultramodern hideout of *Dr. No* (Terence Young, 1962) or the laser room in *Goldfinger* (Guy Hamilton, 1964).[16] Adam's peculiar combination of contemporary shapes with antique furniture and his strange mixture of metal and wood are reminiscent of the tension between the 'googie' cantilevered structures and modern surfaces on the one hand and the telluric embedment that characterizes the Vandamm house on the other.

13 Cavell, "North by Northwest," 263.
14 Old Westbury Gardens, Westbury, Long Island doubles as Townsend's mansion at Glen Cove, Long Island in *North by Northwest*.
15 Rosa, "Burning Down the House: Modern Homes in the Movies," 159. See also Heathcote, "Modernism as Enemy," 20-25.
16 Frayling, *Ken Adam: The Art of Production Design*, 93-101 and 137-91.

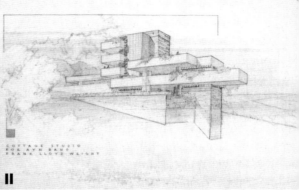

I   II

With its walls of stone and wood, the Goldfinger lair has a touch of Frank Lloyd Wright, which certainly also characterizes the Vandamm house. In particular Wright's iconic Fallingwater (1934-37) is evoked by the horizontalism of the bold design of a cantilever and by the combination of modern forms and materials with natural textures. In addition, Vandamm house is also reminiscent of some of Wright's spectacular designs for hilltop and mountain top Usionian houses of the late 1930s and early 1940s. Perfectly following the disposition of several Wright buildings, Vandamm house was correctly situated just under the top of its hill. Although the dwelling emphatically defies gravity, it is also lodged into the earth. Other features of Wright's Usonian houses that recur in the Vandamm house are the asymmetric floor plan, interpenetrating and free-flowing interior volumes, a centralized fireplace, overlapping roof planes, recessed entries, a fenestration that facilitates real and visual contact with the outdoors, the irregular pattern of limestone that mimics its own sedimentary formation, and the house's massing – heavy with limestone in the rear where the house meets the hillside, light with glass and concrete at the free end of the cantilever.[17] However, Vandamm house also contains elements that do not tally with Wright's style. Instead of the unsupported cantilevers favored by Wright, Vandamm house has steel beams buttressing the cantilever. According to some commentators, "Hitchcock may have felt that a true Wright cantilever would distract audiences from the plot, making them wonder what on earth was holding the house up, instead of focusing on the action."[18] In the event, the beams also served the plot by giving Thornhill a way to climb into the house.

When Hitchcock made *North by Northwest* in the late fifties, Wright had developed into America's most celebrated modern architect. Not only well known among the

17 See Twombly, *Frank Lloyd Wright*; and Wright, "Frank Lloyd Wright and the Domestic Landscape," 80-95.
18 McLendon, "Modernism at the Movies."
19 Neumann, *Film Architecture*, 126-33.
20 Borglum & Zeitner, *Borglum's Unfinished Dream*, 28 and 101.

21 Truffaut, *Hitchcock*, 254.
22 See Sennett, *Setting the Scene*, 181-85.
23 Robert Boyle, quoted in LoBrutto, *By Design*, 9.

I Fallingwater (Frank Lloyd Wright, 1937)
II Ayn Rand Studio (Frank Lloyd Wright, 1946)

professional community of architects, Wright was discussed in mass-market magazines such as *Ladies' Home Journal*, *House Beautiful*, and *House & Garden*, which even devoted entire issues to his work. Not surprisingly, Wright had already been approached by Hollywood in the late forties. Warner Brothers had asked Wright to draw the architecture for *The Fountainhead* (King Vidor, 1949), the story, based on an Ayn Rand novel, of an uncompromising modernist architect starring Gary Cooper.[19] Wright, who had designed a hill top cottage studio for Rand in 1946, declined the assignment due to financial disagreements. In the end, *The Fountainhead* sets and architectural drawings were created by Edward Carrere, who would also design the sets for Hitchcock's *Dial M for Murder*. Wright did not collaborate on *North by Northwest* either, although he had been enthusiastic about Mount Rushmore. He allegedly said that Mount Rushmore seemed to have redesigned itself in response to mankind's prayer and, according to sculptor Gutzon Borglum, Wright had agreed to participate in the design of the (unbuilt) Hall of Records on the other side of the mountain.[20]

Although Hitchcock himself, in the famous Truffaut interview, spoke simply of a "scale model of a house by Frank Lloyd Wright,"[21] the unmistakably Wrightian building was created by MGM set designers William A. Horning, Merrill Pye, Henry Grace, and Frank McKelvey.[22] They worked under the supervision of production designer Robert Boyle, who had collaborated with Hitchcock on *Saboteur* and *Shadow of a Doubt*. Boyle, who later would also design the sets for *The Birds* and *Marnie*, acknowledged the importance of Wright for the design of the Vandamm house: "Every architect is influenced by Frank Lloyd Wright. Most people don't realize that the house was all on Stage Five over at MGM. I knew we had to have a house where Cary Grant would be in a precarious position if he was discovered; he had no way out. It also had to be in a position where he could see everything in the house: he had to see her bedroom, he had to see the living room, he had to see the balcony over the living room, and he had to be able to get down and get away. So this was not a house we could find. The Fallingwater house, which Frank Lloyd Wright designed, was partly cantilevered, but that wasn't what interested me; it was the stonework in the Fallingwater house, which was horizontal striated stone. That was perfect for somebody to get a handhold and climb up; that's why I selected it. I was really influenced by the handholds. Fallingwater jutted out over a little stream. I made the Mount Rushmore house more extravagant, and I really jutted it out."[23]

According to Boyle, in short, some specifically Wrightian characteristics of the Vandamm house, such as the stonework, were incited by the narrative of *North by*

Northwest. For Boyle, this also applied to other aspects of the design, such as the free-flowing interior spaces and the cantilever: "Once you say that it's going to have to canti-lever because he's [Roger Thornhill] going to be in a precarious situation, he has to be in a situation in which he can see into the living room, up onto the balcony, and that she [Eve Kendall] crosses the balcony into the bedroom and he can see her in the bedroom. So it had to be designed like that. If it's just an ordinary porch, or something, it couldn't be. So he has to be in a position where if he's dislodged, he will fall to his death. There has to be some suspense there. And then, cantilevered meant modern, so it just fell into place. I didn't superimpose it, the script superimposed it on me."[24]

24 Robert Boyle in a 1989 interview with Charles Affron, quoted in Affron & Affron, *Sets in Motion*, 66.
25 Robert Boyle, quoted in LoBrutto, *By Design*, 9.
26 Sandy McLendon, "Modernism at the Movies."
27 On modern architecture in Tati, see Abalos, *The Good Life*, 61-83; Borden,

"Material Sounds;" Jacobs, "Reisgids voor Tativille;" Neumann, *Film Architec-ture*, 134-47; Ockman, "Architecture in a Mode of Distraction;" and François Penz, "Architecture in the Films of Jacques Tati."
28 Joseph Rosa, "Burning Down the House," 164. See also Hess, *The Architecture of John Lautner*.

Tyler house (John Lautner, 1953)

Vandamm house turned out to be a masterpiece of cinematic architecture that skillfully combined location shots, matte shots, and a few sections full-scale set pieces. "Of course, in actuality, there is no such place around Mount Rushmore," Boyle later said. "We did certain tricks, which helped. The long shot of Cary Grant going up to the house was done on a back lot. All we had was a road, and the house was a matte painting. Then there's a closer shot, which is another matte in which you see the maid actually close the window and close the curtain. That piece of film was shot on the stage where we had the actual set. The maid closed the curtain, and then that was reduced and put in the matte. So that's a piece of composite filmmaking there." [25]

According to Sandy MacLendon, the parts of the house that were actually built were the living room, part of the bedroom wing, the carport, and a bit of hillside under the living room where the cantilever beams were. Yet, the 'real' architecture was a deception: real limestone was only used in a few places where the camera was very close, the rest of the so-called limestone walls were made of plaster. Since glass reflects camera crews and lights, the expanses of window were mostly without glass. Furthermore, the walls that looked perfectly real and solid were in fact 'breakaways' – walls capable of being unbolted and taken away to accommodate the bulky VistaVision cameras. [26]

The Vandamm house, in short, can be considered a cinematic exaggeration of Wright's architecture. Not unlike the Villa Arpel in Jacques Tati's *Mon oncle*, which was released in the previous year, its architecture displays a kind of exaggerated modernism; a form of architecture that manipulates certain formal features of the icons of modernism – Wright's Fallingwater, Le Corbusier's Villa Savoye, Mies van der Rohe's Farnsworth House – so that a decorative, playful, or funny variant of 'orthodox' modernism is created. [27] In the late 1950s, this kind of approach can also be found in the plastic and sensual work of Oscar Niemeyer or in the designs of Italian modernists such as Luigi Moretti or Carlo Mollino. In addition, it can be traced in the works of several American architects of that era, such as Bruce Goff, Albert Frey, the designers of the Californian Case Study Houses, and, perhaps most of all, John Lautner. Strikingly, Lautner, who had studied with Wright at Taliesin in the 1930s, designed several houses that were used in movies as houses of master criminals. Apart from his 1968 Arthur Elrod Residence in Palm Springs that doubled as Ernst Blofeld's hideout in *Diamonds Are Forever* (Guy Hamilton, 1971), questionable characters also inhabited Lautner houses in *Body Double* (Brian De Palma, 1984), *Lethal Weapon 2* (Richard Donner, 1989), and *The Big Lebowski* (Joel and Ethan Coen, 1998). [28]

As Lautner's dwellings, Vandamm house can be labeled 'contemporary' rather than 'modern' – a notion that, according to Lesley Jackson, should be applied to a large share of American postwar architecture, which disconnected modernism from its ideological and intellectual connotations. The 'contemporary' style was also characterized by a more pragmatic attitude, an interest in comfortable living, an outspoken attention to decorative details, and a preference for warm and soft surfaces.[29] In the late 1950s, these characteristics were perfectly expressed by Julius Schulman's famous architectural photographs. His pictures demonstrated that modernism was capable of creating an improved domestic setting for the rituals of contemporary life. Schulman's widely published beautiful stagings illustrate how postwar modernism was commodified and how it became an inseparable part of the modern American way of life. As Schulman's photographs, Hitchcock's Vandamm house managed to present modern design as something alluring and photogenic. Although its daring modernism is connected to the psychopathology of the master criminal, the luxury and domestic qualities of the Vandamm house, rendered in glorious Technicolor, are unmistakably seductive. Precisely through such photographic and cinematic mediations, the newness of modern design could skillfully be spotlighted and cultivated. Precisely because it is only a cinematic image, Vandamm house touches on the essence of the houses by Lautner, Charles and Ray Eames or other Californian architects of the 1950s, which combined the utopia of the modern movement with the cornucopia of postwar consumer culture.

29 Jackson, *Contemporary*.
See also Ockman, "Toward
a Theory of Normative
Architecture," 142.

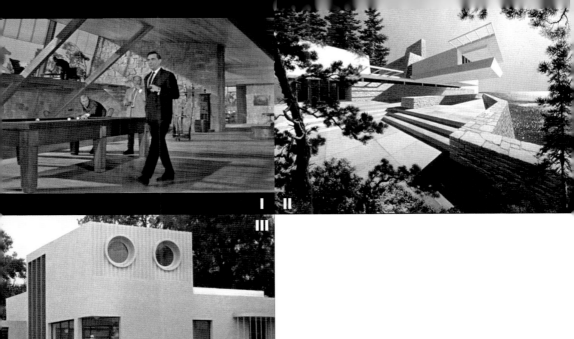

I *Goldfinger* (Guy Hamilton, 1964)
Production design by Ken Adam (Digital Frame)
II *The Fountainhead* (King Vidor, 1948)
Production design by Edward Carrere (Digital Frame)
III *Mon oncle* (Jacques Tati, 1958)
Production design by Jacques Lagrange (Digital Frame)

Appendix:
Hitchcock's Art Directors

Arnold, Norman G. (1892-1964) brother of C. Wilfred Arnold. He did the art direction of *Blackmail* (with C. Wilfred Arnold) and *Juno and the Paycock* (uncredited, with James Marchant). He directed a single film, *They Met in the Dark*, in 1943.

Arnold, C. Wilfred (1889-1957) British art director, who entered the industry in 1920 as a draftsman at Famous Players Lasky, Islington, where his brother Norman was art director. He became an assistant of Hitchcock when he was also designing sets. Having acquired practical experience of film making in Berlin and Munich (as Hitchcock himself), Arnold became the art director of many of Hitchcock's earlier films such as *The Lodger*, *The Ring*, *The Farmer's Wife*, *Champagne*, *The Manxman*, *Blackmail*, *Rich and Strange*, and *Number Seventeen*. According to Michael L. Stephens, "Arnold's designs were economical yet powerful evocations of the tortured, claustrophobic psychology of Hitchcock's characters." Elliott Stein calls the sets of these Hitchcock films "all of quality; those for *Blackmail* are memorable." C. Wilfred Arnold was often otherwise billed as C.W. Arnold, W.C. Arnold, and Wilfred Arnold.

Arrigo, Frank (1918-1974) Arrigo is the art director most associated with Republic westerns of the 1940s and 1950s. With Hein Heckroth, he is the art director of *Torn Curtain*. Occasionally, Arrigo was production manager, assistant director, executive producer, and director of television programs as well.

Austin, John set decorator of *Topaz*. At first specialized in westerns and Eastern exotica, his filmography also includes *A Double Life* (George Cukor, 1947, his first credit), *Secret Beyond the Door* (Fritz Lang, 1948), *Man Without a Star* (King Vidor, 1955), *Touch of Evil* (Orson Welles, 1958), *Coogan's Bluff* (Don Siegel, 1968), and *Paper Moon* (Peter Bogdanovich, 1973).

Basevi, James (1890-1962) Basevi studied architecture in England and was a colonel in World War I. Later, he moved to Canada and then Los Angeles. Shortly after it was founded in 1924, MGM employed Basevi as draftsman in its art department. At MGM, he became head of the special effects department during the transition to sound. In 1937, he joined 20th Century-Fox, first as a special effects specialist, then as a unit art director. At Fox, he formed a partnership with John Ford that would last for decades. Using real locations and sound stages, Basevi designed the realistic, detailed sets of many of Ford's westerns, which created a mythical image of the West (*My Darling Clementine*, *Fort Appache*, *She Wore a Yellow Ribbon*, *The Searchers*). His special effects for Ford's *The Hurricane* (1937) have been called "one of the wonders of the Seventh Art." Basevi also did the art direction of *Lifeboat* (with Maurice Ransford), Hitchcock's only 20th-Century Fox production and one of his notorious single-set pictures. Making the studio tank, in which *Lifeboat* was shot, interesting and convincing was undoubtedly one of his greatest challenges. In the late 1930s and 1940s, Basevi temporarily left the studio to work for independent producers such as Samuel Goldwyn and David Selznick. For the latter Basevi worked as the chief production designer on *Spellbound*. His credits also include *Tobacco Road* (1941), *The Song of Bernadette* (1943) and Selznick's production of *Duel in the Sun* (King Vidor, 1946).

Boyle, Robert (1909) art director (with Jack Otterson) of *Saboteur*, (with John Goodman) of *Shadow of a Doubt*, and production designer of *North by Northwest*, *The Birds*, and *Marnie*. Having graduated from USC in architecture in 1933, Boyle entered the industry as an extra and was eventually hired by Hans Dreier at Paramount as an assistant art director. In 1941 he joined Universal, where one of his first assignments was *Saboteur*, for which he drew the storyboards and in which he managed to evoke the contemporary landscape of rural and metropolitan America. Hitchcock was so impressed by Boyle's accomplishments that he employed him also on *Shadow on a Doubt*, for which Boyle created a small town in which danger lurked in every shadowy corner. After having been a combat photographer during World War II, Boyle worked as an independent production designer in the late 1940s creating other claustrophobic settings for dark mysteries, such as *Nocturne* (Edwin L. Marin, 1946), *Ride the Pink Horse* (Robert Montgomery, 1947), and *They Won't Believe Me* (Irving Pichel, 1947). Apart from his later Hitchcock collaborations, Boyle created in the 1960s other striking images of a small town in crisis, such as J. Lee Thompson's *Cape Fear* (1962), and other examples of paranoid and dark spaces, such as Richard Brooks' *In Cold Blood* (1967). His credits also include *The Wolf Man* (George Waggner, 1941), *It Came from Outer Space* (Jack Arnold, 1953), and *The Shootist* (Don Siegel, 1976).

Bristol, Howard interior decorator of *Rebecca* (art direction by Lyle Wheeler), and set decorator of *Rope* (art direction by Perry Ferguson). His filmography also includes *The Little Foxes* (William Wyler, 1941), *Ball of Fire* (Howard Hawks, 1941), *Sleep My Love* (Douglas Sirk, 1948), *Kiss Me Deadly* (Robert Aldrich, 1955), *Guys and Dolls* (Joseph L. Mankiewicz, 1955), and *Three On a Couch* (Jerry Lewis, 1966).

Bumstead, Henry (1915-2006) art director of *The Man Who Knew Too Much* and *Vertigo* (both with Hal Pereira), and production designer of *Topaz* and *Family Plot*. After graduating at USC, Bumstead started interning at RKO as a draftsman and typesetter in 1935. Two years later he joined Paramount, where he worked under Hans Dreier as a unit art director for over two decades. During his Paramount years, Bumstead is probably best known for the sumptuous visuals of the two mentioned Hitchcock films of the late 1950s. Bumstead, whose career bridges the classical age of Hollywood set design within studios and the more location-oriented style of filmmaking that took hold over the mid-1960s, joined Universal in the early 1960s as a unit art director. Apart from working for two of Hitchcock's Universal movies, he designed sets for *To Kill a Mocking Bird* (Robert Mulligan, 1962), *The War Lord* (Franklin J. Schaffner), *The Sting* (George Roy Hill, 1973), *High Plains Drifter* (Clint Eastwood, 1973), *Unforgiven* (Clint Eastwood, 1993), among many others. He also worked on one of

the rooms in Hitchcock's own house in Los Angeles. For the director's Santa Cruz residence, Bumstead designed some outdoor furniture and iron gates and grilles.

Cain, Syd British art director of the stage and screen, who began as an assistant in 1955 and whose filmography includes *Fahrenheit 451* (François Truffaut, 1966). For Hitchcock he did the production design of *Frenzy*, in which he used the familiar and the mundane to emphasize the horror elements in the story. Michael Stephens calls his work on Hitchcock's penultimate film "one of the most subtle but successful examples of post-studio era scenic design in British cinema." He also worked in various capacities on four James Bond films: *Dr. No* (1962), *From Russia with Love* (1963), *Live and Let Die* (1973), and *Goldeneye* (1995).

Carpenter, Claude (1904-1976) set decorator (with Darrell Silvera) of *Notorious* (art direction by Carroll Clark and Albert S. D'Agostino). Working in Hollywood from 1942 to 1966, his filmography also includes *Experiment Perilous* (Jacques Tourneur, 1944, also with Darrell Silvera and Albert D'Agostino), *Portrait of Jenny* (William Dieterle, 1948), *Gentlemen Prefer Blondes* (Howard Hawks, 1953), and *Carmen Jones* (Otto Preminger, 1954).

Carrere, Edward (1906-1984) art director of *Dial M for Murder*, one of Hitchcock's single-set pictures that was shot in 3-D. Unit director at Warner Brothers in the 1940s and 1950s, mainly for B productions, Carrere also worked on seminal films of the era such as *White Heat* (Raoul Walsh, 1949) and *The Fountainhead* (King Vidor, 1949). For the latter, a film about an idealistic modern architect fighting the establishment, Carrere created some imaginative designs of modernist architecture (made largely through matte paintings and miniatures). His credits also include *Adventures of Don Juan* (Vincent Sherman, 1948), *Sunrise at Campobello* (Vincent J. Donehue, 1960), *Camelot* (Joshua Logan, 1967), and *The Wild Bunch* (Sam Peckinpah, 1969).

Carter, Maurice (1913-2000) assistant set designer (with Albert Jullion, both uncredited) of *The Lady Vanishes* (settings by Alex Vetchinsky). He also designed sets for the 1959 remake of *The 39 Steps* by Ralph Thomas.

Clark, Carroll (1894-1968) associate art director of *Suspicion* (art direction by Van Nest Polglase) and art director (with Albert S. D'Agostino) of *Notorious*. Trained as an architect, Clark entered the industry in the mid-1920s. After working at Pathé, he joined RKO in 1932, where he remained as a unit art director for many years. Together with supervising art director Polglase, Clark created some of the most memorable Art Deco-inspired elegant sets of the era, such as for the Fred Astaire and Ginger Rogers musicals *Flying Down to Rio* (1933), *The Gay Divorcee* (1934), *Top Hat* (1935), *Swing Time* (1936), *Follow the Fleet* (1936), and *Carefree* (1938). In the early 1940s, when Albert D'Agostino replaced Polglase as supervising art director, RKO and Clark turned to a more expressionist style of production design that perfectly answered to the moody, claustrophobic interiors and dark and rain-swept urban landscapes of film noir: *Murder My Sweet* (Edward Dmytryk, 1944), *Strange Bargain* (1949),

A Woman's Secret (Nicholas Ray, 1949), *Angel Face* (Otto Preminger, 1952), *Clash by Night* (Fritz Lang, 1952), *While the City Sleeps* (Fritz Lang, 1956). With the end of RKO in 1956, Clark joined Disney as their supervising art director. At the Disney studio, he helped to define the image of suburban middle-class America.

Clatworthy, Robert (1903-1972) art director (with Joseph Hurley) of *Psycho*. Clatworthy began his career as a unit art director at Paramount in the late 1930s. In the early 1940s, he joined Universal where he assisted Robert Boyle on *Saboteur* and *Shadow of a Doubt*. Despite limited budgets, Clatworthy created some impressive, hard-boiled expressionist sets of alienating nightclubs, dark bars, and menacing cityscapes. His designs of Orson Welles' *Touch of Evil* (1958), which features Janet Leigh in peril at a run-down motel, foreshadow the Bates Motel. His filmography also includes *Phantom Lady* (Robert Siodmak, 1944), *Written on the Wind* (Douglas Sirk, 1956), *The Incredible Shrinking Man* (1957), *That Touch of Mink* (Delbert Mann, 1962), and *Ship of Fools* (Stanley Kramer, 1965).

Comer, Sam (1893-1974) set decorator of Hitchcock's Paramount Pictures: (with Ray Moyer) *Rear Window* (art direction by Hal Pereira and Joseph MacMillan Johnson), (with Arthur Krams) *To Catch a Thief* (art direction by Hal Pereira and Joseph MacMillan Johnson), (with Emile Kuri) *The Trouble with Harry* (art direction by Hal Pereira and John Goodman), (with Arthur Krams) *The Man Who Knew Too Much* (art direction by Hal Pereira and Henry Bumstead), and (with Frank McKelvy) *Vertigo* (art direction by Hal Pereira and Henry Bumstead). His extensive filmography also includes a series of 1940s pictures by Mitchell Leisen (*Hold Back the Dawn*, *Take a Letter Darling*, *No Time for Love*, *Frenchman's Creek*, *Kitty*). In addition, Comer decorated sets for *Love Letters* (William Dieterle, 1945), *Samson and Delilah* (Cecil B. DeMille, 1949), *Sunset Boulevard* (Billy Wilder, 1952), and *The Ten Commandments* (Cecil B. DeMille, 1956) – all of them nominated for or winning the Best Art Direction Oscar.

D'Agostino, Albert S. (1894-1970) art director of *Mr. and Mrs. Smith* (uncredited, with Van Nest Polglase) and *Notorious* (with Carroll Clark). After studying architecture at Columbia University, D'Agostino became a leading stage designer who entered the film industry as an assistant art director at MGM. In 1925, he joined Universal, a studio that would become known for its Gothic horror during the 1930s. D'Agostino, who often combined the Gothic and the modern, joined RKO in 1940 as a unit art director. There, he soon replaced Van Nest Polglase as supervising art director introducing a new, *noirish* style characterized by odd angles and striking lighting effects. *Notorious* clearly displays the characteristics of the influential style of D'Agostino, who also created the designs for Val Lewton's psychological horrors (*Cat People*, *I Walked with a Zombie*, *The Body Snatcher*) and films about uncanny interiors such as *Stranger on the Third Floor* (Boris Ingster, 1940) and *The Spiral Staircase* (Robert Siodmak, 1946). His filmography also includes *The Magnificent Ambersons* (Orson Welles, 1942), *Out of the Past* (Jacques Tourneur, 1947), *The Set-Up*

(Robert Wise, 1949), *On Dangerous Ground* (Nicholas Ray, 1951), and *Clash by Night* (Fritz Lang, 1952).

Dali, Salvador (1904-1989) Spanish surrealist artist who collaborated on the script of Luis Buñuel's *Un chien andalou* (1929). His fascination with dreams, hallucinations, and psychopathology made him an obvious choice to design the dream sequence in Hitchcock's *Spellbound*. For that film, art director James Basevi and effects technician Jack Cosgrove designed sets based on five Dali paintings. He also designed sets and costumes for *Don Juan Tenorio* (Alejandro Perla, 1952).

Evans, Bertram art director of *The Lodger* (with C. Wilfred Arnold) and *Downhill*. His filmography also includes *The Rolling Road* (Graham Cutts, 1927) and *Blighty* (Adrian Brunel, 1927), which were also produced by Michael Balcon for Gainsborough.

Ewing, John (1901-1961) associate art director of *Spellbound* (art direction by James Basevi). Working for various studios, mostly for Universal, 20th-Century Fox and Warner Brothers, his filmography also includes John Brahm's 1944 remake of *The Lodger* (also with James Basevi), *House of Fear* (Joe May, 1939), and Selznick's production of *Duel in the Sun* (King Vidor, 1946).

Ferguson, Perry (1901-1963) art director who designed the ingenious set of Hitchcock's infamous single-set and single-take film *Rope*. With a background in art rather than architecture, Ferguson joined RKO in the early 1930s as a sketch artist and quickly rose to unit art director under Van Nest Polglase's supervision. He was the principal art director for Orson Welles' *Citizen Kane* (1941), which contained some of the most memorable sets of film history. After *Citizen Kane*, Ferguson's best work was seen in Sam Goldwyn productions such as *The North Star* (Lewis Milestone, 1943), *The Pride of the Yankees* (Sam Wood, 1942), *Up in Arms* (Elliott Nugent, 1944), *The Best Years of Our Lives* (William Wyler, 1946), *The Secret Life of Walter Mitty* (Norman Z. McLeod, 1947), and *A Song is Born* (Howard Hawks, 1948). At the end of his life, he mainly worked for the television department of Warner Brothers.

Freeman, Douglas set dresser (uncredited) of *Family Plot* (production design by Henry Bumstead and set decoration by James W. Payne). His credits also include *Magnum Force* (Ted Post, 1973), and *The Towering Inferno* (John Guillermin & Irwin Allan, 1974).

Gausman, Russell A. (1892-1963) set decorator at Universal, he worked for two Hitchcock Universal productions: *Saboteur* (art direction by Jack Otterson and Robert Boyle) and (with Edward R. Robinson) *Shadow of a Doubt* (art direction with John B. Goodman and Robert Boyle). His extensive filmography (over 650 titles), which runs from the 1930s up to 1960, also includes *Helzapoppin* (H.C. Potter, 1941), *Phantom of the Opera* (Arthur Lubin, 1943), *Scarlet Street* (Fritz Lang, 1945), *The Naked City* (Jules Dassin, 1948), and *Spartacus* (Stanley Kubrick, 1960). His most enduring legacy is his baroque over-decoration of Douglas

Sirk's 1950s domestic melodramas *Magnificent Obsession*, *All That Heaven Allows*, *Written on the Wind*, *The Tarnished Angels*, and *Imitation of Life.*

Gilbert, J. Charles British art director of the 1940s. He did the production design of the two shorts Hitchcock made during the Second World War for the British Ministry of Information: *Bon Voyage* and *Aventure Malgache*. He also designed the settings for the 1941 remake of *The Farmer's Wife* directed by Leslie Arliss & Norman Lee.

Golitzen, Alexander (1908-2005) Moscow-born art director of *Foreign Correspondent* for which he designed the working interior of a windmill and a one-acre recreation of a Dutch town, complete with tramcars and a drainage system, the latter needed to deal with the vast amounts of water required for a rain-soaked assassination sequence amid a sea of black umbrellas. For his efforts, Golitzen earned an Academy Award nomination. After graduating as an architect at the University of Wisconsin, Golitzen joined MGM as an illustrator in 1933 on Rouben Mamoulian's *Queen Christina*. For the first decade of his career in motion pictures, Golitzen was mainly an independent working for a number of studios. In 1942, he joined Universal as a unit art director where he became supervising art director in 1954. Although he never developed a personal style, Golitzen's black-and-white films display sympathy for expressionist techniques whereas his color productions show an extravagant sense of contrasting colors. One of the great all-purpose Hollywood designers, Golitzen created great sets for strong directors (Hitchcock, Lang, Ophüls, Siegel) who knew what they wanted. When, in the words of Elliott Stein, "the boss was a producer of the ilk of Ross Hunter, things turned out slick and glossy-to-specification: department-store-chic backgrounds for wax dummy actors – but it was always one of the better stores." His filmography also includes *Stagecoach* (John Ford, 1939), *Wuthering Heights* (William Wyler, 1939), *Scarlet Street* (Fritz Lang, 1945), *Letter from an Unknown Woman* (Max Ophuls, 1948), *Written On the Wind* (Douglas Sirk, 1956), *Touch of Evil* (Orson Welles, 1958), *Spartacus* (Stanley Kubrick, 1960), *To Kill a Mockingbird* (Robert Mulligan, 1962), and *Step Down to Terror* (1958), Henry Keller's remake of *Shadow of a Doubt.*

Goodman, John B. (1901-1991) art director (with Robert Boyle) of *Shadow of a Doubt* and (with Hal Pereira) *The Trouble with Harry*. After briefly studying architecture, Goodman joined Paramount as a draftsman in the early 1920s and remained there as an art director for two decades. In 1943, he joined Universal where he often worked in collaboration with Golitzen. At Universal, he worked on many of the studio's horror films and he also proved a sensible adaptor of Gothic and expressionist styles – as displayed in *Shadow of a Doubt* or Julien Duvivier's *Flesh and Fantasy* (1943). In 1946, he left Universal to work for other studios, mostly Paramount. Hitchcock's Paramount production of *The Trouble with Harry* shows Goodman's imaginative use of color. His credits also include *The Spoilers* (Ray Enright, 1942), *Phantom of the Opera* (Arthur Lubin, 1943), and *The Climax* (George Waggner, 1944).

Grace, Henry (1907-1983) set decorator (with Frank McKelvy) of *North by Northwest* (production design by Robert Boyle, art direction by William A. Horning and Merrill Pye). In the 1950s and early 1960s, his extensive filmography also includes MGM productions by Richard Brooks (*The Blackboard Jungle*, *The Brothers Karamazov*, *Cat on a Hot Tin Roof*), and Vincente Minnelli (*Designing Woman*, *Some Came Running*, *Gigi*, *Home from the Hill*, *The Sandpiper*).

Haworth, Edward S. (1917-1993) art director of two of Hitchcock's Warner Brothers pictures: *Strangers on a Train* and *I Confess*. Haworth had been employed for a number of years as an assistant art director and draftsman at Warners before his debut screen credit for *Strangers on a Train*, which combines actual locations with studio sets. Both Hitchcock pictures and films such as *Invasion of the Body Snatchers* (Don Siegel, 1956) show Haworth's mastery of design for black-and-white photography. Often billed as Ted Haworth, his filmography also includes *Marty* (1955), *Sayonara* (Joshua Logan, 1957) *Some Like It Hot* (Billy Wilder, 1959), *The Professionals* (Richard Brooks, 1966), and some Sam Peckinpah pictures of the early 1970s such as *Junior Bonner*, *The Getaway*, and *Pat Garett and Billy the Kid.*

Heckroth, Hein (1898-1970) production designer of *Torn Curtain*. Heckroth was a prominent stage designer in Germany, principally for the Jooss Ballet, in the 1920s. He left Germany in 1933 and after the war, he became an assistant to Albert Junge, when he worked for The Archers in Great Britain. They both worked on Michael Powell and Emeric Pressburger productions. In the late 1940s, Heckroth succeeded Junge as art director. His filmography includes *The Red Shoes* (1948), *Gone to Earth* (1951), and *The Tales of Hoffman* (1951), pictures by Powell and Pressburger, which, with their richly colored sets, contrast sharply with the bland and subdued colors of *Torn Curtain*, one of Heckroth's last projects.

Heron, Julia (1897-1977) interior decorator of *Foreign Correspondent* (art direction by Alexander Golitzen), who had worked as a set decorator for several Sam Goldwyn productions during the 1930s. In the 1950s, Heron became one of the staff designers on Hitchcock's television work. She designed sets of several episodes of *Alfred Hitchcock Presents* and later of *The Alfred Hitchcock Hour*. Her credits also include *Our Town* (Sam Wood, 1940), *Hangmen also Die* (Fritz Lang, 1943), *The Woman in the Window* (Fritz Lang, 1945), *The Best Years of Our Lives* (1946), and several of Douglas Sirk's melodramas such as *All I Desire* (1953), *All That Heaven Allows* (1955), *Written on the Wind* (1956), and *Imitation of Life* (1959).

Hitchcock, Alfred (1899-1980) Before he started directing films in 1925, Hitchcock was active as an art director. He entered the industry in 1919 when he was employed by the Islington studio of Famous Players-Lasky (later Paramount) as a graphic designer of inter-titles. A few years later, he served as an assistant director, and eventually co-screen-writer and art director on *Woman to Woman* (1923), *The*

White Shadow (1923), *The Passionate Adventure* (1924), *The Prude's Fall* (1924), and *The Blackguard* (1925) – all directed by Graham Cutts and produced by Michael Balcon. The sets of *The Blackguard* were created on the stages of the vast Neubabelsberg studio of UFA in Berlin. In addition, his first credits as director, *The Pleasure Garden* (1925) and *The Mountain Eagle* (1926), were mainly shot in the Emelka studios outside Munich. Hitchcock's lifelong interest in production design has often been interpreted as a result of his personal experiences in the German studios.

Hoesli, John (1919-1997) assistant art director (uncredited) of *Jamaica Inn* (settings by Thomas N. Morahan). His filmography also includes *The African Queen* (John Huston, 1951), and *2001: A Space Odyssey* (Stanley Kubrick, 1968).

Hopkins, George James (1896-1985) set decorator of three of Hitchcock's Warner Brothers productions: *Strangers on a Train* (art direction by Edward S. Haworth), *I Confess* (art direction by Edward S. Haworth), and *Dial M for Murder* (art direction by Edward Carrere). Born in Pasadena, Hopkins attended Occidental College and the Academy of Design in New York and was a scenic designer in the theater before working as an art director of Theda Bara pictures such as *Cleopatra* (1917) and *Salome* (1918) for Realart Studios and Famous Players-Lasky from 1917 to 1919. In 1936, he joined Warner Brothers where he became head set decorator. His credits also include *Casablanca* (Michael Curtiz, 1942), *Mildred Pierce* (Michael Curtiz, 1945), *Deception* (Irving Rapper, 1946), *A Streetcar Named Desire* (Elia Kazan, 1951), and *East of Eden* (Elia Kazan, 1956), *My Fair Lady* (George Cukor, 1964), *Who's Afraid of Virginia Woolf?* (Mike Nichols, 1966), and *Hello, Dolly!* (Gene Kelly, 1969).

Horning, William A. (1904-1959) art director (with Merrill Pye) of *North by Northwest* (production design by Robert Boyle), Hitchcock's only MGM picture. Horning joined MGM in 1931 as a draftsman and in 1936 he became an assistant to Cedric Gibbons, who ran the studio's art department. For about three decades, Horning personally oversaw the set designs for dozens of films at MGM. Horning's role seems to have been largely that of supervisor, overseeing the construction of sets, etc. One of the semi-anonymous studio craftsmen of the Golden Age, who were perfectly willing to do their work with little or no credit and dedicated wholly to the success of the studio, Horning's filmography includes *Fury* (Fritz Lang, 1936), *The Wizzard of Oz* (Victor Fleming, 1939), *Some Came Running* (Vincente Minnelli, 1958), *Gigi* (Vincente Minnelli, 1958), and *Ben Hur* (William Wyler, 1959) – always in collaboration and co-credited with others.

Hughes, Frank Elmo (1891-1947) associate set decorator of *Lifeboat* (art direction by James Basevi and Maurice Ransford, set decoration by Thomas Little). His filmography also includes other Fox films such as *The Song of Bernadette* (Henry King, 1943), *The Ox-Bow Incident* (William Wellman, 1943), and *Hangover Square* (John Brahm, 1945).

Hurley, Joseph F. (1914-1982) art director (with Robert Clatworthy) of *Psycho*. His filmography also includes *Comes a Horseman* (Alan Pakula, 1978), *The China Syndrome* (James Bridges, 1979), and *The Postman Always Rings Twice* (Bob Rafelson, 1981). He spent most of his career as an illustrator.

Irvine, Richard (1910-1976) associate art director (uncredited) of *Foreign Correspondent* (art direction by Alexander Golitzen, interior decoration by Julia Heron). He joined the motion picture industry in the early 1930s. An adaptable designer, working on a wide variety of films, mainly at 20th Century-Fox, Irvine's filmography includes *The Brasher Doubloon* (John Brahm, 1947) and *Miracle on 34th Street* (George Seaton, 1947). During World War II, Irvine joined Disney and he became responsible for planning and designing all new attractions in Disneyland, the four Disney shows at the New York World's Fair, and Walt Disney World in Florida.

Jullion, Albert (1909) art director (with Oscar Werndorff) of *The 39 Steps*, set decorator of *Secret Agent* and *Sabotage* (both art direction by Oscar Werndorff), and assistant set designer (uncredited) of *The Lady Vanishes*. His filmography also includes *Madonna of the Seven Moons* (1945) and *Caravan* (1946), both by Arthur Crabtree.

Junge, Alfred (1886-1964) art director (with Oscar Werndorff) of *Waltzes from Vienna*, the 1934 version of *The Man Who Knew Too Much*, and *Young and Innocent*. Starting his career as a stage designer in the 1910s when the European theater was in the embrace of expressionism, Junge became one of the most important German production designers after he had joined UFA in 1920. According to Edward Carrick, Junge "led the way as an artistic adviser on all points in the development of the film – selecting the camera positions, advising on lighting, and, as shown by so many of his sketches, deciding on the compositions of the figures within the frame." Junge worked for some significant UFA productions such as Paul Leni's *Das Wachsfigurenkabinett* (1924). In the late 1920s, he became the chief production designer of E.A. Dupont, for whom he created the sets of *Moulin Rouge* (1928), *Picadilly* (1929), and *Atlantik* (1929). When Dupont began working in Great Britain, Junge continued as his main designer and he left Germany permanently in 1933. A good organizer, Junge introduced, as it were, the notion of a supervising art director in the British film industries. Apart from his collaboration with Hitchcock, Junge's most important British realizations were his designs for such Powell-Pressburger pictures as *The Life and Death of Colonel Blimp* (1943), *A Matter of Life and Death* (1946), and *Black Narcissus* (1947). In the late 1940s and early 1950s, he headed the department of MGM's British studios.

Krams, Arthur (1912-1985) set decorator of *To Catch a Thief* (art direction by Hal Pereira, Joseph MacMillan Johnson), and the American version of *The Man Who Knew Too Much* (art direction by Hal Pereira and Henry Bumstead) – both with Sam Comer. After working as an interior designer in Chicago and New York, Krams was active in the industry from 1945 to 1969, mostly at MGM and Paramount. His filmography also includes *The Barkleys of Broadway* (Charles Walters, 1949), *Artists and Models* (Frank Tashlin, 1955), *The Rose Tattoo* (Daniel Mann, 1955), and *Gunfight at the O.K. Coral* (John Sturges, 1957).

Kuehl, William L set decorator of *The Wrong Man* (art direction by Paul Sylbert). His list of films, mostly at Warner Brothers, includes *Dark Passage* (Delmer Daves, 1947), *A Kiss in the Dark* (Delmer Daves, 1949), *The Fountainhead* (King Vidor, 1949), *Beyond the Forest* (King Vidor, 1949), *The Damned Don't Cry* (Vincent Sherman, 1950), *The Enforcer* (Britaigne Windust, 1951), and *The Court-Martial of Billy Mitchell* (Otto Preminger, 1955).

Kuri, Emile (1907-2000) Mexican-born interior decorator of *Spellbound* (art direction by James Basevi), and set decorator of *The Paradine Case* (production design by J. McMillan Johnson and art direction by Thomas Morahan), *Rope* (art direction by Perry Ferguson), and *The Trouble with Harry* (art direction by Hal Pereira and John Goodman). Kuri shortly joined the industry in the late 1920s, after having decorated rooms in the Beverly Hills residence of Hal Roach. In the 1940s, he ended up with Selznick working on the sets of *I'll Be Seeing You* (William Dieterle, 1942), *Duel in the Sun* (King Vidor, 1946) and some of Hitchcock's Selznick pictures. Moving frequently from studio to studio, he also collaborated with Hitchcock at Transatlantic and Paramount. His filmography also includes *The Heiress* (William Wyler, 1949), *A Place in the Sun* (George Stevens, 1951), and several Disney films such as *20,000 Leagues Under the Sea* (Richard Fleischer, 1954), and *Mary Poppins* (Robert Stevenson, 1964). Kuri also extensively redesigned Hitchcock's Bel-Air home and, toward the end of *Spellbound*'s shooting schedule, he redecorated the living areas of Ingrid Bergman's house.

Laing, Bob art director of *Frenzy* (production design by Syd Cain). His filmography also includes *On Her Majesty's Secret Service* (Peter Hunt, 1969), *Live and Let Die* (Guy Hamilton, 1973), *Gandhi* (Richard Attenborough, 1982), and *Titanic* (James Cameron, 1997). He often worked in association with production designer Syd Cain.

Little, Thomas (1886-1985) set decorator of *Lifeboat* (art direction by James Basevi and Maurice Ransford). Little began his carreer in a Salt Lake City Theater and entered the film industry with the Robert Brunton Studios. He worked in the art departments of Warner Bros., First National, RKO, Paramount, and Universal before becoming head of Fox' property department until his retirement in 1952. His extensive filmography, which runs from the early 1930s up to the early 1950s, includes *How Green Was My Valley* (John Ford, 1941), *The Ox-Bow Incident* (William Wellman, 1943), *Jane Eyre* (Robert Stevenson, 1944), *Hangover Square* (1945), *Dragonwyck* (Joseph L. Mankiewicz), *Whirlpool* (Otto Preminger, 1949), *House on Telegraph Hill* (Robert Wise, 1951), and John Brahm's remake of *The Lodger* (1944).

McCallum Tait, Kenneth (1915) assistant art director (uncredited) of *Under Capricorn* (production design by Thomas Morahan and set decoration by Philip Stockford). His filmography also includes *The Young Ones* (Sidney J. Fury, 1961), *One Million Years B.C.* (Don Chaffey, 1966) and TV episodes of *The Avengers* (1969).

McKelvey, Frank set decorator who started with Paramount in 1955 and worked (with Sam Comer) for *Vertigo* (art direction by Hal Pereira and Henry Bumstead). He followed Hitchcock to MGM and decorated (with Henry Grace) the sets of *North by Northwest* (production design by Robert Boyle, art direction by William A. Horning and Merrill Pye). His filmography also includes *Wild Harvest* (Tay Garnett, 1947), *Run for Cover* (Nicholas Ray, 1955), *The Misfits* (John Huston, 1961), and 1959 episodes of the TV series *The Twilight Zone*.

McMillan Johnson, Joseph (1912-1990) production designer of *The Paradine Case* (art direction by Thomas Morahan), and art director of *Rear Window* and *To Catch a Thief* (both with Hal Pereira). After studying architecture at USC and the Art Center School in Los Angeles, McMillan Johnson worked for the architect Kem Weber until he was hired by the Selznick Studios in 1938, where he made sketches for *Gone with the Wind* (Victor Fleming, 1939). During the McCarthy era, he left the motion picture industry for about a year and did architectural renderings for many notable architects in the LA area. His filmography also includes *Portrait of Jenny* (William Dieterle, 1948), *Mutiny on the Bounty* (Lewis Milestone, 1962), *The Greatest Story Ever Told* (George Stevens, 1965), and *7 Women* (John Ford, 1966).

Marchant, James art director of *Juno and the Paycock*. In the late 1940s, Marchant designed sets for films by Alfred Goulding (*Dick Barton: Special Agent*, *The Dark Road*), and Godfrey Grayson (*Dr. Morelle: The Case of the Missing Heiress*, *The Adventures of P.C. 49*).

Maxwell, J.B art director of *The Skin Game*.

Mead, John F art director (with Peter Proud) of *Murder*. His filmography also includes *Harmony Heaven* (Thomas Bentley, 1929), *After Office Hours* (Thomas Bentley, 1932), *Abdul the Damned* (Karl Grune, 1935), and *Aren't Men Beasts?* (Graham Cutts, 1937).

Menzies, William Cameron (1896-1957) credited with special production effects for *Foreign Correspondent*. After studying at Yale University and the Arts Student League in New York and his service in the Navy during World War I, Menzies was hired by Anton Grot as an assistant designer at the Fort Lee Studios in New Jersey. Soon after, Menzies left for California where he would become one of the very truly independent art directors in Hollywood's Golden Age. His designs for *The Thief of Baghdad* (Raoul Walsh, 1924) proved immensely important and influential and Menzies himself specialized in fantastic and exotic sets in the late 1920s and early 1930s. Other visually stunning productions by Menzies were *Alice in Wonderland* (Norman Z.

McLeod) and *Things to Come* (1936), which he directed himself. In the late 1930s, Selznick asked Menzies to literally design the production of *Gone With the Wind* (Victor Fleming, 1939). It was for this film, of which Menzies can be considered the true *auteur*, that the credit 'production designer' was conceived, which entails all of the visual details of the production from set designs to camera angles and costume designs. Menzies also oversaw the construction of the sets of *Foreign Correspondent*, which were designed by Alexander Golitzen. However, according to Robert S. Sennett, Menzies' "wit and sense of scale flash all over the film." In addition, Menzies was also responsible for some retakes of *Spellbound*'s dream sequence, refusing the credit because he disliked the sequence. According to Elliott Stein, "identifiably Menziesian perspectives run as visual leitmotifs through nearly forty years of design (e.g. a predilection for broken diagonal barriers which cross the frame like jagged slashes and usually turn up during scenes of tension, grief, and separation in the form of fences, walls, palisades, railings). They can be seen in the Murnau-like designs for *Tempest*, in Griffith's *Lincoln, Kings Row, Our Town* – and both in the lavish *Gone With the Wind* and the fine low-budgeter *Invaders from Mars*." His extensive filmography also includes *The Deep Purple* (Raoul Walsh, 1920), *The Son of the Sheik* (George Fitzmaurice, 1926), *Sadie Thompson* (Raoul Walsh, 1928), *The Thief of Baghdad* (Ludwig Berger and Michael Powell, 1940), *Duel in the Sun* (King Vidor, 1946), and *Invaders from Mars* (1953), which he directed himself.

Milo, George set decorator of *Psycho* (art direction by Joseph Hurley and Robert Clatworthy), *The Birds* (production design by Robert Boyle), *Marnie* (production design by Robert Boyle), and *Torn Curtain* (production design by Hein Heckroth and art direction by Frank Arrigo). He also was set decorator of *Banquo's Chair* (1959) and *Incident at a Corner* (1960), TV episodes directed by Hitchcock himself. Before, in the 1940s, Milo had decorated sets for numerous westerns at Republic.

Morahan, Thomas (1906-1969) art director of *Jamaica Inn, The Paradine Case* (production design by Joseph McMillan Johnson) and *Under Capricorn* – three controversial Hitchcock films, the production design of which, however, is superb. After studying architecture, painting, and sculpture, Morahan joined Vincent Korda as a draftsman in 1933 and worked as his assistant until 1936. One of the leading art directors in Great Britain for three decades, Morahan was an adaptable talent with no noticeable personal style, which explains his relative anonymity. Working on both sides of the Atlantic through 1968, his filmography also includes *Captain Horatio Hornblower* (Raoul Walsh, 1951), *Sons and Lovers* (Jack Cardiff, 1960), and *Those Magnificent Men in Their Flying Machines* (Ken Annakin, 1965).

Moyer, Ray (1898-1986) set decorator (with Sam Comer) of the large and complex single set of *Rear Window* (art direction by Hal Pereira and Joseph MacMillan Johnson). Moyer worked at the Paramount Studios throughout the 1940s, 1950s, and 1960s. In his later years, he worked with John Wayne at Batjac Productions. His filmography

includes *Samson and Delilah* (Cecil B. DeMille, 1949), *Sunset Boulevard* (Billy Wilder, 1950), and *Cleopatra* (Joseph L. Mankiewicz, 1963).

Otterson, Jack (1881-1975) art director (with Robert Boyle) of *Saboteur*. After studying architecture at Yale and collaborating as an architect on designs of the Empire State Building, Otterson joined Fox in 1932 as a sketch artist. In 1936, he moved to Universal, where he was supervising art director from 1937 up until 1943 and where he is best remembered for his atmospheric sets for the studio's horror films. After that, he remained working at Universal as a unit art director on films such as *The Killers* (Robert Siodmak, 1946). In 1946, he resigned to devote himself to painting. His filmography also includes *Magnificent Brute* (John G. Blystone, 1936), *You're a Sweetheart* (David Butler, 1937), *Mad About Music* (Norman Taurog, 1938), *First Love* (Henry Koster, 1939), *Flame of New Orleans* (René Clair, 1941), *The Spoilers* (Ray Enright, 1942), and *Arabian Nights* (John Rawlins, 1942).

Payne, James W set decorator in Hollywood from 1959 of *Family Plot* (production design by Henry Bumstead). His filmography also includes *Come Blow Your Horn* (Bud Yorkin, 1963), *The Oscar* (Russell Rouse, 1966), and *The Sting* (George Roy Hill, 1973).

Pember, Clifford British art director who first worked in Hollywood on *Way Down East* (D.W. Griffith, 1920) and then returned to England for *Easy Virtue*. His credits also include *The Triumph of the Scarlet Pimpernel* (T. Hayes Hunter, 1928), *The Bondman* (Herbert Wilcox, 1929), *The Woman in White* (Herbert Wilcox, 1930), and *The Sign of Four* (Graham Cutts, 1932).

Pereira, Hal (1903-1972) credited as art director of Hitchcock's Paramount films, always in collaboration with unit art directors such as Joseph MacMillan Johnson (*Rear Window* and *To Catch a Thief*), John Goodman (*The Trouble with Harry*), and Henry Bumstead (*The Man Who Knew Too Much* and *Vertigo*). After studying at the University of Illinois, Hal Pereira joined his brother William Pereira's Chicago architectural firm in 1933. Over the following seven years, he specialized in designing film theaters, many of which were recognized as outstanding examples of the form. In the early 1940s, Pereira joined Paramount as an illustrator, where he became a unit art director in 1944 on Billy Wilder's *Double Indemnity*. Switching to Paramount's New York home office in 1946, he handled special assignments as well as the supervision of theater design, both domestically and in South America and overseas. Upon his return to the studio in 1950, he succeeded Hans Dreier as supervising art director perhaps because his exemplary work did not answer to an identifiable personal style. Although most of the designs were probably created by the associate art directors credited with him, Pereira undoubtedly earned some of the credit for the success of the art direction under his supervision. During the course of his career, he worked on some 150 motion pictures and 400 television shows. Between 1952 and 1966, he was nominated for an Academy Award for his work on 23 different pictures. The superb period décor of William Wyler's *Carrie*, made under Pereira's supervision, can be considered one of the finest accomplishments of the Paramount art department of the 1950s.

Platt, Joseph B. (1896-1968) New York industrial and interior designer who decorated the interior sets of several Selznick productions such as *Gone with the Wind* (Victor Fleming, 1939), *Portrait of Jenny* (William Dieterle, 1948) and *Rebecca* (art direction by Lyle Wheeler). In addition, he was set decorator of *The Paradine Case* (production design by Joseph McMillan Johnson and art direction by Thomas Morahan). His filmography also includes *Lady of Burlesque* (William Wellman, 1943). He also did Broadway sets. In the commercial design field, he created Whitman's Sampler box.

Polglase, Van Nest (1898-1968) art director (with Lawrence P. Williams) of *Mr. and Mrs. Smith* and (with Carroll Clark) *Suspicion*. Van Nest Polglase studied architecture at the Beaux Arts School in New York. After practicing the craft in New York City and Cuba for several years in the 1910s, he joined the art department of Famous Players-Lasky (Paramount) in 1919, where he quickly achieved fame as one of the most innovative designers in American cinema. In 1929, Cedric Gibbons hired Polglase as a unit director at MGM. In 1932, Polglase joined RKO where he was supervising art director for the next ten years. As influential a supervising art director as Gibbons was at MGM, Polglase assigned the appropriate projects to unit art directors, approving their drawings, sketches, and designs. Unlike Gibbons at MGM, however, Polglase did not arbitrarily receive credit for every film released by the studio, and he took a more active role overall in designing individual productions. In particular, Polglase became associated with the fixed architectural institution that became known as the B.W.S. (Big White Set) – the glossy and sophisticated Art Deco sets for Fred Astaire and Ginger Roger musicals, which he often designed in collaboration with expert craftsmen such as Carroll Clark: *The Gay Divorcee* (1934), *Top Hat* (1935), *Carefree* (1938) – all directed by Mark Sandrich. For Ginger Rogers, Polglase and the RKO art department even designed a real house. Throughout the 1930s, the sophisticated modernity of these musicals represented the dominant image of RKO although in the majority of the films supervised by Polglase, a more reserved contemporary American style prevailed. When Albert S. D'Agostino joined the studio in 1940, darker and expressionist tendencies came to the fore. The sets of Hitchcock's *Suspicion* perfectly demonstrate this peculiar mix of polished Art Deco and *noirish* atmosphere. In 1943, Polglase joined Columbia as a unit art director and in the early 1950s, he became a freelance art director mainly working for low-budget programmers, many of them directed by Allan Dwan: *Silver Lode* (1954), *Cattle Queen of Montana* (1954), *Tennessee's Partner* (1955). His filmography also includes *Stage Struck* (Allan Dwan, 1925), *Little Women* (George Cukor, 1933), *Bringing Up Baby* (Howard Hawks, 1939), *Citizen Kane* (Orson Welles, 1941), and *Gilda* (Charles Vidor, 1946).

Powell, Michael (1905-1990) famous director who created some idiosyncratic masterpieces with Emeric Pressburger in the 1940s and the early 1950s (*The Life and Death of Colonel Blimp*, *A Matter of Life and Death*, *Black Narcissus*, *The Red Shoes, The Tales of Hoffmann*), collaborated on several early Hitchcock films. Apart from being a still photographer for *Champagne* and *The Manxman*, he was an assistant cameraman of *Blackmail*, to which he also was a contributor to the script (both uncredited). Powell stated that it was he who suggested the final chase over the roof of the British Museum. According to some sources, Powell also worked as a set designer (uncredited) for *Champagne* (art direction by Wilfred Arnold).

Proud, Peter (1913-1989) art director of *Murder* and (with Alfred Junge) *The Man Who Knew Too Much* (uncredited), and assistant art director of *Waltzes from Vienna* (art direction by Alfred Junge and Oscar Werndorff). A former assistant of Alfred Junge, Proud became a master of classical, studio-bound design, who became best known for his collaborations with Hitchcock. He had the reputation of being the designer with the greatest ability for adopting or converting 'stock sets.' Without the resources of the Hollywood studios, Proud managed to create surprisingly effective sets on relatively small stages. His filmography also includes *Something Always Happens* (Michael Powell, 1934), and *The League of Gentlemen* (Basil Dearden, 1947).

Pye, Merrill (1901-1975) art director (with William A. Horning) of *North by Northwest* (production design by Robert Boyle), which was his final credit. In Hollywood from 1925, he came to MGM in 1933 where he became a unit art director for several decades, specializing in musicals. Although Cedric Gibbons usually received the credits for the sleek Art Deco-inspired big white sets of the MGM musicals, they were actually largely the creation of Pye. In 1959, he was assigned to the studio's *Ben Hur* simultaneously with *North by Northwest*, which impressively combines location shots with impressive sets constructed on sound stages. His filmography includes *Broadway Melody* (Harry Beaumont, 1929), *Freaks* (Tod Browning, 1932), *The Great Ziegfeld* (Robert Z. Leonad, 1936), *Babes in Arms* (Busby Berkeley, 1939), *Bathing Beauty* (George Sidney, 1944), *Ziegfeld Follies* (Lemuel Ayers & Roy Del Ruth, 1945), and *Journey to the Center of the Earth* (Henry Levin, 1959). He also worked for television.

Ransford, Maurice (1896-1963) art director of *Lifeboat* (with James Basevi), one of Hitchcock's impressive single set films. After studying architecture at the University of Illinois and practicing the profession in the 1920s, Ransford joined 20th Century-Fox in the early 1930s. He remained his entire career at the studio, where he became the primary art director of the Fox *noirs*, for which he often designed deceptively conventional middle-class interiors as a backdrop for psychological and physical violence: *Hangover Square* (John Brahm, 1945), *Leave Her to Heaven* (John Stahl, 1945), *Somewhere in the Night* (Joseph L. Mankiewicz, 1946), *Panic in the Streets* (Elia Kazan, 1950), *Niagara* (Henry Hathaway, 1953).

Reiber, Ludwig (1904) art director of Hitchcock's two first films, *The Pleasure Garden* and the now lost *The Mountain Eagle* (together with Willy Reiber), both produced at the Munich studios of Emelka (Münchener Lichtspielkunst). He made also the designs for various other Emelka productions directed by Franz Seitz, Louis Ralph, Arthur Bergen, James Bauer, Willy Reiber, and Karl Grune, among others. His filmography also includes *Decision Before Dawn* (Anatole Litvak, 1951), and *Paths of Glory* (Stanley Kubrick, 1957).

Robinson, Edward R. (1893-1979) associate set decorator (with Russell A. Gausman) of *Shadow of a Doubt* (art direction by John Goodman and Robert Boyle). Robinson decorated sets of numerous Universal productions in the 1940s. His filmography includes *The Spoilers* (Ray Enright, 1942), *Flesh and Fantasy* (Julien Duvivier, 1943), *The Killers* (Robert Siodmak, 1946), and *Ruthless* (Edgar G. Ulmer, 1948).

Silvera, Darrell (1900-1983) set decorator of the three films Hitchcock made for RKO, where he was head of the prop department: *Mr. and Mrs. Smith* (art direction by Van Nest Polglase), *Suspicion* (art direction by Van Nest Polglase and Carroll Clark), and (with Claude Carpenter) *Notorious* (art direction by Carroll Clark and Albert S. D'Agostino). He joined the studio when he was seventeen but he earned his first RKO credit in 1936. From then onwards, he decorated numerous sets under Polglase's and D'Agostino's supervision until the studio ended in 1956. Polglase's chief set decorator on at least five of the Astaire-Rogers pictures, Silvera had at times as many as 110 set decorators, including furniture men and carpet men, working under him. He later became a freelance set decorator. His filmography includes *Citizen Kane* (Orson Welles, 1941), *The Magnificent Ambersons* (Orson Welles, 1942), *Experiment Perilous* (Jacques Tourneur, 1944), and *The Man with the Golden Arm* (Otto Preminger, 1955).

Stockford, Philip set decorator of *Under Capricorn* (production design by Thomas Morahan). His filmography also includes *The First Gentleman* (Alberto Cavalcanti, 1948) and *The Queen of Spades* (Thorold Dickinson, 1949).

Sylbert, Paul (1928) art director of *The Wrong Man*. Sylbert was also production designer of such films as *A Face in the Crowd* (Elia Kazan, 1957 – together with his twin brother Richard Sylbert), *One Flew Over the Cuckoo's Nest* (Milos Forman, 1975), *Hardcore* (Paul Schrader, 1979), and *Blow Out* (Brian De Palma, 1981). In addition, Paul Sylbert also directed films for both the screen and television.

Verity, Terence (1913) British art director of *Stage Fright*, who had studied architecture in London. His filmography also includes *Corridor of Mirrors* (Terence Young, 1948), *The Hasty Heart* (Vincent Sherman, 1949), *Duel in the Jungle* (George Marshall, 1954), *The Dark Avenger* (Henry Levin, 1955), *The Naked Earth* (Vincent Sherman, 1958), and *The Devil's Disciple* (Guy Hamilton, 1959).

Vetchinsky, Alex (1905-1986) art director of *The Lady Vanishes*, for which, in addition to designing the cramped carriages of the steam train, he also provided the train station and the rustic hotel seen at the beginning of the film. One of the leading English art directors, Vetchinsky's career spanned five decades. In the 1920s, he designed productions for several notable slapstick comedies starring Will Hay and the Crazy Gang. In the 1930s and 1940s, Vetchinsky worked mostly at Gainsborough designing sets for several films by Carol Reed, such as *A Girl Must Live* (1939), *Girl in the News* (1940), *Night Train to Munich* (1940), and *The Young Mr. Pitt* (1942).

Wakefield, Simon set dresser of *Frenzy* (production design by Syd Cain, art direction by Bob Laing). His filmography includes *An American Werewolf in London* (John Landis, 1981) and some 1969 episodes of the TV series *The Avengers*.

Werndorff, Oscar M. (1887-1938) aka Otto Werndorff, Oskar Friedrich Werndorff, he is the art director (with Alfred Junge) of *Waltzes from Vienna*, *The 39 Steps* (with Albert Jullion), *Secret Agent*, and *Sabotage*. Born in Vienna, Werndorff studied architecture and worked as a building designer in the 1910s. According to some sources he once held the prestigious post of chief architect to the last emperor of Austria. In the early 1920s, he entered the industry by designing sets that combined expressionist and conventional elements. His greatest triumph of that era is *Varieté* (1925) by E.A. Dupont, who started to work in England in the late 1920s. In the 1930s, Werndorff moved to the United Kingdom, where he worked on Hitchcock's Gaumont productions, which were almost entirely shot in the studio.

Wheeler, Lyle (1905-1990) art director of *Rebecca*. After studying industrial and architectural design at the University of Southern California, Wheeler worked as an architect, industrial designer, and magazine illustrator in the 1920s. After having been employed as a sketch artist and assistant art director by MGM for about six years, Wheeler joined Selznick International Pictures in 1935. Although Wheeler's style was more realistic, Selznick demanded that he create the sort of massive and richly decorated sets that could compete with Cedric Gibbon's overblown MGM sets. In particular, Wheeler designed the highly stylized sets for Selznick's color productions *The Garden of Allah* (Richard Boleslawski, 1936), *A Star is Born* (William A. Wellman, 1937), *Nothing Sacred* (William A. Wellman, 1937), and, most notably, *Gone With the Wind* (Victor Fleming, 1939). Also for Selznick, Wheeler designed the impressive sets of Hitchcock's *Rebecca*. In 1941, Wheeler returned to MGM as a unit art director but joined 20th-Century Fox in 1943, where, four years later, he became one of the great supervising art directors of Hollywood's Golden Age. As a supervisor (until 1962), Wheeler assigned the appropriate art director to a project and approved of his designs. In this capacity, Wheeler received numerous screen credits and many Oscar nominations and awards. In contrast with Gibbons at MGM, however, Wheeler would often personally work on individual productions. This is the case with some of Otto Preminger films of the late 1940s and early 1950s, such as

Whirlpool and *Where the Sidewalk Ends*. In the early 1960s, he worked as a production designer at Columbia and other studios. His extensive filmography also includes *Man in the Attic*, Hugo Fregonese's 1953 remake of *The Lodger*.

Whitlock, Albert (1915-1999) Although not an art director in the strictest sense, Whitlock contributed largely to the creation of Hitchcock's cinematic spaces as the man responsible for the 'pictorial designs,' 'special effects,' or 'special photographic effects.' He began a life-long association with Hitchcock, doing all the signs for *The 39 Steps* and assisting in the miniature effects for *The Man Who Knew Too Much* (uncredited). At Gaumont British, Whitlock had started as a sign painter, then switched to painting art titles, then scenic backdrops and miniatures. After having worked as an assistant to a visiting German crew which was making Schufftan process shots, Whitlock started doing matte work and he subsequently became one of the most skilled matte artists in the history of motion pictures. Mastering an impressionistic approach to matte painting, Whitlock developed a trademark technique of working on the original negative and adding moving elements such as clouds or waves to give more life to mattes. In 1954, he came to the United States to work for Disney and in 1961 he moved to Universal, where he created mattes for *The Birds*, *Marnie*, *Torn Curtain*, *Topaz*, *Frenzy*, and *Family Plot*. He also acted in Mel Brooks' Hitchcock pastiche *High Anxiety* (1977).

Williams, Lawrence Paul (1905-1996) associate art director of *Mr. and Mrs. Smith* (art direction by Van Nest Polglase). His filmography also includes *Brief Encounter* (David Lean, 1945) and several pictures directed by Herbert Wilcox, both in England and in Hollywood under an arangement with RKO, such as *The Woman in White* (1929), *The Loves of Robert Burns* (1930), *Carnival* (1931), *Nell Gwyn* (1934), *Victoria The Great* (1937), *Sixty Glorious Years* (1938), *Nurse Edith Cavell* (1939), *Irene* (1940), and *Sunny* (1941).

Filmography

List of films directed by Alfred Hitchcock with indication of producers, art directors, production designers, and set decorators.

For more complete listings of cast and crew, see Sloan (1993), McGilligan (2003), or the Internet Movie Database (www.imdb.com). For DVD releases of Hitchcock films and comparisons between various editions, see http://www.daveyp.com/hitchcock/wiki

The Pleasure Garden (1925)
Produced by Michael Balcon and Erich Pommer for Gainsborough and Münchener Lichtspielkunst
Art Direction: Ludwig Reiber

The Mountain Eagle (1926)
Produced by Michael Balcon for Gainsborough and Münchener Lichtspielkunst
Art Direction: Willy Reiber, Ludwig Reiber

The Lodger: A Story of the London Fog (1926)
Produced by Michael Balcon and Carlyle Blackwell for Gainsborough
Art Direction: C. Wilfred Arnold, Bertram Evans

Downhill (1927)
Produced by C.M. Woolf and Michael Balcon for Gainsborough
Art Direction: Bertram Evans

The Ring (1927)
Produced by John Maxwell for British International Pictures
Art Direction: C. Wilfred Arnold

Easy Virtue (1927)
Produced by C.M. Woolf & Michael Balcon for Gainsborough
Art Direction: Clifford Pember

The Farmer's Wife (1928)
Produced by John Maxwell for British International Pictures
Art Direction: C. Wilfred Arnold

Champagne (1928)
Produced by John Maxwell for British International Pictures
Art Direction: C. Wilfred Arnold
Set Designer: Michael Powell (uncredited)

The Manxman (1929)
Produced by John Maxwell for British International Pictures
Art Direction: C. Wilfred Arnold

Blackmail (1929)
Produced by John Maxwell for British International Pictures
Art Direction: C. Wilfred Arnold, Norman Arnold

Juno and the Paycock (1930)
Produced by John Maxwell for British International
Pictures
Art Direction: James Marchant, Norman G. Arnold
(uncredited)

Elstree Calling (1930)
Directed by Alfred Hitchcock, André Charlot,
Jack Hulbert, and Paul Murray (Hitchcock directed
"sketches and other interpolated items.")
Produced by John Maxwell for British International
Pictures

Murder (1930)
Produced by John Maxwell for British International
Pictures
Art Direction: John F. Mead, Peter Proud

The Skin Game (1931)
Produced by John Maxwell for British International
Pictures
Art Direction: J.B. Maxwell

Rich and Strange (1932)
Produced by John Maxwell for British International
Pictures
Art Direction: C. Wilfred Arnold

Number Seventeen (1932)
Produced by Leon M. Lion and John Maxwell for British
International Pictures
Art Direction: C. Wilfred Arnold

Waltzes from Vienna (1933)
Produced by Thomas Charles Arnold for Tom Arnold
Productions/Gaumont-British
Art Direction: Alfred Junge, Oscar Werndorff
Assistant Art Direction: Peter Proud

The Man Who Knew Too Much (1934)
Produced by Michael Balcon and Ivor Montagu for
Gaumont British
Art Direction: Alfred Junge, Peter Proud (uncredited)

The 39 Steps (1935)
Produced by Michael Balcon and Ivor Montagu for
Gaumont British
Art Direction: Albert Jullion, Oscar Werndorff

Secret Agent (1936)
Produced by Michael Balcon and Ivor Montagu for
Gaumont British
Art Direction: Oscar Werndorff
Set Decoration: Albert Jullion

Sabotage (1936)
Produced by Michael Balcon and Ivor Montagu for
Gaumont British
Art Direction: Oscar Werndorff
Set Decoration: Albert Jullion

Young and Innocent (1937)
Produced by Edward Black for Gaumont British
Art Direction: Alfred Junge

The Lady Vanishes (1938)
Produced by Edward Black for Gaumont British
Settings: Alex Vetchinsky
Assistant Set Design: Maurice Carter (uncredited),
Albert Jullion (uncredited)

Jamaica Inn (1939)
Produced by Erich Pommer and Charles Laughton for
Mayflower Pictures
Settings: Thomas N. Morahan
Assistant Art Director: John Hoesli (uncredited)

Rebecca (1940)
Produced by David O. Selznick for Selznick International
Pictures
Art Direction: Lyle Wheeler
Interiors: Joseph B. Platt
Interior Decoration: Howard Bristol

Foreign Correspondent (1940)
Produced by Walter Wanger for Walter Wanger
Productions – United Artists
Art Direction: Alexander Golitzen
Associate Art Direction: Richard Irvine (uncredited)
Interior Decoration: Julia Heron
Constructor: Oscar Brodin (uncredited)

Mr. and Mrs. Smith (1941)
Produced by Harry E. Edington for RKO
Art Direction: Van Nest Polglase, Albert S. D'Agostino
(uncredited)
Associate Art Direction: Lawrence P. Williams
Set Decoration: Darrell Silvera

Suspicion (1941)
Produced by Harry E. Edington for RKO
Art Direction: Van Nest Polglase
Associate Art Direction: Carroll Clark
Set Decoration: Darrell Silvera

Saboteur (1942)
Produced by Jack H. Skirball for Frank Lloyd Productions
– Universal
Art Direction: Jack Otterson
Associate Art Direction: Robert Boyle
Set Decoration: Russell A. Gausman

Shadow of a Doubt (1943)
Produced by Jack H. Skirball for Universal – Skirball
Productions
Art Direction: John B. Goodman
Associate Art Direction: Robert Boyle
Set Decoration: Russell A. Gausman
Associate Set Decoration: Edward R. Robinson

Lifeboat (1943)
Produced by Kenneth MacGowan for
Twentieth -Century Fox
Art Direction: James Basevi, Maurice Ransford
Set Decoration : Thomas Little
Associate Set Decoration : Frank E. Hughes

Bon Voyage (1944)
Produced by the British Ministry of Information for
Phoenix Films
Production Design: J. Charles Gilbert

Aventure Malgache (1944)
Produced by the British Ministry of Information for
Phoenix Films
Production Design: J. Charles Gilbert

Spellbound (1945)
Produced by David O. Selznick for Selznick International
Pictures
Art Direction: James Basevi
Associate Art Direction: John Ewing
Interior Decoration: Emile Kuri
Dream Sequence Design: Salvador Dali

Notorious (1946)
Produced by Alfred Hitchcock for RKO
Art Direction: Carroll Clark, Albert S. D'Agostino
Set Decoration: Darrell Silvera, Claude Carpenter

The Paradine Case (1947)
Produced by David O. Selznick for Selznick International
Pictures
Production Design: Joseph McMillan Johnson
Art Direction: Thomas Morahan
Interiors: Joseph B. Platt
Set Decoration: Emile Kuri

Rope (1948)
Produced by Alfred Hitchcock & Sidney Bernstein for
Transatlantic Pictures
Art Direction: Perry Ferguson
Set Decoration: Emile Kuri, Howard Bristol

Under Capricorn (1949)
Produced by Alfred Hitchcock & Sidney Bernstein for
Transatlantic Pictures
Production Design: Thomas Morahan
Set Decoration: Philip Stockford
Assistant Art Direction: Kenneth McCallum Tait
(uncredited)

Stage Fright (1950)
Produced by Alfred Hitchcock for Warner Brothers
Art Direction: Terence Verity

Strangers on a Train (1951)
Produced by Alfred Hitchcock for Warner Brothers
Art Direction: Edward S. Haworth
Set Decoration: George James Hopkins

I Confess (1952)
Produced by Alfred Hitchcock for Warner Brothers
Art Direction: Edward S. Haworth
Set Decoration: George James Hopkins

Dial M for Murder (1954)
Produced by Alfred Hitchcock for Warner Brothers
Art Direction: Edward Carrere
Set Decoration: George James Hopkins

Rear Window (1954)
Produced by Alfred Hitchcock for Paramount
Art Direction: Hal Pereira, Joseph MacMillan Johnson
Set Decoration: Sam Comer, Ray Moyer

To Catch a Thief (1955)
Produced by Alfred Hitchcock for Paramount
Art Direction: Hal Pereira, Joseph MacMillan Johnson
Set Decoration: Sam Comer, Arthur Krams

The Trouble with Harry (1956)
Produced by Alfred Hitchcock for Paramount
Art Direction: Hal Pereira, John Goodman
Set Decoration: Sam Comer, Emile Kuri

The Man Who Knew Too Much (1956)
Produced by Alfred Hitchcock for Paramount
Art Direction: Hal Pereira, Henry Bumstead
Set Decoration: Sam Comer, Arthur Krams

The Wrong Man (1957)
Produced by Alfred Hitchcock for Warner Brothers
Art Direction: Paul Sylbert
Set Decoration: William L. Kuehl

Vertigo (1958)
Produced by Alfred Hitchcock for Paramount
Art Direction: Hal Pereira, Henry Bumstead
Set Decoration: Sam Comer, Frank McKelvy

North by Northwest (1959)
Produced by Alfred Hitchcock for Metro-Goldwyn-Mayer
Production Design: Robert Boyle
Art Direction: William A. Horning, Merrill Pye
Set Decoration: Henry Grace, Frank McKelvy

Psycho (1960)
Produced by Alfred Hitchcock for Paramount – Shamley
Productions
Art Direction: Joseph Hurley, Robert Clatworthy
Set Decoration: George Milo

The Birds (1963)
Produced by Alfred Hitchcock for Universal
Production Design: Robert Boyle
Set Decoration: George Milo

Marnie (1964)
Produced by Alfred Hitchcock for Universal
Production Design: Robert Boyle
Set Decoration: George Milo

Torn Curtain (1966)
Produced by Alfred Hitchcock for Universal
Production Design: Hein Heckroth
Art Direction: Frank Arrigo
Set Decoration: George Milo

Topaz (1969)
Produced by Alfred Hitchcock for Universal
Production Design: Henry Bumstead
Set Decoration: John Austin

Frenzy (1972)
Produced by Alfred Hitchcock for Universal
Production Design: Syd Cain
Art Direction: Bob Laing
Set Dresser: Simon Wakefield

Family Plot (1976)
Produced by Alfred Hitchcock for Universal
Production Design: Henry Bumstead
Set Decoration: James W. Payne
Set Dresser: Douglas Freeman (uncredited)

Bibliography

Abalos, Iñaki, *The Good Life: A Guided Visit to the Houses of Modernity* (Barcelona: Editorial Gustavo Gili, 2001).

Abel, Richard, "*Notorious*: Perversion par Excellence," in Marshall Deutelbaum & Leland Poague (eds.), *A Hitchcock Reader* (Ames: Iowa State University Press, 1986), 162-69.

Adorno Theodor W., "Valéry Proust Museum," in *Prisms* (Cambridge, MA: MIT Press, 1997), 173-86.

Affron, Charles and Mirella Jona Affron, *Sets in Motion: Art Direction and Film Narrative* (New Brunswick, NJ: Rutgers University Press, 1995).

Albrecht, Donald, *Designing Dreams: Modern Architecture in the Movies* (London: Thames & Hudson, 1986).

"All Around the Town with *The Wrong Man*: Hitchcock Troupe Shoots New Thriller at Surface and Underground Sites," *New York Times* (29 April 1956).

Allen, Richard, "Hitchcock, or the Pleasures of Meta-skepticism," in Richard Allen & S. Ishii Gonzalès (eds.), *Alfred Hitchcock: Centenary Essays* (London: BFI Publishing, 1999), 221-37.

AlSayyad, Nezar, *Cinematic Urbanism: A History of the Modern From Reel to Real* (New York: Routledge, 2006).

Atkinson, David, "Hitchcock's Techniques Tell *Rear Window* Story," *American Cinematographer* (January 1990), 34-40.

Auiler, Dan, *Hitchcock's Notebooks: An Authorized and Illustrated Look Inside the Creative Mind of Alfred Hitchcock* (New York: HarperCollins, 1999).

Auiler, Dan, *Vertigo: The Making of a Hitchcock Classic* (New York: St. Martin's Griffin, 2000).

Bachelard, Gaston, *La poétique de l'espace* (Paris: Presses Universitaires de France, 1957).

Barr, Charles, *English Hitchcock* (Moffat: Cameron & Hollis, 1999).

Barsacq, Léon, *Caligari's Cabinet and Other Grand Illusions: A History of Film Design* (Boston: New York Graphic Society, 1976).

Bass, David, "Insiders and Outsiders: Latent Urban Thinking in Movies of Modern Rome," in François Penz & Maureen Thomas (eds.), *Cinema & Architecture: Méliès, Mallet-Stevens, Multimedia* (London: BFI Publishing, 1997), 84-99.

Bauso, Thomas M., "*Rope*: Hitchcock's Unkindest Cut," in Walter Raubicheck & Walter Srebnick (eds.), *Hitchcock's Rereleased Films: From Rope to Vertigo* (Detroit: Wayne State University Press, 1991), 226-39.

Bazin, André, *What Is Cinema?* (Berekely: University of California Press, 1971).

Bellour, Raymond, *The Analysis of Film* (Bloomington: Indiana University Press, 2000).

Belton, John, "Alfred Hitchcock's *Under Capricorn*: Montage Entranced by Mise-en-Scène," *Quarterly Review of Film Studies* (Fall 1981), 365-83.

Belton, John, "The Space of *Rear Window*," in Walter Raubicheck & Walter Srebnick (eds.), *Hitchcock's Rereleased Films* (Detroit: Wayne State University Press, 1991), 76-94.

Benjamin, Walter, *Gesammelte Schriften* (Frankfurt: Suhrkamp, 1982).

Bogdanovich, Peter, *The Cinema of Alfred Hitchcock*

(New York: The Museum of Modern Art, 1963).

Bogdanovich, Peter, *Who the Devil Made It: Conversations with Legendary Film Directors* (New York: Ballantine Books, 1997).

Bondil-Poupard, Nathalie, "Alfred Hitchcock: An Artist in Spite of Himself," in Dominique Païni & Guy Cogeval (eds.), *Hitchcock and Art: Fatal Coincidences* (Montreal: The Montreal Museum of Fine Arts, 2000), 179-88.

Bonitzer, Pascal, "Hitchcockian Suspense," in Slavoj Zizek (ed.), *Everything You Always Wanted to Know About Lacan But Were Afraid to Ask Hitchcock* (London: Verso, 1992), 15-30.

Bonitzer, Pascal, "Notorious," in Slavoj Zizek (ed.), *Everything You Always Wanted to Know About Lacan But Were Afraid to Ask Hitchcock* (London: Verso, 1992), 151-54.

Borden, Iain, "Material Sounds: Jacques Tati and Modern Architecture," in Bob Fear (ed.), *Architecture + Film II* (*Architectural Design*) 70 (2000), 26-31.

Borglum, Lincoln & Jane Culp Zeitner, *Borglum's Unfinished Dream: Mount Rushmore* (Aberdeen, S. Dakota: North Plains Press, 1976).

Boyer, M. Christine, *Manhattan Manners: Architecture and Style 1850-1900* (New York: Rizzoli, 1985).

Brady, John, "An Interview with Ernest Lehman," in James Naremore (ed.), *North by Northwest* (New Brunswick, NJ: Rutgers University Press, 1993), 186-88.

Brill, Lesley W., "Hitchcock's *The Lodger*," in Marshall Deutelbaum & Leland Poague (eds.), *A Hitchcock Reader* (Ames: Iowa State University Press, 1986), 67-77.

Brill, Lesley, *The Hitchcock Romance: Love and Irony in Hitchcock's Films* (Princeton, NJ: Princeton University Press, 1988).

Bronfen, Elisabeth, *Home In Hollywood: The Imaginary Geography of Cinema* (New York: Columbia University Press, 2004).

Brougher, Kerry, "Hitch-Hiking in Dreamscapes," in *Notorious: Alfred Hitchcock and Contemporary Art* (Oxford: Museum of Modern Art, 1999), 7-20.

Bulgakowa, Oksana (ed.), *Eisenstein und Deutschland: Texte, Briefe, Dokumente* (Berlin: Akademie der Künste, 1998).

California (Michelin Tourist Guide, 1999).

CAMUS Project, *Five Parishes, Their People, and Places: A History of the Villages of Castor, Ailsworth, Marholm with Milton, Upton and Sutton* (Castor, Peterborough: The Rectory, 2004).

Carcassonne, Philippe, "L'ordre et l'insécurité du monde," *Cinématographe* 59 (July-August, 1980), 13-16.

Cardiff, Jack, *Magic Hour* (London: Faber and Faber, 1996).

Cardiff, Jack, "The Problems of Lighting and Photographing *Under Capricorn*," *American Cinematographer* 30, 10 (October 1949), 358-59, 382.

Carrick, Edward, *Art and Design in the British Film: A Pictorial Directory of British Art Directors and Their Work* (London: Dennis Dobson, 1948).

Cavell, Stanley, "North by Northwest," in Marshall Deutelbaum and Leland Poague (eds.), *A Hitchcock Reader* (Ames: Iowa State University Press, 1986), 249-64.

Chabrol, Claude & Eric Rohmer, *Hitchcock: The First Forty-Four Films* (Oxford: Roundhouse Publishing, 1979).

Chabrol, Marguerite, "Variations sur le huis clos: les espaces theâtraux complexes au cinéma de *Drôle de drame* à *Gosford Park*," in Anne Goliot-Lété (ed.), *Le film architect* (Paris: L'Harmattan, 2005), 29-45.

Chion, Michel, "Alfred Hitchcock's *Rear Window*: The Fourth Side," in John Belton (ed.), *Alfred Hitchcock's Rear Window* (Cambridge: Cambridge University Press, 2000), 110-17.

Codrington, Andrea, "Modernist Malice," http://www.cabinetmagazine.org/issues/5/

Cogeval, Guy, "What Brings You to the Museum, Mr. Hitchcock?," in Dominique Païni & Guy Cogeval (eds.), *Hitchcock and Art: Fatal Coincidences* (Montreal: Montreal Museum of Fine Arts, 2000), 21-38.

Cohen, Paula Marantz, *Alfred Hitchcock: The Legacy of Victorianism* (Lexington: The University Press of Kentucky, 1995).

Cohen, Tom, *Hitchcock's Cryptonymies* (Minneapolis: University of Minnesota Press, 2005).

Colomina, Beatriz, "The Split Wall: Domestic Voyeurism," in Beatriz Colomina (ed.), *Sexuality & Space* (New York: Princeton Architectural Press, 1992), 73-130.

Conrad, Peter, *The Hitchcock Murders* (London: Faber & Faber, 2000).

Corber, Robert, *In the Name of National Security: Hitchcock, Homophobia, and the Political Construction of Gender in Postwar America* (Durham, NC: Duke University Press, 1993).

Corliss, Mary and Carlos Clarens, "Designed for Film: The Hollywood Art Director," *Film Comment* (May/June 1978), 25-60.

Counts, Kyle B., "The Making of Alfred Hitchcock's *The Birds*: The Complete Story Behind the Precursor of Modern Horror Films," *Cinefantastique* (Fall 1980), 14-35.

"Court is Turned into a Movie Set," *New York Times* (9 April 1956).

Curtis, Scott, "The Making of *Rear Window*," in John Belton (ed.), *Alfred Hitchcock's Rear Window* (Cambridge: Cambridge University Press, 2000), 21-56.

Dal Co, Francesco, *Figures of Architecture and Thought: German Architecture Culture 1880-1920* (New York: Rizzoli, 1990).

Deleuze, Gilles, *Cinema 1: The Movement-Image* (London: The Athlone Press, 1996).

Deutelbaum, Marshall, "Finding the Right Man in *The Wrong Man*," in Marshall Deutelbaum & Leland Poague (eds.), *A Hitchcock Reader* (Ames: Iowa State University Press, 1986), 207-218.

Deutelbaum, Marshall, "Seeing in *Saboteur*," *Literature/Film Quarterly* 12, 1 (1984), 58-64.

Dixon, Roger & Stefan Muthesius, *Victorian Architecture* (London: Thames & Hudson, 1985).

Doane, Mary Ann, *The Desire to Desire: The Woman's Film of the 1940s* (Bloomington & Indianapolis: Indiana University Press, 1987).

Dolar, Mladen, "A Father Who is Not Quite Dead," in Slavoj Zizek (ed.), *Everything You Always Wanted to*

Know About Lacan… But Were Afraid to Ask Hitchcock (London: Verso, 1992), 143-50.

Dorr, John, *An Oral History of the Motion Picture in America* (Regents of the University of California, Special Collections, University of California at Los Angeles, 1969).

Douchet, Jean, "Hitch et son public," *Cahiers du cinéma* 113 (1960), 7-15.

Douchet, Jean, *Alfred Hitchcock* (Paris: Herne, 1967).

Duncan, Carol, *Civilizing Rituals: Inside Public Art Museums* (London: Routledge, 1995).

Durgnat, Raymond, *A Long Hard Look at 'Psycho'* (London: BFI Publishing, 2002).

Durgnat, Raymond, *The Strange Case of Alfred Hitchcock or The Plain Man's Hitchcock* (Cambridge, MA: MIT Press, 1974).

Durgnat, Raymond, "The Subconscious: From Pleasure Castle to Libido Motel," in Alain Silver & James Ursini (eds.), *Horror Film Reader* (New York: Limelight Editions, 2000), 39-49.

Edelman, Lee, "Hitchcock's Future," in Richard Allen & S. Ishii Gonzalès (eds.), *Alfred Hitchcock: Centenary Essays* (London: BFI Publishing, 1999), 239-58.

Edwards, Kyle Dawson, "Brand-Name Literature: Film Adaptation and Selznick International Pictures' *Rebecca* (1940)," *Cinema Journal* 45, 3 (Spring 2006), 32-58.

Eisenstein, Sergei, "The Montage of Film Attractions," in Peter Lehman (ed.), *Defining Cinema* (London: The Athlone Press, 1997), 17-36.

Elsaesser, Thomas, "Mirror, Muse, Medusa: *Experiment Perilous*," *Iris* 14/15 (Autumn 1992), 147-59.

Elsaesser, Thomas, "Tales of Sound and Fury: Observations on the Family Drama," (1972) in Christine Gledhill (ed.), *Home Is Where the Heart Is: Studies in Melodrama and the Woman's Film* (London: British Film Institute, 1987), 43-69.

Ettedgui, Peter, *Production Design and Art Direction* (Woburn, MA: Focal Press, 1999).

Fawell, John, *Hitchcock's Rear Window: The Well Made Film* (Carbondale: Southern Illinois University Press, 2000).

Felleman, Susan, *Art in the Cinematic Imagination* (Austin: University of Texas Press, 2006).

Fletcher, John, "Primal Scenes and the Female Gothic: *Rebecca* and *Gaslight*," *Screen* 36, 4 (Winter 1995), 341-70.

Foster, Frederick, "Hitch Didn't Want it Arty," *American Cinematographer* (February 1957), 84-85, 112-14.

Foucault, Michel, *Surveiller et punir: Naissance de la prison* (Paris: Gallimard, 1975).

Frayling, Christopher, *Ken Adam: The Art of Production Design* (London: Faber & Faber, 2005).

Freedman, Jonathan, "From *Spellbound* to *Vertigo*: Alfred Hitchcock and Therapeutic Culture in America," in Jonathan Freedman & Richard Millington (eds.), *Hitchcock's America* (New York: Oxford University Press, 1999), 77-98.

Freud, Sigmund, "The Uncanny" (1919), in *The Standard Edition of the Complete Psychological Works of Sigmund Freud* (London: Hogarth Press, 1955), 17, 217-52.

Frisby, David, *Simmel and Since: Essays on Georg Simmel's Social Theory* (London: Routledge, 1992).

Funck, Jean, "Fonctions et significations de l'escalier dans le cinéma d'Alfred Hitchcock," *Positif* (December 1984), 30-35.

Gallefant, Ed, "Black Satin: Fantasy, Murder, and the Couple in *Gaslight* and *Rebecca*," *Screen* 29, 3 (Summer 1988), 84-103.

Garncarz, Joseph, "German Hitchcock," *Hitchcock Annual* (2000-2001), 73-99.

Gavin, Arthur E., "Rear Window," *American Cinematographer* (February 1954), 76-78, 97.

Gay, Peter, *The Education of the Senses: The Bourgeois Experience* (London: W.W. Norton & Company, 1999).

Giblin, Gary, *Alfred Hitchcock's London: A Reference Guide to Locations* (Baltimore: Midnight Marquee Press, 2006).

Giedion, Siegfried, *Space, Time, and Architecture: The Growth of a New Tradition* (Cambridge, MA: Harvard University Press, 1967).

Gilbert, Sandra & Susan Gubar, *The Madwoman in the Attic: The Woman Writer and Nineteenth-Century Imagination* (New Haven: Yale University Press, 1979).

Girouard, Mark, *The Victorian Country House* (New Haven: Yale University Press, 1979).

Girouard, Mark, *Life in the English Country House: A Social and Architectural History* (New Haven: Yale University Press, 1978).

Godard, Jean-Luc, "Georges Franju," in Tom Milne (ed.), *Godard on Godard* (New York: Da Capo Press, 1972), 99-101.

Godard, Jean-Luc, *Histoire(s) du cinéma* (Paris, Gallimard: 1998).

Godard, Jean-Luc, "The Wrong Man," in Tom Milne (ed.), *Godard on Godard* (New York: Da Capo Press, 1972), 48-55.

Goffman, Erving, *Behavior in Public Spaces* (New York: The Free Press, 1963).

Goffman, Erving, *The Presentation of Self in Everyday Life* (New York: Anchor Books, 1959).

Goliot, Anne, "Introduction à une narratologie de l'espace: *Gaslight* ou le récit-architecte," *Iris* 12 (1991), 71-83.

Goodwin, James, *Eisenstein, Cinema, and History* (Urbana: University of Illinois Press, 1993).

Gottlieb, Sidney, "Early Hitchcock: The German Influence," *Hitchcock Annual* (1999-2000), 100-130.

Gottlieb, Sidney (ed.), *Hitchcock on Hitchcock: Selected Writings and Interviews* (London: Faber & Faber, 1995).

Gottlieb, Sidney, "Unknown Hitchcock: The Unrealized Projects," in Richard Allen and Sam Ishii-Gonzalez (eds.), *Hitchcock: Past and Future* (London: Routledge, 2004), 85-106.

Haeffner, Nicholas, *Alfred Hitchcock* (Harlow: Pearson Longman, 2005).

Handlin, David P., *American Architecture* (London: Thames & Hudson, 1985).

Harris, Steven & Debora Berke (eds.), *Architecture of the Everyday* (New York: Princeton Architectural Press, 1997).

Harris, Thomas, "*Rear Window* and *Blow-Up*: Hitchcock's Straightforwardness vs Antonioni's

Ambiguity," *Literature/Film Quarterly* 15/1 (1987), 60-63.

Heath, Stephen, "Narrative Space," *Screen* 17, 3 (Autumn 1976), 68-112.

Heathcote, Edwin, "Modernism as Enemy: Film and the Portrayal of Modern Architecture," in Bob Fear (ed.), *Architecture + Film II* (*Architectural Design*) 70 (2000), 20-25.

Heisner, Beverly, *Hollywood Art: Art Direction in the Days of the Great Studios* (Jefferson, NC: McFarland & Company, 1990).

Hemmeter, Thomas, "Twisted Writing: *Rope* as an Experimental Film," in Walter Raubicheck & Walter Srebnick (eds.), *Hitchcock's Rereleased Films: From Rope to Vertigo* (Detroit: Wayne State University Press, 1991), 253-65.

Hesketh, Robert Fermor (ed.), *Architecture of the British Empire* (London: Weidenfeld and Nicolson, 1986).

Hess, Alan, *The Architecture of John Lautner* (New York: Universe Publishing, 1999).

Hitchcock, Alfred, "After-Dinner Speech at the Screen Producers Guild Dinner," (1965) in Sidney Gottlieb (ed.), *Hitchcock on Hitchcock: Selected Writings and Interviews* (London: Faber & Faber, 1995), 54-58.

Hitchcock, Alfred, "Direction," (1937) in Sidney Gottlieb (ed.), *Hitchcock on Hitchcock: Selected Writings and Interviews* (London: Faber & Faber, 1995), 253-61.

Hitchcock, Alfred, "Let 'Em Play God," (1948) in Sidney Gottlieb (ed.), *Hitchcock on Hitchcock: Selected Writings and Interviews* (London: Faber & Faber, 1995), 113-15.

Hitchcock, Alfred, "Life Among Stars," (1937) in Sidney Gottlieb (ed.), *Hitchcock on Hitchcock: Selected Writings and Interviews* (London: Faber & Faber, 1995), 27-50.

Hitchcock, Alfred, "My Most Exciting Picture," (1948) in Sidney Gottlieb (ed.), *Hitchcock on Hitchcock: Selected Writings and Interviews* (London: Faber & Faber, 1995), 275-84.

Hitchcock, Alfred, "Murder – With English on It," in Sidney Gottlieb (ed.), *Hitchcock on Hitchcock: Selected Writings and Interviews* (London: Faber & Faber, 1995), 133-37.

Hitchcock, Alfred, "More Cabbages, Fewer Kings: A Believer in the Little Man," (1937) in Sidney Gottlieb (ed.), *Hitchcock on Hitchcock: Selected Writings and Interviews* (London: Faber & Faber, 1995), 176-78.

Hitchcock, Alfred, "On Film Production," *Encyclopaedia Britannica* vol. 15 (1965), 907-911. Reprinted in Sidney Gottlieb (ed.), *Hitchcock on Hitchcock* (London: Faber & Faber, 1995), 210-226.

Hitchcock, Alfred, "Production Methods Compared," *American Cinematographer* (May 1949), 162-63 and 182.

Hitchcock, Alfred, "Search for the Sun," (1937), in Sidney Gottlieb (ed.), *Hitchcock on Hitchcock: Selected Writings and Interviews* (London: Faber & Faber, 1995), 250-52.

Hitchcock, Alfred, "On Style," originally published in *Cinema* 1, 5 (August-September 1963), 4-8, 34-35. Reprinted in Sidney Gottlieb (ed.), *Hitchcock on Hitchcock: Selected Writings and Interviews* (London: Faber & Faber, 1995), 285-302.

Hitchcock, Henry-Russell, *Architecture: Nineteenth and Twentieth Centuries* (London: Penguin Books, 1990).

"Alfred Hitchcock – Director: On TV or at the Movies,

Suspense Is Golden," *Newsweek* (June 11, 1956), 105-108.

"Hitchcock at Work," *Take One* 5, 2 (May 1976), 31-35.

Horowitz, Margaret M., "*The Birds*: A Mother's Love," in Marshall Deutelbaum & Leland Poague (eds.), *A Hitchcock Reader* (Ames: Iowa State University Press, 1986), 279-87.

Horton, Andrew, *Henry Bumstead and the World of Hollywood Art Direction* (Austin: University of Texas Press, 2003).

Hunter, Evan, *Me and Hitch* (London: Faber & Faber, 1997).

Hurley, Neil P., *Soul in Suspense: Hitchcock's Fright and Delight* (Metuchen, NJ: The Scarecrow Press, 1993).

Hyde, Thomas, "The Moral Universe of Hitchcock's *Spellbound*," in Marshall Deutelbaum & Leland Poague (eds.), *A Hitchcock Reader* (Ames: Iowa State University Press, 1986), 153-61.

Irwin, David, *Neoclassicism* (London: Phaidon, 1997).

Ishii-Gonzalez, Sam, "Hitchcock with Deleuze," in Richard Allen and Sam Ishii-Gonzalez (eds.), *Hitchcock: Past and Future* (London: Routledge, 2004), 128-45.

Jackson, Lesley, *Contemporary: Architecture and Interiors of the 1950s* (London: Phaidon Press, 1994).

Jacobs, Steven, "From Flaneur to Chauffeur: Driving Through Cinematic Cities," in Christian Emden, Catherine Keen, and David Midgley (eds.), *Imagining the City* (Oxford: Peter Lang, 2006), 213-28.

Jacobs, Steven, "Interieur en introspectie: architectuur en huiselijkheid in de Gothic Romance Film," *De Witte Raaf* 103 (May 2003), 15-17.

Jacobs, Steven, "Reisgids voor Tativille: Architectuur en stad in het werk van Jacques Tati," *Andere Sinema* 160 (October 2001), 104-123.

Jacobs, Steven, "Sightseeing Fright: Alfred Hitchcock's Monuments and Museums," *Journal of Architecture*, 11, 5 (2006), 595-602.

Jameson, Fredric, "Spatial Systems in *North by Northwest*," in Slavoj Zizek (ed.), *Everything You Always Wanted to Know About Lacan But Were Afraid to Ask Hitchcock* (London: Verso, 1992), 47-72.

Kapsis, Robert E., *Hitchcock: The Making of a Reputation* (Chicago: The University of Chicago Press, 1992).

Kehr, David, "Hitch's Riddle," *Film Comment* (May-June 1984), 9-18.

King, Anthony D., *The Bungalow: The Production of a Global Culture* (Oxford: Oxford University Press, 1995).

Klinger, Barbara, "*Psycho*: The Institutionalization of Female Sexuality," in Marshall Deutelbaum & Leland Poague (eds.), *A Hitchcock Reader* (Ames: Iowa State University Press, 1986), 332-39.

Kolker, Robert, "The Form, Structure, and Influence of *Psycho*," in Robert Kolker (ed.), *Alfred Hitchcock's Psycho: A Casebook* (New York: Oxford University Press, 2004), 206-55.

Kracauer, Siegfried, "The Hotel Lobby," in *The Mass Ornament: Weimar Essays* (Cambridge, MA: Harvard University Press, 1995), 173-85.

Kraft, Jeff & Aaron Leventhal, *Footsteps in the Fog: Alfred*

Hitchcock's San Francisco (Santa Monica: Santa Monica Press, 2002).

Krohn, Bill, *Hitchcock at Work* (London: Phaidon, 2000).

Krohn, Bill, "Le musée secret de M. Hitchcock," *Cahiers du cinéma* 559 (July-August 2001), 66-71.

Kuri, Emile, *Memoirs* (Calabasas, California, 1989).

Kuter, Leo, "Production Designer," *The Society of Motion Picture Art Directors Bulletin* (March 1951), 11-13, 16.

Lefebvre, Henri, *The Production of Space* (1974) (Oxford: Blackwell, 1991).

Leff, Leonard J., "Hitchcock at Metro," in Marshall Deutelbaum & Leland Poague (eds.), *A Hitchcock Reader* (Ames: Iowa State University Press, 1986), 41-61.

Leff, Leonard J., *Hitchcock and Selznick: The Rich and Strange Collaboration of Alfred Hitchcock and David O. Selznick in Hollywood* (Berkeley: University of California Press, 1987).

Leitch, Thomas M., *The Encyclopedia of Alfred Hitchcock* (New York: Checkmark Books, 2002).

Leitch, Thomas M., *Find the Director and Other Hitchcock Games* (Athens: The University of Georgia Press, 1991).

Levey, Michael, *Painting and Sculpture in France 1700-1789* (New Haven: Yale University Press, 1993).

Levy, Emanuel, *Small-Town America in Film: The Decline and Fall of Community* (New York: Continuum, 1991).

Liebs, Chester, *Main Street to Miracle Mile* (Boston: Little Brown, 1985).

Liehm, Mira, *Passion and Defiance: Film in Italy from 1942 to the Present* (Berkeley: University of California Press, 1984).

Lightman, Herb A., "Hitchcock Talks About Lights, Camera, Action," *American Cinematographer* (May 1967), 332-35.

LoBrutto, Vincent, *By Design: Interviews with Film Production Designers* (Westport, Connecticut: Praeger, 1992).

Lofland, Lyn H., *A World of Strangers: Order and Action in Urban Public Space* (New York: Basic Books, 1973).

Loring, Charles, "Filming *Torn Curtain* by Reflected Light," *American Cinematographer* (October 1966), 680-83.

Lüdi, Heidi & Toni Lüdi, *Movie Worlds: Production Design in Film* (Stuttgart: Edition Axel Menges, 2000).

Lunde, Erik S. & Douglas A. Noverr, "Saying It With Pictures: Alfred Hitchcock and Painterly Images in *Psycho*," in Paul Loukides & Linda K. Fuller (eds.), *Beyond the Stars: Studies in American Popular Fiction Film: Volume 3: The Material World in American Popular Film* (Bowling Green: Bowling Green State University Popular Press, 1993).

McAlester, Virginia & Lee McAlester, *A Field Guide to American Houses* (New York: Knopf, 2005).

MacCannel, Dean, *The Tourist: A New Theory of the Leisure Class* (1976) (Berkeley: University of California Press, 1999).

McElhaney, Joe, "The Object and the Face: *Notorious*, Bergman, and the Close-Up," in Richard Allen & Sam Ishii-Gonzales (eds.), *Hitchcock: Past and Future* (London: Routledge, 2004), 64-84.

McElhaney, Joe, "Touching the Surface: Marnie, Melodrama, Modernism," in Richard Allen & S. Ishii Gonzales (eds.), *Alfred Hitchcock: Centenary Essays* (London: BFI Publishing, 1999), 86-105.

McGilligan, Patrick, *Alfred Hitchcock: A Life in Darkness and Light* (New York: Regan Books, 2003).

MacKinnon, Kenneth, *Hollywood's Small Towns: An Introduction to the American Small-Town Movie* (Metuchen, NJ: The Scarecrow Press, 1984).

McLaughlin, James, "All in the Family: Alfred Hitchcock's *Shadow of a Doubt*," in Marshall Deutelbaum & Leland Poague (eds.), *A Hitchcock Reader* (Ames: Iowa State University Press, 1986), 141-52.

McLendon, Sandy, "Modernism at the Movies: The Vandamm House in Alfred Hitchcock's *North by Northwest*," http://www.jetsetmodern.com/modatmovies.htm

McLeod, Mary, "Everyday and 'Other' Spaces," in Debra Coleman, Elizabeth Danze, and Carol Henderson (eds.), *Architecture and Feminism* (New York: Princeton Architectural Press, 1996), 1-37.

Mallet-Stevens, Robert, "Le décor" (1929), in *Iris* 12 (1991), 129-37.

Mandelbaum, Howard & Eric Myers, *Forties Screen Style: A Celebration of High Pastiche in Hollywood* (Santa Monica: Hennessey & Ingalls, 2000).

Marker, Chris, "A free replay: notes sur *Vertigo*," *Positif* (June 1994), 79-84.

Marx, Leo, *The Machine in the Garden* (New York: Oxford University Press, 1964).

Michie, Elsie B., "Unveiling Maternal Desires: Hitchcock and American Domesticity," in Jonathan Freedman & Richard Millington (eds.), *Hitchcock's America* (New York: Oxford University Press, 1999), 29-54.

Midding, Gerhard, "Aus angemessen bequemer Distanz: Dekors und Schauplätze bei Hitchcock," in Lars-Olav Beier & Georg Seesslen (eds.), *Alfred Hitchcock* (Berlin: Bertz, 1999), 125-44.

Middleton, Robin & David Watkin, *Neoclassical and 19th Century Architecture* (London: Faber & Faber, 1980).

Millington, Richard H., "Hitchcock and American Character: The Comedy of Self-Construction in *North by Northwest*," in Jonathan Freedman & Richard H. Millington (eds.), *Hitchcock's America* (New York: Oxford University Press, 1999), 135-54.

Modleski, Tania, *The Women Who Knew Too Much: Hitchcock and Feminist Theory* (New York: Routledge, 1989).

Monaco, James, *How to Read a Film: The Art, Technology, Language, History, and Theory of Film and Media* (New York: Oxford University Press, 1981).

Morris, Christopher D., *The Hanging Figure: On Suspense and the Films of Alfred Hitchcock* (Westport, Connecticut: Praeger, 2002).

Morrison, James, "Hitchcock's Ireland: the Performance of Irish Identity in *Juno and the Paycock* and *Under Capricorn*," in Richard Allen & Sam Ishii-Gonzales (eds.), *Hitchcock: Past and Future* (London: Routledge, 2004), 193-210.

Mulvey, Laura, "Pandora: Topographies of the Mask and

Curiosity," in Beatriz Colomina (ed.), *Sexuality & Space* (New York: Princeton Architectural Press, 1992), 53-72.

Mulvey, Laura, "Visual Pleasures and Narrative Cinema," in *Visual and Other Pleasures* (Bloomington: Indiana University Press, 1989), 14-26.

Muthesius, Hermann, *Das englische Haus: Entwicklung, Bedingungen, Anlage, Aufbau, Einrichtung und Innenraum. Bd. 1-3.* (1904-1905) (Berlin: Gebr. Mann Verlag, 1999).

Naremore, James, "Hitchcock and Humor," in Richard Allen & Sam Ishii-Gonzales (eds.), *Hitchcock: Past and Future* (London: Routledge, 2004), 22-36.

Naremore, James, "Hitchcock at the Margins of Noir," in Richard Allen and S. Ishii Gonzalès (eds.), *Alfred Hitchcock Centenary Essays* (London: BFI Publishing, 1999), 263-77.

Neumann, Dietrich, *Film Architecture: From Metropolis to Blade Runner* (Munich: Prestel, 1999).

Newhouse, Victoria, *Wallace K. Harrison: Architect* (New York: Rizzoli, 1989).

Newhouse, Victoria, *Towards a New Museum* (New York: The Monacelli Press, 1998).

Niemeyer, Oscar, *Dialogo Pré-Socratico* (Sao Paolo: Instituto Lina Bo e P.M. Bardi, 1998).

Ockman, Joan, "Architecture in a Mode of Distraction: Eight Takes on Jacques Tati's *Playtime*," in Mark Lamster (ed.), *Architecture and Film* (New York: Princeton Architectural Press, 2000), 171-196.

Ockman, Joan, "Toward a Theory of Normative Architecture," in Steven Harris & Deborah Berke (eds.), *Architecture of the Everyday* (New York: Princeton Architectural Press, 1997), 122-52.

Öhner, Vrääth & Marc Ries, "Bildbau," in Helmut Weihsmann, *Cinetecture: Film, Architektur, Moderne* (Wien: PVS Verleger, 1995), 31-36.

Olsen, Donald, *The City as a Work of Art: London, Paris, Vienna* (New Haven: Yale University Press, 1986).

Orr, John, *Hitchcock and 20th Century Cinema* (London: Wallflower, 2005).

Paglia, Camille, *The Birds* (London: BFI Publishing, 1998).

Païni, Dominique, "The Wandering Gaze: Hitchcock's Use of Transparencies," in *Hitchcock and Art: Fatal Coincidences* (Montreal: The Montreal Museum of Fine Arts, 2001), 51-78.

Pallasmaa, Juahani, *The Architecture of the Image: Existential Space in Cinema* (Helsinki: Rakenustieto Oy, 2001).

Penz, François, "Architecture in the Films of Jacques Tati," in François Penz & Maureen Thomas (eds.), *Cinema & Architecture: Méliès, Mallet-Stevens, Multimedia* (London: BFI Publishing, 1997), 62-69.

Perkins, V.F., "Rope," *Movie 7* (February-March 1963), 11-13.

Peucker, Brigitte, "The Cut of Representation: Painting and Sculpture in Hitchcock," in Richard Allen and S. Ishi Gonzalès (eds.), *Alfred Hitchcock: Centenary Essays* (London: British Film Institute, 1999), 141-56.

Peucker, Brigitte, *Incorporating Images: Film and the Rival Arts* (Princeton NJ: Princeton University Press, 1995).

Pevsner Nikolaus, *A History of Building Types* (London: Thames & Hudson, 1976).

Piso, Michele, "Mark's Marnie," in Marshall Deutelbaum & Leland Poague (eds.), *A Hitchcock Reader* (Ames: Iowa State University, 1986), 288-303.

Poague, Leland, "Links in a Chain: *Psycho* and Film Classicism," in Marshall Deutelbaum & Leland Poague (eds.), *A Hitchcock Reader* (Ames: Iowa State University Press, 1986), 340-49.

Pomerance, Murray, *An Eye for Hitchcock* (New Brunswick, NJ: Rutgers University Press, 2004).

Praz, Mario, *An Illustrated History of Interior Decoration: From Pompeii to Art Nouveau* (London: Thames & Hudson, 1994).

Pugin, Augustus Welbin, *True Principles of Pointed or Christian Architecture* (London, 1841).

Ramirez, Juan Antonio, *Architecture for the Screen: A Critical Study of Set Design in Hollywood's Golden Age* (Jefferson, NC: McFarland & Company, 2004)

Rebello, Stephen, *Alfred Hitchcock and the Making of Psycho* (New York: St. Martin's Griffin, 1990).

Rebello, Stephen, "Psycho," *Cinefantastique* (October 1986), 57-80.

Reed, Christopher, (ed.), *Not at Home: The Suppression of Domesticity in Modern Art and Architecture* (London: Thames & Hudson, 1996).

Renov, Michael, "From Identification to Ideology: The Male System of *Notorious*," in David Boyd (ed.), *Perspectives on Hitchcock* (New York: Simon & Schuster Macmillan, 1995), 103-111.

Riley, Terence & Peter Reed (eds.), *Frank Lloyd Wright: Architect* (New York: The Museum of Modern Art, 1994).

Ringel, Harry, "*Blackmail*: The Opening of Hitchcock's Surrealist Eye," *Film Heritage* vol 9, 2 (Winter 1973-74), 17-23.

Rosa, Joseph, "Burning Down the House: Modern Homes in the Movies," in Mark Lamster (ed.), *Architecture and Film* (New York: Princeton Architectural Press, 2000), 159-67.

Rosenblatt, Bettina, "Doubles and Doubt in Hitchcock: The German Connection," in Richard Allen & Sam Ishii Gonzales (eds.), *Hitchcock: Past and Future* (London: Routledge, 2004), 37-63.

Rothman, William, *Hitchcock: The Murderous Gaze* (Cambridge, MA: Harvard University Press, 1982).

Ruskin, John, *Sesame and Lilies* (1856) (Leipzig: Bernhard Tauchnitz, 1906).

Ryall, Tom, *Blackmail* (London: BFI Publishing, 1993).

Rykwert, Joseph, *The Necessity of Artifice* (London: Academy Editions, 1982).

Samuels, Robert, "Epilogue: *Psycho* and the Horror of the Bi-Textual Unconscious," in Robert Kolker (ed.), *Alfred Hitchcock's Psycho: A Casebook* (New York: Oxford University Press, 2004), 149-62.

Sanders, James, *Celluloid Skyline: New York and the Movies* (New York: Alfred A. Knopf, 2001).

Sarris, Andrew, *The American Cinema: Directors and*

Directions 1929-1968 (New York: Da Capo, 1996).

Schlör, Joachim, *Nights in the Big City: Paris, Berlin, London 1840-1930* (London: Reaktion Books, 1998).

Searing, Helen, "The Development of a Museum Typology," in Suzanne Stephens (ed.), *Building the New Museum* (New York: The Architectural League, 1986), 14-23.

Sennett, Robert S., *Setting the Scene: The Great Hollywood Art Directors* (New York: Abrams, 1994).

Sharff, Stefan, *The Art of Looking in Hitchcock's Rear Window* (New York: Limelight editions, 1997).

Sharff, Stefan, *Hitchcock's High Vernacular: Theory and Practice* (New York: Columbia University Press, 1991).

Sheridan, Bart, "Three And A Half Minute Take: How Dramatic Continuous Scene in Hitchcock's *Paradine Case* Was Photographed by Lee Garmes, ASC, Using New Multi-Directional Camera Dolly," *American Cinematographer* (September 1948), 305-314.

Silver, Alain, "Fragments of the Mirror: Hitchcock's Noir Landscape," in Alain Silver & James Ursini (eds.), *Film Noir Reader 2* (New York: Limelight Editions, 1999), 107-28.

Sloan, Jane E., *Alfred Hitchcock: A Filmography and Bibliography* (Berkeley: University of California Press, 1995).

Smith, Susan, "Disruption, Destruction, Denial: Hitchcock as Saboteur," in Richard Allen & S. Ishii Gonzalez (eds.), *Alfred Hitchcock: Centenary Essays* (London: BFI Publishing, 1999), 45-58.

Smith, Susan, *Hitchcock: Suspense, Humour, and Tone* (London: BFI Publishing, 2000).

Spigel, Lynn, "From Theatre to Space Ship: Metaphors of Suburban Domesticity in Postwar America," in Roger Silverstone (ed.), *Visons of Suburbia* (London: Routledge, 1997), 217-39.

Spoto, Donald, *The Art of Alfred Hitchcock: Fifty Years of His Motion Pictures* (New York: Anchor Books, 1992).

Spoto, Donald, *The Dark Side of Genius: Alfred Hitchcock* (London: Plexus, 1983).

Stam, Robert & Roberta Pearson, "Hitchcock's *Rear Window*: Reflexivity and the Critique of Voyeurism," in Marshall Deutelbaum & Leland Poague (eds.), *A Hitchcock Reader* (Ames: Iowa State University Press, 1986), 193-206.

Stam, Robert, Robert Burgoyne, and Sandy Flitterman-Lewis, *New Vocabularies in Film Semiotics* (London: Routledge, 1992).

Stein, Elliott, "Filmographies of Art Directors and Production Designers," in Léon Barsacq, *Caligari's Cabinet and Other Grand Illusions: A History of Film Design* (Boston: New York Graphic Society, 1976), 195-244.

Stephens, Michael L., *Art Directors in Cinema: A Worldwide Biographical Dictionary* (Jefferson, NC: McFarland & Company, 1998).

Stern, Robert A.M., Gregory Gilmartin, and John Massengale, *New York 1900: Metropolitan Architecture and Urbanism* (New York: Rizzoli, 1995).

Stern, Robert A.M., Gregory Gilmartin, and Thomas Mellins, *New York 1930: Architecture and Urbanism Between the Two World Wars* (New York: Rizzoli, 1987).

Stern, Robert A.M., Thomas Mellins & David Fishman, *New York 1960: Architecture and Urbanism Between the Second World War and the Bicentennial* (New York: The Monacelli Press, 1995).

Sterritt, David, *The Films of Alfred Hitchcock* (Cambridge: Cambridge University Press, 1993).

Strauss, Marc Raymond, *Alfred Hitchcock's Silent Films* (Jefferson, NC: McFarland, 2004).

Tanski, Julia, "The Symbolist Woman in Hitchcock's Films," in Dominique Païni & Guy Cogeval (eds.), *Hitchcock and Art: Fatal Coincidences* (Montreal: The Montreal Museum of Fine Arts, 2000), 147-54.

Tashiro, C.S., *Pretty Pictures: Production Design and the History of Film* (Austin: University of Texas Press, 1998).

Taylor, John Russell, *Hitch: The Life and Times of Alfred Hitchcock* (New York: Da Capo Press, 1996).

Tiersten, Lisa, "The Chic Interior and the Feminine Modern: Home Decorating as High Art in Turn-of-the-Century Paris," in Christopher Reed (ed.), *Not at Home: The Suppression of Domesticity in Modern Art and Architecture* (London: Thames & Hudson, 1996), 18-32.

Toles, George, "If Thine Eye Offended Thee…": *Psycho* and the Art of Infection," in Robert Kolker (ed.), *Alfred Hitchcock's Psycho: A Casebook* (New York: Oxford University Press, 2004), 120-45.

Truffaut, François, *Hitchcock* (New York: Simon & Schuster, 1984).

Trumpener, Katie, "Fragments of the Mirror: Self-Reference, Mise-en-Abyme, *Vertigo*," in Walter Raubicheck & Walter Srebnick (eds.), *Hitchcock's Rereleased Films* (Detroit: Wayne State University Press, 1991), 175-88.

Tschumi, Bernard, *Architecture in/of Motion* (Rotterdam: NAi Publishers, 1997).

Turner, George E., "Du Maurier + Selznick + Hitchcock = *Rebecca*: Haunted Romance Hovers over Manderley," *American Cinematographer* (July 1997).

Turner, George E., "Hitchcock's Mastery is Beyond Doubt," *American Cinematographer* 74, 5 (May 1993), 62-67.

Turner, George E., "*Rope*: Something Different," *American Cinematographer* 66 (March 1985), 34-40.

Turner, George E., "*Saboteur*: Hitchcock Set Free," *American Cinematographer* 74, 11 (November/ December 1993), 67-72/88-93.

Twombly, Robert C., *Frank Lloyd Wright: His Life and His Architecture* (New York: John Wiley and Sons, 1979).

Urry, John, *The Tourist Gaze: Leisure and Travel in Contemporary Societies* (London: Sage, 1990).

Vernet, Marc, "Espace (Structuration de l')," in *Lectures du film* (Paris: Editions Albatros, 1976), 86-95.

Vidler, Anthony, *The Architectural Uncanny: Essays in the Modern Unhomely* (Cambridge, MA: MIT Press, 1992).

Wakefield, David, *French Eighteenth-Century Painting* (London: Gordon Fraser, 1984).

Waldman, Diane, "Architectural Metaphor in the Gothic Romance Film," *Iris* 12 (1991): 55-70.

Waldman, Diane, "The Childish, the Insane, and the Ugly:

The Representation of Modern Art in Popular Films and Fiction in the Forties," *Wide Angle* 5 (1982), 52-65.

Walker, John A., *Art and Artists on Screen* (Manchester: Manchester University Press, 1993).

Walker, Michael, *Hitchcock's Motifs* (Amsterdam: Amsterdam University Press, 2005).

Watkin, David, *English Architecture* (London: Thames & Hudson, 2001).

Weis, Elisabeth, *The Silent Scream: Alfred Hitchcock's Sound Track* (Rutherford: Fairleigh Dickinson University Press, 1982).

Wigley, Mark, "Untitled: The Housing of Gender," in Beatriz Colomina (ed.), *Sexuality & Space* (New York: Princeton Architectural Press, 1992), 327-38.

Willensky, Elliot & Norval White, *AIA Guide to New York City* (San Diego: Harcourt Brace Jovanovich Publishers, 1988).

Wilson, Shelagh, "Monsters and Monstrosities: Grotesque Taste and Victorian Design," in Colin Trodd, Paul Barlow & David Amigani (eds.), *Victorian Culture and the Idea of the Grotesque* (Aldershot: Ashgate, 1999), 143-62.

Wollen, Peter, "Architecture and Film: Places and Non-Places," in *Paris Hollywood: Writings on Film* (London: Verso, 2002), 199-215.

Wollen Peter, "*Rope*: Three Hypotheses," in Richard Allen & Sam Ishii-Gonzales (eds.), *Alfred Hitchcock: Centenary Essays* (London: BFI, 1999), 75-85.

Wood, Robin, *Hitchcock's Films Revisited* (New York: Columbia University Press, 1989).

Worland, Rick, "Before and After the Fact: Writing and Reading Hitchcock's *Suspicion*," *Cinema Journal* 41, 4 (2002), 3-26.

Wright, Gwendolyn, "Frank Lloyd Wright and the Domestic Landscape," in Terence Riley & Peter Reed (eds.), *Frank Lloyd Wright: Architect* (New York: The Museum of Modern Art, 1994), 80-95.

Yacowar, Maurice, *Hitchcock's British Films* (Hamden, Connecticut: Archon Books, 1977).

Yacowar, Maurice, "Hitchcock's Imagery and Art," in Marshall Deutelbaum & Leland Poague (eds.), *A Hitchcock Reader* (Ames: Iowa State University Press, 1986), 16-26.

Yates, Virginia, "*Rope* Sets a Precedent," *American Cinematographer* (July 1948), 230 and 246.

Zirnite, Dennis, "Hitchcock on the Level: The Heights of Spatial Tension," *Film Criticism* 10, 3 (Spring 1986): 2-21.

Zizek, Slavoj, "In His Bold Gaze My Ruin is Writ Large," in Slavoj Zizek (ed.), *Everything You Always Wanted to Know About Lacan (But Were Afraid to Ask Hitchcock)* (London and New York: Verso, 1992), 211-72.

Zizek, Slavoj, "The Hitchcockian Blot," Richard Allen & S. Ishii Gonzalès (eds.), *Alfred Hitchcock: Centenary Essays* (London: BFI Publishing, 1999), 123-40.

Zizek, Slavoj, "Is There a Proper Way to Remake a Hitchcock Film?," in Richard Allen & Sam Ishii Gonzales (eds.), *Hitchcock: Past and Future* (London: Routledge, 2004), 257-74.

Zupancic, Alenka, "A perfect Place to Die: Theatre in Hitchcock's Films," in Slavoj Zizek (ed.), *Everything You Always Wanted to Know About Lacan But Were Afraid to Ask Hitchcock* (London: Verso, 1992), 73-105.

Index

338

he Wrong House: The Architecture of Alfred Hitchcock was made possible with the support of the Hogeschool Sint-Lukas Brussel, the Ghent Urban Studies Team (GUST) at the University of Ghent, the Royal Film Archive Brussels, and deSingel International Arts Campus Antwerp

This book was published in conjunction with the exhibition *The Wrong House, Suspense in Architecture: Alfred Hitchcock / PauHof (Wolfgang Pauzenberger & Michael Hofstätter)*, 20 September - 25 November 2007 in deSingel International Arts Campus Antwerp (Curators: Steven Jacobs and Moritz Küng)

Architectural drawings by Annelies Staessen and Steven Jacobs (general coordination); Wesley Aelbrecht (Wendice Apartment: 103); Anna Barborini (Aysgarth House: 195); Bartel Bruneel (Bunting House: 66-67); David Claus (Verloc House & Bijou Cinema: 85; Newton House: 92-93; Jeffries Apartment & Courtyard: 278-81; Vandamm House: 297-98; Bates House & Motel: 118-20); Thomas De Keyser (Anthony House: 261); Bruno Poelaert (Paradine House: 231; Keane House: 243); Annelies Staessen (House Number 17: 78-79); and Linde Vertriest (Manderley: 174-75; Brandon-Phillip Penthouse: 267; Minyago Yugilla: 249; Brenner House: 136-37; Hayworth House: 151)

Source Credits of Photographs: Academy of Motion Picture Arts and Sciences: 14 I, 19, 117, 127 II, 128 I, 128 II, 133 VII, 135, 190 III, 190 IV, 303, 304; British Film Institute: 20 I, 87, 167 I, 167 II, 167 V, 170 II, 256 V, 259 II; Fine Arts Museums of San Francisco: 62 II; Royal Film Archive Brussels: 17 I, 17 II, 20 II, 27 I, 31 I, 31 II, 32, 35, 91 IV, 91 V, 127 I, 140 I, 140 II, 141 III, 155 IV, 161 VI, 161 VII, 170 III, 170 IV, 170 VII, 226 VI, 235 III, 235 IV, 247 III, 247 VII, 254 IV, 255 XII, 265 IV, 269 II, 269 IV, 269 V, 273 I, 273 II, 283 I, 283 II, 284; Time & Life Pictures, Getty Images (Gjon Mili): 101; *American Cinematographer* (1948): 275 II; *American Cinematographer* (1949): 259 I; Girouard (1978): 173 II, 254 II; Girouard (1979): 182 I, 182 II, 182 III, 185 III; Hess (1999): 310; Horton (2003): 24; *Magasin pittoresque* (1883): 295; Neumann (1999): 308 II; *New Yorker* (1940): 177 VI; Niemeyer (1998): 301; Riley (1994): 308 I; *Rope* (Warner Brothers Press Release Leaflet): 14 II, 275 I; Watkin (2001): 173 I, 254 I; All other illustrations are screen shots of DVDs

Book design by Piet Gerards Ontwerpers, Amsterdam (Piet Gerards and Maud van Rossum)

Printed by Snoeck Ducaju, Antwerpen

ISBN 978 90 6450 637 6
www.010publishers.nl